THE INVISIBLE HANDS

THE INVISIBLE HANDS

*Hedge Funds Off the Record—
Rethinking Real Money*

Steven Drobny

Foreword by Jared Diamond

WILEY

John Wiley & Sons, Inc.

Published by John Wiley & Sons, Inc., Hoboken, New Jersey.
Published simultaneously in Canada.

For general information on our other products and services or for technical support, please contact our Customer Care Department within the United States at (800) 762-2974, outside the United States at (317) 572-3993 or fax (317) 572-4002.

Wiley also publishes its books in a variety of electronic formats. Some content that appears in print may not be available in electronic books. For more information about Wiley products, visit our Web site at www.wiley.com.

Library of Congress Cataloging-in-Publication Data

Drobny, Steven.
  The invisible hands : hedge funds off the record—rethinking real money /
Steven Drobny; foreword by Jared Diamond.
      p.   cm.
    Includes bibliographical references and index.
    ISBN 978-0-470-60753-4 (cloth)
  1. Hedge funds. 2. Mutual funds. 3. Investment advisors. 4. Portfolio management.
I. Title.
  HG4530.D743 2010
  332.64'524–dc22

                                                                    2009054061

Printed in the United States of America.

10 9 8 7 6 5 4 3 2 1

For the taxpayer.

The whole problem with the world is that fools and fanatics are always so certain of themselves, but wiser people so full of doubts.

—Bertrand Russell

Investors are the big gamblers. They make a bet, stay with it, and if it goes the wrong way, they lose it all.

—Jesse Livermore

Only after disaster can we be resurrected.

—Tyler Durden

Argue for your limitations and they're yours.

—Richard Bach

Contents

Foreword

Question: What is the difference between a Peruvian peasant farmer and a Harvard or Yale endowment manager?

Answer: The peasant is the one who understands risk-sensitive investing and sound investment goals.

That question and answer illustrate why I, as a mere impractical academic historian, find the practical world of investment fascinating.

I got my first peek into the mystery-wrapped world of hedge funds several years ago, when Steven Drobny invited me to give the opening address at his annual conference for hedge fund managers. That initial peek aroused my curiosity. It led me to return to his conference in the following year as an observer, to meet some of Steven's colleagues and invited managers, to read Steven's previous book, *Inside the House of Money*, and to enjoy brunches with Steven from time to time, where we talk about anything from hedge funds and raising children to fixing the world.

One reason why I became fascinated in the world of investing was the parallels that I saw between investing and history. The issue of risk is acute in both of those spheres. Endowment and hedge fund managers evaluate upside and downside risk to the money they manage for other people, and they make or lose money as a result of those evaluations. The historical and modern peoples whom I study assess upside and downside risk to their own resources that they manage, and they and their families survive or die as a result of those evaluations.

For example, in the Middle Ages, the Norse on the island of Greenland, descended from Viking settlers who colonized Greenland in the year AD 984, made decisions each year about how many of their cows to cull in the fall. They knew the amount of hay that they had harvested during the previous summer, and knew the length of each individual winter (hence the demand for hay to feed the cows over the winter) over many past decades, but did not know the length of the particular winter lying ahead. If they still had hay left in the spring, that meant that they had culled a certain unnecessary quantity of cows, and they could have brought more cows through the winter, then produced more milk, cheese, and meat as a result and been less hungry the following year. If they instead found themselves running out of hay during the winter, that meant they had culled too few cows in the fall, meaning they would have to start sacrificing cows in the winter, ending up with fewer cows in the spring than if they had culled more cows already in the fall.

For about 376 years, the Greenland Norse made those annual decisions about risk-sensitive investment in cow herds sufficiently well that they flourished. But around year AD 1360 there was a particularly cold series of winters for which their hay gamble proved to be a bad miscalculation, with the result that all their cows died during one winter, and all of the thousand or so Norse of Greenland's Western Settlement starved to death in the late winter. Hedge fund managers will undoubtedly empathize with the dilemma that the Norse faced, and with their temptation to be greedy and to invest in many cows in their winter herd. But managers will be grateful, when their own risk calculations prove to be in error, that they themselves lose only their investors' money and don't lose their own lives.

Another reason why I was fascinated with what I learned about the world of investments was the parallels between investment managers and modern farming peoples. For instance, studies of modern Peruvian peasants resolved a mystery that long puzzled medieval historians, and that should have puzzled college investment managers. Each medieval peasant family didn't cultivate one large plot of ground; instead, they cultivated up to several dozen little strips of land scattered in several different directions from their hut, despite the obvious inefficiency of wasting time on traveling and carrying supplies between strips, as well as the waste of land inevitably left uncultivated at boundaries between adjacent strips belonging to different peasants. A possible explanation for the peasants' apparently irrationally stupid behavior was that they were practicing the virtue of diversification praised by modern financial managers: don't put all your eggs in one basket but instead diversify your portfolio. In any given year, all the strips in a single field may fail because of pest infestation, local climate, or thieves. You (the peasant family) are less likely to starve if you plant different scattered strips.

That idea of diversification is plausible, but only recently did economic historians and agronomists discover how sophisticated are the underlying calculations performed unconsciously by peasants. Modern Peruvian peasants scatter their strips of land as did medieval English peasants. Any individual Peruvian peasant owns between 9 and 26 different strips, whose yields of potatoes and other crops vary from year to year independently of each other and partly unpredictably. The peasants can't store significant quantities of potatoes from one year to the next; their food needs have to be satisfied by the current year's harvest. In analogy to the medieval Norse farmers' need for hay, the modern Peruvian peasants must succeed in obtaining a certain minimum potato harvest amounting to about 680,000 calories in every single year, otherwise they and their families end up starving. For 20 different peasants owning a total of 488 strips, the anthropologist Carol Goland measured the potato yields in successive years, then used those measured years to calculate the yield that each peasant would have harvested each year by cultivating only 1, or 2, or 3 . . . etc. strips, with total area held constant but with yield per acre equal to the value for each possible combination of the 1, 2, 3 etc. actual strips. She also measured the calories invested in travel between 1, 2, 3 . . . strips, in order to obtain the net calories remaining to the peasant for each combination.

Four interesting conclusions emerged from Goland's study. First, the long-term time-averaged potato harvest decreased with subdivision of the peasant's land, in agreement with the expectations of horrified western agronomists who urged the peasants to consolidate their strips, and for several reasons including wasted travel time. Second, the year-to-year variance in potato harvest decreased with increasing subdivision of the peasant's land, as expected from the principle "don't put all your eggs in one basket." But, because of that variance, the third conclusion was that the frequency of the years with a harvest so low as to cause starvation was highest for a single strip and decreased with subdivision to reach zero at a certain number of strips varying between 4 and 13, depending on the particular peasant's land. Finally, each individual peasant planted 2 or 3 strips more than the number required to reduce the risk of starvation to zero.

In short, the peasants do *not* aim at maximizing long-term time-averaged yield, even though that is an appropriate goal for investors not spending their earnings and just investing to pay for luxuries on a rainy day in the distant future. Instead, the peasants only maximize long-term yield insofar as that is consistent with their overriding goal of eliminating their risk of starving in any given year, and throwing in a small safety margin for that calculation. It seems to me that the Harvard and Yale endowment managers are in a position analogous to that of the peasants, and would have done better to set a goal of maximizing yield only above a certain minimal level. As a Harvard graduate myself, I receive my college's periodic mailings, the tone of which has recently changed from pride in Harvard's wisdom to tales of woe. Harvard, like Peruvian peasants, uses endowment income for current needs; in fact, as it turns out, a considerable fraction of college expenses is paid from the endowment each year. As a result, Harvard has had to impose a hiring freeze, and recently it had to cancel its plan for a new science campus.

Naturally, Peruvian peasants did not perform the sophisticated statistical analysis that Carol Goland performed retrospectively. Instead, they arrived at their solution of optimizing strip numbers to avoid starvation on the basis of long experience. They had observed some greedy but lazy peasants with overconsolidated holdings who glutted themselves for many years, only to starve to death in a bad year. Likewise, they observed other peasants with overspread holdings who never starved but also never glutted, while still others discovered a happy medium of strip numbers that permitted frequent modest gluts and never any starvation. Should you suspect that the peasants really did use a pocket calculator and a friendly visiting mathematical modeler, birds such as sparrows, which certainly don't have pocket calculators, also make similar risk-sensitive decisions such that they are never starving.

Steven Drobny's latest book is about the Peruvian peasants of the hedge-fund world: that minority of managers who made money or at least preserved capital during the *Annus horribilis* of 2008, while greedier managers who had accumulated major gluts and perhaps even achieved higher long-term time-averaged returns in previous happy years lost disastrously or went bankrupt. Hence, anyone interested in the world of finance and making money will pour over this book to extract some powerful lessons: What can I do to emulate those successful guys and gals in order to make money or preserve capital, even under the worst conditions, and become rich and famous?

But this book will also fascinate anyone interested in people. My other interest in the hedge fund world is for that reason. When Steven Drobny introduced me to his world of colleagues and clients, I found myself comparing them with the many creative scientists, architects, composers, artists, and business people whom I have interviewed. I wondered: What makes these people tick? How did their childhood experiences shape their adult professional success? Because a person's abilities change with age, do most hedge fund managers become washed up by age 40, or does a 60-year-old manager still have ways of succeeding in a world of cutthroat young managers who need less sleep and who received a more recent technological education? Are they managing money in order to become rich, to stoke their ego, to acquire flashy cars and supermodel dates, or to satisfy some other motivation?

With Steven Drobny's kind help, I interviewed some hedge fund managers (including a couple that Steven interviewed for this book) just for my own curiosity. I was struck by the fact that, although all the managers were quite different from each other, each had a broader life philosophy that he or she applied to the world of hedge funds in particular. Each had childhood experiences, things that their parents did or didn't do for them, that shaped them as future managers, although their parents could have hardly anticipated that outcome. All of them became managers partly for fun and curiosity. They want to understand how the world works, and they want to keep testing their evolving hypotheses about the world's workings against reality. All are still active in their 40s, 50s, and 60s. Yes, the 28-year-old whiz kids can get by with less sleep, while saddled with less knowledge about dated technologies, and have been schooled in the latest technologies. But "older" managers whom I interviewed enjoyed the advantage of having used their years to try out more things, and having seen more ups and downs. They are in the position of the peasant who remembers that dry summer 17 years ago, and who isn't deceived by the recent runs of wet summers into assuming that summer will always be wet. Some of the managers whom I met expect still to be managing money when they are 80 years old. They fulfilled their own lifetime financial needs long ago, but they may never fulfill their curiosity about how the world works, nor the fun they derive from testing their ideas.

My own interviews were casual ones, by an interviewer (i.e., me) ignorant of the subject matter. Steven Drobny's book consists of 13 long interviews, eleven anonymous and two of named managers. No one is better qualified than Steven to probe the subject matter, and to place his interviewed managers in a broad context, both as investors and as human beings. Whether you are curious about money or people, you are certain to love this book.

Jared Diamond
Professor of Geography and Environment Health Sciences, UCLA
Author of numerous books including *Guns, Germs and Steel,*
Collapse, The Third Chimpanzee, and *Why is Sex Fun?*

Preface

2008 was an unmitigated disaster for most investors, including un-levered "real money" investors—the focus of this book. Markets around the world, from real estate to equities to commodities to credit, posted huge declines, taking down with them some of the world's most venerable financial institutions, a wide variety of alternative asset managers (hedge funds, private equity, venture capital, and real asset managers), and a host of real money accounts (pension funds, insurance companies, endowments, foundations, family offices, and sovereign wealth funds). Almost everyone lost money in 2008, and in many cases more than anyone imagined possible.

Anger and confusion linger in the aftermath of the crisis, but are by no means limited to market players. Main Street is reeling as homes and jobs have been lost, savings have evaporated, and many assumptions governing the stability of modern society have been challenged. Governments around the world have responded with all sorts of innovative monetary and fiscal stimulus, generating even more uncertainty about the future. At the same time, the social contracts between governments and their citizens are being called into question as Social Security, health care, and pensions loom as potential financial crises for the taxpayer.

Meanwhile, a full year after the crash of '08, nearly everyone in the markets—from savvy hedge fund managers to small private investors with retirement accounts to policy makers—still struggle to understand what went wrong. While the debate over who or what deserves blame will likely rage for decades, the world has not ended and investors must now adapt and adjust to the new reality. The crisis of 2008 has called many investment mantras into question—notably the Endowment Model (diversifying into illiquid equity and equity-like investments) and others including stocks for the long term, buy the dip, buy and hold, and dollar cost averaging—yet no new model has taken root. The crisis of 2008 did, however, supply the financial community with an abundance of new information with regards to portfolio construction, in particular around risk, liquidity, and time horizons.

After such an extreme year in the markets, reactions in the real money world have been polarized: some have learned valuable lessons and are incorporating them in their approach, whereas others are operating as if it is business as usual, completely dismissing 2008 as a one-in-a-hundred-year storm that has passed. Although this latter camp may well prove correct in the near-term, history has taught us that extreme events happen more frequently than predicted, both on the downside and the upside. What if 2010 or 2011 offers an environment similar to or worse than 2008? Ignoring or discounting the lessons of 2008 is quite simply poor risk management.

One of the more significant questions facing all investors is whether a three-decade tail wind for risk assets—due to falling inflation and declining interest rates—could be over, now that the main economic blocks (United States, Europe, Japan) have no inflation and near-zero interest rates. Fiscal deficits, increasing public sector debts, private sector deleveraging, and populist and protectionist politics around the globe all point to increased volatility and a move away from "price stability." Still, real money accounts have an overwhelming proportion of their portfolio in equity and equity-like investments.

The status quo for real money management is no longer tenable. It is not acceptable to obscure losses and volatility behind benchmarks, long-term time horizons, or relative performance numbers. Losing less than peers or benchmarks does not provide the annual cash flow needs of pensioners, universities, and charities. Poor portfolio construction by these funds creates a potential cost to society and the taxpayer that is too great to ignore.

"The most powerful force in the world is compound interest," Albert Einstein is said to have declared. However, he neglected to mention that avoiding large drawdowns—which can wipe out years of performance—is an important implicit part of this phenomenon. Building better portfolios and properly managing risk are the first lines of defense against large drawdowns, which should be the primary concern of anyone managing capital against annual cash needs.

It is time to rethink real money management, and a good place to start is with portfolio managers who fared well in 2008, either by posting strong performance or by preserving capital. Risk management was the key differentiator and global macro hedge fund managers were, in aggregate, one of the few investment categories that managed risk effectively through the crisis. Although there is always a wide disparity in performance among global macro managers due to its broad mandate, there was a clear delineation in 2008: funds that focused on risk made money or at least preserved capital, whereas most funds that remained entrenched in long-held views suffered debilitating losses. Because my professional network includes many of the world's leading global macro hedge fund managers, I decided to reach out to those who performed in 2008 to see if any lessons were transferable to real money and other investors.

My last book, *Inside the House of Money: Top Hedge Fund Traders on Profiting in the Global Markets* (John Wiley & Sons), published in 2006, captured the process behind global macro investing through a series of interviews with some of the top global macro hedge fund traders at the time. Many of these managers foresaw the coming credit crunch, and elements of this foresight were captured through the animated discussions in the book. This book seeks to ignite a discussion about portfolio management in light of the lessons learned in 2008. Through another series of interviews, this time with top global hedge fund traders who managed risk well through 2008 and into 2009, the book highlights certain valuable elements of the global macro approach that could be applied to other mandates within money management.

The Invisible Hands begins by defining and discussing the importance of real money management. It then discusses the evolution of real money management and raises some important questions about how real money portfolios are constructed. Next, the experts speak for themselves. First, my business partner Dr. Andres Drobny, "The Researcher," discusses where the global economy is headed. Then, "The Family Office Manager," Jim Leitner, addresses the lessons he learned in 2008 and offers his own thoughts on rethinking real money. Next, the "Invisible Hands"—10 anonymous global macro hedge fund managers, the Philosopher, the House, the Professor, et al—discuss how they approach money management, how they managed to make money or avoid large losses in the crisis, and how they would address some of the challenges faced by real money managers. Finally, "The Pensioner" gives a view from the inside of the real money world and offers prescriptions for his peers.

I chose the anonymous route to increase candor as well as keep the focus on the ideas as opposed to the personalities. Many of the managers featured in this book actively shun publicity and have little to gain from revealing their money-making process. Few are seeking new investors and most have seen their assets under management grow dramatically as a result of strong 2008 performance. Nevertheless, they agreed to take part in this project because they recognize the important societal implications of real money performance.

To give some context amidst the anonymity, the hedge funds represented by the 10 anonymous managers herein manage over $100 billion of capital. The interviewees represent half a dozen different nationalities, and are based in various financial centers around the world. All have strong historical track records and all but two of the managers made money in 2008, with the exceptions still having preserved capital, finishing the year roughly flat (i.e., percentage losses in the single digits). None of the managers had a good year in 2008 that stood out against their historical performance due to either one significant bet or a long-standing bearish bias. This is a collection of discussions with outstanding risk managers.

This book is meant to serve as a catalyst for a deeper discussion on the future of real money management. It does not presume to possess a silver bullet, as no such thing exists. The goal is to provide an understanding of how successful global macro hedge fund managers navigated the most significant financial crisis of our lifetimes and to offer suggestions for how real money managers and all investors can incorporate certain elements of the macro approach into their own investment process. For all of our benefit, I hope this book makes progress toward that end.

Steven Drobny
Manhattan Beach, California
December 2009

Part One

REAL MONEY AND THE CRASH OF '08

Those who cannot remember the past are condemned to repeat it.

—George Santayana

Chapter 1

Rethinking Real Money

I. Why Real Money?

Real money is a commonly used term in the financial markets to denote a fully funded, long-only traditional asset manager. Real money managers are often referred to as institutional investors. The term real money means the money is managed on an unlevered basis. This contrasts with hedge funds, which often manage money using borrowed funds or leverage. Real money funds can and often do employ leverage, but they normally attain leverage on a nonrecourse basis (e.g., investing as a limited partner in a fund that is levered). Examples of real money managers are public and private pension funds, university endowments, insurance company portfolios, foundations, family offices, sovereign wealth funds, and mutual funds.

This book focuses on the mistakes made and lessons learned in 2008 and attempts to incite a dialogue about how to construct better portfolios in the real money world. For this reason, mutual funds will be excluded from the discussion, since they are usually managed under strict mandates and asset class restrictions, rather than as broad portfolios where asset allocation decisions dominate the investment process.

Real money funds are important and worth analyzing because: (1) they are some of the largest pools of capital in the world; (2) they have a direct impact on the functioning of society; (3) they lost staggering amounts of money in 2008; and (4) in many cases, these funds are ultimately backstopped by the taxpayer if they fail to deliver their promises. Real money funds are in crisis and are "too big to fail."

Size

Real money funds comprise a majority of world's managed assets, which totaled $62 trillion at the end of 2008. Within this grouping, pensions are by far the largest category, at $24 trillion, with U.S. pensions at $15 trillion, or almost one-quarter of total managed assets (see Figure 1.1).

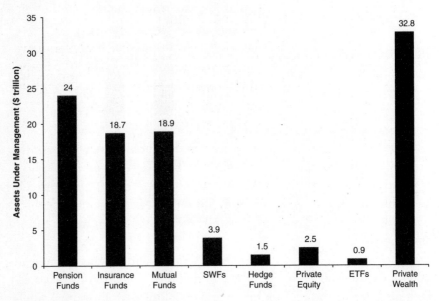

Figure 1.1 Global Fund Management Industry, End of 2008
SOURCE: IFSL estimates.

Impact on Society

Much of real money exists to deliver the promise of future retirement benefits, to support education, to guarantee the payouts from insurance agreements, to support charitable activities, and even to back national interests. In short, real money is the foundation for many important aspects of modern society. Pensions form an important part of the fundamental social contract between workers and employers, both in the public and private sectors. Public pensions in particular help ensure that basic societal functions are populated by competent people. Some of these functions include: police officers, firemen, judges, sanitation workers, teachers, health workers, politicians, and soldiers, amongst many others. To give an example of how real money affects society, after the crash of 2008, Philadelphia city officials threatened to lay off workers and cut sanitation and public safety services unless they could delay pension contributions. Stories such as these will likely become much more prevalent over the next few years.

2008 Losses

During the financial crisis, real money accounts suffered immense drawdowns. Pension funds globally saw their assets fall by almost 20 percent, while university endowments in the United States lost 26 percent on average. More surprisingly, because of the severity of investment losses, many institutions were forced to modify their operations to reflect a new reality: universities laid off staff, froze or cut salaries, issued debt, reduced financial aid, and suspended building projects; pensions increased employee and employer contributions, raised retirement ages, and cut benefits; charitable foundations canceled grants and delayed new programs; families curtailed spending and in many cases have been forced to sell assets.

The severe losses in 2008 also exposed some fundamental flaws in how real money portfolios are managed. Portfolio construction methodologies failed to account for both worst-case scenarios and potential illiquidity. A primary lesson of this experience is that the pain of investment losses is not linear; there is a kink, after which point losses begin to force changes in behavior. As a result, short-term investment performance has consequences even for "long-term" investors.

Taxpayer

Although all real money accounts are important to society in one way or another, pensions are the largest and arguably the most important. Well before the crisis of 2008, demographic challenges had been steadily putting pressure on pension systems in the developed world. Nevertheless, at the end of 2007, after an extended bull run for assets, many plans were fully funded, whereas at the end of 2008 most had become significantly underfunded.

Although a university going bust or a charitable foundation closing down is tragic for those directly involved, the effect would be relatively isolated. On the other hand, a pension fund going bust has implications for taxpayers. In the United States, the taxpayer is the explicit backstop for public pension funds and the implicit backstop for corporate pension funds, the latter of which are guaranteed by the Pension Benefit Guaranty Corp. (PBGC), a federal agency, The PBGC is currently facing its own crisis, with a reported deficit of $33.5 billion at midyear 2009, a more than tripling of the $11 billion deficit reported at midyear 2008. The deficit is the largest in the agency's 35-year history. More importantly, without confidence by workers that their benefits are intact, society breaks down.

In Ohio, for instance, the teachers pension system reported that it could take 41 years for its investments to meet its liabilities to retirees based on actuarial assessments—and this was *before* 2008. During the 2008–2009 fiscal year, the pension fund lost 31 percent, prompting officials to claim that they would never be able to meet liabilities. Because of the inherent complexity and subjectivity associated with calculating the funding levels for pension funds, the true costs are often disguised in the near-term (see box on page 7).

The shortfall associated with underfunded pensions can be made up by either investment performance or pension reform (i.e., changing the structure of the pension in some way). Yet pension reform amounts to fiscal tightening at a time when the global economy is weak and personal budgets are stretched. At the same time, these decisions are made by politicians, whose tenure in office does not compel them to make difficult, long-term decisions. Because voters do not opt for more tax or less benefits, the problems are often ignored, growing bigger by the day. Pensions loom as the next big financial crisis.

But crises often bring about change. We now have new information, which raises many important questions about what to do going forward. In order to understand more clearly what happened in 2008 and be able to formulate a plan for where we go from here, it is worthwhile to examine a brief history of real money, focusing on the U.S. pension world because it is the largest pool of funds and the biggest risk to the taxpayers of the world's largest economy.

Pension Funding Levels

Pension plans have two primary elements: (1) the future benefit obligations earned through employee service; and (2) the plan assets available to meet the liabilities owed to the beneficiaries. The challenge in assessing the health of pension plans is that both future liabilities and returns are estimates.

Since the payments to beneficiaries will be made far into the future, actuarial assumptions are required to estimate mortality rates, medical costs, and future salary increases. The future stream of assumed payments is discounted into a single present value estimate, whereby the discount rate is determined by reference to a benchmark yield. The higher the discount rate, the lower the benefit obligations. Very small changes in the discount rate have enormous real dollar implications for estimated funding levels.

Likewise, the value of plan assets available in the future to meet the pension obligations is also an estimate. The future value calculation is a function of expected returns on plan assets. Expected long-term returns are often developed using historical or "assumed" rates of return. In sum, it's a big guessing game.

II. The Evolution of Real Money

In the Beginning, There Were Bonds

Although pensions have existed for hundreds of years, the current structure took shape after 1948. In that year, the U.S. National Labor Relations Board (NLRB) ruled that corporate pensions must be included in contract negotiations between employers and employees. Before the ruling, the amount of capital allocated to an employee pension scheme, if such a plan even existed, was at the employers' discretion. This ruling defined how much a corporation must contribute to the employee pension plan annually, regardless of company performance and profits. As a result, money began to consistently move into pension funds, creating significant growth in assets and eventually leading to the large, powerful, professionally managed institutions that exist today (see Figure 1.2).

At the time, pension assets were managed very conservatively; fixed interest on bonds was matched to meet fixed commitments to pensioners—simple asset/liability matching. Bonds were selected from preapproved "legal lists" of securities, and it was common to have a limit for equities. In 1949, public and private pension assets in the United

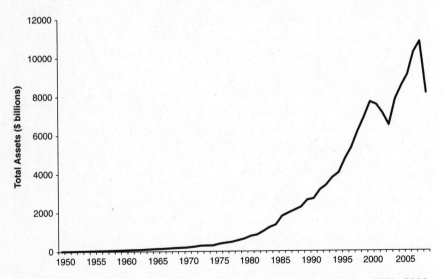

Figure 1.2   Growth of US Public and Private Pension Fund Assets, 1950–2008
Source: Federal Reserve Flow of Funds.

States were $15.7 billion. The asset mix was roughly half in government bonds, and half in other fixed income and insurance company fixed annuity investment products. There was minimal exposure to equities.

Along Came Inflation

By 1970, public and corporate pension fund assets in the United States reached $211.7 billion, the majority of which was concentrated in fixed income. Beginning with the 1973–1974 oil embargo, wave after wave of commodity price-induced inflation roiled fixed interest portfolios through the remainder of the decade. Nevertheless, assets continued to pour into pension funds because of strict commitments mandated on employers.

At the end of the decade, U.S. pension funds had $649 billion in total assets, and the outperformance of equities versus bonds during the previous ten years did not go unnoticed by pension fund managers. While bond portfolios got destroyed, equities at least managed to preserve capital in real terms (see Figure 1.3). Panicked and weary pension fund managers began rethinking their portfolios, and the shift out of bonds

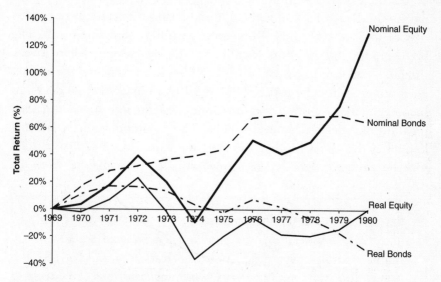

Figure 1.3 U.S. Stocks and Bonds, 1970s

SOURCE: Bloomberg; U.S. Bureau of Labor Statistics, http://www.bls.gov/CPI/; and *Damodaran Online*, http://pages.stern.nyu.edu/~adamodar/.

into stocks began in earnest. By 1980, corporate pensions had 45 percent of their assets in equities, while public pensions had 16 percent. In many cases, public plans were still capped as to how much equities they could own. The largest U.S. pension fund, the California Public Employees' Retirement System (CalPERS), for example, had a maximum allocation to equities of 25 percent, which was eventually lifted in 1984.

The 60–40 Model and the Great Moderation

Through the 1980s and 1990s, pensions continued to shift their assets out of bonds and into stocks, ultimately moving toward the now ubiquitous 60–40 policy portfolio (60 percent in stocks and 40 percent in bonds, often domestic only). The 60–40 model which became the standard benchmark by which to judge portfolio performance. The shift into stocks, and corresponding increase in risk, occurred in lock step with Federal Reserve Chairman Paul Volcker's famous battle with inflation, which saw the fed funds rate peak at 20 percent in 1981. In 1980, the so-called "misery index"—unemployment plus inflation—peaked at 20 percent.

As the excess pessimism of the 1970s gave way to excess optimism during the Reagan 1980s and euphoria during the technology revolution of the late 1990s, 60–40 pension portfolios performed well. The big decisions that investors faced at this time were whether to tweak the 60–40 allocation to, say, 65–35 or 55–45. In actuality, the market environment throughout the 1980s and 1990s rendered these decisions inconsequential as both stocks and bonds benefited greatly from falling inflation and declining interest rates. The environment later became known as the Great Moderation, and was summed up well in a 2004 speech by then–Federal Reserve Governor Ben Bernanke (see box).

Bernanke on the Great Moderation

The Great Moderation, the substantial decline in macroeconomic volatility over the past twenty years, is a striking economic development. Whether the dominant cause of the Great Moderation is structural change, improved monetary policy, or simply good luck is an important question about which no consensus has yet formed. I have argued today that improved monetary policy has likely made an important contribution not only to the reduced volatility of inflation (which is not particularly controversial) but to the reduced volatility of output as well. Moreover, because a change in the monetary policy regime has pervasive effects, I have suggested that some of the effects of improved monetary policies may have been misidentified as exogenous changes in economic structure or in the distribution of economic shocks. This conclusion on my part makes me optimistic for the future, because I am confident that monetary policymakers will not forget the lessons of the 1970s.

SOURCE: Board of Governors of the Federal Reserve System, www.federalreserve.gov; February 20, 2004.

By 1998, U.S. pension assets totaled more than $6.9 trillion, 438 times the 1949 figure. Pensions were larger than the national debt and growing faster. Because of their immense buying power, pensions became powerful market players in terms of shareholder activism, governance, and reform (see Figure 1.4).

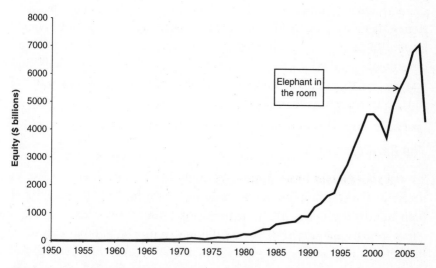

Figure 1.4 Equity Assets Owned by US Public and Private Pensions, 1950–2008
SOURCE: Federal Reserve Flow of Funds.

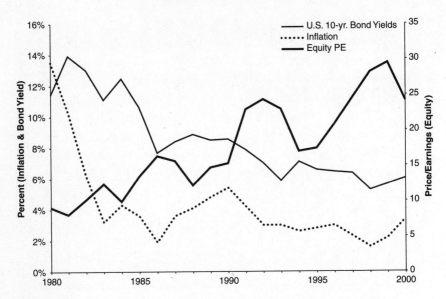

Figure 1.5   Interest Rates, Inflation and Equity Multiples, 1980–2000
SOURCE: Bloomberg; Federal Reserve System, http://www.federalreserve.gov/datadownload/; and U.S.
Bureau of Labor Statistics, http://www.bls.gov/bls/.

For two decades, the trend in equity markets was almost straight up, producing an entire generation of real money investors conditioned to buy any dip and remain invested in equities for the long term. Academics such as Jeremy Siegel of the University of Pennsylvania and bank strategists such as Abbey Joseph Cohen of Goldman Sachs became cheerleaders for the idea of owning equities for the long term, while banks and consultants peddled the story. Pensions, other real money investors, and retail investors all made money in this environment. It was a wonderful time to be invested (see Figure 1.5).

The Dot-Com Crash

As real money was becoming increasingly loaded up on equity risk in their 60–40 portfolios (stocks can be anywhere from 2 to 10 times riskier than bonds depending on what proxies are used), two decades of declining inflation and interest rates culminated in a technology-led stock market bubble that finally popped in March 2000. After the peak, global equity markets declined relentlessly year after year, finally bottoming in

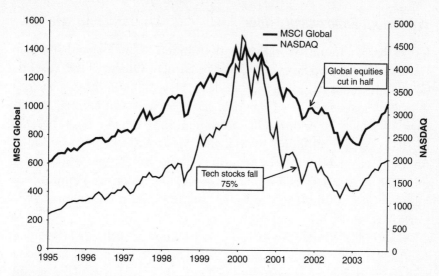

Figure 1.6 MSCI Global and NASDAQ, 1995–2003
SOURCE: Bloomberg.

early 2003. Stocks generally lost half their value while in-vogue technology stocks dropped 75 percent from peak to trough (see Figure 1.6). Just as they had in the 1970s with bonds, real money managers became painfully aware of the equity concentration risk in their portfolios and began to look for a better, less risky approach. Pensions were facing serious underfunding issues and all investors were looking for new answers. Amidst the carnage, the two largest university endowments—Harvard and Yale—rode through the dot-com bust unscathed, causing many investors to explore what these large, sophisticated real money investors were up to (see Table 1.1).

Table 1.1 Equity Returns versus Harvard and Yale Endowments

Fiscal Year (July 1–June 30)	S&P500	MSCI Global	Harvard	Yale
2000	7.3%	11.0%	32.2%	41.0%
2001	−14.8%	−21.3%	−2.7%	9.2%
2002	−18.0%	−16.3%	−0.5%	0.7%
2003	0.3%	−4.1%	12.5%	8.8%

SOURCE: Bloomberg and Mebane Faber, *The Ivy Portfolio* (Wiley).

We Are All Endowments Now

Just as the real money world's attention shifted to the Harvard and Yale Endowments, David Swensen, Chief Investment Officer of the Yale Endowment, published a seminal work in May 2000, entitled *Pioneering Portfolio Management: An Unconventional Approach to Institutional Investment,* in which he outlined his investment process. The book became the bible of the real money world, and dog-eared copies can be found on the desks or bookshelves of most real money managers. Soon after its publication, investors from family offices to pensions and foundations began trying to emulate Yale by creating their own endowment-style portfolios.

The "Yale Model" soon came to be known as the "Endowment Model" as the portfolio management style became pervasive among university endowment portfolios. The Endowment Model, as it was popularly interpreted, is a broadly diversified portfolio, though with a heavy equity orientation, which seeks to earn a premium for taking on illiquidity risk. The argument behind the equity and "equity-like" orientation is that stocks produce the highest returns over time. This fundamental concept has roots in the very foundations of capitalism: risky equity capital should earn more than less risky bonds. The argument for seeking out illiquidity risk comes from financial theory, which states that investors are paid a premium for assuming the risk of illiquid assets (you should be compensated for not being able to sell something when you want). Illiquid investments include publicly traded illiquid securities and a host of "alternatives," including private equity, real estate, venture capital, infrastructure, physical commodities and real assets such as timber, mines, etc. The focus on illiquid assets made the Endowment Model particularly attractive to funds that—at least in theory—had extremely long time horizons, such as endowments and pensions.

David Swensen took over the Yale Endowment in 1985, when total assets stood at $1.3 billion, and started to shift the portfolio towards illiquid alternative assets aggressively after 1990 (see Table 1.2). He grew assets to a reported peak of $22.87 billion by June 30, 2008, a truly remarkable achievement. During his tenure, he shifted Yale's endowment from a classic policy portfolio (80–20 in this case) focused primarily on

Table 1.2 Yale Endowment Portfolio Composition

Asset Class	1985	1990	2008
Domestic equity	61.6%	48.0%	10.1%
Foreign equity	6.3%	15.2%	15.2%
Absolute return	0%	0%	25.1%
Private equity	3.2%	6.7%	20.2%
Real assets	8.5%	8.0%	29.3%
Fixed income	10.3%	21.2%	4.0%
Cash	10.1%	0.9%	−3.9%

SOURCE: Mebane Faber, *The Ivy Portfolio* (Wiley).

listed equities to an illiquid, equity-oriented portfolio invested in a broad array of alternative assets, primarily managed by external managers. His extraordinary performance included only one negative year (−0.2 percent in fiscal 1988), so it is hardly surprising that other investors with similar mandates sought to emulate him.

In the years following the dot-com bust in 2000, and accelerating after 2003, slow-moving investment committees across the real money spectrum shifted their portfolios from the 60–40 model to versions of the Endowment Model, again spurred on by consultants and banks selling both expertise and products. Aggressive real money managers at pension funds and university endowments such as Stanford, Duke, Notre Dame, MIT, and Princeton pushed their portfolios towards high percentages of illiquid assets and alternatives, in turn becoming the industry stars that others sought to emulate. David Swensen followed up his first book with a retail investor version in 2005, entitled *Unconventional Success: A Fundamental Approach to Personal Investment,* in which he addressed how individual investors can mimic the Yale portfolio using low-cost instruments available to retail investors such as Exchange-Traded Funds. Meanwhile, new money management firms headed by former endowment chiefs created endowment-style funds that were sold to retail investors through mass distribution channels.

With so many real money and retail investors piling into the Endowment Model, the assets of partially liquid and illiquid alternative asset managers exploded. Central banks, fighting the last battle—the dot-com bust—kept interest rates low, adding fuel to the fire.

Assets of hedge funds grew from $237 billion in 2000 to over $2 trillion in 2007. Private equity grew from $511 billion with another $450 billion committed in 2003, to $1.5 trillion with another $1 trillion committed in 2008. Investment in commodity indexes grew from $70 billion in 2005 to $180 billion in 2007 and real estate became a worldwide bubble. Yet, as real money investors sought diversification through the same methodology, their portfolios were in fact becoming more correlated to each other while portfolio risks were becoming more concentrated and increasingly dependent upon illiquid equity-like investments. Crowding was becoming an issue, yet the primary concern of real money investors at the time was getting capacity in the "best" managers. This stampede led investors to accept worsening terms, such as longer lockups, less transparency, higher fees, and others that served to increase the overall risk profile of their funds. Indeed, crowding is not a surprise since real money managers often share the same consultants and occasionally the same board members.

In a May 31, 2007 interview in *Fortune*, Harvard's endowment chief at the time, Mohamed El-Erian, was asked about the major investment challenges facing Harvard Management Corporation. He had this to say:

> More people are replicating what we do. The endowment model is very much in vogue. There have been many articles in the press trumpeting how well endowments like Harvard's and Yale's have performed. And David Swensen, who brilliantly heads up Yale's endowment with impressive long-term performance, has written a great book showing how endowment management is done. So now lots of central banks and pension funds are trying to become more like endowments. The space is becoming more crowded.

The Crash of '08

Just as real money investors became fully invested in portfolios resembling the Endowment Model—with hopes of achieving excess returns with low risk—along came the crash of '08, reminding everyone that excess returns are only generated by taking on more risk, even if that risk remains hidden for a period of time. From a peak in October 2007 to a trough in March 2009, global equities declined by almost 60 percent, taking down equity-oriented portfolios with them (see Figure 1.7).

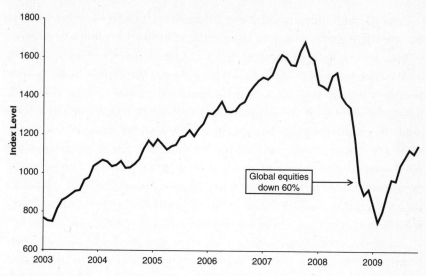

Figure 1.7   MSCI Global, 2003–2009
SOURCE: Bloomberg.

During the fiscal year to June 30, 2009 (which most university endowments report on), the S&P 500 was down 26 percent, while most real
money investors suffered losses in the 20 to 40 percent range. Worse, a
substantial portion of the remaining assets were illiquid. It was not un-
common to find real money managers stuck in portfolios that were 50 to
100 percent illiquid, making cash obligations difficult to meet. The valuation of illiquid assets is approximate in the best of times, and they could
continue to drag down performance for years to come as valuations crys-
talize. There have been many attempts to sell illiquid assets in secondary
markets, and the deals that have been reported were a fraction of the
valuations on the books of other portfolios. Some private equity funds
have reportedly traded hands for as low as 20 to 30 cents on the dollar.

    The crash of '08 highlighted flaws in the Endowment Model,
namely: (1) diversification with a high equity orientation is not really diversification; (2) valuation matters, whether it applies to equities,
real estate, or liquidity; (3) investing in certain limited partnerships is a
form of leverage; and (4) time horizons are not as long as previously
envisioned for investors with annual liquidity needs.

    First, when you diversify your portfolio but retain an equity and
equity-like orientation, you are not really diversified; all the risk eggs

remain in the equity basket. For example, if you are invested in international equities, long/short equity hedge funds with a long bias, private equity, and venture capital, you essentially have a one-way bet on the returns of equities. Similarly, real assets offer equity-like exposure because they are dependent on the nominal growth in the economy. Ironically, the Endowment Model usurped the prevalence of the 60–40 policy portfolio precisely because it was supposed to offer an alternative to equity-centric investing. But not only did the concentration for the Endowment Model remain in equities, it went further, concentrating the equity risk in illiquid investments that were often levered. The asset allocation for Yale in 2008 (see Table 1.2.) had 99.9 percent of the portfolio invested in equity and equity-like assets (4 percent in bonds but −3.9 percent in cash; the portfolio was leveraged outright by 3.9 percent, and presumably the actual leverage was much higher due to committed but yet uncalled allocations to private equity, venture capital, and other funds).

The argument that equities outperform other asset classes in the long term often fails to mention the risk undertaken to achieve that outperformance. Taking risk into account, history offers an alternative answer to the claim that equities always outperform in the long term. Through October 2009, 10-year U.S. government bonds have outperformed the S&P 500 for the past 5 and 10 years. Twenty-year returns of stocks and bonds are almost equivalent, but bonds have less than half the volatility. (See Table 1.3.) Further, from 1900–2000, equities and bonds

Table 1.3   U.S. Equities and U.S. Government Bonds, Annualized Returns and Volatility through October 2009

	Returns		Volatility	
Time Period	**U.S. 10-yr Bonds**	**S&P 500**	**U.S. 10-yr Bonds**	**S&P 500**
5 years	8.08%	−1.12%	7.36%	22.11%
10 years	8.17%	−1.71%	6.81%	20.05%
15 years	8.03%	7.49%	8.52%	21.55%
20 years	7.77%	7.79%	8.48%	19.43%
25 years	8.91%	10.13%	9.50%	18.37%
30 years	9.15%	10.75%	10.04%	17.50%

SOURCE: Bloomberg; and *Damodaran Online,* http://pages.stern.nyu.edu/~adamodar/.

in the United States have generated almost identical nominal returns on a risk-adjusted basis, with bonds slightly outperforming.

Second, 2008 was a reminder that valuation matters. Part of the success of Yale and Harvard could be attributed to their recognition two decades ago that illiquid assets were cheap. As early entrants, they were able to benefit from the increased valuations of illiquids as followers drove up prices. Another part of their success could be a function of the extremely favorable macro environment, which saw declining interest rates and declining inflation for the past three decades. Put another way, it is not at all clear that what transpired will continue to transpire. Sticking to one investment style regardless of valuation or environment is dangerous, but that is exactly what real money managers did.

Third, although real money portfolios do not assume outright leverage, they often attain leverage through allocations to external managers. In this sense, they were implicitly leveraged through their private equity, venture capital, real estate, and other investments that required advanced commitments, giving a portion of their portfolio a short option-like profile. It became common practice for real money managers looking to invest in these areas to "over-commit" by up to two times the target allocation in order to achieve their desired portfolio allocation, as commitments are called. These types of funds draw down (i.e., ask for or "call") the money committed to them as opportunities are identified. As such, only a fraction of a commitment may be used at any one time, and it can take years to fully deploy a commitment. Private equity and venture capital opportunities tend to produce cash flows only after several years because it takes time to generate value and exit the investments. Investors counted on these cash flows from prior investments to fund new capital calls, creating a recycling process. However, in 2008 and 2009, cash flows from successful exits dried up while capital calls continued. This served to increase real money managers' exposure requiring cash precisely when it was in short supply.

For example, on June 15, 2009, CalPERS announced they were raising their investment target to private equity from 10 percent to 14 percent. Of course, their private equity allocation had already risen above their target because of capital calls and the "denominator effect." On June 30, 2009, CalPERS had $21.8 billion of its $180.9 billion portfolio allocated to private equity, with another $22.5 billion committed—an implicitly levered exposure of 25 percent to private equity.

Fourth, the conventional wisdom that real money managers are "long-term" investors is misguided. Just as all of the equity instruments were correlated on the way up and the way down, so, too, were the illiquid assets. Although the illiquid investments remained illiquid, many formerly liquid investments also became illiquid as real money and levered investors alike all attempted to sell at the same time. Such a worst-case scenario was not considered despite the time-worn adage that liquidity is never there when you need it most. Even if these illiquid assets wind up performing well over time, institutions had short- to medium-term cash obligations that they could not honor due to the illiquid nature of their portfolios, calling into question the true time horizons of these investors.

The difference between the 2000–2003 period—when endowments performed—and the 2008 period—when they didn't—was a function of crowding and the sheer size and percentage of assets dedicated to illiquids and alternatives (often through leverage).

Less Endowed

The large endowments gained a following because of strong performance, but significant losses in 2008 cast doubt upon the quality of that performance. Caught with high proportions of "equity-like" and illiquid investments, they gave back years of gains (see Table 1.4 and Table 1.5). Excess returns require high risks, and the bill finally came due. The majority of Yale's outperformance over the past decade came from private equity and real assets, which currently make up half of the endowment portfolio (see Figure 1.8). It is worth questioning how much of Yale's (and other endowments') past outperformance was attributable to superior manager selection and better portfolio construction, and how much was simply a function of leverage, both explicit and implicit.

Yale University saw its endowment assets fall from almost $23 billion to $16.3 billion for fiscal year 2008–2009, a decline of almost 30 percent. As a result of investment losses and illiquidity, Yale postponed $2 billion in construction projects and trimmed 600 jobs through voluntary resignations and firings. Harvard University saw its endowment assets

Table 1.4 Annual Long–Term Performance of Harvard and Yale Endowments Compared to Other Assets, 1991–2008 (June 30 Fiscal Year End)

1991–2008	Harvard	Yale	S&P500	MSCI World	Barclays AGG	Commodities	HFRI Macro	HFRI FoFs
Return	14.7%	16.0%	9.6%	5.7%	7.1%	3.8%	14.9%	9.4%
Volatility	9.5%	10.0%	15.4%	13.3%	4.6%	14.3%	11.7%	6.8%
Sharpe (5%)	1.06	1.14	0.37	0.11	0.47	−0.02	0.89	0.67
Best Year	32.2%	41.0%	34.7%	22.0%	14.0%	46.6%	44.9%	21.0%
Worst Year	−2.7%	0.7%	−18.0%	−21.3%	−1.3%	−12.0%	4.2%	−0.2%

SOURCE: Mebane Faber, *The Ivy Portfolio* (Wiley), Bloomberg, HFR.

Table 1.5 Annual Long-Term Performance of Harvard and Yale Endowments Compared to Other Assets, 1991–2009 (June 30 Fiscal Year End)

1991–2009	Harvard	Yale	S&P500	MSCI World	Lehman AGG	Commodities	HFRI Macro	HFRI FoFs
Return	11.9%	13.4%	7.3%	3.3%	7.0%	0.3%	14.1%	7.9%
Volatility	13.4%	13.5%	17.2%	15.6%	4.5%	18.1%	11.9%	8.7%
Sharpe (5%)	0.58	0.68	0.22	−0.03	0.47	−0.17	0.81	0.37
Best Year	32.2%	41.0%	34.7%	22.0%	14.0%	46.6%	44.9%	21.0%
Worst Year	−27.3%	−24.6%	−26.2%	−31.2%	−1.3%	−46.0%	−0.2%	−15.2%

Source: Mebane Faber, *The Ivy Portfolio* (Wiley), Bloomberg, HFR.

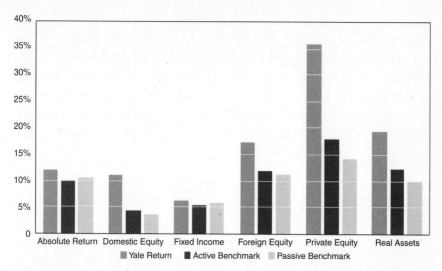

Figure 1.8   Yale Asset Class Results Trounce Benchmarks, 1998–2008
Source: *The Yale Endowment 2008 Investment Report,* http://www.yale.edu/investments/.

decline from a peak of $36.9 billion to $26 billion over the same period, also a decline of almost 30 percent. Similarly, Harvard has frozen
teacher salaries, announced layoffs, and curtailed construction projects
in the wake of its investment losses and portfolio illiquidity. One of the
projects it cancelled was a $1 billion science center across the Charles
River on its new Allston campus, a controversial decision that has spurred
protests from the local community. On top of these woes, Harvard issued
$2.5 billion in bonds to generate additional liquidity, in essence levering
up the university, which is now saddled with $5.98 billion in total debt.

After 2008, even David Swensen acknowledged the need to rethink
some aspects of his approach. In a May 2009 interview on *Consuelo
Mack WealthTrack* (PBS), Swensen remarked, "I'm not sure that the
crisis has caused us to conclude that we would do things differently, but
it certainly highlighted the importance of liquidity." Yet in the same
answer, he added, "One of the things that I've said consistently, and I
still continue to believe to be true, is that investors get paid unreasonable
amounts for accepting illiquidity in their portfolios."

While that may or may not be true, illiquidity needs to be reconsidered on a risk-adjusted basis, which includes the analysis of stressed
scenarios and the impact on the overall portfolio in light of annual cash

liabilities. Although the Endowment Model is not dead, the flaws and shortcomings exposed in 2008 need to be considered and adjusted for when building real money portfolios. Whether the performance of endowment style portfolios snap back quickly or not doesn't matter; we have learned that risk-adjusted returns and drawdowns are important. If large drawdowns force action beyond the portfolio level (i.e., if the underlying institutions must take action because of portfolio losses), then it makes sense to do whatever is necessary to cut off that risk.

Public Pension Goes Endowment

In the fall of 2006, I was invited to attend an offsite meeting for a state pension fund that had just been given clearance, through a November 2006 ballot vote, to invest outside of the United States for the first time. The vote essentially gave them carte blanche to invest in anything. For years, the double-digit billion dollar pension fund had invested half its assets in U.S. listed equities and half in U.S. government bonds. After the vote, the state treasurer wasted no time hiring a CIO from another comparable pension fund, where he had implemented the Endowment Model. The two-day offsite was organized as an opportunity for consultants, product providers, other experts, and constituents to discuss the way forward. Having just published my first book, I was invited to speak about global macro—I did not have an investment product to sell at the time, and was allowed to stay through all of the presentations (most product providers were asked to leave after making their pitch). I saw bond mutual funds, funds of hedge funds, enhanced index products, private equity funds, and others present their wares, all from leading firms. Most importantly, I saw the pension's consultants describe how they were going to convert a pie chart with two slices (stocks and bonds) into one with dozens of slices and a sprinkling of portable alpha (leverage) here and an over-commitment to private equity there. Despite the obvious complications and challenges with transitioning such a large pool of capital, the plan was to execute this major shift in asset allocation as quickly as possible, through swaps, special purpose vehicles, and block trades. It all sounded so easy. The plan was agreed and initiated during 2007, just in time for the credit crisis. During 2008, the pension's total assets fell by a third and much of the remaining assets are illiquid. Still, despite getting absolutely crushed, they won an industry award for sweeping reform and leading edge design implementation. Meanwhile, had the 2006 vote not passed and the original portfolio remained intact, pension assets would be approximately 20 percent higher today, equating to a few billion dollars.

Pensions Are Different

Whatever pension-cost surprises are in store for shareholders down the road, these jolts will be surpassed many times over by those experienced by taxpayers. Public pension promises are huge and, in many cases, funding is woefully inadequate. Because the fuse on this time bomb is long, politicians flinch from inflicting tax pain, given that problems will only become apparent long after these officials have departed. Promises involving very early retirement—sometimes to those in their low 40s—and generous cost-of-living adjustments are easy for these officials to make. In a world where people are living longer and inflation is certain, those promises will be anything but easy to keep.
—Warren Buffett, *Berkshire Hathaway 2007 Letter*

While troubles with endowments and universities are worrisome, endowments only represent a little more than $400 billion of capital. Pensions, however, are almost 60 times larger in terms of assets and they more directly impact a wider proportion of society because the taxpayer ultimately foots the bill for their shortcomings. Over the past decade, pension funds piled headlong into the Endowment Model, the ultimate verdict for which is still out; but pensions could wind up being the real losers. For years, demographic challenges have been putting stress on the pension system, and 2008 investment losses exacerbated these issues. According to Watson Wyatt, the 11 largest pension markets saw assets fall by 19 percent in 2008. The consultancy noted a "significant deterioration in solvency, raising the probability of plan defaults and producing pressures for revised strategies."

CalPERS is emblematic of the broader pension world. For its funding calculations, it has been reporting an expected rate of return of 7.75 percent for the past eight years, and 8.25 percent prior to that. Meanwhile, the actual annualized return over the past decade—from fiscal year 2000 to fiscal year 2009—is only 2.46 percent, and in 2008, it lost over 27 percent. CalPERS, combined with its cross-town rival, CalSTRS (the second largest pension in the United States), had reported peak assets of $436 billion in late 2007, and suffered a peak-to-trough drawdown of $164 billion by early 2009. The California state taxpayer is the backstop.

By way of comparison, when the Orange County pension fund blew up in 1994 amidst great scandal, losses only amounted to $1.64 billion, yet services were cut drastically. Today, California has a budget crisis that has seen state worker furloughs, payments in the form of IOUs, layoffs, and other services cut. California already has the one of the highest state income tax rates in the United States at 10.55 percent, and has been losing businesses and state residents (taxpayers) for years. Not a very solid backstop.

But it is not all dire. Some forward-thinking pension fund managers are asking good questions about the looming issues. At a September 2009 meeting in Sacramento with Joseph Dear, the newly appointed CIO of CalPERS, we discussed the daunting issues facing California pensions. Faced with significant underfunding and demographic challenges, a pension has two options to address the situation: (1) increase contribution levels, reduce benefits, or inject cash from outside sources; and/or (2) improve investment performance. Dear had this to say during our discussion:

> One of the really big questions I am trying to address is how to do asset allocation in this environment because the standard method that we use, that is sold by consultants and is deemed prudent is predicated on a set of assumptions which are empirically false. The whole edifice is built on the assumption that returns are normally distributed and that this is a formula driven exercise whereby returns, volatilities and correlations can be derived by looking at history. As a result, everyone's portfolio ends up looking like everyone else so it is deemed okay if

you lose money along with everyone else. But it does not adequately address risk. It does not adequately address inter time period funding issues whereby the 20 year horizon may work but you may run out of money in the intermediate period. The main question I am faced with is how to run a large pension fund in light of these issues.

Addressing the "risk" side of the equation head-on is a step in the right direction.

III. RETHINKING REAL MONEY—MACRO PRINCIPLES

One of the main conclusions to come out of this book is that the accepted standard practice of real money no longer works. Real money management needs to be rethought as the old methodologies have failed. The massive growth of real money funds took place in a very benign environment where inflation was falling and virtually all assets performed well. In such conditions, static rule based strategies such as buy and hold, stocks for the long run, and the Endowment Model worked. But in a new, less benign world of higher volatility, a change in standard practice is required.

Despite the widespread pain and colossal losses endured by most investors in 2008, there were a few bright spots. Global macro hedge funds, in aggregate, proved resilient by effectively managing risk and keeping a sharp focus on liquidity. The most successful made substantial gains, in large part due to tactical risk management techniques. In aggregate, global macro hedge funds, as measured by the HFRI Macro Index, returned 4.83 percent in 2008 and were up 4.03 percent for 2009. Since 1990, the HFRI Macro Index has returned an average of approximately 14 percent annually with annualized monthly volatility of 7.8 percent and only one losing calendar year—down 4.3 percent in 1994 (see Figure 1.9).

One of the primary factors enabling global macro funds to exhibit such strong long-term performance is the avoidance of significant drawdowns. Consistently compounding positive returns leads to strong long-term performance, whereas significant, even if infrequent, drawdowns destroy performance. Because of the phenomenon of negative compounding, big losses are very hard to recover from. "Siegel's Paradox"

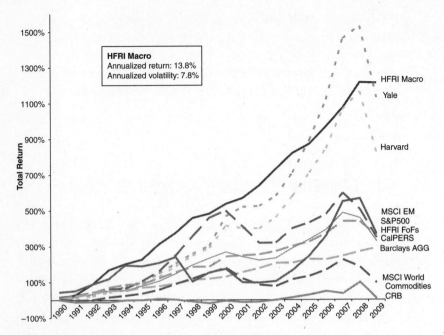

Figure 1.9 Cumulative Returns, 1990–2009
SOURCE: Bloomberg; HFR, *CalPERS Annual Reports*, http://www.calpers.ca.gov/; and Mebane Faber, *The Ivy Portfolio* (Wiley).

explains how gains and losses are not symmetric, losses are much worse. For example, a loss of 50 percent requires a gain of 100 percent just to break even. In other words, the bigger the hole, the harder it is to dig out of (see Table 1.6).

This book offers a contribution towards a new model for real money management leaning heavily on the methods used by many global macro hedge funds and by looking at the lessons learned in 2008. Although I spoke with many real money managers for background on this project, few had the performance in 2008 that would warrant their inclusion. When discussing the concept of this book with a chief investment officer at a billion dollar university endowment, he said:

> Who are you interviewing for the real money part? Most people got smoked—including me—and don't warrant an interview. We should have all just been long 50 percent emerging market equities and 50 percent government bonds for the last 6–7 years and learned to surf.

Table 1.6 Siegel's Paradox

Losses	Returns Needed to Get Back to Even
0%	0%
−10%	11%
−20%	25%
−30%	43%
−40%	67%
−50%	100%
−60%	150%
−70%	233%
−80%	400%
−90%	900%

Instead, we did all this work to fool ourselves into thinking we found the next best manager since Medallion, and we completely missed out on the macro.

Even Yale endowment chief David Swensen recognized the need to take a more forward-looking, global macro approach. In the May 2009 interview on *Consuelo Mack WealthTrack* (PBS), Swensen said:

One of the difficulties of this current crisis is that we have to think about securities markets more from a top-down basis or macro basis than is the case when we're not facing the type of crisis we lived through in the past six or nine months or a year. I am religiously bottom up in everything we do . . . but the crisis forces you to think top-down in ways that would, I think, be unproductive in normal circumstances, but are absolutely necessary in the midst of a crisis. You have to think about the functioning of the credit system. You have to think about the potential impact of monetary policy on markets over the next 5 or 10 or 15 years.

The question is: Why wait for a crisis to take a global macro approach when arguably it is already too late? Why not incorporate certain global macro principles into a real money investment approach, melding the best from both worlds? Understanding how global macro managers avoided large losses and made money in 2008 offers a unique opportunity for new ideas and approaches to be adopted by real money managers and all investors.

The real successes of 2008 occurred when managers took decisive action rather than sat still and hoped that everything would be okay in the long run. The way that global macro managers approach risk distinguishes them from other hedge fund strategies and real money managers. Regardless of valuation metrics or the general attractiveness of an opportunity, a macro manager will always want to know how much he can lose in his portfolio at any given time. The entire portfolio construction process is anchored in risk: What will this specific trade strategy add in terms of overall risk to the portfolio? What are the true risks assumed for each position? In a worst-case scenario, how much can the portfolio or the position lose?

Analyzing the world through a risk prism in no small way enabled macro managers to avoid the pitfalls that befell other investors during 2008. Steadily compounding positive returns while avoiding large drawdowns may sound boring, but it is an effective way to build capital over the long-term. Ironically, conventional wisdom in the investment world holds that global macro hedge funds are risky while real money funds are prudent and safe.

It is now clear that real money managers need to reorient their thought process and approach towards improving the portfolio construction process, especially if they have annual cash needs. Specifically, a more forward looking risk-based approach should be at the foundation of real money portfolios. Real money managers should:

1. **Replace return targets with risk-adjusted return targets.** Big drawdowns and volatility matter. Focusing on return targets misses the damage to performance caused by large drawdowns and high volatility. Portfolios should be constructed such that extreme worst-case scenarios are accounted for and dealt with in the investment process, either through the use of overlays, hedges to cut off tail risk, or less aggressive asset allocation with truly diversifying exposures.

2. **Look forward, not backward.** Historical asset class or fund performance is not a good indicator of the future. Real money portfolios should not be constructed to fit the recent past no matter how comfortable that may be. The macro environment matters greatly

and should be considered first and foremost when constructing portfolios.

3. **Rethink liquidity.** Do not undervalue liquidity when the world looks benign and volatility remains low. Low probability events by definition escape most models, but this does not mean that they should be ignored. On the contrary, it is the fiduciary duty of real money managers to manage to potential scenarios where liquidity can disappear. Similarly, real money managers should not overvalue the return received from taking on illiquidity. Time horizons are much shorter than generally believed.

The following interviews offer a wealth of new ideas and strategies for rethinking real money. While I don't pretend to have all the answers, this book is a good starting point for developing a new model and framework for real money managers.

Chapter 2

The Researcher

Dr. Andres Drobny
Drobny Global Advisors

To get a handle on where we are in today's markets—the issues, drivers, and looming uncertainties—I headed across town to sit down for another session with my business partner and resident guru—"The Researcher"—Dr. Andres Drobny (no relation). When we sat down to conduct his interview for *Inside the House of Money* in 2005, his central premise was that "it all ends in tears."

His roots as a trained economist led him to point out building imbalances and disequilibrium in the global economy during the past few years, factors which pointed to an impending crisis—although the timing or exact cause eluded him. In late 2008, I witnessed him buy equities for the first time since I have known him—and not just any equities, but emerging market equities. Besides being my business partner, his rare skill set as former academic economist, Wall Street chief economist, and proprietary trader make him well-placed to comment on the macroeconomic backdrop that anchors all of the following interviews.

In running the research business at Drobny Global, Andres has built a franchise around the "favorite trade." His research pieces, ad hoc discussions, and macro conferences all revolve around crystallizing macroeconomic views, themes, and ideas into hard trade ideas: which market, instruments, and time horizon should be selected to express a given idea. The concept of having to bring one best idea to the table and justify it to an audience of peers strengthens the research process and forces managers to think deeply about both the macroeconomic chain of causality and the detailed expression of a specific trade, the latter of which needs to value downside risk above all else.

Dr. Drobny has used this methodology to hold a living discourse on world markets with the best in the business over the last decade, giving him a unique vantage point from which to see the gamut of how different traders express good risk/reward trades.

It did, in fact, end in tears (see box).

How did you know?

It had to end in tears because there was too much private sector debt buildup. It is ironic now that people talk about government debt as being a problem. Private sector debt is the real problem. The government can almost always fund its debt if it decides to print money; the private sector cannot. Private sector debt just kept growing and growing, but my timing was way off. I thought it was over in 2000, after the equity bubble burst, but the Great Macro Experiment restarted it. The next leg up, especially the 2005–2007 phase, really surprised me. We are now onto the second phase of the Great Macro Experiment. (See Figure 2.1.)

It All Ends in Tears

My main hypothesis has been that it all ends in tears. Ultimately, if there is a sufficient recovery, interest rates go up to a point that assets get knocked and we head back to deflation. Or assets on their own give up and burst. The only other way out of all this debt is to devalue it via genuine goods price inflation, but that seems hard to achieve. If the authorities are lucky, they will be able to muddle through with lowish inflation, stable asset values, and okay growth over a long period, but during that process the world economy will be very vulnerable. It's never been accomplished before, but maybe this time things are different.

Today, the pessimists are actually now the optimists. The pessimist says house prices are going to collapse. Think about it. It's actually not that pessimistic because if assets give without interest rates going up, then interest rates can stay low, helping cushion the process. So, oddly enough, the optimistic case may turn out to produce the worst outcome. Interest rates will have to rise more than is priced into the markets, which could cause a nasty tumble in assets and, ultimately, the global economy.

SOURCE: *Inside the House of Money* (John Wiley & Sons, 2006).

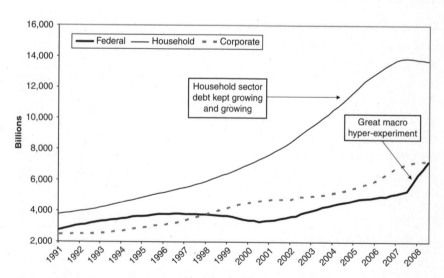

Figure 2.1 U.S. Debt by Sector, 1991–2008
SOURCE: Bloomberg.

Explain what you mean by the Great Macro Experiment.

Debt-fueled overconsumption has historically resulted in a depression, a deep and prolonged recession, or in the case of Japan, a very long stagnation. The common argument, put forward especially by monetarists, is that these episodes occurred and persisted because monetary policy was not eased fast enough or far enough. The Great Macro Experiment, therefore, is an attempt to use aggressive reflationary policies to overcome the effects of debt deflation after the equity bubble burst. We still seem to be in the midst of the Great Macro Experiment, although it is the next phase. It is a hyper-experiment now.

The Experiment started with Greenspan, who preemptively and aggressively cut interest rates to head off the looming recession/depression in 2001–2003. It was a real-time experiment; it had never been done before. From 2003 to 2007, it appeared to have worked as easy money helped fuel another leg to the property and asset boom. I underestimated the potency of easy money when asset deflation emerges, perhaps because there was still another asset to inflate: property (see Figure 2.2). The hyper-experiment today, which includes the use of quantitative easing (QE) and bailouts, is a renewed attempt to prevent a cascade of

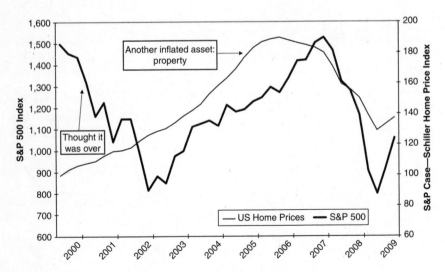

Figure 2.2   U.S. Home Prices and S&P 500 Index, 2000–2009
SOURCE: Bloomberg.

defaults and preempt a deepening recession and possibly a prolonged depression.

It is very important, however, not to neglect the role of fiscal policy. The conventional argument is that Greenspan's monetary policy was too easy, which created conditions for the equity bubble of the mid- to late 1990s and the housing bubble of 2002–2007. But fiscal policy also played a role, especially in the housing bubble. The Bush tax cuts early in the decade accelerated a redistribution of income towards the rich—the investing classes—and this redistribution added fuel to the original asset bubble. Greenspan takes most of the blame, but the fiscal element is often overlooked in the analysis of these events. Fiscal policy matters. Keynes taught us that, although the monetarists led us to forget it.

Look back at the Great Depression. The popular explanation is that tight monetary policy and the gold standard produced and prolonged the Great Depression. But few seem to be aware that taxes were progressively cut during the first half of the 1920s, which culminated in big tax cuts in 1925, especially for higher income earners (see Table 2.1). When taxes were cut in 1925, an asset bubble and spending boom ensued, ultimately leading to the crash of 1929 (see Figure 2.3). More recently, Bush cut taxes at the start of this decade, culminating in the big cuts of 2003. Again an asset bubble ensued and a crash emerged in 2008 (see Figure 2.4). This redistribution towards the investing classes helped maintain and arguably added a new leg to the bubble in both episodes.

However, in 1931–1932, taxes were increased and spending was cut as Hoover tried to balance the budget. Simultaneously, monetary policy was tightened. The monetary and fiscal measures combined to send

Table 2.1   U.S. Tax Policy, 1992–1936

Income ($)	1922	1925	1932	1936
5,000	8%	3%	8%	8%
25,000	18%	12%	18%	21%
50,000	31%	18%	31%	35%
100,000	56%	25%	56%	62%

SOURCE: Tax Foundation.

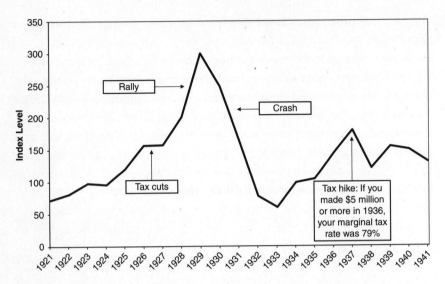

Figure 2.3   Dow Jones Industrial Average, 1921–1941
SOURCE: Bloomberg.

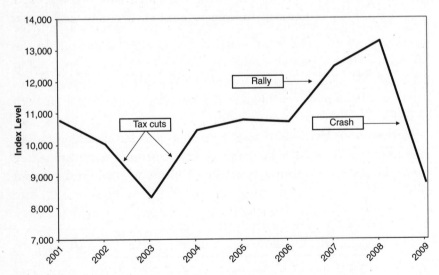

Figure 2.4   Dow Jones Industrial Average, 2001–2009
SOURCE: Bloomberg.

the U.S. economy into another deeper downturn in 1932, just when there was hope that things were starting to improve. Monetary and fiscal policies were eased aggressively when FDR was elected and took office in 1933, and recovery ensued. Given the depth of the downturn, the recovery was especially vigorous during the first few years. The Great Macro Experiment, then, is both an attempt to avoid a 1931–1932–style downturn and an effort to prompt an FDR-type vigorous recovery. It is not an easy task to do both.

Isn't all that private sector debt still out there?

Sure, the excess debt is still out there, and it will not go away quickly. But it is getting smaller, not bigger—it is a stock versus flow issue. Although the stock remains very high, it is falling rather than increasing because households are paying back debt or defaulting. That is a critical difference. It is the equivalent of saying that the savings ratio in the debtor countries has increased. So yes, there is still excess debt out there, but it is probably falling now. Because of this, although things feel worse now, the situation is actually improving compared with two years ago. This is a crucial element in making investment decisions and in part explains why I am no longer bearish equities.

Is there any exception to your claim that government debt can always be funded by printing money?

Many people think there is a limit on public debt, but I am not so sure. Apart from a country constrained by a gold standard or fixed exchange rate, the only scenario where the government might not be able to fund its debt is an inflationary scenario. However, that scenario only seems likely to emerge after the policies succeed in promoting growth. One of the reasons that a much-anticipated financing problem has never materialized in Japan is that reflationary policies failed to stimulate a sustained rebound and a return of inflation. Interest rates have remained low and funding the deficit has been surprisingly easy.

Consider what happens if the public debt and financing fears prove correct and bond markets start to tank. This is an issue that came up during a debate at our recent conference in London (see box). Without inflation, rising nominal bond yields push up real yields and deflate the economy; bonds become more attractive again and buyers bring yields back down. Without inflation, it is hard to get a bond rout. It is only when inflation rises that government financing becomes a real and sustained problem for bond markets. That is when bonds no longer get cheaper as they sell off and nominal yields rise, which is when you get a real bond crisis.

Drobny Global Conference, London, October 2009

The day ended with a new event: the first ever Drobny Debate. Niall Ferguson (Harvard University) and Hugh Hendry (Eclectica Asset Management) squared up to make the case: bullish or bearish bonds? Oh wow! It produced many good laughs. And, several powerful moments. One still reverberated at the bar after the event. Niall was asked whether his bear bond view is predicated on rising inflation. He answered "no"; it is fundamentally a supply issue. Hence real yields should rise as bonds sell off.

The questioner responded sharply: in such circumstances, a rise in price will beget demand. Lower bond prices and higher real returns will bring out more buyers, and an equilibrium will be found at a higher real yield. Hugh Hendry's face suddenly lit up and he pronounced, "Then Niall and I agree!" This is precisely what happened in 1931, he argued, when real rates rose in a downturn, which became the catalyst for the next steep decline in financial markets and the global economy.

Now, whether rising yields today would produce a 1931-type crack is an interesting question. In 1931, real interest rates rose as fiscal policy was being tightened. That proved a disastrous combo. But, fiscal policy today is aggressively stimulative. That may make the global economy more resilient to higher real yields. As long, that is, as the fiscal stimulus is sustained.

But, what about the other tail? The bond collapse, the old Latam-type default and devaluation scenario? The question revealed that the bear bond story *must* incorporate a view on inflation. *For bond markets to truly collapse, and a Latam-type financial crisis to ensue, you need both rising nominal yields and steady to lower real yields.* That is, rising inflation. That's how you get to a bond crisis, since bonds don't actually get cheaper as prices fall. That's the disaster scenario. Without this, rising bond yields leads to higher real yields, which attracts more buyers and/or increasingly restricts borrowing and thus economic activity. Notice, then, that the simple hedge to the bond disaster scenario is to buy break-even inflation. That option wasn't really available in Latam-type bond defaults.

Both participants are to be congratulated for taking the event seriously, doing it with humor and, most of all, for helping deepen our understanding of a topic that is all too often handled in a cavalier and sloppy manner. Hugh acquitted himself well against a genuine international heavyweight. Niall is also highly commended for taking on Hugh on his own turf. And, for defending a view initially expressed back in April, when yields generally were 50 to 100 basis points lower. A very well played "away" game. Bravo!

SOURCE: *Drobny Global Monitor,* October 30, 2009.

What, then, happens if we have inflation or hyperinflation, as some are predicting?

These are the new "bond vigilantes" (see box). They have a point, but you do not want to skip any steps here. The path to hyperinflation may well involve an initial period of healthy-looking recovery. It takes a long time for hyperinflation to take root. Things can look good for a while at first. Hyperinflations typically start when a fiscal deficit gets monetized, so the vigilantes are right to be alert to the dangers. But, the bond disaster story has to go through the path of better growth and a better outlook for some time. The process, even if the vigilantes are right, is likely to take a good deal longer than generally assumed.

Bond Vigilantes

Bond vigilante is a term given to bond market participants who, in reaction to inflationary monetary and fiscal policies, effectuate a "protest" in U.S. Treasury markets, pushing up yields. From the fall of 1993 to the fall of 1994, 10-year Treasury yields climbed from 5.2 percent to over 8.0 percent, in part because of concerns about the federal deficit. James Carville, one of Clinton's top political advisors, said, "I used to think that if there was reincarnation, I wanted to come back as the president or the pope or as a .400 baseball hitter. But now I would like to come back as the bond market. You can intimidate everybody."

Can the Hyper-Great Macro Experiment—with quantitative easing, bank bailouts, and other creative measures—have a happy ending?

Perhaps, though it may have more to do with fiscal policy than monetary issues from here. It is critical that an expansionary fiscal policy is maintained for long enough. Monetary stimulus may become less necessary over time and be slowly withdrawn, but fiscal stimulus will have to be maintained for longer to make sure overall demand growth is sustained as household debt repayments proceed. That will likely depend on the political will of the population. In a democratic society, the population may have limited appetite for sustaining fiscal stimulus. The key is to take away fiscal stimulus at the right time: after it starts to work and the multipliers are taking over. The U.S. authorities seem to be looking at 2011–2012 to remove some of the stimulus, which is the timing set by the Bush tax cut sunset provisions. Their hope is that the stimulus starts to work, growth resumes, and the deficit starts coming down, allowing for a modest fiscal tightening without threatening the recovery. It is a delicate situation. Meanwhile, there are people out there right now saying that the U.S. government should be balancing the budget. Oh wow! That is precisely what they did in 1931–1932, which was a disaster. They argue that it was monetary tightening that created the second wave of the Great Depression. Although it is true that monetary tightening made things worse, fiscal policy was also being tightened at that time, and that is precisely the wrong thing to do when the private sector is retrenching.

If the economy has a double dip, some think it could be significantly worse than the crisis of 2008 because all of the bullets have been fired. Interest rates are at zero, and fiscal stimulus, TARP [Troubled Asset Relief Program], and other programs are unlikely to get additional support.

That is possible, which leads to one of my concerns about what Obama and other policy makers have done. One of the lessons from the 1930s and the New Deal is that it is much easier for fiscal policy to succeed after you have gone through a really nasty downturn. The question is whether the downturn of 2008–2009 was nasty enough. Obama keeps using the phrase "save or create jobs," but you never get any credit for saving jobs. It is possible that he did not let things get bad enough early on, limiting the potential for a strong rebound, in which case the danger is a loss of credibility and a possible rebellion against additional fiscal stimulus. This is also part of the Great Macro Experiment. It is not just whether the policy authorities did too much or too little, but whether they acted too fast and too soon to retain popular support for the stimulus efforts.

What are the implications of the crisis and the recovery outside the U.S.?

That is one of the things I got very wrong. Look at how well many countries outside the U.S. are doing; it is the decoupling theory. I thought a crisis in debtor countries would drag down surplus countries as well. Not for long, it seems. China is the most obvious example; their fiscal stimulus was huge and so far pretty effective. With perfect hindsight, it makes sense; in a global savings glut environment, when interest rates stay low, you want faster domestic demand in the high savings/creditor countries. That leans against contracting demand growth in the debtor economies. As the U.S. consumer spends less out of income, the Chinese consumer spends more. That helps absorb excess capacity in China and helps limit the global downturn. Increased savings in the U.S.—leading to a narrowing of the U.S. current account deficit—is matched by increased spending and a narrower surplus abroad. I underestimated this possibility before seeing it happen in 2008–2009, and it enhances the potential for the global economy to muddle through this crisis.

So when you say fiscal policy is often underestimated or underappreciated, you are not just speaking about the U.S.?

No, it is everywhere. Again, China is a great example. Their stimulus was largely fiscal; monetary policy was relatively passive through all this. China did not cut rates aggressively, nor did they have to bail out the banking system all at once. They never faced a potential domino effect of failing banks. The same is true for much of non-Japan Asia. Countries that did not face a banking crisis did not have the same type of monetary policy response. Aggressive monetary stimulus generally occurred in the debtor countries, such as the U.S. and UK. In the euro region, monetary policy stimulus occurred mainly because Spain, Ireland, and several Eastern European debtor countries were in deep trouble. And while Switzerland is a creditor country, they needed an easier monetary policy mainly because they have a finance-based economy and their banks were in trouble as well. China, however, remains a good example of how powerful and effective fiscal policy can be in this type of environment.

That being said, it is not clear what happens next because it depends in part on future policy actions and in part on whether the Great Macro Experiment succeeds. What I can say, though, is that the risk of inflation has increased compared to a year or two ago. Again, we are better off today than we were two years ago, just before the crash of '08. A process of adjustment is underway, and that increases the risk of inflation. But a lurch back into deflation is very possible as well, especially if the policy makers take their feet off the fiscal accelerator.

What exactly do you mean when you say we are better off now than two years ago?

I am not saying that our wealth or income is higher. Rather, I am saying that the world is now in an adjustment period, where a process towards solving the underlying problems is underway. This compares with pre-2008, when we were creating bigger and bigger problems. Because debtors are deleveraging and creditors are spending more, we are moving towards a more sustainable equilibrium. There is a better chance now that things will work out, especially given the policy response. Hence, the probability has increased that the outcome will be inflationary rather than deflationary. Whether you think that the absolute probability of inflation is high or low, you should admit that it has increased in favor of inflation. There is also a higher probability of a middle ground outcome, whereby we muddle through with 4 to 5 percent nominal growth in the U.S. for a prolonged period. Such a scenario is possible because decoupling has greater potential than I originally thought, and because the authorities have responded aggressively as the private sectors in debtor countries are rebuilding savings. The savings ratio has been increased in the debtor countries and this has involved a painful adjustment in consumption levels. That makes the outlook better, not worse.

Speaking of things getting better, you went long Asian equities in late 2008 during the heart of the crisis. I thought you were an equity perma-bear. What made you buy stocks?

I went from bearish equities—especially emerging market equities—to neutral, which meant I had to buy some. I bought Asia for several reasons. The first reason is price—prices came down hard even though stimulus was already starting. That struck me as an opportunity simply because policy might buoy the market. Second, Asia already had cheap currencies, and many became even cheaper. But most importantly, I had to admit that I had been wrong. My bearish view on emerging market equities since 2004 had been very painful. Emerging market equities exploded. And look at one of my conclusions today: that the decoupling idea might actually prove correct. So part of it was recognizing that I might have been very wrong about emerging markets and the sustainability of decoupling. When we got the price adjustment, I saw the opportunity to correct what increasingly seemed a mistake.

What lessons did you learn in 2008?

The primary lesson was the value of liquidity—I learned how important it is to have liquid positions. Liquidity helps avoid making bad decisions in a crisis, and provides funding potential to take advantage of extreme prices. The lesson of liquidity relates as much to owning a house at the personal level as to owning assets in a hedge fund or having exposure

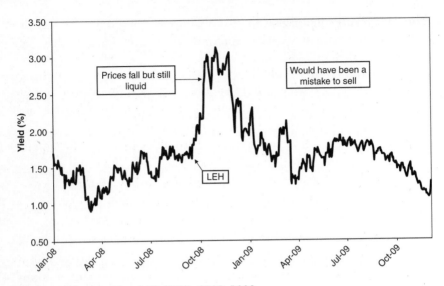

Figure 2.5   Ten Year U.S. TIPS, 2008–2009
SOURCE: Bloomberg.

to a fund that is invested in illiquid assets. As we saw during the crash, markets can totally shut down. I am not talking about prices just going against you, which is what happened with TIPS (see box). You still could have sold TIPS during the crisis, even though it would have been a mistake (see Figure 2.5). Some assets became totally illiquid; you could not sell them at virtually any price. I cannot remember a time when that happened in our lifetimes. The lesson of the importance of liquidity will be remembered by the survivors and will likely not be forgotten for a generation.

TIPS

Treasury Inflation-Protected Securities (TIPS) are inflation-indexed bonds issued by the U.S. Treasury. The principal is adjusted to the Consumer Price Index, the commonly used measure of inflation. The coupon rate is constant, but generates a different amount of interest when multiplied by the inflation-adjusted principal, thus protecting the holder against inflation. Inflation-indexed bonds in foreign countries are also referred to as *linkers* because of their link to inflation rates.

How do you value liquidity?

I don't know how to value it per se, or what the excess return should be for holding an illiquid instrument. I do know that the position has to be exceptionally small and nonmaterial to make it in my portfolio. In general, I want to be in instruments that I can get out of quickly if I have to. You cannot hedge illiquidity in any way other than staying liquid. I suppose you can sell correlated liquid variables to cover the illiquid assets that you own, but that creates additional risks. This, by the way, was another reason why I had the confidence to buy equities: I knew that some people were selling to hedge illiquid holdings, which meant that equities were probably overshooting to the downside.

Another lesson learned from 2008 is the importance of good risk management techniques. You could have had the right view but missed the move, or worse, got run over in the crisis. Views sometimes count very little, whereas good risk management always counts a lot. The top performers in 2008 were able to put on good risk-versus-reward bets at the right time, and had the liquidity to do so due to good risk management.

The old style of risk management suggests establishing a "diversified" portfolio with different asset weightings based on risk tolerance and time profile, which does not really work in this environment. If you are 60 years old, you are theoretically supposed to increase your bond weighting. But if you did that at the beginning of 2009—decreased your equities and increased your bonds—you virtually committed suicide. And if the inflation hawks are right, this may prove to be a really bad trade for a long period, even if your timing is reasonably good. People still seem stuck on what worked from 1980 to 2000 and arguably until 2007. That was an amazing period and I am not at all sure that what worked will continue to work going forward.

Does the real money management world have to change as a result of the crisis?

Yes, because again, the crash has given us new information. People were introduced in real-time to what economists call the "corner solution." In the idealized, perfectly functioning world imagined in traditional economic theory, economic agents optimize subject only to a budget constraint such as maximizing profits or investment returns. That is a first best solution. But 2008 revealed the dangers posed by extreme investment losses and the potential for default and bankruptcy. This suggests the optimization exercise should incorporate an additional constraint of avoiding losses and drawdowns so large that they imperil the existence of an economic entity (e.g., banks and insurance companies) or cause a very severe dislocation in spending for entities with fixed spending commitments (pension, endowments, foundations). That implies a solution to the optimization exercise where risk-adjusted returns and volatility play a role. It is a second-best solution, but one that helps reduce the potential for a catastrophic outcome.

This was neatly illustrated in a recent discussion I had with Larry Bacow, president of my alma mater, Tufts University. He mentioned that the universities with large endowments suffered disproportionately in the crash and now face significant cutbacks in spending as a result. Universities with smaller endowments experienced smaller losses and thus felt less pain in the crash. Bacow concluded that the more a university relies on endowment returns to fund its spending, the lower the risk profile of that endowment should be. Yet, in practice, the opposite seems to have been the case: the bigger the endowment, the greater the risk it assumed. The experience of 2008 reveals that this needs to change, he argued. His idea is a powerful one, and it applies to pension funds as well as university endowments. For a pension or endowment, the greater the dependence of the operating budget on investment returns, the lower the risk profile should be, not the other way around. That helps avoid the "corner solution" of bankruptcy, default, or draconian spending cuts.

If you had to put on one trade right now for the next 10 years, what would it be?

I guess it would have to be TIPS. I am tempted by Asian equities, but the safety margin of TIPS is what drives my decision. I am painfully close to the age of 60 so I need to consider safety first. TIPS have been an undervalued asset class and some of the smartest guys I know have been bullish since 1998, when these instruments first came on the scene in the U.S. In those days real yields were pretty high, so I could see how TIPS would work because of the potential for a decline in real yields. But, until monetary policy is tightened aggressively, TIPS still look pretty good, even with real yields down considerably. If you are afraid of a bond catastrophe, then you want to own break-even inflation; that is, you want to be long TIPS against nominal bonds. As we discussed earlier, the path to a bond crisis must involve higher inflation, so break-even inflation should adjust (see box). Another beauty of TIPS is the principal guarantee in the event of deflation. You get a floor in a deflation scenario and protection in the case of a bond rout due to rising inflation. Because TIPS offer a positive yield over inflation—more than what is offered by short-dated Treasuries—they seem a decent place to hold wealth.

Break-Even Inflation

Break-even inflation is the difference between the nominal yield on a fixed rate investment and the real yield, where the latter is reflected in the yield spread between nominal bonds and an inflation-linked investment of similar maturity and credit quality.

SOURCE: Inflation-Linked.com.

What do you think about real estate?

Real estate is a spread trade now. The great trade, if it were liquid and you could do it, would be to buy repossession property in the U.S. and sell high-end property, like oceanfront. That trade has both legs going in its favor right now. Repossession property has fallen back near 2000 price levels, at least here in California, and is now trading in pretty high volume. The price of oceanfront property is still three to five times 2000 levels, and precious little turnover is taking place these days. This trade also captures the notion that widening income dispersion—a trend that has been running since 1980 and supported higher end property prices—has run its course and has started to reverse. And, by selling oceanfront, you own an implicit call on global warming! Obviously, and unfortunately, this is not a trade that you can really put on, although it does suggest renting oceanfront rather than buying until prices adjust.

What about the U.S. dollar—is the dollar's status as the world's reserve currency on the wane?

The idea that the dollar's reserve currency status is disappearing is something I used to believe in, but now I am not so sure. In order for that to happen, the public sector would have to begin dumping its dollars, or at least no longer accumulate dollars. If the underlying U.S. trade deficit has fallen, then the public sector will likely be accumulating fewer dollars. In other words, faster consumption growth in China and Asia is an alternative to both reserve accumulation and nominal currency appreciation.

My view on the direction of the dollar has also changed. I have been bearish the dollar for a long time. It has been in a downtrend since 1970. But that downtrend was associated with excess U.S. growth, insufficient U.S. savings, and a growing U.S. trade deficit. That process could well be reversing. The dollar looks terrible right now because the U.S. has zero interest rates, which certainly weighs it down, but the underlying elements of the dollar are better now than they have been for a generation. It is already pretty cheap and the U.S. trade deficit is narrowing as households retrench. Further, a U.S. recovery based on infrastructure spending and redistribution of income towards the lower income segments of the population is a growth model that has more domestic spending absorption and less import leakage. Add to that the accelerated growth in China, and all of it points to a trend narrowing U.S. trade deficit. So the structural factors for the dollar have improved significantly. The cyclical issue is that interest rates are at zero, so the U.S. has no interest rate spread advantage anymore. The day that you get a rebound in the U.S. economy sufficient to change interest rate expectations is the day that you could get a very powerful move up in the dollar. I abandoned my longstanding bearish dollar stance back in 2004 or 2005 and have been both long and short the dollar since then. I am still officially neutral, but I am leaning towards a bullish bias going forward.

The following is from your chapter in **Inside the House of Money:** *"I find it hard to believe I'll ever be bullish the dollar. . . . The only reason to be bullish the dollar is if real U.S. interest rates get very high.*

That would both attract capital inflows and hold back spending and thus the excess demand in the economy."

Yikes! That is also something we can put on the list of lessons learned: never say never. The crash of '08 created an additional dimension by reducing the U.S. trade deficit without the inhibiting effect of higher real rates. I may have underestimated the power of the crash in turning around the U.S. trade deficit, and thus helping to correct the big underlying structural problem for the dollar. We still most likely need higher interest rates to get a true bull market in the dollar, but the upside potential is much better now than it has been in a long time.

It seems as if there is a big global dollar carry trade going on whereby everyone is long something and short the dollar. As such, could a big dollar rally cause a double dip?

I do not think so. First, the U.S. has a trade deficit, so there has to be a long dollar position out there. Somebody owns a lot of dollars and we know who that is: many of the world's central banks. It is correct, though, that the private sector now likely has a short dollar position, but the public sector is long dollars. Whether any dollar rally is associated with a double dip depends on why the dollar has turned. If it is the 2008 model of falling growth, renewed asset deflation, and a falling U.S. trade deficit, then sure, that sounds like a scenario for a double dip. But if the U.S. dollar turns because fiscal expansion in the U.S. leads to stronger growth, and an unwind of the friendly Fed policy, then a dollar rally will probably not be associated with a double dip.

The fundamental point here is that the U.S. trade deficit fell in 2008 by considerably more than ever could have been expected, which is new information. Moreover, the decoupling idea seems to have a higher probability than before. Initially, that can create a dollar downdraft for cyclical reasons, whereby the rest of the world grows faster than the U.S. Structurally, however, it is a big positive for the dollar.

Has anything else changed as a result of the crisis?

Many, many things have changed because of the crisis. In the big picture, it is certainly a mistake to believe that it's business as usual or that little has changed. Some have argued that we have experienced a shock and will now return to good old tried and tested models. I don't believe this at all. Rather, the path ahead remains very unclear to me and it depends critically on the outlook for fiscal policy.

If you were a deflationist before the crash, then you really have to accept that the speed and extent of the policy reaction may have changed the outlook. It has to have changed things at the margin. Holding on to old views and failing to acknowledge this change seem rigid and dangerous. Equally, those who were caught bullish growth and long equities into the crash should also have learned a valuable lesson. Being proven wrong provides great information content. This is perhaps the greatest lesson of all from the crash: change your views as facts change. It is important to recognize and accept when things don't work out as you expect. If you are proven wrong, adjust your outlook accordingly. To persistently hold on to views, regardless of changing reality, is a recipe for failure and constant distress.

Chapter 3

The Family Office Manager

Jim Leitner
Falcon Management

"The Family Office Manager" is the most popular chapter in *Inside the House of Money*. The original interview was assembled from a series of discussions with Jim Leitner, who described his approach as attempting to combine the best of hedge fund investing with the best of real money management. In light of what happened to the real money world in 2008, those conversations provided the inspiration for this book.

Leitner got into the markets as a money broker, scribbling prices on the chalkboard of a New York trading floor while still in school. He moved on to become a proprietary trader in London, focused principally on interest rates and currencies, and later moved out the risk spectrum into equities, then frontier emerging markets. He ran the European trading desk at a major bank and then branched off on his own to run managed accounts for some of the most famous investors in the world.

Eventually, having accumulated enough capital, he whittled his investor base down to just himself and set up his own family office behind a gas station in suburban New Jersey. It was there that he developed the unique absolute return strategy for managing his own money, a strategy he has employed to great success for the past decade. He focuses truly on absolute returns, preferring to express trades through option structures wherever possible, limiting downside risk and making it easy to sleep at night. Leitner has also been a member of the Yale Endowment Investment Committee since 2004, where he has witnessed firsthand the development of the celebrated Endowment Model, adopted by so many real money managers in recent years.

I conducted this interview on October 15, 2009, the same day that Leitner's latest iteration went live: a hedge fund in which he has accepted limited outside capital for the first time in years. Because the line of potential investors in his fund was long and varied, he had the luxury of choosing those who seemed best aligned with his own goals of long-term capital appreciation and charitable giving, the latter of which is exemplified by the Leitner Center for International Law and Justice, which he supports at Fordham Law School (www.leitnercenter.org). Due to excess demand, the fund was immediately oversubscribed; he is closed to new investors.

The excitement was palpable on launch day in his newer Wyckoff, New Jersey, office, where he has been practicing aikido and running his family office since 2001, having finally moved from the shadow of the gas station. The energy on the trading floor contrasted starkly with the early morning gloom outside as his team celebrated its first trade: a bet on 10-year U.S. Treasuries ahead of the September consumer price inflation (CPI) number. Leitner thought that market expectations were incorrect and made a bet that government bonds should rally if inflation came in lower than expected. Minutes later, the CPI number printed in line with expectations, yet Treasuries still rallied. Leitner quickly closed the trade according to his risk management plan and, despite being wrong on the inflation number, still managed to make a profit on his new fund's first trade. Classic Jim Leitner.

Because of his varied background not only trading multiple instruments in multiple asset classes around the world, but also working inside a variety of investment vehicles, from bank prop desks to family offices to university endowments to hedge funds, Leitner can speak to many of the issues faced by a host of different investors today. His edge comes from his ability to forecast macro trends on a longer-term basis, coupled with his skill at aggressive tactical trading, structuring themes and trades with good risk-versus-reward characteristics in the shorter term. Most important, however, is Leitner's focus on risk management. Because all of his money is in the fund, he never wants to lose more than 20 percent and structures his portfolio to make sure that under no possible scenario can he ever exceed this loss threshold.

After the inaugural trade of his new hedge fund, Jim and I retired to a conference room filled with books about finance, economics, philosophy, history, and philanthropy to talk about lessons learned in 2008 and his own thoughts on rethinking real money.

From mid-2008 to mid-2009, you took a year off and went to cash. Is going to cash the key differentiator between hedge funds and real money?

I certainly think so. Over the last 10 years, real money investors have clearly drifted to the Yale model, which has come to be known as the Endowment Model. This model, as it is popularized, basically considers cash "trash," such that any cash balance is considered wasted capital. Historically, that makes perfect sense; cash always gives the lowest return when modeling on a backward-looking basis. If you look back 100 years, for example, cash was clearly an underperforming strategy. You would have been better off in medium-term or long-term bonds, and certainly much better off in equity and equity-like instruments. And this is generally how people construct their efficient portfolio frontier: by looking backwards. So there has been a push to hold the lowest possible cash balance.

Hedge fund managers, on the other hand, always have cash. I have been running my personal account since 1997, during which time my average cash balance has been 25 percent, whereas the high was probably 90 percent. To an absolute return investor, cash is an essential asset. When other assets have negative returns forecast over the next 6 or 12 months, there is no reason to not hold a low return cash portfolio. As an absolute return macro manager, I believe in tactical asset allocation and that clearly distinguished my approach from the Endowment Model, where asset allocation is never done tactically. The Endowment Model's core approach consists of a long-term process where equity-like returns are being generated in a diversified portfolio.

How do you value cash?

The prevailing wisdom looks at cash on a historical basis, which completely neglects the inherent opportunity costs associated with a lack of cash. By this I mean simply that cash affords you flexibility; if you have cash, you can allocate that cash when attractive opportunities arise. By taking a backward look at cash, you wind up focusing on the rate it has earned historically. The correct way to measure the return on cash is more dynamic: cash is bounded on the lower side by its actual return, whereas the upper side possesses an additional element of positive return received from having the ability to take advantage of unique opportunities.

Look at 2008 as an example. A lot of assets collapsed in value, creating ample opportunities for those with cash to deploy. Mortgage-related bonds, emerging market corporate bonds, and some country-related Eurobonds all got absolutely trashed. For instance, Ghanaian Eurobonds traded at 59 cents on the dollar, although there was no reason to believe that the Ghanaian government would have any difficulty paying interest and principal on these securities. Buying them led to a quick 72 percent return on invested capital over about 10 months. How can you consider cash trash when it affords these kinds of opportunities?

The popularity of the Endowment Model has led to increasing sums of money being allocated to illiquid assets, implicit in which is the belief that the return on these assets outweighs the costs of illiquidity. However, in a tail event, when all risk assets are dropping and correlations have gone to one, being long illiquid assets makes it virtually impossible to capitalize on other assets that might be trading at bargain-basement prices. In 2008, how many real money funds were able to buy assets that had gone down 70 percent in only a few quarters?

Running the Endowment Model makes it very difficult to tactically move into really cheap assets because there is no available cash. You would have to redeem from a fund or an illiquid investment before reallocating to take advantage of truly exceptional opportunities, a process that takes time. The Endowment Model encourages long-term investment in illiquid assets because these assets, on average, should pay a slightly higher expected return. When you put those slighter higher expected returns in an optimization model, it recommends a higher allocation to illiquid assets. If you have a 100-year time horizon, it probably makes very good sense to have high exposure to illiquids. But it is very difficult to redeem from a manager, especially when that manager traffics in an illiquid market. Number one, it is difficult, in good conscience, to ask a manager for your money back due to your own issues. Number two, even if you do ask for it back, it doesn't happen that quickly. You cannot redeem from a real estate manager, an oil and gas manager, or a lumber or forestry manager at the snap of the fingers. Sure, theoretically you can redeem from an absolute return portfolio, but even most hedge fund redemptions—assuming the manager does not impose a gate or suspend the redemptions—have at least a 30-day notice period. Quarterly redemptions are much more common, and many funds offered slightly cheaper terms to institutional investors in exchange for longer lockups. The increased illiquidity came at a price, and that price seemed okay at a time when illiquidity was valued independent of its implicit opportunity cost, but this is no longer the case. Cash and liquidity have been undervalued by the real money crowd, and 2008 exposed that.

Looking back at Japan in 1990 or at the United States in 1929, the value of cash looked pretty good 20 or 30 years after these events. Yet for the last 20 to 30 years in the U.S., cash looks like a pretty bad investment.

Correct. But what will cash be worth over the next 30 years? Who knows? The higher asset prices go, the more I feel compelled to reduce exposure to risk assets and raise cash balances. Assets are mean reverting over the long term. In 1929, when everything was booming, it would have been great to sell your portfolio and raise cash in order to reinvest in 1933. (See Figure 3.1.) In Russia, where the markets went up tenfold between 1992 and 1997, it would have been great to take your money out to be able to reinvest in 1999, when the market was down 90 percent. (See Figure 3.2.)

Holding cash when markets are cheap is expensive, and holding cash when markets are expensive is cheap. Since markets had gotten expensive

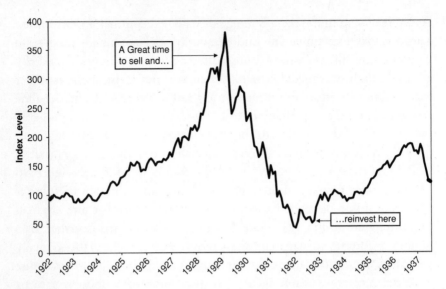

Figure 3.1 Dow Jones Industrial Average, 1922–1937
Source: Bloomberg.

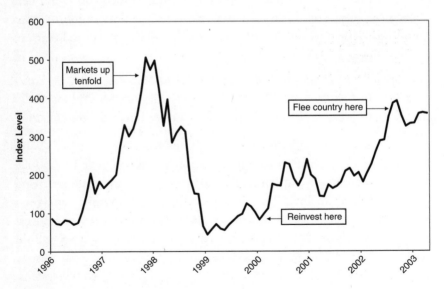

Figure 3.2 Russia (RTSI$) Index, 1996–2003
Source: Bloomberg.

in 2007, having more cash on the books made sense. But today, markets are no longer that expensive; things have come down a lot since the end of 2007. Prices have come off the bottom, but if you look forward, we now have positive expected value again—in terms of earning equity-like risk premia—because we are starting at a lower price. At this point there are clearly some values to be found.

What is the appropriate cash level for an endowment or pension?

That's a very difficult question, and the answer depends on the size of the underlying fund. Hedge funds can use derivatives to take risks and get exposure over a whole portfolio, while still allowing them to hold cash. They can buy options to be long markets or do swaps without having to put up much cash. But endowments typically don't have in-house trading staff, so they rely more on outside managers. As a result, it is probably more expensive for them to run cash on their books than for a macro fund, the latter of which can always gain risk exposure through the derivatives markets, curtailing opportunity costs.

The crux here really comes down to understanding that managing capital involves thinking about both return and risk. It seems to me that real money managers spend a lot more time thinking about returns than about how to manage downside risk. The investment process seems to be driven by a need to generate certain returns rather than a need to avoid absolute levels of loss on deployed capital.

Real money funds run an efficient frontier using long-term historical correlations and returns (see box on page 60). They may use forecasted returns, but they don't actually look at correlations over very short periods of time. Over long periods of time, correlations might show you that emerging market equities and U.S. equities have a low correlation. If you owned emerging market equities and U.S. equities from 1970 to 2000, you did okay because there were cycles when the U.S. was doing better and cycles when emerging markets were doing better, so having both in your portfolio worked fine. But if you look at your downside volatility in the tails, things become highly correlated. If you are using long-term correlations of 0.3 or 0.5, but in the tail the correlation goes to one, then your models are effectively telling you to take more risk than you should be taking if you care about short-term returns. If you ran your models based on correlations of one, it would bring the efficient frontier in and tell you to take less risk.

From 2000 to 2007, everyone was piling into the Endowment Model and moving out on the risk curve, thinking that diversification was the only risk management tool. And they were led down this path because of long-term historical return correlations. Though over a short period of time, when the downside tail correlation went to one, they were all over invested, and even worse, they were also overinvested in the same assets, exacerbating the pain.

Efficient Frontier

The Efficient Frontier is formed by plotting the risk and return of all possible portfolio combinations. The portfolios that have the highest return for a given level of risk are the optimal portfolios and make up the efficient frontier. Portfolios above the curve would be impossible to construct. Those that are below the curve are suboptimal. According to Modern Portfolio Theory (MPT), a rational investor would only hold a portfolio on the efficient frontier.

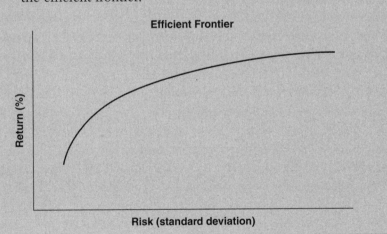

We all know that correlations go to one in a disaster, yet it still catches people out. What can investors do to prepare for downside tail events?

I am thinking more and more about the linkage between leverage and cash, particularly how and when to employ leverage. In general, I had always thought that leverage is a bad thing. A leveraged portfolio will be blown up quickly if leverage is defined as borrowing more to do the same thing. But 2008 forced me to think about the benefit of taking on leverage to do something different (e.g., borrow to purchase only those assets that, at least historically, have had negative correlations). In the large tail events for risk assets, government bonds have always gone up. Of course, it is impossible to say if this was due to a flight to quality or if it was a rational expectation that anticipated a weaker economy and lower interest rates.

Regardless, we began thinking about purchasing a portfolio of bonds using leverage to mitigate the downside volatility of a real money portfolio oriented toward the Endowment Model with more than 90 percent of its risk in equity-like investments. We ran some simulations and discovered that even a tiny 5 percent leveraged allocation to long U.S. government fixed income would, over time, generate more absolute return, better ratios of return-to-worst-drawdown, and less significant absolute worst drawdown levels. We then conducted a simple study that adds leveraged bond positions to a portfolio of 100 percent long domestic U.S. equities. The back test results, from 1992 to 2009, show that adding 100 percent leverage to buy U.S. Treasuries increased annual yield by almost 5 percent while reducing the worst drawdown by 10 percent. Back-testing other periods, such as 1940 to 1980, yield less conclusive results; but it is clear more analytical work needs to be done in this area. It is also much too facile to say that leverage is bad in every occasion. Logically, since bonds can be repo'd at the cash rate and have a risk premium over cash, over time the cost of such insurance should actually be a positive to the fund (see box). (See Table 3.1.)

Bond Repurchase Agreement, or "Repo"

A form of short-term borrowing in which a party sells securities and immediately agrees to buy them back at a fixed price on some future date, where the difference between the forward price and the spot price represents interest on the loan. Treasury securities, corporate bonds, and stocks can be used in repo transactions. Repos can be done as overnight, term (with a

(continued)

specified end date), or open (no end date). For the party selling the security (and agreeing to repurchase it in the future) it is a repo, whereas for the party on the other end of the transaction, (buying the security and agreeing to sell in the future) it is a reverse repo. The repo market is a key cornerstone of the cash management process for market participants and banks. The Federal Reserve uses the repo market as part of its open market operations to manage the money supply.

In doing this analysis, are you guilty of investing in the rear view mirror?

We very well might be fighting the last battle, which is why a fundamental discretionary thought process and plausible scenario analysis is so important. Obviously, there is a risk that in the next tail event, government bonds become perfectly correlated with stocks. That is the scenario where people withdraw from a country because of the same source of macro instability that drives investors to sell all assets, even "safe" government bonds. Looking around the world, this happens when a country starts being perceived as too risky and investors try to flee all assets in the country. Let us assume it happens in the U.S., whereby foreigners are selling all U.S. assets. In that scenario, levering U.S. bonds on top of stocks would not work. Instead, maybe we should be levering a foreign bond portfolio on top of a U.S.-centric equity portfolio. In a scenario where everyone is trying to exit U.S. assets, the dollar is going down and foreign bonds gain in currency value. From 1992 through 1999, it would have been better to add a portfolio of half U.S. and half Japanese bonds than just U.S. bonds. But that advantage does not hold up for the more recent back tests from 2000 through 2009. Nevertheless, the idea of international bond diversification is definitely worth exploring in greater detail. (See Table 3.1.)

Being cognizant of what everyone else is doing seems to be a big part of your analysis.

Identifying crowded positions, themes, or even portfolio approaches is an important part of our process. It is also important to realize that

Table 3.1 Back Tests

Model	Start Date	End Date	Yield	Info Ratio	Worst Drawdown
100% stocks	1992	2009	7.66%	0.39	55.25%
100% stocks + 100% U.S. bonds	1992	2009	12.41%	0.59	45.89%
100% stocks + 50% U.S. bonds + 50% JGB	1992	2009	11.36%	0.57	48.90%
100% stocks	1992	1999	19.51%	1.29	19.19%
100% stocks + 100% U.S. bonds	1992	1999	22.45%	1.14	19.38%
100% stocks + 50% U.S. bonds + 50% JGB	1992	1999	24.27%	1.39	15.32%
100% stocks	2000	2009	−1.15%	−0.05	55.25%
100% stocks + 100% U.S. bonds	2000	2009	4.66%	0.21	45.89%
100% stocks + 50% U.S. bonds + 50% JGB	2000	2009	1.75	0.08	48.90%

SOURCE: Falcon.

diversification only works when you have assets that are valued differently; when some things are cheap and other things are expensive. If everything is expensive, everything will go down, so it doesn't really matter if you own different things for diversification's sake. Some things might go down less than others, but that does not give you any positive benefits in terms of making money. The key is finding cheap things that will go up in scenarios where everything else is going down. And historically, the only asset that has really done that is government fixed income.

It's easy to replicate and model portfolios with leveraged government bond positions or bond option positions, and the most interesting thing about this kind of leverage is that historically, it adds value to portfolios. It's like receiving free insurance because the bond risk premium is positive. If you buy a portfolio of government bonds and fund it by borrowing cash, if there is an upward sloping yield curve on average, over the business cycle or over any long period of time, that portfolio will make money. Hence you are buying insurance that, on average, makes you money. It is an incredibly interesting idea because normally insurance costs you money.

In 2007, we were looking at all kinds of things to hedge an equity portfolio in a bad event. Credit spreads were tight, so we viewed betting on credit spread wideners as an out-of-the-money put on stocks. We thought that credit spreads would only blow out if equities really came down hard since companies would still pay off their debt in a milder scenario. So we ran various scenarios for stocks and looked at credit spreads, S&P puts and put spreads, forward-starting volatility, and other ways to think about how to hedge an equity portfolio. Every single one of those strategies had negative carry, where you had to pay to get that insurance protection. But by being long government bonds, you actually get paid. It is an interesting, positive carry way to hedge an equity tail event that historically would have added value to a portfolio.

U.S. government bonds were yielding around 5 percent in 2007 while inflation was around 2 percent. That risk premium was neither excessively expensive nor excessively cheap, but I knew that other assets were expensive. So trimming back expensive assets to raise cash levels would have been prudent. The key question with respect to holding cash is: Do you have to have cash, or can you have government bonds instead? What kind of extra risks are you taking by having a government bond? Government bonds really are totally liquid. If you own a U.S. 10-year bond or a U.S. two-year note, is that not more or less the same as owning cash? Instantaneously, you can buy or sell billions and billions of dollars of them. So I am loath to just call it cash because of the nexus between cash and cash-like instruments.

So real money managers should use a valuation approach to raise or lower equity and equity-like exposures and cash and cash-like exposures?

Exactly. As equity and equity-like assets get to be more and more expensive, you want to have more and more cash and cash-like assets in your portfolio because the volatility on the downside can increase. If we think of valuations as departures from long-term fair value, then many approaches have been shown to allow better forecasting of returns in equities—at least better than a random walk. For judging valuation levels, I would start with price-to-earnings multiples, price-to-book multiples, or whatever kind of fundamental earnings model you want to use. Tobin's Q ratio, as demonstrated by Andrew Smithers' work, has correctly identified over- and undervalued episodes in the U.S. equity market, and the use of cyclically adjusted price to earnings ratios has worked in a similar manner. Everybody on the Street generates these kinds of numbers, and you can take an average of them or develop your own metric. I am not that smart, so I just try to talk to enough people to get a sense of what fundamental value might be. From recent discussions, markets now have positive risk premia again, though the recent rally in equities has probably put us back over fair value on a shorter time frame. Two years ago, there was not a great deal of risk premium to be had if you were intelligently looking forward. At that time, there was really no reason to be involved in most markets.

Jeremy Grantham, of Grantham, Mayo, Van Otterloo & Co. (GMO), has done a great thing the past decade. In the late 1990s, he took serious career risk by saying that the U.S. equity market was too expensive and dot-coms had driven the whole market too high. He refused to invest in that area and for a few years he underperformed, losing a considerable amount of assets as a result. But those assets came back in spades after 2000 when he was proven right. It wasn't market timing in the sense that he said tech stocks would come down in the next quarter. Rather, he was saying that because tech stocks had gotten expensive, there was no reason to be in them at prevailing valuation levels.

A good analogy is trying to forecast the weather. If you ask me today, on October 15, what the weather will be like going forward, I can tell you with confidence that on January 15, it will probably be colder. I don't know if it will be a really cold day on January 15, and I don't know if January 10 or January 20 will be the really cold day. I have no idea if there will be a lot of snow or no snow. But I do know that the average temperature in January is highly likely to be lower than the temperature today.

Forecasting returns is similar. You are not saying that the stock market tomorrow or next week will be higher or lower, but over the next 7 or 10 years, there is value. If you can do that, then you can orient your portfolio toward the cheaper areas of the market and put yourself in a position to capture that value. And if you cannot find cheaper areas of the market, then you should have more cash. That is basically what it boils down to.

To say that valuation really doesn't matter because you have a very long-term horizon is irresponsible. Sure, if you have a long enough time horizon, risk premia can never be too low. If I have a 300-year time horizon, even a 1 percent risk premium will compound to eventually generate some returns.

In reality, it was pretty clear that U.S. equities were overpriced in 2000, when growth stocks were trading at ridiculous multiples and the dot-com bubble had driven one segment of the market to such extreme levels that the entire market became overvalued. What does that tell us about the experience 2007–2008? At the beginning of this period, all risk assets were no longer cheap. There was no real diversification in owning a portfolio of overvalued assets. That is the true lesson. Overvaluation becomes a risk factor that must be addressed directly in portfolio construction. Addressing over- and undervaluations in the market is difficult, and stepping away from valuation analysis by hiding behind the efficient market hypothesis—which says that tactical asset allocation is impossible—is simply just avoiding the hard work.

What other flaws in the real money world were exposed in 2008?

We learned that there is a problem with the long-term modeling done by real money funds. Because portfolios are constructed based on a long-term time frame, correlations are analyzed over the past 20 or 30 years. But real money funds actually do have annual cash demands. University endowments pay out a portion of their budgets, and pension funds have annual payouts to pensioners. So the portfolio is run for the long term, but the annual cash demands impose certain short-term constraints, making it important to manage downside volatility.

Another reason to manage downside volatility in the short term is because we all get psychologically damaged when we suffer large losses. There is the career risk element. Maybe it doesn't affect someone like David Swensen at Yale Endowment, who has incredible standing and has done an amazing job over 20 years, but for most people in this business, there is a high degree of career risk. Losing a lot on the downside or underperforming on the upside will eventually lead to management getting fired or being told to act differently. There is also the issue of negative compounding. In 2008, many hedge fund managers dropped 40 percent, which means to get back to unchanged, you have to make 67 percent, something that is not easy to do after such a big loss. You are nervous about what you are doing; you do not want to lose another 10 percent, and even if you manage to make 67 percent over a few years, you will still be flat. You have a zero compound return. And that doesn't account for annual cash outflows, which means getting back to even takes even longer.

Those annual cash flows are important because a university's annual operating budget, for example, cannot suddenly withstand 30 percent less cash. As such, the volatility has to flow into the investment account, not the budget. While you might have a portfolio that you expect to perform fine over the next 20 to 30 years, based on various forecasts and historical assumptions, if for whatever reason that portfolio drops by 60 percent and you're suddenly paying out that much less cash to the university budget, that's a real problem. Even if you are certain you will be fine 30 years later by compounding at 6 percent per annum, the university's budgeting process will remain significantly constrained over the next few years. Put another way, if you are down 60 percent and are paying out the same cash the university was expecting before your drawdown, it becomes a much higher percentage of the portfolio. That creates real constraints. Because of this bifurcation between short-term cash needs and long-term investment performance, it is imperative to start thinking more about managing downside volatility over the shorter term.

Global equities were down 60 percent from the peak at one point in 2009. These things tend to happen more often than the normal distribution predicts they will happen. I am agnostic about whether such a scenario reproduces itself or not. Rather, my job is to assume that it could happen again and make sure that if it does, my portfolio does not blow up. If I can do that without sacrificing a large amount of return, then I should.

I try to maximize return given an unwillingness to bear too much downside risk. I am not willing to lose more than 10 percent in any one month or 20 percent in any given year. These figures are based on a psychological recognition that it would be extremely difficult to dig myself out of a hole deeper than 20 percent. Further, without setting some kind of absolute stop to the amount of capital I am willing to lose, I am implicitly saying that in a diversified portfolio, it is impossible to imagine a total destruction of capital. Yet such a claim runs counter to historical evidence. Why do we not have very wealthy Roman families who have compounded their capital over millennia? While I am not sure what my focus on truncating downside risk has cost me over time in terms of lost opportunity, I am certain that I have not maximized return. But at least I can be sure that I will be around for future opportunities.

Would I be surprised if what happened in 2008 happened again in 2010? I would be a bit surprised, but not absolutely shocked. We have some underlying problems that have not gone away. The U.S. consumer needs to become more savings driven. A rebalancing must take place in the world, whereby surplus countries become more domestic demand driven and deficit countries like the U.S. begin to save more. As that rebalancing occurs, it is bound to create breaking points where you get sudden shocks and volatility occurs.

Should real money funds manage to a risk target rather than a return target?

Managing downside risk using methods other than just diversification is important. That is the crux of what absolute return investing is about, and all investors should take an absolute return approach. This is not to say that absolute return managers are smarter about investing because I don't think we are. Real money managers are just as smart as hedge fund managers. The difference is we don't try to forecast our returns and we try hard to cut off the left tails. When we really screw up, we lose 10 percent, but are then 95 percent in cash so we cannot blow up two months in a row.

Maybe this methodology is not possible for the likes of CalPERS because the assets are just too large. Maybe real money funds over a certain asset size cannot be true absolute return managers. However, there are still ways to truncate the downside, which has to do with figuring out ways to buy insurance in an uncorrelated sense. While there are times when you just have to pay for insurance to protect your portfolio, if you can figure out other strategies, which are uncorrelated, you might be able to take on more risk through leverage, actually reducing the risk in tail events. Running more risk in normal times means you are running at a slightly higher volatility. But when a true crisis hits and the markets collapse, you have the protection when you need it.

Does asset allocation work in a world where extreme events happen more often than predicted?

Asset allocation works if you put in the correct forward-looking returns. If you knew what the returns were going to be, the models would come back with perfect portfolios. The problem is not with asset allocation but with figuring out what returns and what correlations to use. Should you be using 30-year correlations when you are nervous about the one week when all markets collapse simultaneously? Should you be using long-term forecasts for equity risk premia when the next equity risk premium could be negative?

We use tactical asset allocation models to manage a portion of our capital and help our research process. These models help in two ways. First, they provide us with an independent yardstick, which we try to outperform. Second, we think of our tactical asset allocation model as an unbiased observer of the markets, which we use to give us some sense of the market's momentum. They are price-based, momentum-driven models that have been running since about 2005, and have produced consistently positive results. Even our longer term model broke even in 2008, and it is only allowed to be long assets because in the long term you want to earn risk premium. After being down about 8 percent by the fall of 2008, it switched heavily into U.S. fixed income and recouped its losses by year-end. Our shorter-term trading model did far better. It was able to generate positive returns on the year since it is allowed to go long and short all asset categories except for cash, which, because we do not take leverage, is constrained to always be zero or long.

Tactical asset allocation has worked for us both in the model sense and in the discretionary sense. But then again, we are small and nimble, so we can do it. There are many models of tactical asset allocation that seem to work, and I have discussed them at Drobny Conferences. We have done momentum models on returns, on correlations, and have even run efficient frontiers that, using ETFs, generate returns very similar to what Yale has generated through its asset allocation process and successful manager selection. So I believe that tactical asset allocation works, though it is very difficult to make it work for very large investors like CalPERS or for the entire investment industry.

While we think about valuation, we do not actually utilize valuation-driven models for asset allocation. Valuation-driven tactical asset allocation models need a much longer time frame because of the difficulty of forecasting when assets will actually revert to fair value. This is a flaw in our system that we plan to work on over the next few years, whereby we can bring together valuation and momentum-driven strategies in a coherent unit.

If size is the enemy of flexibility, what should large real money funds like CalPERS, with $200 billion in assets, do?

I am spending a lot of time thinking about this whole idea of leveraged bonds overlaying equity-like portfolios in order to protect the portfolio from sharp downward market spikes when correlations go to one or negative one. I am also thinking a lot about using foreign currency diversification to protect a U.S. equity centric portfolio from a real run on the U.S. Tactically moving around the weights in any meaningful way, however, would be counterproductive on that asset size. Slippage to the market would be enormous. What they need is much better portfolio construction and more thinking about portfolio protection.

Along those lines, all real money managers need to rethink their approach to private equity and real assets, which have been responsible for much of the big endowments' past success. The usual fundraising process in the private equity and real asset arenas centers around a commitment process, under which investors are asked to make capital available to the fund manager often years before the capital needs to be drawn down. Under such a regime, commitments are an implicit call on the future resources of the investor. In a world where the size and income of the investor has dropped precipitously in 2008, commitments in general have remained unchanged. This method of precommitments reminds me of the overleveraged consumer who loses his job and whose debt level remains constant, leading to a plethora of macroeconomic imbalances. Commitments of this nature need to be rethought. A process where the size of the commitment varies or is linked to the absolute size of the investor can be imagined. In this scenario, commitments would shrink proportionally as the investor's asset base shrinks, shifting some of the problem from the investor to the asset manager. The asset manager is better placed to deal with the volatility of his capital base since his investments have not yet been made. Having the asset manager reduce potential investments before they have been made would appear much easier than the investor having to sell assets to fund capital calls.

How should a real money fund manage its portfolios with respect to inflation?

It comes back to time frame. In the short-term, equities and inflation are uncorrelated. Sometimes equities will go up, sometimes equities will go down. As a matter of fact, it's probably more likely that, as inflation rises, equities initially go down. In the long term, however, many studies show that equities and inflation are very correlated. Hence, an equity-oriented portfolio, over the long term, should perform fine. Real money managers should not be all that nervous about long-term inflation since the majority of their portfolios are in equities. What they should be nervous about, however, is managing the short-term volatility of the portfolio in the interim.

Let's take a scenario where we are moving from a benign level of inflation toward more drastic levels of high inflation. If you look at market history around the world, you find many emerging markets that have gone through this. Turkey is a good example. The Turkish stock market index (ISE 100) started at one in 1986. Today it is at 55,000. But if you chart that in real terms from 1988 to today, it's basically flat. The ISE 100 with CPI subtracted out has not gone anywhere. If you had invested in '88 and were living in Turkey, at least you still have the same purchasing power. You didn't lose any money. Meanwhile, if you had kept your money in Turkish government bonds or in cash, you would be toast. So the equity impact was actually very positive. (See Figure 3.3.)

The same thing happened in Zimbabwe where, if you had any money, the only way to hedge against hyperinflation was to be long real assets. The equity market in Zimbabwe went up with inflation, even though inflation was running in the trillions as money was being printed faster than people could spend it. Equities skyrocketed because equity indices are denominated in nominal terms. (See Figure 3.4.)

Today, the S&P 500 is around 1,000. Sticking with the Turkish stock market example, it went from 1 to 10 to 55,000. Extrapolating

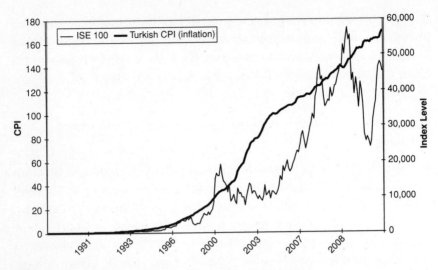

Figure 3.3 Turkish Inflation and Equities, 1990–2009
SOURCE: Bloomberg.

that performance for the S&P would equate to it going from 1,000 to 10,000 to 55 million. Today we can buy 10-year, 10,000 strike S&P calls for 14 basis points and hedge out any hyperinflation risk over the next 10 years. We think it's unlikely that there will be any inflation in the next year or two. But in five years, who knows? For 1.4 basis

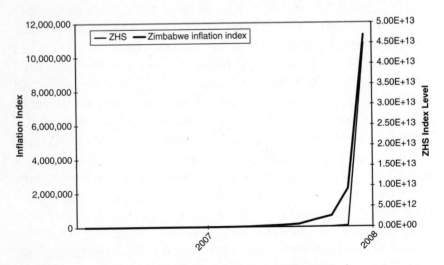

Figure 3.4 Zimbabwean Inflation and Equities, 2006–2008
SOURCE: Bloomberg.

points a year for 10 years, I am perfectly happy to buy hyperinflation protection. The lesson to be learned here is that equity indices are priced in nominal dollars, not inflation-adjusted real dollars, which means that a long-duration call option on the local equity index implicitly includes an option on future inflation.

There are some other very interesting ways to hedge long-term inflation. If you look at the research, dividends and inflation are 90 percent correlated over the long term, and an active dividend swap market exists. Today's Dow Jones Eurostoxx 50 index dividends are trading at about 115 euros for 2009. For 2018—nine years forward—that same dividend can be bought at 110, implying five euros less dividends nine years from now. If there is any kind of inflation in Europe over the next nine years, dividends will be higher, not lower. The correlation might not work week-by-week or quarter-by-quarter, but over nine years, inflation will send these dividends higher. What is the risk? How much lower could they be? Well, it's possible that dividends could be cut over the next nine years if we have deflation. But if you look at Japan, for a proxy, the country has been in a terrible state for the last 19 years and yet deflation has remained fairly low. Over the last decade, deflation was minus 40 basis points, which is negligible. If you assume that a scenario like that is your worst-case scenario, then buying 2018 dividends in Europe is a very cheap inflation hedge. And the trade also gives you foreign currency exposure, which would be nice for a U.S.–centric real money manager who would get the double benefit of the dollar going down in a hyperinflation scenario. (See Figure 3.5.)

Meanwhile, Japanese inflation-protected bonds now imply 100 basis points of deflation annually for the next 10 years. This is a number that Japan has not experienced during any of the 10-year periods starting in 1990, when their bubble burst. So owning these bonds is another cheap hedge to inflation.

There are many ways to think about inflation and many ways to use nominal forward markets to hedge inflation. The most interesting one to me is buying really long-dated out-of-the-money equity index call options for cheap. You can even break up the equity market into subindices and make long-dated bets on natural resource-linked equities, oil services stocks, or foreign stock markets that are more natural resource driven to get more of a direct inflation exposure. The point is that equities are a good hedge to inflation over the long term.

Figure 3.5   Rolling 10-Year Japanese Inflation, 1987–2008
SOURCE: Bloomberg.

Is there anything else you learned from 2008?

Investing is the art and science of extracting risk premia from financial markets over time. 2008 taught us to look around the entire investment universe to find risk premia, both cheap ones to invest in and expensive ones to use as insurance policies against the underlying portfolio. In the summer of 2007, investment grade bonds (IG8) were trading at a 35 basis point spread to Treasuries. These were incredibly tight spreads, which showed that the market was not expecting any increase in risk premium and was trading entirely complacently. It also provided a beautiful asymmetric bet to use as insurance. By investing in positions that would profit from spread widening, you risked about 10 basis points of further tightening, while the eventual widening in 2008 took the spread out to almost 300 basis points. This was in a market that was entirely liquid and allowed even a large manager to establish positions of sufficient size to be meaningful.

Looking further back not too many years ago, the credit default swap (CDS) contracts on European sovereign credits with 10-year maturities were trading at 5 basis points. The loss from paying on a CDS is limited to the interest rate charged, which in this case was 5 basis points a year for

10 years. Yet many of these moved to levels over 80 basis points during 2008. This resembles an insurance contract with limited downside, but asymmetric upside in the event of material changes to the investment universe.

For an example of an asymmetric bet available today, look at Sweden. The central bank of Sweden, the Riksbank, has announced they do not plan to raise rates before June 2010. The one-year interest rate is currently 87 basis points, whereas the one-year interest rate in one year's time is 2.52 percent, and the one-year interest rate in two years' time is 3.50 percent. Right now, due to the steep upward sloping forward yield curve, you can buy receiver swaptions on one-year interest rates struck at 1.8 percent that will increase in value six times if one-year interest rates remain unchanged. This is not a bad payout for a world with very low rates because the global economy remains weak or stock markets have sold off again.

These examples call for real money investment committees to widen their search for risk premia beyond the usual assets covered, and be willing to use option-like derivatives to purchase potential upside for a portfolio that works especially well during periods of crisis. Focusing on 2007–2008 brings into stark focus the possibility of buying cheap insurance when the market is willing to sell it, before the horse has left the barn.

Part Two

The Invisible Hands

[E]very individual necessarily labours to render the annual revenue of the society as great as he can. He generally, indeed, neither intends to promote the public interest, nor knows how much he is promoting it. By preferring the support of domestic to that of foreign industry, he intends only his own security; and by directing that industry in such a manner as its produce may be of the greatest value, he intends only his own gain, and he is in this, as in many other cases, led by an invisible hand to promote an end which was no part of his intention. Nor is it always the worse for the society that it was no part of it. By pursuing his own interest he frequently promotes that of the society more effectually than when he really intends to promote it. I have never known much good done by those who affected to trade for the public good.

—Adam Smith

Chapter 4

The House

I headed off the beaten path of financial capitals to Stockholm to meet a fixed income specialist and pioneer in Swedish financial markets. On a gorgeous, late summer day, we strolled around town, discussing the credit crisis, China, pension funds, and a myriad of things that had taken place over the previous 18 months. This manager builds a diverse portfolio of small bets, all reasonably independent of each other, where on average he feels he has a slight edge. This process led him to once present his fund to his investors as a casino, although he was quick to note he was the house, not the gambler. After all, as Steve Wynn once said: "The only way to win in a casino is to own one."

Overlooking the marina, we ate roe and fresh fish, as my mind raced to keep abreast of "The House's" thought process, a rare combination of rapid-fire connections, pragmatic wisdom, and deep analysis. Where trading often conjures images of taking outsized bets and winning, over time his game is won through superior portfolio construction. Later, in his office, we dug more deeply into some of the systemic issues that continue to plague the world economy and certain challenges that real money managers face within that environment. He thinks real money managers should use their inherent strengths and more effectively manage their endemic weaknesses, adopting innovative portfolio management techniques to address the uncertain road ahead.

How did you get into this business?

I started off in the business doing market making and then prop trading within the fixed income division at a bank. After that it seemed rather natural to take the next step to start a hedge fund.

As a young kid I liked to play poker, bridge, and other games. While these games no longer excite me, I now get a similar high taking risk in the markets, especially from the analysis behind the risk taking. Markets are an intense, intellectual game with real consequences and, when properly done, with real benefits both for the risk takers and society. I find markets fascinating, particularly the macro elements because of the interplay between the international economy and geopolitics. I love forming an idea of what is happening in the world and in markets, identifying the best risk/reward, thinking about how to strip out all the unnecessary risk, how to protect against other risks, and how to construct a portfolio. Then you put on trades based on this analysis and see the result. I love the feedback of being right or wrong.

How does the feedback of being right or wrong affect you?

It annoys me when I'm wrong—I get upset with myself when I feel that I'm making mistakes. It is important to clarify that losing money and making mistakes are not the same thing. Likewise, making money and doing the right things are also not necessarily the same. I can have a period during which I'm making really nice money, yet feel that I screwed up because I didn't read the markets well. Perhaps I had been looking for a different scenario to play out, or I did not have the optimal positions, or my position sizing or hedging could have been better. Similarly, I could be losing money, yet be very happy with myself because something unexpected happened and I had on some protection which worked really well, limiting my losses. Or perhaps I readjusted my views, positions, and hedges in such a way that I had very small losses and stand ready to take advantage of new opportunities to make a lot of money going forward. My market timing has never been good so I avoid short-term trading and do not try to time strategies. This probably saves some agony and regret, which can be important for your focus.

The importance of psychology—your own psychology and that of other market participants—is underestimated by most institutional investors. And it is much more difficult to understand your own psychology than the markets' psychology. It takes a much longer time to truly understand how you work, how you function psychologically in various environments, and how you manage this psychology and your risk as you monitor the markets. You can only learn this over time.

At what point in your career did you know you had skill?

Does one ever know? I would say that 10 years ago, a really good or a really bad run affected me more psychologically than it does today. I still get annoyed when I feel that I do not understand what is going on in the markets, or when I feel that I am making mistakes. But I don't get too annoyed by losing money.

Many years ago, I was making markets in Swedish government bonds for a bank. Because the Swedish government bond market was new at the time, I had read all the books I could find on the subject, and had gone to the U.S. to sit with primary dealers to learn more about bond trading. I thought I had a fairly good idea of what was going on. I had made a lot of money as a market maker and prop trader before that so I was fairly confident in my abilities.

Then, within the Swedish bond market, I introduced a standardized forward market where originally I was the sole market maker. Clients or other banks could trade with me and I kept the balance of the exposure, which I could translate through the repo market, also newly created. I could hedge whatever I wanted, and at one point saw an opportunity to short the Swedish government bond market on an absolute basis, something that had probably never been done before—the tools had not been available. People had been underweight duration against the benchmark before, but I actually went outright short at one stage and made money on the trade. I thought I was really smart because I had made money in all types of markets, even with newly created instruments. Many heard about our bank making money in an environment of rising rates; the president of the bank called down to the trading floor to congratulate me, and I was starting to believe that I was really smart. Of course, I increased the short position just when rates started to turn and quickly lost the bulk of what I had previously made. I went from thinking that I was able to walk on water to thinking maybe I am not very good at this after all.

After such a humiliating experience where I saw my risk capital cut significantly, I promised myself that I would never put myself in such a situation again. I slowly began to develop an understanding for what risk taking was really all about, using my love for the markets to test concepts such as sizing, risk, and so on. I was forced to accept the fact that markets are a very psychological game as well as a risk management game. Traders have to be able to handle risk, not only that which is inherently in the market, but also that which is specific to their portfolio and their circumstances. I have been trying to improve on this ever since, and I have been at it for 25 years now.

If you were asked to run one of the Swedish AP pension funds as part of your social welfare duty, how would you go about it?

The AP funds are a bit special, but if I were running a typical public pension fund, I would start by trying to identify my natural advantages and disadvantages, some of which are obvious, others less so.

The most obvious advantages of a pension fund are its balance sheet and its credit worthiness. Pension funds have a very long-term investment horizon and a great deal of liquidity, although I am not sure they fully appreciate it. There are very few pension funds that take full advantage of their liquidity position.

The most obvious disadvantage, however, is that a pension fund is highly constrained in its investment universe, making it far less flexible than a hedge fund. Pensions are subject to explicit external constraints by regulators, as well as more implicit constraints if they manage to a benchmark, which most do. These constraints often lead pension boards to impose strict guidelines for portfolio construction, exacerbating the problem. Further, although pension boards can have investment pro-fessionals, they can also be populated by people outside the investment business further handicapping them in terms of knowledge and expertise. There are also certain ancillary constraints in the realm of political risk or public relations that tend to complicate matters further. Finally, their rather stiff governing structure usually makes them slow-moving players in the markets, which can be a disadvantage.

The quality of investment talent within a pension fund is also likely to be a disadvantage. Usually talent flows to areas where it gets the best pay and the most interesting challenges. I imagine that due to competition from hedge funds, banks, and other asset managers, it is very difficult to retain top talent at a public pension fund. While this is certainly not true 100 percent of the time, as there are some very good people in the long-only community, on average the best talent will tend to flow to better paying and less constrained environments.

As an analogy, you would not expect a really talented football player to stay on his local team in a midsized town that no one has heard of. If someone has world-class talent, he will likely end up playing professional football in a Champions League club, which pays much more and has much greater exposure. All players want to reach their full potential, and will generally go where they can get not only the best coaches and facilities, but also be able to play with and against others of their caliber. The same applies to the investment community. If someone really has an outstanding talent that distinguishes him, whether that be intellect, mathematical aptitude, a talent for reading market psychology, or a mixture of other factors, this person will probably migrate to where he gets the best reward for his effort, where he will be able to play amongst the best and thus get even better, and where he is the least constrained.

So the weaknesses in the real money world are structural. How would you go about maximizing the strengths, such as the strong balance sheet and credit worthiness that you mentioned?

The most obvious way is to get paid for pockets of illiquidity in the market, and the easiest way of doing that is by investing in safe but less liquid securities. This is one way of being what Myron Scholes calls a liquidity provider to the market, something difficult to be if you are a leveraged player with redemptions, like a hedge fund. A liquidity provider should ideally have long-term money, say for the next 20 or

30 years, maybe forever. This is an underutilized resource among most pension funds, who often think that being fully invested means they have 100 percent of their assets allocated and thus no more liquidity. But you can get additional liquidity from repo'ing bonds, selling equities and simultaneously buying them back forward, shifting into instruments with cheap embedded leverage, and many other creative ways.

You can pick up very safe extra return just by repo'ing special securities and lending equities that are in demand, and this also provides liquidity to the market. If you do it the right way with the right counterparties and with the correct haircuts, it's risk-free income.

If I were managing a real money portfolio, I would try to pick up extra return from activities where I provide some kind of risk-free liquidity from both short- and long-term usage of my balance sheet. The market is willing to pay for this service, and it will probably be even more willing to do so going forward as bank balance sheets remain constrained. The long-term real money players should be the ultimate private sector providers of liquidity to the system. They should take advantage of getting paid for liquidity much more systematically than they do today. They are leaving the easy money on the table.

To sum it up, I would not try to outguess the market in the short- or medium-term; I would outsource that to others who have a better institutional setup. I would, however, use the strength of my balance sheet to pick up extra return. And over multiyear horizons, I would strive to be overweight cheap asset classes and underweight expensive ones, a strategy where a long-term horizon and a common sense approach is useful. But I am glad I do not have to do it for real. I am sure it is much easier sitting on the outside having a view on how it should be done.

Isn't levering up a portfolio with illiquid assets what caused so much trouble for investors in 2008, especially in the endowment and pension world?

I am not saying that you should go into illiquids of all types. Rather, I am primarily talking about risk-free illiquidity, or very low-risk illiquidity. Of course, illiquid risky assets are a totally different ballgame.

An interesting new example of what I am talking about is high-yielding government guaranteed bonds issued by financial institutions on the back of the credit crisis. The yields are high because the instruments are less liquid, but they are government guaranteed. Another example is government bonds that have recently been trading above LIBOR (see box). Buying a long-term government bond issued by a credit worthy country above LIBOR is essentially a very-long-term arbitrage. To capture the profits over the investment horizon, you need to be able to withstand mark-to-market losses along the way. Real money players who have a long-term time horizon are best suited to do these types of trades. These are excellent risk-reward trades, and everyone with a long-term time horizon should have these types of trades in their portfolio.

LIBOR

The London Inter Bank Offer Rate is an interest rate at which banks can borrow funds, in marketable size, from other banks in the London interbank market. The LIBOR is fixed on a daily basis by the British Bankers' Association. The LIBOR is derived from a filtered average of the world's most creditworthy banks' interbank deposit rates for larger loans with maturities between overnight and one full year. The LIBOR is the world's most widely used benchmark for short-term interest rates. It's important because it is the rate at which the world's most preferred borrowers are able to borrow money. It is also the rate upon which rates for less preferred borrowers are based. For example, a multinational corporation with a very good credit rating may be able to borrow money for one year at LIBOR plus a small spread. Countries that rely on the LIBOR for a reference rate include the United States, Canada, Switzerland and the United Kingdom.

SOURCE: *Forbes Investopedia.*

What are your thoughts on diversification, which didn't provide much safety in 2008?

I am a great fan of diversification. It is one of the few free lunches that we have in the markets. But I would certainly not argue in favor of diversifying a very large percentage of the portfolio in private equity, real estate, and other similar illiquid investments. This is a fairly dangerous strategy, and I am not so sure you get paid much, if anything, for the illiquidity component you take on. These vehicles largely pay out traditional risk premia that can be found in the public markets through much simpler, more liquid instruments.

Many investors do not use diversification efficiently. There are pension funds that have 80 or 90 percent of their assets invested in equities, arguing that in the long term, this will result in higher returns compared to a more traditional portfolio. This cannot be a smart way of constructing a portfolio. Diversification into more asset classes, perhaps using instruments with embedded leverage, can produce the same or even higher returns with less risk.

If you are talking about diversification in the endowment model sense, we may have just witnessed a version of what [George] Soros calls "reflexivity," whereby people's behavior affects both the real economy and the markets through a feedback loop (see box). If everyone is looking for the same type of diversification for the same reasons using the same instruments, less diversification would automatically result when you need it most. Five or 10 years ago, it was reasonably important to know how crowded your trades were. Recently it has been absolutely essential. During 2008, knowing how others were positioned in your trades was a matter of life or death. Determining whether you were alone in a trade or if it was crowded made all the difference in the world.

Reflexivity

The concept of reflexivity is very simple. In situations that have thinking participants, there is a two-way interaction between the participants' thinking and the situation in which they participate. On the one hand, participants seek to understand reality; on the other, they seek to bring about a desired outcome. The two functions work in the opposite directions: in the cognitive function reality is the given; in the participating function, the participants' understanding is the constant. The two functions can interfere with each other by rendering what is supposed

> to be given, contingent. I call the interference between the
> two functions "reflexivity." I envision reflexivity as a feedback
> loop between the participants' understanding and the situation
> in which they participate, and I contend that the concept of
> reflexivity is crucial to understanding situations that have think-
> ing participants. Reflexivity renders the participants' under-
> standing imperfect and ensures that their actions will have
> unintended consequences.
>
> SOURCE: George Soros, *Alchemy of Finance*.

What else do most institutional investors get wrong?

All of us are less mentally disciplined than we should be. It is amazing
how much time we can spend hoping an investment pans out, rather
than looking at all sides of the argument—analyzing the downside, all
the risks, and valuing it relative to other types of investments. It is also
crucial to reappraise a situation as the fundamentals or the prices change.
It is easy to just fall in love with a trade, believing it is going to make
a lot of money, or more dangerously, underestimating how much it can
lose. It is a typical human mistake of which we are all guilty at times.

Most investors look at relatively few factors or variables, and even
on the more sophisticated end of the spectrum, I am sometimes struck
by the reasoning they employ on risk. Some of them even equate risk
and volatility. Volatility is a useful concept in most situations, but risk is
something much more complex. Many investors rely on basic rules of
thumb rather than reasoning and analysis built on sound financial theory.
Many assumptions are made without any regard to whether they have
any logical backing or not. A good example would be the assumption
that equities always generate good long-term returns, regardless of the
price at which you buy them. This is total baloney. But people tend to
believe clichés and stories rather than logic and science.

For example, many people think the expected return of an asset is
determined by its risk. That is getting it the wrong way around. The
right way to look at it is: The expected return is a function of the risk
premium of the asset at a given price. This is different than saying return

is a function of risk, unless you are naïve enough to think that all markets are perfectly priced all the time.

A risky asset priced with a small risk premium is just a bad investment. For example, buying equities listed on Nasdaq in 1999 was not a good idea. These shares certainly had high risk but were not priced to compensate for that. Rather, they were priced for a low future return. We had a repeat of that in credit markets in 2007, when people could not get enough of risky bonds that were clearly priced for very poor long-term returns. Saying that equities or other risky assets will always deliver high returns in the long term is just incorrect. Price matters. Valuation matters.

Knowing basic financial theory and its limitations can help avoid sloppy thinking. But you don't necessarily need to be an expert on all of this stuff, and I am most certainly not an expert. I do, however, believe I have a good grasp of the logic that forms the building blocks of how financial instruments are priced and how the macro environment affects financial markets. Long-term winners in financial markets use common sense. Less blind faith in models and a more common-sense approach would have helped many players during the past few years.

Should institutional investors use outside advisors to help plug their knowledge gap?

In theory, yes, but not all consultants and rating institutions are up to their jobs. They are simply not experts in the subjects in which they claim expertise. Some of them do not have a clue what they are doing, yet they still peddle advice to pension fund boards and institutions that, in many cases, know even less than they do. That is a recipe for disaster, and that is exactly what happened recently in credit markets. First the rating agencies declared that a leveraged CDO was triple-A rated, that Iceland was triple-A rated, that a host of stuff was higher quality than it really was, and frankly a child should have known better. But the agencies peddled these opinions to the boards of institutions, which, in turn, happily bought them and promptly lost a lot of money. It's unbelievable, really.

The following is an amusing story about sloppy thinking and bad assumptions. I heard about a pension fund that bought a chunk of inflation-protected government bonds, locking in a real return of 2 percent for the next 30 years. However, in their asset and liability model, they simultaneously assumed that these were going to deliver a 4 percent real return since this was the return these bonds had delivered historically. What happened to common sense?

If you were allocating money to hedge funds, what characteristics would you look for?

I would like to know how the decision makers at the fund truly think, and I don't necessarily mean what their market views are right now. Rather, what is their view of the world? How has this view evolved over the past few years? What does risk mean to them? How do they think about risk? What do they think risk means for others in the markets? What types of risk are important? How do they think about managing risk? How do they think about pricing in financial markets more broadly?

It is extremely important to understand how people think. Obviously, an observable track record would also be important, but a good track record should not automatically justify an investment. I would need to hear the story behind the numbers: how money was made, how much risk was taken, etc. So I would like to see a combination of people whose thinking is logical, consistent, and sounds as if they would be alpha extracting over time (see box). Then I would want the track record to verify it.

Alpha Versus Beta

In modern portfolio theory (MPT), there are five basic statistical measurements: beta, alpha, standard deviation (volatility), R-squared (correlation), and the Sharpe ratio (return/risk). Beta measures both the correlation and volatility of a fund or security to a benchmark. For example, if a fund has a beta of 2.0 in relation to the S&P 500, the fund's returns are on average double those of the S&P. If a fund has a beta of -0.5, the fund's

(continued)

returns are on average half those of the S&P, and in the opposite direction.

Alpha is a risk-adjusted measure of the excess return of a fund or manager relative to an applicable benchmark. The excess return is the difference between the fund's actual return and the fund's predicted return, the latter of which is defined by its beta to the benchmark. In hedge fund parlance, alpha represents the value that a portfolio manager adds to or subtracts from a fund's return through active management, thus connoting a manager's skill (or lack thereof).

Is alpha extraction a zero-sum game?

Alpha, by definition, is a zero-sum game—or at least by my definition. Before costs, that is. I don't think there is that much alpha in hedge fund indices. Some hedge funds extract true alpha rather consistently, while others generate none, or even pay alpha. Then they hide it through beta, sometimes through difficult-to-see exotic betas.

Alpha seeking is, however, a positive sum game for society. You need to have people in there chasing alpha to make markets more efficient. And by efficiency I am not talking about providing liquidity to the market. Rather, you need to have people constantly trying to evaluate the right price, who are ready to trade on that belief, pushing the market towards equilibrium in a price discovery process. That way we get better allocation of resources in the real economy and fewer bubbles. If there had been more John Paulsons in the market during the last few years, and fewer gullible institutional investors in subprime, the global economy would have been much better off. But alpha in a strict sense is a zero-sum game, although with beneficial externalities for society.

What else did you learn in 2008?

Markets can go to even worse extremes than I thought possible. I was surprised to see the extent of arbitrage opportunities that emerged, although I was not very surprised by the extent of either stock market weakness or credit spread widening. While the moves in both equities and credit were of a larger magnitude than I had anticipated, they remained within what I thought were reasonable norms and a reasonable probability scenario. But I would have definitely put an extremely low probability on the market offering up so many outright risk-free arbitrages.

Often these risk-free arbitrage opportunities arise during the worst moments of a crisis when liquidity is scarce. Should a real money fund manager keep a certain amount of dry powder in reserve for such events?

Yes, always, always, always keep dry powder. That is one of the most important things in the money management business, and in all risk management. Never allow yourself to be painted into a corner, whether by the market, a regulation, a counterparty, or anything. You never want someone else to decide your fate. You must retain some flexibility at all times, and this comes at a cost that may include paying premium for option protection or leaving a certain allocation to low yielding cash or cash-like instruments. But it is worth it over the long term. If you do not take steps to protect yourself from high-impact, unforeseen events, then I would argue that you are doing more betting than investing and risk management.

How would you protect yourself from high-impact, unforeseen events in a real money vehicle?

I would start by defining an overall acceptable level of risk, which would come from my stipulated statutes and from the specific mandate that I have been given by the fund's trustees. I should be able to construct a portfolio that is fairly close to that risk level not only in terms of volatility and value-at-risk, but also from a maximum drawdown perspective, which may in fact be a better measure of risk.

Several questions need to be addressed: What is my specific mandate? Are we expected to deliver a real or nominal return? Do we guarantee a minimum level of return? Am I expected to perform at least in line with my peers at other pension funds, or can I deviate for a few years? This last part is important because I need to be able to underweight expensive assets that may be in a bubble, which often means underperforming in the short-term. But avoiding owning overpriced assets obviously pays off in the long term, and also provides a hedge against bad times since you will not be in trouble at the same time as others. The question is whether the fund's sponsors have the stomach for this strategy. You can look rather stupid on the sidelines when everyone else is surfing the bubble.

Once I have these questions answered, I would set up an overall risk limit and a number of risk parameters, constructing a portfolio that is as efficient as possible within the constraints that I have outlined with my trustees. And to me, that means that the portfolio is well diversified. I would not feel constrained by the size of the balance sheet, per se; I do not believe that the mix of the underlying assets has to add up to 100 percent. If I had a lot of low-risk assets in the portfolio, such as illiquid government guaranteed bonds, I could use some type of gearing and my total assets could then be above 100 percent of the fund's equity. If, on the other hand, I thought the best value was in some of the more risky assets such as equities or corporate bonds, then I would have a significant amount invested passively in cash or T-bills and the active risk assets would be much less than 100 percent of the fund.

Can you give me an example of how a real money fund could safely lever up?

As I mentioned earlier, my guess is that many real money funds think they are more constrained by their balance sheet than they truly are. They are often not allowed to borrow, but there are other techniques available to get liquidity and flexibility. In a simple example, let us assume that you conclude that the optimal portfolio mix, based on your set of assumptions, is: 35 percent equities, 15 percent corporate bonds, 10 percent real estate, 15 percent alternatives, and 25 percent government bonds. Let us say it turns out that this portfolio has a risk that is only 80 percent of the risk level that you have deemed appropriate for your particular pension fund. No problem. Keep the mix the same but increase all positions by 25 percent, making total underlying assets 125 percent. You can put that portfolio on without much of a problem, because you can get a lot of leverage out of the market, especially with respect to bonds and public equities. Most pension funds could use swaps or futures to get exposure, both of which require little cash. If these instruments pose a problem, I would guess almost all would be allowed to buy ETFs (exchange-traded funds), some of which have embedded leverage. Buying high beta versions of instruments would be another alternative.

Identifying an optimal portfolio and then borrowing or lending to adjust risk levels is well-known standard financial theory. But pension funds are not always constructing efficient portfolios, and they are losing out because they could generate a higher return without taking on more risk. Put another way, they could get the same return with less risk.

How would you manage risk in this hypothetical portfolio through a year like 2008?

You always need to have some kind of insurance on to make sure that you never end up in a scenario where someone else makes a decision for you. For example, you would not want to be forced to cut equity exposure when equities are really cheap, which is exactly what many real money funds did in late 2008 or early 2009. Make sure from the outset that you never end up in such a position. A typical way of doing this is having trades on that you can be fairly sure will benefit from increased turmoil. Those trades were very easy to find a couple of years ago, when the risk of a financial crisis was priced at almost zero—it was ridiculous.

At present, it is much more difficult to find these trades, but some are still around. A trade that is always available, although not always smart, is risk reversals in the equity market, whereby you give away some upside to protect the downside. You write some calls to buy some puts for zero premium. You pay for this over time because calls are often cheaper than puts, and for good reasons. But if you are not willing to give away any upside return by buying some insurance, then you have to accept the cost of being very wrong sometimes, at which point you will lose all flexibility in how you handle the portfolio. That is simply not good risk management. If you are not willing to pay some insurance all the time, I would argue that you are not doing your job as a fiduciary.

Can you give me an example of the value of liquidity and flexibility?

At the end of 2008, the market was more or less giving free money to players with strong balance sheets. There were a large number of arbitrage opportunities out there in the markets. We know that when markets are stressed they often become dysfunctional. If you have flexibility in turbulent markets, the market will pay you for that flexibility. As one of the few left standing, you can capitalize on all the mistakes and mispricings that arise. It was rather extreme in the case of fixed income arbitrage where hundred-dollar bills were lying around everywhere just waiting to be picked up by someone who had the balance-sheet capacity to do it. Similarly, imagine how many sweet deals Warren Buffett was offered in the fall of 2008, besides GE and Goldman Sachs, just because everyone knew he was sitting on such a large cash pile. If only he knew how to check his voicemail (see box).

If you plan on being in the markets for a long time, regardless if you are a hedge fund, pension fund, or whatever, you can be fairly sure that if you are not paying insurance for downside protection, you will be forced out at some point. You will make a huge mistake, which will kill your historical track record, and in many cases you will not be allowed to trade again because you will be fired, lose your reputation, etc. The best way to avoid such a scenario is by never playing for more than you can lose. Never play for so much that you might not be allowed to play again.

Buffett, Lehman, and A Voicemail

As you can imagine, Warren Buffett was hearing from a lot of people on that crazy weekend exactly a year ago, when the financial world was falling apart. AIG, desperate to come up with $18 billion, begged him for help. "Don't waste your time on me," he told them. "I'm not going to be able to do anything for you." And around 6 PM on that Saturday night, as Buffett was rushing out to a social engagement in Edmonton, Alberta, he got a call from Bob Diamond, the head of Barclays Capital. Diamond was trying to buy Lehman Brothers and rescue it from oblivion, but he was having trouble with British authorities. So he had come up with another plan, one in which Buffett would provide insurance that might make it all work. It was all too complicated for Buffett to take in a quick phone call, so he asked Diamond to fax him the details. Buffett got back to his hotel room around midnight and was surprised to find . . . nothing. Lehman went under, and within days, the world was in a full-blown financial crisis.

Fast forward 10 months. Buffett, who admits he never has really learned the basics of his cell phone, asked his daughter Susan about a little indicator he had noticed on the screen: "Can you figure out what's on there?" It turned out to be the message from Diamond that he had been waiting for that night.

I asked him whether, in retrospect, he might have gone for the deal. He pulled the simple little Samsung phone out of his pocket and pondered it for a moment. It's entirely possible, he suggested. "I don't know." And we never will.

Source: Karen Tumulty, "If Only Warren Buffett Knew How to Work His Cellphone . . . ," *Swampland: A Blog about Politics,* September 15, 2009, http://swampland.blogs.time.com/2009/09/15/warren-buffett-could-have-saved-lehma/.

How do you make sure that you are around to keep playing in your hedge fund?

We tend to be long volatility and look for trades that make money in difficult markets, during down swings in risky assets and in times of increased volatility. We like to be long the tails, the black swans. In general, however, we run a fairly low-risk fund. We try to avoid being hurt by catastrophic scenarios because the survivors are usually granted a license to print money for a while.

Do you spend more time thinking about how it could all go wrong or how you are going to make money?

We spend more time on how to make money. We are in the business of making money, so that is where the whole process starts. We are not here to avoid losing money. But although we are here to make money, we have the constraint of wanting to limit losses. Our focus switches when we identify a macro scenario or environment that is not good for us. During these times we think more about the downside and how to protect the portfolio.

To prepare for a macro scenario or an environment that is not good for you, do you conduct stress tests on your portfolio?

Yes, we always run our portfolios over a number of different stress scenarios, under multiple time frames, and across multiple potential scenarios, both qualitatively and quantitatively with an emphasis on qualitative. We run them over the September 11 period, the LTCM period, and other time periods. We will certainly be running them over the Lehman scenario once that falls out of our current time series. Risk management has to be both qualitative and quantitative, and we try to have an intuitive feel for how our portfolio behaves under different scenarios and circumstances. Then we look at what the numbers are telling us, and we want the numbers to tell us something that is close to what our logic, experience, and gut feeling tell us. If they are not the same, we get nervous and check to see if there is a calculation error, if we made a faulty assumption somewhere, or if something is clearly different this time.

We spend a great deal of time thinking about different scenarios. We are not that interested in history in the sense that what happened in the past can happen exactly the same way today. That is nonsensical thinking. These are evolving situations and the background factors are never the same. But it's still useful to have an idea about the history; ignorance of it is not a good strategy.

When modeling potential future scenarios, do you play around with historical and future correlations and volatilities?

Yes, but during turbulent times in the markets, we typically assume that correlations and volatilities are unknown going forward. Sometimes it is fairly easy to map out what type of correlations will evolve going forward, but other times you don't have a clue. At the first signs of market distress in this latest crisis, it was not difficult to realize that we might be heading into a storm. There were balance-sheet problems, weak growth, a troubled financial sector, the specter of disinflation or deflation, declining credit availability, etc. You could have constructed a scenario from that and have had a good idea what correlations would be.

But in some cases, the logical correlations were overridden by market technical factors. At the time of the Lehman collapse we owned some long-dated fixed income options where volatility was trading at all-time lows. But volatility actually fell further, a rather strange occurrence, since all other implied volatilities in the marketplace increased sharply for obvious reasons. Yet the reason for this was very technical: These cheap long-dated, long vega positions were held by leveraged players who were forced out of their positions under stress, and there were few natural buyers on the other side. That is a typical example of why you want to have your cash cushion to be able to put on or add to positions in times of stress as we did in this example. The great part about that trade was that it had a clearly defined downside barrier. If fixed income volatility went to zero forever—which is a rather stupid assumption—the maximum loss was bearable while the upside was fairly large.

Did you alter your time horizon or any other aspects of your strategy or process during 2008?

We have had some trades on for three or four years, and others that were on and off intraday. On average, our time horizon is a few months. During 2008, for trades where we were concerned about liquidity or availability of funding, our time horizon had to be very short. We were very worried about balance sheet availability. As it turned out, there was always some type of balance sheet available for us, even though it was somewhat constrained and much more expensive than it typically is. Apart from that, during the crisis we had a time horizon that was longer than normal, putting on trades that we knew were absolutely mispriced, such as the long fixed income volatility trade or short-dated assets like government bonds at LIBOR plus 80, which is ridiculous. We didn't have a clue whether these mispricings would correct or whether we would have to sit on them until maturity to get paid. We basically told ourselves that if we had to sit on them for three to five years, so be it. They might correct sooner, but if they don't, we thought we would have the balance sheet, the funds, and the stability to carry them to maturity if needed.

During the second half of 2008, we lost a lot of money buying even more insurance protection than usual and reducing our balance sheet, which meant incurring significant transaction costs. We exited the year with a balance sheet that was roughly three times our equity, with virtually all government bonds. This level of leverage is insignificant for a fund that primarily trades government bonds. Meanwhile, we went into the mispriced trades much too early. With three- to five-year U.S. TIPS trading even with LIBOR, we knew that we could fund those at LIBOR minus 50 at the time. After we put the trade on, it went to LIBOR plus 20, then to plus 40, plus 60, plus 80, all the way up to LIBOR plus 100 briefly. That clearly was not a very good time for us. We lost a lot of money in those positions and others. But at LIBOR plus 100, the market seemed to be pricing some risk of the U.S. government defaulting on its own dollar debt over the next few years. We thought that was extremely unlikely because if all else fails they can print the dollars needed. So we were confident that we would make money on the trade as long as we had financing available. We never thought of cutting that position. Rather, we sized all of our positions such that none was big enough to cause problems. Indeed, although we had several other positions at the same time that were in deep trouble because of very illogical mispricings and arbitrages that were getting worse, they didn't cause us too much trouble because they were reasonably sized.

Another step we took early in the crisis was to reduce all the positions that had something to do with macro views, apart from those that we thought would be protective for us in a very bad scenario for the arbitrages. We avoided complexity and positions that might distract us, and strived to have an easy-to-understand portfolio. We thought we could get squeezed a bit more, whereby the TIPS trade might go from LIBOR plus 100 to LIBOR plus 200. But we needed the staying power to be able to stay in these trades even if it got somewhat worse. We needed to have the liquidity and the balance sheet to be able to hang on to them. That was our strategy at the time. Then we put more of those arbitrage trades on at the beginning of 2009.

It sounds as if you structure your portfolio with a lot of small trades.

Exactly. On average, we have more than a hundred different positions on at any given time. Because most of these positions have a few legs to them, the number of financial instruments that we have in the portfolio is often more than 500. The bulk of the trade ideas are internally generated, even though we spend a lot of time talking to market participants, reading, etc. In our 10-year overview to investors, I presented our fund as a casino, although I was quick to point out that we were talking about the house, not the gambler. We view ourselves as trying to put on many bets that are reasonably independent of each other, where we feel that on average we have a slight edge. If we are able to live up to that, we will be making money over time, and that is what we have done so far. This approach also reduces our downside risk because rather than trying to take out all of our profit at once, we are trying to accumulate a number of small profits slowly.

Why does the market or banks allow you to be the casino—shouldn't the banks be the casinos?

Yes, I agree with where you are going. A few years ago, banks were the casinos—they were big casinos. They have a better institutional setup than hedge funds for being the house, helped by their flow business and ultimately their access to central bank financing. In some niches over longer time horizons I actually think the insurance sector, and pension sector—as we discussed to some extent—may have an even better structure for being the house, but the investment banks definitely had the best position. They took full advantage of their position, making a lot of money, but there was always something left over for the rest of us. As we now know, most of the investment banks got overconfident, acting not only as the casino operator but also the big player at the table, and this last part burned them.

Bank balance sheets are one of the casualties of the crash of 2008. A few years back, balance sheet availability was not an issue in the market. The banks were not paying much attention to the size of their balance sheets, and neither was the market. The equity analysts and the credit analysts were just looking at capital adequacy ratios. If you added a small amount of leverage based on government bonds, that counted as zero, and still counts as zero in the Basel II framework for bank capital ratios. The bank lends money to the hedge fund against very high-grade collateral and borrows from another bank, from the Fed, or from whomever, and just sets its balance sheet in between. There is no risk and no liquidity constraint to that trade and it doesn't require any cash, but it will end up on the balance sheet.

The equity and credit analysts are now looking at the leverage ratios of the banks. They want to see lower leverage and smaller balance sheets. Many banks used to have a leverage ratio—defined as total assets to equity—of 30, so present levels of about 20 do not look so bad. Repos are clearly a casualty of this process, however, as low margin business has been pushed out. There is no longer free availability of cash against high-grade collateral. The availability is still there, but it's not unlimited the way it used to be and it now comes with a cost attached to it. That cost is for using and expanding the bank's balance sheet while they are trying to keep it lean. This presents opportunities for others.

When you are looking for trade ideas for your fund, do you focus more on the macro big picture or the micro story within certain financial instruments?

In times like these, when there is free money around due to huge mispricings, trying to out-guess the macro market is not a priority. Rather, we take the easy money and focus on the almost risk-free part. We concentrate on finding optimal ways to express arbitrage and arbitrage-like trades.

Under more normal circumstances you need both. We are always trying to find the best relative value trades, which sometimes are not far away from true arbitrages, although we probably spend more time thinking about the macro scenarios and try to anticipate them. We are actually spending a lot of time thinking about the macro scenarios now as well, but we are not running much risk on them because we think it's very unclear what's going to happen.

A couple of years ago, we ran a lot of macro risk because we were more or less convinced that we were in a credit bubble. We had a position on for a credit bubble blow-up, which also served as a way of getting insurance for other types of positions that we were running to make money until the bubble cracked.

How did you recognize we were in a credit bubble?

The bubble was easy to see just from looking at the price of credit products. We thought interest rates had been too low for much too long following the dot-com crash, and credit had expanded too quickly to be sustainable from a macro perspective. Some of the borrowers were probably too weak and credit was probably too freely available, but those were just backup signs. The pricing of credit products was totally ridiculous at one stage.

Can you give me an example of ridiculous credit pricing?

Some CDOs, if you stripped out all the leverage, offered a yield pick-up of maybe 10 basis points after fees. You can get paid more than that just for being a risk-free liquidity provider to the market. But at that stage many investors thought it was a better idea to take a mispriced risk premium—much too low both by logical standards and historical standards—and leverage it multiple times, creating an illiquid product that would incur leveraged losses should something go awry. As an investment strategy, it did not look very clever. Even if you believed we were in a new world without business cycles or defaults, some credit products had already been priced for such a world, leaving you with little upside and enormous downside. So you had to be short these, either outright or spread against other risky assets where pricing was more reasonable.

We had trades on where we were buying protection against losses on tranches of credit indices. As an example, we paid what was at the time a very small yearly premium for being compensated for all the losses between 6 percent and 9 percent of a credit index. This trade behaves like an option, whereby you pay a small amount annually, which is your maximum downside, and you have a big maximum payout, which, although limited since it's a spread, could be huge—in some cases 500 times your money. That would only happen if the companies in the index showed massive defaults over the next few years. Losing 6 or even 9 percent on an index of credit investments means that times are really bad, probably the Great Depression revisited or something close to it. However unlikely a scenario, even a probability of once every 500 years meant that people selling the protection were not adequately compensated. They could maybe hope to break even over that period, but were not being compensated for the risk. Should it happen more often than predicted, say once every 50 or 100 years, they would be totally screwed. The sellers of these types of optionality trades were basically selling tail risk—catastrophe risk options at a price that was much too low. Risking survival for a few pennies is incredibly bad risk management.

The problem with buying those types of hedges is if the option becomes worth a lot, it is unlikely that the counterparty who sold it to you would still be around to pay. We almost saw that with AIG.

Correct, absolutely. You can mitigate this to some extent by moving collateral back and forth daily, but you would still have counterparty risk. We put them on with exactly that thought process in mind and thus exited the trades well before that became an issue. We also spread our trades around against many counterparties, further mitigating such risks. The introduction of central clearing for these instruments is going to help a lot.

And I presume you recognized the credit bubble in 2004–2005?

We put on our first trades betting against the bubble in the second half of 2005, which was much too early and cost us money through 2006. We stayed with them, though, actually adding a bit in the first part of 2007, especially in the second quarter when we really thought we saw signs of an impending collapse. We had thought so before, but protection got even cheaper as the situation was clearly worsening. (See Figure 4.1.)

In hindsight, I didn't realize that the credit bubble was as big as it was, especially within certain areas such as subprime. (See Figure 4.2.) We generally had a vague idea that it was all going horribly wrong, but I didn't have any details. Although we never traded subprime, we just looked at market pricing, calculated the price of likely defaults over cycles, and looked at the risk premia in that market, which was totally ridiculous. It was the same as trading the Nasdaq at 5,000, whereby you do a calculation on the back of an envelope and you can only come to one conclusion—the price is horribly wrong, it's horribly mispriced.

But the NASDAQ was already mispriced in 1997. It was definitely mispriced in 1998, then more so in 1999.

Sometimes these things take time. For our credit bubble trades, we received the first installment of our payoff two years after we first entered

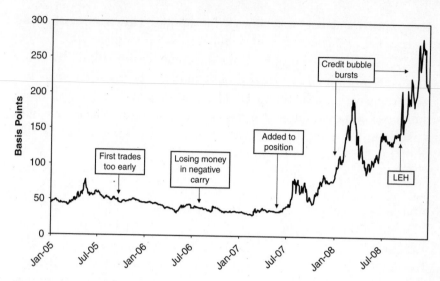

Figure 4.1   CDX Generic Credit Spreads, 2005–2008
SOURCE: Bloomberg.

the positions. One of the reasons we had staying power is that we structured the trade through option-like structures. Even though credit default swaps are not technically options, they behave like options. You can lose the bulk of what you paid for CDS, but when spreads become really tight you don't need to sell them because your downside becomes

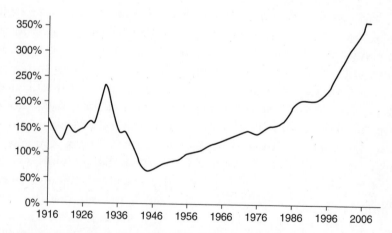

Figure 4.2   Total Credit Market as a Percentage of GDP, 1916–2006
SOURCE: U.S. Department of Commerce; and Federal Reserve System.

very limited and you still have all the upside. This is especially true for tranches.

We had many discussions about the counterparty risk on these instruments. We weren't worried about counterparty risk short-term, but we were worried that things could get a lot worse, which, all other things equal, should imply that spreads widen even more and we would make even more money. But we weren't sure that we would be able to find willing buyers who would accept the counterparty risk that we were carrying against the major U.S. and European banks. So we decided early on that we would exit these trades fairly quickly and move on to other similar types of exposures in more reliable and liquid markets.

One of the relatively easy trades to do once credit started to crack was going long the front end of fixed income curves—two-year U.S. Treasury Notes, German *Schatz* contracts, or something similar. Because we like to spread our bets around, we expressed that through options and outright directional positions in various markets, but volatility was already becoming fairly expensive. We were also running more long-term long volatility exposures as part of our blow-up scenario in many parts of the portfolio, which paid off handsomely.

Now that the credit bubble has burst and banks and financials have imploded, what is next?

We have huge deflationary forces that up until recently were self-reinforcing. These forces were only mitigated by record government interventions with liquidity provisions, interest rate cuts, quantitative easing, and fiscal stimulus. Now we have two enormous forces struggling against each other: one deflationary—the economy and the financial system—and one reflationary—stimulus of various types. We haven't got a clue how these will play out, and it's rather difficult balancing them. Quantitative easing, probably the correct course for central banks, is a difficult beast to control if market psychology turns quickly or if the real economy improves faster than expected. Because timely exit strategies will be tricky to implement, it is likely that they will come too early or too late. The most likely scenario is too late because political pressure will mitigate doing anything too early. If you consider the responsibility and institutional setup of most central banks, most of their decision makers would argue that it would be a bigger mistake to cut stimulus too early rather than too late. On balance, then, the risk is that it will be withdrawn too late, even though both scenarios are plausible. We are following a number of indicators and different possible scenarios, waiting to see which seems to be getting the upper hand before taking a strong view in the markets.

So you have multiple scenarios that you are tracking: (A) the world is okay; (B) the Great Depression; and (C) bad inflation?

These are all possible scenarios. There is the inflation scenario and the deflation scenario. There is a protectionist scenario. There is a too much stimulus scenario, which is an inflationary scenario. There is a central banks getting less independent scenario. Since there are many different ingredients out there right now, many forces that we are not used to evaluating, we have to be patient.

For the first time in centuries, Asia is the most important economic player on the margin. Right now, China is more important for the global economy than the U.S. But I have no idea whether Chinese growth rates are sustainable. We are just trying to follow the data and be ready once one of the scenarios becomes dominant.

Protectionism is also a great danger, and the worse the global economy looks, the greater this danger is. We have seen tendencies towards protectionism over the past six months and are following these developments closely. More of an economic downturn would certainly increase the risks of a very bad depression-like scenario, because of both real economic implications as well as psychological ones. More protectionism in the system would mean that real growth will be lower than expected, which, in turn, would mean that the debt problem is bigger than expected, which would lead to more deleveraging, more problems in the financial system, and so on. At that point, everyone will be aware that the politicians have screwed up, making a bad situation worse by resorting to protectionism and other beggar-thy-neighbor policies, which can lead to even more political populism and radicalism. This is a really bad scenario.

As market conditions have improved since March 2009, the risks you describe seem less likely. Nevertheless, are you starting to purchase protection against these types of extreme scenarios as protection becomes cheap again?

We always have some type of protection against extreme scenarios, but right now we are carrying it more as insurance than as a true position. Two years ago it was one of our main positions. We do not have big insurance policies on at this stage, although we are starting to think about it, as it may be time to put them on again. We have been playing for the rather benign scenario as our main portfolio scenario, with mispriced relative value and arbitrage trades dominating our portfolio. We are running rather low risk at this stage, as we think the environment is very uncertain.

The consensus view at the moment is that unprecedented fiscal stimulus and quantitative easing automatically leads to inflation. Do you believe that?

It is not automatic, but the likelihood of both very inflationary and deflationary scenarios is much higher now than usual. I would not rule out deflationary scenarios at all. Assuming that we get a renewed slump in 2010 after the end of the inventory correction, a slowdown in Asia without any pickup in economic activity in the Western world, and politicians moving towards protectionism, a highly deflationary scenario is very possible.

But big budget deficits do not automatically lead to inflation. Japan is a good example here, with one of the biggest government debts in the world. We have only seen deflation there. Of course, it could ultimately lead to an inflation scenario in Japan, but this is not necessarily the case. Many people say that if you create excess reserves or buy back government debt on the scale of what the Fed or the Bank of England are doing right now, it will inevitably lead to inflation. But I do not agree with this thinking, either. Although it certainly increases the risk of such scenarios, as long as you can keep liquidity under control by paying interest on excess reserves, it will not necessarily translate into increased lending, risk taking, and inflation. And even if it does, there are ways of controlling that.

Although we are definitely playing with fire, we were forced to do so in order to contain the collapse that we experienced in global activity. Policy makers are conducting real-time experiments with the economy because they have no choice. It is going to be tricky calibrating this scenario—very tricky.

How can you hedge against protectionism?

Protectionism causes all risky assets to underperform dramatically. You would want to own the short end of most sovereign bond markets because when you enter into protectionist scenarios, countries will want to ease their monetary conditions and devalue their currency against everyone else.

Do fiat currencies inevitably lead to instability?

I would not say that instability is inevitable. However, mishandling a fiat currency system like the current one can bring collapse. We did not run our system in a controlled way, but rather allowed the system to get overextended on credit. You could argue that the political logic assumes politicians will bail out the system to save the economy from totally collapsing under their watch, regardless of what the costs are afterwards. The fact that the long-term costs and consequences are unknown strengthens the politicians' case for intervening now. Some claim that we will inevitably have to pay the price of past excesses and the least bad option is to do it now. Others argue that we must try to prevent today's economic correction from translating into total disaster, depression, and mayhem. There might be something to each of these arguments, and only time will tell. But it is very plain to me that the politicians and the central bankers will at this stage do more or less whatever it takes to avoid that collapse happening now, under their watch. They will not let nebulous long-term economic consequences get in the way.

What are your thoughts on the status of the dollar as the world's reserve currency?

The dollar is certainly challenged, and will remain so for a number of reasons. A better longer-term solution for the world is probably more than one reserve currency. But unless the U.S. really mismanages things from here, the dollar will remain the world's number one reserve currency 5 and 10 years down the road. It just might not enjoy such a wide margin of dominance in the future.

Is this current bailout going to create the mother of all moral hazards? Are the actions of the Bernanke Fed a highly levered version of the Greenspan put?

The idea that central banks can fine-tune everything, that they have perfected their game such that risk premia should be much lower, has been proven false. Perhaps it was exactly the other way around: central banks lowered risk premia enough to spark a bubble in credit markets (see box).

Paradox of Perfection

I was talking with a hedge fund manager in Stockholm recently about this phenomenon and together we came up with the term "paradox of perfection," meaning that as central bankers have perfected their game, paradoxically, that perfection has encouraged excessive risk taking and created other issues and imbalances elsewhere.

SOURCE: *Inside the House of Money* (John Wiley & Sons, 2006).

I am not overly worried about new financial bubbles forming in the next few years. Sure, there are some scenarios where that could happen, particularly if we assume that we haven't learned any lessons from 2008. For example, in order to get us out of this hole, we go back to leveraging up the consumer's balance sheet. Because of sluggish overall growth, this might be allowed to go on for a few years, whereby interest rates remain low, consumer lending and debt grows strongly, and asset prices rise. Such a scenario would fuel the build-up for the mother of all bubbles, and would require a really painful adjustment at some stage. But hopefully this is not the way things play out. As long as we price risk reasonably, the risk of bubbles should be lower. We will have a better capitalized banking and financial system going forward, and hopefully smarter regulation.

The weak link could be the level of interest rates. Staying too low for too long will mean trouble at some point in the future. It is not obvious that we can normalize global interest rates without running into a host of problems, and the longer we wait before we try, the more difficult it could be. Another worry is how quickly the market and policy makers forget about the crisis. If everything looks okay in a few years, will we be underpricing risk again? Will we be leveraging up again? That is a rather scary scenario.

Even though I see little risk of any big financial bubble over the next few years, psychological bubbles can form in some submarkets, and inflation could become a prime example. I can easily see an inflation paranoia developing whereby people become convinced that we have a big inflation problem ahead of us, which may or may not be correct. If the reasonably strong round of economic statistics continues and intensifies, people will say that there is too much stimulus in the system and the Fed has lost control. They could say that the Fed needs to hike interest rates to 3 or 5 percent immediately in order to avoid runaway inflation, but they are politically constrained from doing so. Commodities might be booming. The market could easily get into some kind of inflation panic at that stage. In this uncertain environment, it is so easy to tell stories rather than perform deep analyses, like the DOW 36,000 fairy tale during the late 1990s equity boom. This time it might be conspiracy theories with regards to the Fed or something like that. All kinds of B.S. tend to permeate in uncertain and troubling times, yet people still buy into that stuff.

If we do have inflation, or even hyperinflation as some predict, what is the best way for real money managers to hedge it?

I would assume that most real money investors have some type of inflation protection in their asset mix as the neutral portfolio to start with. This might be inflation-linked bonds or inflation swaps, for example. If inflation starts taking off, these instruments will become very expensive, so managers should be looking for other instruments as well. Real assets of various types would perform less poorly than other investments. Highly leveraged real estate, for example, could be interesting, as you inflate away all the debt.

Commodities would be relatively fine, including gold. It is easy to envision a psychological bubble building in gold, especially in the inflation type scenarios that we have been discussing, or in a deflation scenario characterized by excess protectionism. Many people will begin questioning the credit worthiness of sovereign borrowers and their willingness to uphold the value of their currencies, which strengthens the case for gold, an asset generally perceived good in risk aversion scenarios. It is a small market that can be pushed around so strong buying could generate outsized price moves.

Longer-dated nominal bonds will obviously be a total catastrophe in an inflation scenario, so you have to be underweight those if you think the risk of inflation is increasing. But the opposite holds true in a deflationary scenario. This game was never meant to be easy.

If you were to follow your passion and go deep sea fishing for the next 10 years, and you had to put all of your wealth into one trade, what would it be?

Well, I hope I will never have to bet everything on one card without being able to adjust my views for 10 years. But if I had no choice, I would say residential real estate in the U.S., focusing on cheaper markets with rock-bottom prices such as Florida or California—but not the fancy addresses. Housing in parts of the U.S. is cheap relative to the rest of the world. And housing is not only a financial asset, it has utility because you can live in it. If I keep the house up well or have someone that looks after it, I uphold that utility value and I would argue it will turn out to be a solid investment in any kind of normalization or rebound. And if we don't see such a normalization or rebound for 10 years, then the downside at this price level is lower than other risky assets, so the trade has relatively good risk versus reward characteristics. Farmland is another idea where prices in many cases have come off significantly, and there is also utility to it that could be worth a lot in some extreme scenarios.

So you have an inflation hedge and an Armageddon hedge?

Exactly. In an unlikely worst-case scenario, I have a place to live where I can farm and fish and in the much more likely scenario where prices have normalized, I will have made a profit.

Chapter 5

The Philosopher

E rudition drives "The Philosopher's" process. In following the philosophies of Karl Popper as much as George Soros, the Philosopher seeks not what is true, but rather what is more fit, in the sense of a range of conjectures that can be evaluated. In other words, he focuses on what is priced into the market and how that pricing may change, rather than on what the "right" answer might eventually be. In this vein, he is the ultimate hypothesis tester. You can sit down with the Philosopher and discuss history, economics, politics, philosophy, and a host of other topics, but in his trading world, probability reigns supreme.

When the world financial system broke down in 2008, policy makers responded by implementing creative strategies to halt the collapse, and suddenly the plumbing behind the system—the money markets—became critical to understanding events and their consequences. Long neglected as an unsexy area of global finance, money markets became a focal point.

The Philosopher's savvy is rooted in his unique approach, which combines his deep knowledge of the financial system with a ruthless attention to philosophical logic. Starting off as a money markets bank prop trader taught him the inner workings of the plumbing that underpins the global financial system. He learned the ropes taking true, directional macro risks, then going on to work with some of the biggest names in the hedge fund business, and ultimately striking out on his own, where he now sits atop a multibillion dollar macro-hedge fund.

How did you get into the markets?

I read *Reminiscences of a Stock Operator* by Edwin Lefèvre when I was 17, which was in 1987, the year the stock market crashed. It proved to be a formative experience. I read the book in the summer, the stock market crashed in the fall, and as I watched television, I realized that many people were not making much sense. I began to read everything I could about financial markets and joined a bank straight out of college, which was when I started trading.

At age 17 you knew that people were talking nonsense?

I thought, well, if a schoolboy can form a coherent view that differs from the expert consensus, then maybe I should go into the markets. Markets appeared to combine my two loves, which were economics and competitive games. I played hockey and cricket, but it was the intellectual, strategy games such as chess and bridge that I really loved. These days, the only sport I play is golf.

What was your first job in the markets?

I started off on the trading floor as one of those coffee-fetching trainees. I soon joined the money markets desk, which was very unfashionable, but it was the only desk on the floor that actually took proprietary macro directional risk. I wanted to learn about the plumbing of the markets so that I could understand how to interpret central bank policy and position for interest rate moves. I started taking proprietary risk, and as I did well, my position limits were increased.

When did you know you were a good trader?

When I first started, I was not at all sure I was any good—many other trainees were faster than me at giving rapid explanations as to why certain things happened in the markets, things that were not at all obvious to me. For example, to me, there were a number of factors that could explain why USD/JPY was going up and while it was not at all clear to me, my peers would quickly come up with highly plausible answers. It took me some time to realize that most market explanations are really rationalizations, making up simple stories to explain complex situations. But markets are not that simple.

My first very profitable year was 1994, which was when I began to think that I could actually play this game. Although I started as a junior coffee fetcher, I was one of the top performers on the floor during the big bond crash of '94, when many other traders got crushed. (See Figure 5.1.)

You must have been one of the few macro traders to make money in 1994.

Maybe my success was due in part to youth and ignorance, but I was also helped enormously by some very smart and supportive senior traders on

Figure 5.1 Bond Market Rout of 1994
SOURCE: Bloomberg.

my desk who also did very well that year. The scenario certainly seemed quite straightforward: Because the economy had been doing well, it was pretty clear that central banks would hike rates, pushing up yields. Perhaps some traders who had been around longer became too obsessed with positive carry and a belief in their value-driven fundamental models. Ironically, the trades that often make traders lots and lots of money are the very trades that blow them up in the end because they stay in them too long. In some ways, I feel quite lucky that my first big year was an atypical big year for a macro trader. It makes it much harder to get stuck in a pattern as it is clearly not optimal to get addicted to making big money in bear markets and crashes—these events are too rare.

What did you learn from working on a trading floor?

Although my style is mainly self-taught, I still learned a lot from watching the people around me. One of the beautiful things about working on the trading floor is that you are sitting in a big open room with some very good traders. I was always fascinated by how people made money, and I would try to reverse engineer their processes, although my results were often quite different from theirs. Sometimes their self-awareness was lacking, whereby they did not understand that their ability to take money out of a market was in part due to their trading style being conducive to the particular market environment. This is why you often see people have a stellar two- or three-year run, then never make money again. I learned early on from a study of my peers that it is useful to have a variety of styles to be able to adapt to and profit in all types of markets. The biggest macro question is always: "What type of market are we in?" If I know that, then I can implement the style and type of trading that suits that specific market.

What do you miss from the trading floor now that you run your own hedge fund in an office with less people around?

When I was younger I used to enjoy the noise level of the trading floor, even though given my auspicious start the rest of my time on the floor proved to be somewhat anticlimactic. My first week on the floor was when the United Kingdom dropped out of the European Exchange Rate Mechanism (ERM). (See Figure 5.2.) The noise level was at a fever pitch

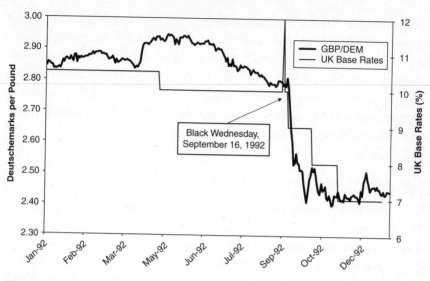

Figure 5.2 The United Kingdom Dropping out of ERM, 1992
SOURCE: Bloomberg.

at that time, and everything since has seemed quite calm in comparison. More broadly, however, the information you receive on a trading floor tends to be just noise, so in terms of information there is little that I miss.

How do you define information, and what sources of information do you use?

My team and I try to develop a hypothesis about how the world is working and how it could work in the future. Therefore, information to us is a collection of theories and ideas, together with evidence that either supports or falsifies these theories and ideas. Information can come from fundamental economic drivers, such as growth, inflation, and other variables, or it can come from more technical, market-based factors such as flows, liquidity, etc. Building a team of smart people who can effectively filter and analyze this information is key, but the really tricky part is making the right linkages to develop the analysis into tradable themes.

We are not engaged in what I describe as "vision macro," whereby one tries to work out some kind of single truth about how the world works. Rather, we form a probabilistic set of hypotheses about how the world could look and what might drive markets going forward, focusing on the market impact in all scenarios and looking for good risk-versus-reward trades around these hypotheses. A great book that describes this process is *The Alchemy of Finance* by George Soros, in which he describes and demonstrates how he uses hypothesis formation and testing, ideas that come from the philosopher Karl Popper.

Can you give me an example of how this process works in practice?

Some people can trade markets using only numbers, prices on a screen, but this approach does not work for me. The numbers have to mean something—I have to understand the fundamental drivers behind the numbers. And while fundamentals are important, they are only one of many important inputs to the process. Just as a Value-at-Risk (VaR) model alone cannot tell you what your overall risk is, economic analysis alone cannot tell you where the bond market should be.

Let us use an interest rate trade around central bank policy as a straightforward example to illustrate my process. Economic drivers will create the framework: What is the outlook for growth, inflation, employment, and other key variables? What will the reaction of the central bank be? We then build a model of the potential outcomes of these economic drivers, weighting them according to probabilistic assumptions about our expectations. We look at what the central bank could do in each scenario, comparing this with market prices to see if there are any interesting differences. When differences exist, we then think about what can drive those differences to widen or converge.

It is important to note that a key element to this exercise is the fact that what other people believe will happen is just as important as the eventual outcome. A market is not a truth mechanism, but rather an interaction of human beings whereby their expectations, beliefs, hopes, and fears shape overall market prices. People in the private equity business can decide if something is a good idea or not if held to maturity. My horizon is much shorter term.

A good example of this psychological element can be seen in inflation. At the end of 2008, U.S. government fixed income was pricing in deflation forever (see Figure 5.3). At that point, the only thing of

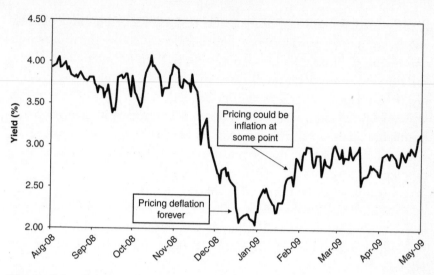

Figure 5.3 Ten-Year U.S. Government Bonds, 2008–2009
SOURCE: Bloomberg.

interest to me was the question of whether people might think that there could be inflation at some point in the future. Quantitative easing made it easy to answer this question affirmatively, because there are many monetarists in the world who believe that the quantity of money is the driver of inflation. Whether they are right or not is a problem for the future—what is important to me is that such people exist today. Their existence makes the market pricing for U.S. long bonds completely lopsided. Such pricing only makes sense if you are a died-in-the-wool output gapper who believes that when unemployment goes up, inflation goes down, end of story. Market prices reflect the probability of potential future outcomes at that moment, not the outcomes themselves. Some people do not believe in the output gap theory of inflation, and these people believe that pricing for U.S. bonds should be somewhere else. Because these two divergent schools of thought exist, it is possible that market sentiment can shift from deflation to inflation and that pricing will follow.

One way to think about my process is to view markets in terms of the range of reasonable opinions. The opinion that we are going to have declining and low inflation for the next decade is entirely reasonable. The opinion that we are going to have inflation because central banks have printed trillions of dollars is also reasonable. While most pundits and many market participants try to decide which potential outcome will be the right one, I am much more interested in finding out where the market is mispricing the skew of probabilities. If the market is pricing that inflation will go to the moon, then I will start talking about unemployment rates, wages going down, and how we are going to have disinflation. If you tell me the markets are pricing deflation forever, I will start talking about the quantity theory of money, explaining how this skews outcomes the other way. Most market participants I know do not think in these terms. The market is extremely poor at pricing macroeconomics. People always talk about being forward looking, but few actually are. People tell stories to rationalize historical price action more frequently than they use potential future hypotheses to work out where prices could be.

Do you view your job as predicting sentiment?

Yes, that is a very reasonable way of describing it. But by sentiment I do not mean some kind of vague general feeling or emotion. I mean the reflection of people's beliefs, which are based on something real and tangible, which will change their actions. Although beliefs tend to be driven by fundamentals, people and markets are very slow to fully incorporate macro information, and when they do the results can be overly dramatic. The uncertain nature of the economic future and our flawed attempts to understand it are a permanent source of market mispricing. The economy is not easily predictable, but the reactions of policy makers and the persistent errors in human expectations are. The natural extension of Keynes' beauty contest is that animal spirits are not irrational and because they are not irrational they can be anticipated (see box). To illustrate this idea let's imagine there are two states of the world, and although each is quite reasonable, one is more likely than the other. Unfortunately, the human brain is not wired to understand probability very well. We are particularly bad at understanding low probability events, which we tend to think of as either inevitable or impossible. Therefore, a very small change in the underlying fundamental probability can sometimes cause wild swings in sentiment because the potential outcome went from impossible to inevitable, whereas the underlying fundamentals did not move substantially. Shifts in sentiment cause markets to move much more frequently and violently than shifts in fundamentals do.

Beauty Contest

The concept of a "beauty contest" in financial speak comes from a passage that John Maynard Keynes wrote in *The General Theory of Employment, Interest, and Money* (1935) to describe the behavior of stock market participants. Keynes compared the art of selecting stocks to correctly predicting the winner of a beauty contest held by a number of the English newspapers of the day. The newspapers would publish photographs of one hundred or so women and ask readers to choose which five would match the consensus selections of the other readers. Keynes wrote, "It is not a case of choosing those [faces] which, to the best of one's judgment, are really the prettiest, nor even those which average opinion genuinely thinks the prettiest. We have reached the third degree where we devote our intelligences to anticipating what average opinion expects the average opinion to be. And there are some, I believe, who practise the fourth, fifth and higher degrees." In other words, selecting a winning investment becomes a psychological game of predicting what investments others will select. Keynes believed that, ultimately, investment and market prices are determined by the herd-like "animal spirit" of investors.

Most economic and market research is overly focused on core outcomes. If you ask people what they think will happen in the future, they will often tell you what they think is most likely to happen. For example, let's say that something, "A," has a 60 percent probability of occurring. If you ask 10 different people what will happen, they will all tell you that "A" will happen. Then you post a poll saying everyone believes that "A" will happen. But if you change the 60 percent to 40 percent and ask people the same question, they will respond that "B" will happen. Changing the probability only 20 percent swung the "expected outcome" from

100 percent "A" to 100 percent "B." This is how I see my role in terms of predicting market sentiment. I do not go around asking people how they are feeling, but I look for cases where a small change in fundamentals could cause a large change in how people perceive the fundamentals.

There have been large swings in sentiment during the past few years. How do you stay ahead of these swings when they are driven by only small changes in fundamentals?

It is impossible to accurately predict an outcome all the time, which is where money management discipline comes in. Again, everything is a hypothesis-testing exercise. If the hypothesis is falsified and I am wrong, then I cut the position. I am not trying to get everything right, but I want to be sure that I limit my losses when I am wrong.

How do you achieve that positive asymmetry in outcomes?

Sometimes I use options, although options are often quite misunderstood. I buy options when they are cheap, not for insurance. Buying insurance when it is too expensive is not a very good way to manage money over the long term. There were times in 2008 when options were ludicrously cheap, making them great things to own. But if you trade primarily in liquid markets, you can truncate the downside through stop losses just as easily as using options.

How many hypotheses or positions do you typically run?

We commonly run 10 to 15 themes, where each theme is made up of one to ten different trades. Potential themes can be around central bank policy, yield curve shape, the dollar, credit spreads, or anything else in the traditional directional macro space. From a risk management perspective, we are looking for common risk factors, as well as historical and potential correlations. From a trade level perspective, we are most concerned about changing volatility, whereas from a portfolio perspective, the biggest concern is always a change in correlation. Although you may think that you have 10 independent positions, a regime change can mean that you really have just one trade, which is exactly the risk management lesson that struck many people in 2008.

Why do you think that happened in 2008?

The main reason is liquidity, which is a common risk factor that most people still omit from their analysis. This baffles me. Maybe I am colored by the early stages of my career during the ERM crisis, which was all about liquidity. During the event, the FX markets were driven by central banks squeezing liquidity to force speculators from betting against the currencies. The 1997 Asia crisis was clearly a liquidity crisis, and the 1994 bond crash can also be viewed as a liquidity crisis. Markets just gapped away.

If you have not actively traded in a liquidity crisis, it can be very difficult to understand. Many markets that had never before had any type of crisis suffered liquidity crises in 2008. For example, many people in the large U.S. markets thought a liquidity crisis was something endemic to emerging markets and thus were totally unprepared. Liquidity is a perpetual common risk factor across a broad variety of markets, but because in normal times it is invisible, econometric models and academia often assume the risk does not exist.

How do you measure liquidity and how do you prepare for potential illiquidity?

I trade the most liquid strategy in the most liquid markets in the world. Nevertheless, I try to stay at least twice as paranoid as the market. There are many trades that others deem great opportunities—but I will not engage in them because they have negative skew risk, meaning they can become illiquid very quickly.

For example, the potential for a liquidity crisis in 2008 was well flagged. In August 2007, when LIBOR spiked, it was clear that we were in a systemic banking crisis. It was also obvious that the leverage would have to unwind, which would trigger a liquidity problem causing more unwinding. A full year later, however, people were still in denial that balance sheets were overleveraged and that banks were in trouble. (See Figure 5.4.)

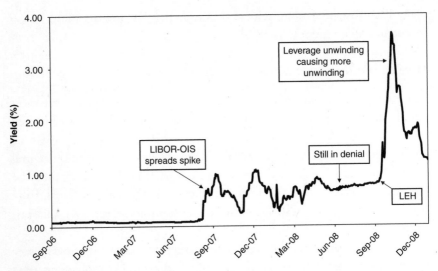

Figure 5.4   Three-Month LIBOR—Overnight Indexed Swap (OIS) Spreads, 2006–2008
SOURCE: Bloomberg.

When people saw LIBOR spike in the summer of 2007, what should they have done to mitigate their illiquidity risk?

They should have sold anything that was illiquid or had the potential to become illiquid. It was the only way out, and some people did sell their illiquid positions. There are some really smart people who did brilliantly during both the boom times and the bust. There are not that many, but they exist so it was possible. When you are in something that is illiquid, you really have to decide if you can hold it to maturity. If you hold something to maturity and have secured financing then you do not need to care about liquidity. If you do not have to worry about mark-to-market, you will be fine. You do not, however, want to fool yourself into thinking that you are liquid when in fact you are not. Many of the credit products offer ample opportunities for this type of delusion. If you are not going to hold these products until maturity, then you are essentially trading on the greater fool theory. At some point, you have to sell it to someone else. If you are planning to sell it during the bull market, then you will be fine—but most people do not, and collectively it is logically impossible. If you wait until it all starts rolling over, it's too late. Once a market becomes illiquid, there is no bid and there is no way out.

I never engage in illiquid strategies because I always think about the entire plan for a trade, particularly the exit strategy if things go wrong. For me, if a trade starts going wrong and its hypothesis is looking falsified, I exit. This type of behavior is difficult in illiquid strategies.

Why do investors engage in illiquid strategies when they could stick with liquid ones?

These investors would correctly point out that this strategy has histori- cally been highly profitable and that if you believe in efficient markets there should rationally exist a risk premium, which the truly illiquidity tolerant investor can earn. But the problem with many of these strategies is their overuse, which largely comes down to benchmarking. What gets you fired? Does losing money get you fired, or does underperform- ing your benchmark get you fired? If underperforming your benchmark gets you fired, then do not be surprised if people act according to this in- centive structure and eventually have a huge absolute return drawdown. The only way to avoid the drawdown catastrophe is to get out early, and getting out early means you have at least some period of underper- formance, which can potentially be long. If you do get fired, someone else will be hired to take your place who will chase the benchmark, which is why blowups like 2008 happen. Behavior follows incentive structures, and the incentive structures were strongly weighted towards taking excessive liquidity risk prior to 2008.

How would you change the incentive structures?

I am not sure the incentive structures have to be changed. Rather, the people setting the incentive structures just need to be happy with the consequences. If you are an endowment and you do not really care about a drawdown, then that is fine. If you want to invest long term, drawdowns do not matter, so ignore the mark-to-market. With a long- term time horizon, you want to sell risk premium systematically forever if you do not believe that you have skill at discretion and timing. And this is a perfectly reasonable thing to do. Just do not be surprised when you drop 30 percent, because it will happen at some point.

You said you run 10 to 15 themes and if you are wrong, you stop out.
How do you set stops, and how do you manage risk at the portfolio level?

We are always looking for evidence that a hypothesis can be falsified. I prefer saying "hypothesis falsified" rather than "stop loss" because there are many potential reasons for a falsified hypothesis. One piece of evidence is losing money, whereby the market goes through some level that you think it should not have. This is a market test, but fundamentals can change as well. For example, there are many trades that make money for all the wrong reasons. I always keep in mind why I did a given trade, and if those reasons are no longer valid, I take the trade off. You do not have to wait until a trade has lost money before cutting it. At a thematic level, when a hypothesis is falsified, we cut the position.

In the second quarter of 2008, I was bullish UK fixed income on the hypothesis that rates would be cut dramatically because the UK economy was deteriorating rapidly. Instead, the market started trading as though inflation was the primary concern, and I was forced to think about the fact that commodity prices were still going through the roof and the inflation profile was becoming extremely worrying. And if this was the key driver, rather than the growth outlook, then UK rates could go a lot higher. The hypothesis was proved wrong partly through price action and partly through high inflation numbers. We got out of the trade well before it hit a stop loss because the fundamental hypothesis was falsified. (See Figure 5.5.)

What is more difficult is when you have no hypothesis falsification at any thematic level. There are no specific stop losses, yet the overall portfolio is losing money. When that happens, we reduce risk overall, obeying specific triggers we have in place for drawdowns. If I have one of these drawdowns, I have done something wrong and need to reduce risk and reassess.

Let's say I am running 10 themes where none of them have hit their individual stop loss or had their hypothesis falsified, yet the portfolio is down significantly. In this case, there are likely two main things that I have gotten wrong: (1) sizing, which means I have misunderstood the volatility input; and (2) correlation of themes within the portfolio. If the correlation amongst the themes in the portfolio is higher than expected,

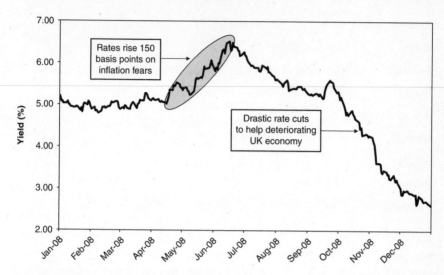

Figure 5.5 Two–Year UK Swap Rates, 2008
SOURCE: Bloomberg.

I will be running too much risk and need to reduce the sizing of all the trades.

When I am wrong, I cut risk and move on. I am adamant about being in only the most liquid markets precisely because I want to reserve the right to be wrong. Illiquid markets put a lot of pressure on you to be right.

When you put on a trade, do you worry about being wrong first and foremost?

I focus on risk versus reward, but it is primarily potential loss that I worry about, as potential losses are the killers. A trade certainly has to have the potential to make a lot of money, but knowing the downside risk and when you are wrong is really the most important thing. A classic example of false discipline is something like this that happens on trading floors all the time:

Boss: *What have you got on?*

Trader: *I'm long USD/JPY, but don't worry, I've got a stop 1 percent lower.*

A day later

Boss: *How's it going in USD/JPY?*

Trader: *Oh, I got stopped out. Hit my limit. I'm out.*

Boss: *Okay, fine.*

A day later

Boss: *What are you doing now?*

Trader: *Long USD/JPY.*

Boss: *Oh, really?*

Trader: *It's okay. I've got a 1 percent stop on it . . .*

And they do the same trade over and over again. The trader had a stop loss, but did not really believe in it and never felt he was wrong being long USD/JPY. This type of trader has the illusion of discipline, which they read about in trading books. They will talk about stop losses, discipline, all those good trading habits and methods. But running stops off of pain thresholds is a terrible way to run money. If a trade goes to your pain threshold stop level, you will get out because you told yourself you should, because you are disciplined. But because all the fundamentals and technicals still look okay, and often even better, there is nothing to prevent you from doing the trade again once the pain has subsided.

This is why I prefer hypothesis testing. To stop out of a trade, you have to believe you are wrong, that your entire rationale for the trade is wrong. I always think in advance about what it will take for me to believe I am wrong. Then I can work backwards to determine my conviction and how much I am willing to lose on the trade, which leads to the potential sizing of a position.

When you play golf, do you visualize every shot?

I do, actually. I believe in visualization, and the analogies between golf and trading go beyond just visualizing the trade. With golf, you can only control your process, not the result. You can control your swing, but you cannot control where the ball goes—there are too many variables. You can make a great shot but the ball could take a bad bounce and go in a bunker, or take a great bounce and go in the hole. Once the ball leaves your club after impact, you lose control and become subject to myriad imperfections on the course. Trading can be similar. You can have a great trade that loses money, or conversely a terrible trade that makes money. Regardless, the process is the only thing that you can control, never the result. My process is such that we will occasionally lose money, but over time, on average, we will make money. I try not to get too worried about good patches or bad patches in the shorter term, but rather always come back to focusing on the investment process and how we make money over time.

How do you generate trade ideas?

There are two generic ways to think about trade ideas. The most common is what I would call *fundamentals to market*, which is bottom–up analysis of economics and fundamentals. It is comparing values and catalysts for what is happening versus what is priced into markets. An example of this approach would be the Fed funds trade I presented at your conference in Budapest (October 23, 2008). It was a purely fundamentally driven trade idea, which was that Fed funds were going to trade close to zero before year end due to the Fed's inability to mop up excess liquidity at positive rates. The market did not understand this at the time, and what I loved about the trade was that many people at the conference were telling me I was wrong, but no one could articulate why. I thought the market was expressing strong confidence in the Fed's ability to maintain a floor in rates, which was actually highly improbable given the technical plumbing of the system. So this is an example of something that was driven by fundamental analysis, which resulted in a good trade idea. (See Figure 5.6.)

The second type of trade is more markets driven, which I could call *markets to fundamentals*. These trades result from markets going a certain direction due to some underlying driver, which for one reason or another presents an opportunity for good risk-versus-reward trades. To find this type of idea, I will unashamedly beg, borrow, and steal from any source. If anyone has a great idea, I will listen to it. We source such trades formally through our trading desk, which continually tries to find interesting ideas from other people. We read independent and Street research, where people have hypotheses and ideas that stimulate our own

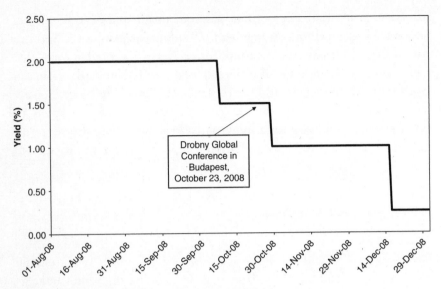

Figure 5.6   Fed Funds Target Rate, Fall 2008
SOURCE: Bloomberg.

efforts to find out if what they say is true. Then my process goes two ways. First, I think of the potential implications if a given hypothesis is true, then only afterwards try to work out in what circumstances it could in fact be true or not. If you start by trying to determine whether an idea is true or not, it becomes too easy to believe nothing and ultimately do nothing, or to only do trades which become fixations. By the time something is clearly true, it is already largely priced in. I prefer to force myself to act based on situations that might be true if the risk/reward characteristics are favorable enough. Another source of ideas can come from looking at other people's ideas inversely. Sometimes ideas are so bad that the opposite is true, and that, too, is valuable information. If someone comes in and pitches that you should buy credit because of a ridiculous structure and reason, your eyes light up and you think, wow, a great trade might be going the opposite way.

What is your time horizon for your trades?

My time horizon is one to three months for most trades, although the fundamental analysis that drives them tends to be quite a bit longer term than that. Many factors can play out in terms of evolving fundamentals and changing perceptions in the marketplace in a one- to three-month horizon. Less than one month can be too random, whereas horizons beyond one year fall more into the vision or held-to-maturity category.

What percentage of your trades make money?

We have a hit ratio of around 50 percent. Although 2008 was a pretty good year, we still had a hit ratio of around 50 percent. It all comes down to trade structure and risk versus reward. If you have a hit ratio of 50 percent and an average payoff of three-to-one, then you make a lot of money. Perhaps surprisingly, I actually find that it is helpful to be wrong half the time. Stopping out of a trade is psychologically much easier when you reserve the right to be wrong half the time.

Trading must be more psychologically challenging for traders who depend on a high hit ratio because at some point we all get it very wrong. They might be consistently right for five years in row, but then they miss one year and their performance suffers tremendously or they just blow up. I, on the other hand, can have miss after miss after miss, and I am okay because I make sure none of these individual misses can ever sink me.

What was your worst miss ever?

The worst trades are mainly opportunity cost problems, which tend to be misses around the end of bubbles. In 1999 and 2006, for example, I did not really make any money. Although both of these years ended positive, I could have made a lot more money going with the direction of the bubble. However, in both cases I got a little stuck on fundamental value—prices were so high that I struggled to get involved.

Our result in 2007 was better, partly because I recognized my mistakes in 1999 and 2006 and realized that a bubble is something that you cannot fade because it can always last longer than you think. What you should absolutely avoid during bubbles is buying assets that are already too expensive and that risk becoming illiquid. If you are going to play a bubble, you have to be invested in the most liquid products that correlate to the bubble, so that you can get out when you want. For example, in

2007 I happily made money trading commodity currencies until August, at which point I just got out. We had a change in view, and I flipped my book in a day.

Where is the next bubble?

I do not yet know where the next bubble will be. I am generally not a great bubble follower, but I would like to make some money from the next one and make sure I do not get short too early. I was not involved in the dot-com or housing bubbles. Bubbles in general are difficult for me and I suspect that will continue to be the case. The people who make the most in a bubble are always the true believers who buy irrespective of value. But these tend to be the same people who lose the most at the end as well. Over time a lot of money can be made out of bubbles, but I will never become evangelical, claiming how this time it is different, the world has changed, because it doesn't change.

I imagine that the vast majority of my focus and risk will remain on themes and strategies that have nothing to do with the next bubble. This is where we generate our returns over time. Too many people obsess about finding the next bubble because they want to get quick returns without doing too much work. I am happy to run a portfolio that is "bubble-neutral," meaning I do not rely upon timing the coming crash. But the large bubbles are difficult to avoid since they affect so many markets. In order to engage in any strategies connected to a bubble, I would have to find a liquid product that relates to the bubble. As long as you are in liquid products, you can get out when things start to crash—although the obvious problem is that everyone else probably thinks the same thing. Surprisingly, in the big bubbles you can sometimes be months late getting out and still survive. The Nasdaq peaked in March 2000 and declined steadily for the next two-and-a-half years. The credit crash of 2008 began in the summer of 2007. By the summer of 2008, many thought they had cut risk, although they really had not. Most of the losses occurred in the second half of 2008, which was a full year after the bubble had clearly popped.

One of the major benefits of a directional strategy is that our leverage can be kept very low. Most other strategies are far more dependent upon leverage, which means that they run far greater correlation risk and have a far greater reliance upon their prime broker, allowing them to maintain their leverage. In order to truly understand your risk, you have to volatility-adjust and correlation-adjust your positions. Too many managers neglected to do this in 2008, which cost them dearly even though they thought they had cut risk. Reducing gross equity exposure from two times to one time is not reducing risk if volatility has jumped from 20 percent to 80 percent and correlations have become uncertain. Overall risk could have doubled or, depending on the correlations, even shot up tenfold, at which point it is probably too late to adjust.

Tell me about your worst trade, not your worst miss. What lessons did you learn?

My overriding ambition is to never have a career-ending trade, so the opportunity cost ones tend to be the worst. I have a long list of trades that perhaps I should have done which I did not, and I try to learn from that. With a hit ratio of 50 percent, I am full of trades that lost money, and they, too, are learning experiences.

My worst trading period was in 2006 when I severely misread the intentions of the Fed—I thought they would continue their hiking cycle given how little effect it was having. But instead of trying to combat the bubble they decided to accommodate it, which meant that it extended further than I anticipated. In addition to losing money being bearish bonds, I was long too much volatility, and being long volatility at that time was a terrible trade. Volatility collapsed during the rally in risky assets and being long volatility was a countertrend trade. Countertrend trading is very dangerous, and this trade reminded me that you have to wait until the trend is exhausted to get involved. (See Figure 5.7.)

What part of the cycle are we in now?

I always try to be open-minded about where we are in a cycle. As we stand right now, the financial markets crisis is over. The deleveraging problem is over because governments have successfully backstopped the banks. Of course, whether the government should have done this or not is a different question, and it is not my job to answer that. With the deleveraging crisis off the table, the most likely scenario is an economic malaise similar to Japan in the 1990s, although a potential

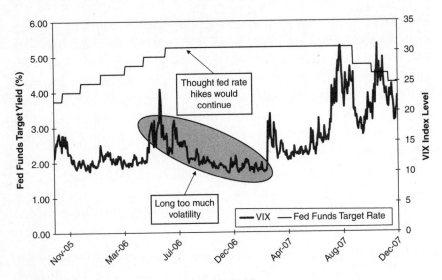

Figure 5.7 VIX and Fed Funds, 2005–2007
SOURCE: Bloomberg.

alternative to such a hypothesis is increased policy activism. Because a Japanese-style economic malaise is not acceptable to most, there is the potential of a 1970s outcome resulting from overstimulation of the economy. Politicians will choose inflation over stagnation any day but stagflation is something they might well regret. Although I am reluctant to make longer-term predictions, I think the U.S. is more likely to eventually end up with an inflationary outcome, whereas Europe will remain deflationary.

The combination of these scenarios creates a very interesting macro environment whereby two major economic blocks are diverging. The synchronization of global economies is really what drove the reduction in volatility across global markets over the past decade. Increased synchronization is quite easy in a low inflationary or declining inflationary environment. But if you move to an environment with credit and balance sheet problems, like the one we are in now, you can have much greater policy divergence. Every major central bank in the world over the last 10 years has been inflation targeting, and this may well cease to be the driver going forward. The ECB may target inflation, whereas the Fed may target growth, for example. Congress is already trying to pass legislation to end the Fed's independence. Of course, the Fed is not really independent anyway, but this kind of policy divergence will drive real economic divergence, which, in turn, will drive volatility and broader change. Macro is much more interesting than most other investing strategies in this type of environment.

What is it that makes macro more interesting in diverging and volatile markets?

Global macro is agnostic to market direction; you just want things to happen. Many other investing strategies, however, are essentially bull market strategies, performing better when markets go up and volatility is low and declining. A lot of money has gone into bull market strategies, particularly in the last five or so years, because we have been in a prolonged bull market cycle for the past 20 years. So it is no surprise that many people invest with a bull market style because such a style has been very profitable for a long time. But it is important to remember that many strategies that were relatively successful in the 1960s went bust in the 1970s, with macro persisting successfully through this time. Many people managed money very successfully in the late 1960s, the go-go years. But how many proved profitable through both the 1960s and the 1970s? Most notably, Warren Buffett and George Soros. Although their styles are very different, both are able to take advantage of volatility and both have approaches conducive to that kind of market. Buffett says, "I love Mr. Market because he gives me the opportunity to buy assets when they get too cheap." And Soros says, "Reflexivity means prices go up and they go down. The world changes and I'll adapt by reinventing myself over and over again depending on the environment."

If you went to play golf for the next 10 years and had to put all your money in one trade, what would it be?

That would be a terrible punishment but I would probably buy inflation-linked debt. I do not believe in a free lunch in that you can earn excess returns risklessly. Therefore, I will take the risk-free rate unless I am allowed to manage it actively myself. There is nothing that I can predict over the next 10 years.

I take it you do not believe that diversification is the only free lunch in finance?

No, of course not. Diversification is mainly a method for reducing volatility and the confusion comes from the fact that finance professors teach that volatility and risk mean the same thing. Diversification is not an effective method of reducing drawdowns. Moreover, diversification as a strategy can make you complacent, leading you to believe that you have mitigated certain risks that you really have not. You have to ask yourself what you can really diversify, and where. Some risks cannot be diversified away, so unfortunately people tend to ignore them rather than highlight them. For example, it is very difficult to diversify liquidity risk in any way apart from being in liquid products only. But that is not diversification—that just means you are only invested in liquid assets.

It is only okay to invest in illiquid instruments if you do not care about drawdowns. A Warren Buffett-style of buying assets when they are cheap and holding them forever is fine if you are unlevered and do not care about drawdowns. It is a good way to think about long-term investing but you cannot implement it if you risk redemptions. That is not my business. It is utterly inappropriate for a hedge fund offering regular liquidity to its investors to move too far out the liquidity spectrum.

If asked, could you run a large unlevered pool of capital, such as a pension or large endowment with no redemptions?

Could I do it? Absolutely. But it would be critical to define several issues upfront. Who is my boss? What am I being paid to do? The pensioners have not signed over all of their money to me so that I can implement whatever strategy I want. That is not the deal. You must have a clearly defined mandate with buy-in from all of the constituents. Do the pensioners care about drawdowns or not? Do they care about benchmarking the performance or not? Questions such as these would help to define the parameters of my mandate.

In my hedge fund, I care a lot about drawdowns, but I do not care much about benchmarks. In contrast to someone who manages versus a benchmark, I would much rather have a small positive return when my peer group is up more than me than be down small when my peer group is down a lot. I don't want to have any down years ever. I am in the absolute return business, which over long periods is how everyone should manage money.

Generating a true absolute return with no benchmark in a pension fund would have to mean that a manager cannot be fired for under-performing a given benchmark over the short- and medium-term. But I realize this is a tough call for a board of trustees, which is why I do not presume to tell pension fund managers how they should run money. Pensions have a very different mandate than I do.

Let's say you run a charitable foundation for an individual who aspires to change the world. The individual wants long-term capital preservation, with returns of about 5 percent a year over inflation to cover annual donations. How would you do that?

I would have a very similar model to Soros Fund Management. Soros, to me, is a great endowment fund that is mostly externally managed through a large number of portfolio managers picking up risk premia. They will buy farms in South America, engage in private equity, do emerging market equities, etc. Because it is truly a go anywhere, do anything type of mandate, the portfolio can outperform during bull markets. But there is someone at the top who can make a big macro call when necessary. From time to time, George will say, "Hmm, this is not going well," exit the bad stuff and put on a macro overlay to hedge the rest of the fund. Soros was nicely profitable in 2008, after having been up a lot in 2007. That is genius. The fact that Soros managed to make a lot of money through the bubble and then still made a bit in the crash is brilliant. It is a great way to manage money in the long term. Big drawdowns kill your compound returns, so you have to avoid them.

I want to avoid big drawdowns at all costs. Making the big macro calls when it counts is key, and few can actually do it. It is possible for Soros because the fund is his money. There is no career risk or board to report to. If George is wrong and he winds up being flat while everyone else is up 20 or 30 percent, he will be disappointed, but he cannot be fired, and he did not lose capital. George Soros is successful, and is getting richer still, because he manages money to minimize drawdowns and to maximize compounding over the long term. Compounding is the most powerful force in finance, whereas negative compounding is murderous. A down–50 percent year can take decades to recover from, whereas a series of small up years will compound to great returns over time.

What is the right formula for a fund like CalPERS, then? Should they have different groups capturing risk premia and then tactically overlay?

That is how I would do it, and I think this is a common model. The problem is that you have to believe in manager skill and discretion in order to make the bigger macro call. It is not clear to me that everyone should have that mandate. If you do not believe you have skill, defined as the ability to time markets, it would probably be better over time to use a risk premium type approach.

If risk premia are too high, buy things that have risk premia embedded in them. This is a good way to make money. A major challenge for pension funds is overcoming the myth that equities always outperform. Finance myths such as this and others have greatly compromised pension performance.

What are some other myths?

The idea that price does not matter is clearly a myth, and this is what drives people to buy equities regardless of the price level. I do not believe this idea. If you bought equities 10 years ago, you would be flat today. So that would not have been a good idea. Buy and hold was not a sensible strategy for the last decade. The problem with buy and hold is that you may have to wait a long time for your opportunity. A long only, "see what happens" type of strategy is probably best addressed by buying an index. You can run this strategy with a lean, low-cost staff. You basically resign yourself to the fact that you do not have market timing skill and opt instead for cheap beta through an index.

A real money manager thinks about the world through the Capital Asset Pricing Model, which is a diversified efficient frontier model of managing money. In this model, you want noncorrelated assets with decent returns, and I would say there are three types of return streams. The first is beta. Everyone knows what beta is—it is S&P500 or something equivalent. Then there is what I will call "beta-plus," or "hard-to-access beta." It is hard-to-access private equity, distressed real estate, mines in Ghana, and other types of illiquid assets. The last type of return stream is alpha, which includes macro.

A lot of people think alpha or macro means tactically trading beta, but that is not necessarily the case. That definition is enormously limited and in bull markets would mean macro managers correlate to everyone else. The macro stream to which I refer is comprised of things that are different than beta or beta-plus. For example, discerning which country will hike rates first has no relation to beta, and it is not even tactically trading beta. Rather, it has to do with global economics and central bank reaction functions. It has nothing to do with beta.

People began writing books about beta-plus, which became the holy grail of how to invest, the fashionable thing that you absolutely had to do if you were a long-term real money investor. If you have assets that are hard to access and difficult to understand, these assets will, by definition, be cheap. When this anomaly is widely recognized, money piles in, allowing the early entrants to make a fortune. Eventually, however, the assets are no longer cheap, yet the early movers are showing impressive excess returns. If they experience excess returns for a period of years, they may start to believe that they are generating alpha and that the excess returns will carry on forever. But the excess return only exists because the asset was hard to access, making it cheap. Once product providers catch on to the demand and enough capital flows into hard-to-access assets, these assets eventually become expensive. David Swenson of the Yale Endowment wrote a great book about how there are excess returns to be made from investing in illiquid assets, which was absolutely true when he started, but was no longer the case by the summer of 2007—at which point the opposite had become true. A bubble had been created during a bull market in illiquid assets, and people started to think that they had to be invested in these types of assets. All the smart money is invested this way, all the sexy money is in this, all the rich people are in this, and everyone just follows along. And then there is a crash.

Real money became dominated by beta-plus, but to excel in the long term, you need an alpha component. Deciding when to be involved in the beta-plus assets is a macro call, a decision about where you are in the cycle; where to be and how to be. Many people think that investing is all about earning risk premia. Although this approach is not entirely wrong, it is severely limited. There is so much more to investing than that, and the people who have done really well over long periods have recognized that there is more to it than just beta-plus.

You have to be smart enough to make the macro call to get out of the beta-plus assets once you recognize danger in the macro environment, and great money managers have this ability. The trick is making lots of money in bull markets without becoming a true believer. None of the survivors become true believers. Truth exists up to a certain price and you become classified as a true believer once price loses its importance in your thought process. You have to be conscious of price.

What major changes would you implement for pension fund investing?

I would strongly push to move away from benchmarking. To give you an example, the UK gilt curve is sharply inverted because pension funds are forced to buy long-term fixed income assets according to the regulatory framework. They know it is not economically sensible, but because of regulation and accounting, they are forced to do things they know are not in the best interest of their pensioners. As a fund manager, this must be a tough spot in which to find yourself. No one thinks buying 40-year gilts is a good idea, but that is how the accounting works. There is a lot of pressure to avoid volatility in the reported value of your pension pool. In some ways, pension funds face more mark-to-market pressure than I do.

If you worked for a pension fund that allocates to hedge funds, what would you look for in hedge funds?

The most important thing to me would be that a manager is generating true alpha, not simply beta or beta-plus, both of which I could get more cheaply on my own. Hedge fund is a broad term that comprises great funds and terrible funds, and looking at a manager's track record alone makes it difficult to differentiate between the two. This is why manager selection is challenging. A fund running a consistently large net equity long will obviously have a high correlation to beta, so justifying a 2-and-20 fee structure is difficult. On average, hedge funds have somewhat moved away from generating alpha, but this problem has been exacerbated by benchmarking. It is still possible to find managers who generate alpha, but alpha will underperform in a raging bull market, where people with big net long positions are the big performers. Selecting managers based purely on higher returns, without trying to gauge whether those returns are beta or not moves the entire industry closer to beta generation by default. Hedge funds did so poorly in 2008 precisely because they had more beta than anyone thought. They had more beta than they had 10 years ago. But for the 5 years up until 2008, beta was the easy money, far easier than alpha.

What else did you learn in 2008?

2008 was mostly a validation of my paranoia, and it was in some ways reassuring to see risk premia return to the market. When you run money conservatively, always thinking that such a severe market environment is possible, you tend to feel a bit vindicated when it occurs. 2008 was a reminder that it really matters to care about liquidity and correlation, that it matters to worry about a large range of risk indicators rather than just one, that counterparty risk is important, that your balance sheet is important. Most of these lessons are as old as the hills, which is why I really cannot understand all this talk about black swans. When the same thing happens over and over again, how can you be surprised?

"Black swan" may have become the most confusing phrase in markets. Nassim Taleb's recent use of the term is commonly understood to denote an unlikely and unforeseeable event, but this is not the main story of 2008. I saw a crisis as highly likely given people's beliefs and behaviors. Many people seem to use the "black swan" idea to reassure themselves when some bad things happened that they did not expect. They use it to claim that it was not their fault, which I do not think was Taleb's meaning. Too often, people use it to avoid taking responsibility for their actions by claiming the events—and their losses—in 2008 were unforeseeable, whereas in fact their hypothesis of how markets worked was just disproved. The other hypotheses always existed. The metaphor of the black swan is of course an old one and was used by Karl Popper in the 1930s to illustrate the fallacy of induction. It is an example of something that can falsify a hypothesis. If you have a hypothesis that all swans are white, a single black swan falsifies that hypothesis. In this usage, the existence of a black swan is of course neither unforeseeable nor even a low probability event, since hypotheses are falsified all the time. It is as though the recent "black swan" is not taken as a falsification but instead as confirmation that swans are generally white and so we should carry on as before, which is a perverse interpretation of either Popper or Taleb.

Did 2008 invalidate the endowment model?

I do not think 2008 invalidates what I call the beta-plus approach, which will always have an important place in investing. If I were building an endowment portfolio I would have beta, and I would have beta-plus if it were cheap. All of these assets will equal nominal GDP in the long term, and this is what real money is trying to capture. If you believe in growth and capitalism, you should own some assets. The beauty of alpha is that you can have it as an overlay. If you believe in skill, you can make more than nominal GDP. Without skill, nominal GDP is a perfectly good benchmark in the long term.

What 2008 did invalidate, however, are the beliefs that markets are efficient, capitalism is naturally stable, and policymakers can control the economy. Policy makers may have good intentions, but they do not have as much power as many assumed. I learned this lesson a long time ago during my first week in the business, when the head of the trading floor asked me if I thought sterling would drop out of the ERM [the European Exchange Rate Mechanism] or not. I felt I gave him a coherent story about how the British pound was going to stay in the ERM because it was a priority for the Conservative government to keep it in since the implications of falling out would be disastrous for them. About three hours later, when the UK dropped out of the ERM, I learned that policy makers do not have that kind of control.

For this reason, it is a false sense of complacency to believe that central bankers can control inflation. Of course they cannot control inflation—they can influence it, but they cannot control it. Again, people tend to go from thinking that central bankers are omniscient to thinking that they are impotent. And neither is true. Central bankers have influence but not control. Many people were surprised to learn in 2008 that the world is not as safe as they had thought. They do not have someone looking after them to ensure that everything will be okay.

How does increased policy activity affect your portfolio?

Policy activity is one of our bread-and-butter sources of returns. Most of the policy activity in 2008 was very predictable and very reasonable. For example, we know that the Fed is an activist, pro-growth central bank. Fed Governor Mishkin gave a speech in January 2008 in which he laid out the whole game plan (see box). He said they would be decisive, early, would proactively cut off risks, and sort it all out later. And what happened? The Fed cut interest rates a lot. They got aggressive early and they are now trying to clean it all up. They told us they would act this way.

Fed Governor Mishkin Speech

The monetary policy that is appropriate during an episode of financial market disruption is likely to be quite different than in times of normal market functioning. When financial markets experience a significant disruption, a systematic approach to risk management requires policymakers to be preemptive in responding to the macroeconomic implications of incoming financial market information, and decisive actions may be required to reduce the likelihood of an adverse feedback loop. The central bank also needs to exhibit flexibility—that is, less inertia than would otherwise be typical—not only in moving decisively to reduce downside risks arising from a financial market disruption, but also in being prepared to take back some of that insurance in response to a recovery in financial markets or an upward shift in inflation risks.

Finally, while I have argued that monetary policy needs to be decisive and timely in responding to a financial market disruption, a lot of art as well as science is involved in determining the severity and duration of the disruption and the associated implications for the macroeconomy (Mishkin, 2007c). Indeed, assessing the macroeconomic risks to output and inflation in such circumstances remains among the most difficult challenges

(continued)

faced by monetary policymakers. Furthermore, a central bank may well be able to employ non-monetary tools—such as liquidity provision—to help alleviate the adverse impact from financial disruptions. All of these considerations must be taken into account in determining the most appropriate course of monetary policy.

SOURCE: Federal Reserve System, www.federalreserve.gov, Jan 11, 2008.

On the flipside, with respect to the plumbing of monetary policy, the ECB is a brand new central bank, with a brand-spanking-new way of managing money markets. Their approach is much more flexible and effective because they have a better understanding of liquidity. They were able to inject liquidity into markets very quickly. The Fed, on the other hand, has an antiquated system it does not even understand itself. So it was very clear that the Fed would not be able to add liquidity, whereas the ECB would be able to. This meant that although the Fed was more aggressive in its policy rate actions, it was far less effective than the ECB in actually getting liquidity into the market. Meanwhile, we also knew that the Bank of England would be volatile because it is more academic in nature, and its academic approach kept being proved wrong. It had a view it was convinced was optimal, yet it proved so catastrophic that it was repeatedly forced into dramatic policy shifts. The Bank of England has been the most dramatic flip-flopper in terms of how to approach the process, whereas the Fed and ECB have been more consistent, each with different results and different aims. This mismatch creates opportunity for an alpha-seeking macro fund.

Broadening the discussion to government policy makers, things such as TARP getting voted down and then voted for, or the banning of short selling, or allowing Lehman to go bust and then bailing out AIG a few days later—these things seemed pretty random.

They were far from random—many were quite predictable. But this is not the same as saying they were easy. It was clear the week before it happened that Lehman would be let go. Our fund had battened down the hatches the week before, so we did not have a single deal open with Lehman. We cut leverage in preparation for the big impending storm because U.S. Treasury Secretary Paulson was very clear that he would not bail out Lehman. The mistake was that not many people believed him because they had learned the wrong lesson from Bear Stearns. In fact, most people still seem to misunderstand the difference between a firm seen to be valuable but illiquid and one that is insolvent. In the first case, the lender of last resort can fix it, whereas in the second case, you need the taxpayer. Where I got it wrong was by misunderstanding that policy makers would allow everything to descend into near anarchy. I thought it would be bad, but I did not fully appreciate the extent of the disorder.

It is not clear to me that the policy makers fully understood the implications of their actions. There are markets and then there is plumbing, and they did not understand the plumbing. But very few people understand the plumbing, because none of the sexy jobs on Wall Street involve doing the plumbing. I am very lucky to have had a few un-sexy jobs over my career, which taught me how a bank actually works, how funding actually works. Big bond traders rarely think about how to fund their position because someone else at the firm does that for them. They do not care about how the money moves around the world because it always just happens. They think it is magical and robust, while in actuality it is quite archaic and fragile.

Other aspects of the Lehman episode surprised me as well. The government knew that it lacked a legal infrastructure around the collapse of Lehman because Bernanke had given a speech about it in March 2008, when Bear Stearns was bailed out (see box on page 144). It was one of the reasons he cited to justify the bailout of Bear Stearns. The thing that disappointed me about policy makers was that in the six-month period between Bear and Lehman, no mechanism was set up to deal with the collapse of a broker-dealer. I thought they would do for Lehman what they did for AIG: conservatorship. I do not think they realized it until it happened, but if AIG went under, everyone would have gone under. You could not pretend there was any way of isolating AIG. They could misunderstand Lehman and think it was isolated.

Bernanke on Bear Stearns

The Primary Dealer Credit Facility was put in place in the wake of the near-failure of Bear Stearns, a large investment bank. On March 13, Bear Stearns advised the Federal Reserve and other government agencies that its liquidity position had significantly deteriorated and that it would have to file for Chapter 11 bankruptcy the next day unless alternative sources of funds became available. This news raised difficult questions of public policy. Normally, the market sorts out which companies survive and which fail, and that is as it should be. However, the issues raised here extended well beyond the fate of one company. Our financial system is extremely complex and interconnected, and Bear Stearns participated extensively in a range of critical markets. With financial conditions fragile, the sudden failure of Bear Stearns likely would have led to a chaotic unwinding of positions in those markets and could have severely shaken confidence. The company's failure could also have cast doubt on the financial positions of some of Bear Stearns' thousands of counterparties and perhaps of companies with similar businesses. Given the current exceptional pressures on the global economy and financial system, the damage caused by a default by Bear Stearns could have been severe and extremely difficult to contain. Moreover, the adverse effects would not have been confined to the financial system but would have been felt broadly in the real economy through its effects on asset values and credit availability. To prevent a disorderly failure of Bear Stearns and the unpredictable but likely severe consequences of such a failure for market functioning and the broader economy, the Federal Reserve, in close consultation with the Treasury Department, agreed to provide funding to Bear Stearns through JPMorgan Chase. Over the following weekend, JPMorgan Chase agreed to purchase Bear Stearns and assumed Bear's financial obligations.

SOURCE: Federal Reserve System, www.federalreserve.gov, April 2, 2008.

I am really looking forward to reading the book that tells what really happened the week of the Lehman collapse, because there are stories that Hank Paulson called up all his friends at the broker-dealers and asked, "If Lehman goes under are you okay?" And they said, "Yeah, we're fine." They were fine because they had CDS—they were hedged. But, of course he called the wrong people, as the main issue was really about *rehypothecation*, something few understand (see box). The counterparties were absolutely fine. It was all the customers of Lehman that got killed, and they were the ones that were fundamentally needed to provide market liquidity.

Hypothecation

Hypothecation is the pledging of securities or other assets as collateral to secure a loan, such as a debit balance or a margin account. For example, hedge funds hypothecate securities to their prime brokers in exchange for margin or leverage. *Rehypothecation* is the pledging of securities in customer margin accounts as collateral for a brokerage's bank loan. Rehypothecation occurs when a bank takes securities that have been pledged to them as collateral and uses them as collateral to obtain further loans for the bank. For example, broker dealers rehypothecate customer securities to commercial banks in exchange for loans or credit lines.

Would you like to be a policy maker some day?

I could imagine being an advisor. Last year I was happy to talk to anyone who would listen about how things should be fixed and what actions should be taken. What disappointed me was that there was no effective mechanism for senior policy makers to learn from market participants, the latter of whom understood the financial market plumbing. Many important policy decisions in 2008 were critically dependent upon understanding the practical functioning of markets. Unfortunately, because most senior bankers do not understand this well, they likely provided poor information when asked by policy makers.

I do not think that I could become a central banker. I am temperamentally suited to say what I think, and it is very difficult for policy makers to say what they think. Central bankers have a tough job, especially with modern media forcing them to be extremely careful about every single word they use. That would not work for me.

I run a macro fund, and I reserve the right to be wrong. My hit ratio is only 50 percent. I get things wrong, change my mind, and move on. Central bankers are not allowed to do that—it is very hard for a central banker to say, "That rate cut last year, that was a mistake. I shouldn't have done that." When people hear that, central bankers lose credibility. People want to believe in some wise old person that gets things right all the time.

Do you think Bernanke has gotten things right?

Bernanke's success or error will be decided after the next crash as we find out if it is possible to keep re-inflating bubble after bubble. I am personally pretty skeptical of that idea. I thought the Fed was making a mistake when they spiked the punchbowl rather than taking it away in 2006, at which time the risk party was in full swing. During the crisis of 2008, Bernanke got some things right and other things wrong. He is a smart person with integrity, and I have sympathy for him because of the numerous almost impossible situations he was put in—he had a U.S. Treasury that ceased to function. Because there was a vacuum within Treasury, the Fed was forced to do many jobs it should not have been asked to do. The Fed should not have been saving Bear Stearns, but if they did not, who would have?

You are probably the first person with whom I have spoken in the last year that has not mentioned Asia. Why is that?

There is no particularly strong reason. At the moment, I find the things going on around G10 policy to be the most interesting. Asia is mainly a long-term bull story and because I offer investors monthly liquidity in my fund, I am not looking for this kind of trade. I do have Asia trades on, however. I am bullish Asian currencies, but they are trades, not investments. China/Asia is an interesting story, but my fund is a liquid product alpha vehicle. Our investors invest in us for specific reasons, and we do not want to have style drift, whereby we turn into long-term visionaries about Asia. In the long term, maybe it is true that China takes over the world—but that is a beta-plus story.

Chapter 6

The Bond Trader

P rior to the budget surpluses and the equity bull market of the late 1990s, the trading desks of the big bond houses were the epicenters of financial markets. In the wake of 2008, with the ensuing fiscal deficits and exploding government debt issuance, fixed income markets have once again taken center stage.

"The Bond Trader" generated strong positive performance for his investors through 2008 and 2009. For over two decades, he has stuck to his guns, specializing in fixed income and never posting a single losing year. He is very simply best of breed, although his process is not easy to pin down because of its extreme flexibility and adaptability to different conditions. He implements different processes and risk management approaches depending on the prevailing market environment, and most efforts to understand how he does what he does result in a simple: "It depends." As Keynes once said: "When the facts change, I change my mind. What do you do, sir?"

The Bond Trader exemplifies macro trading at its finest: flexible, extremely liquid, hyperfocused on the downside risks, and adaptive to changing facts and market conditions. Where many hedge fund investors in recent years have sought to understand strategies based on narrowly defined criteria, The Bond Trader proves that sometimes, talent is unquantifiable.

As we sat down for breakfast, he placed his two BlackBerries on the table, remaining fully wired into markets almost intravenously. Although the current complexity and uncertainty of global macro markets have led some to stake claims on very specific, extreme outcomes, the Bond Trader says that such thinking does not concern him. When pressed on how he will address the road ahead, well, "It depends."

What did you learn in 2008?

Things can move much quicker than we expect. The speed of events was surprising.

Why did so many investors lose money in 2008?

First, their structure or style often didn't allow them to act quickly enough to limit the damage. Second, there has been a persistent "buy the dips" mentality in the market, which proved a disaster in 2008. Lastly, many investors owned a lot of illiquid positions which were expensive to get out of in 2008.

2008 was a year of illiquidity, volatility, and falling asset prices, whereas 2009 has mostly been a year of recovery. Very few investors made money in both years. How have you been able to make money in both of these very different market environments?

Because we did not have the three issues I just mentioned, we were able to start 2009 without any legacy problems or positions, and this gave us a clean slate to operate in a market with less competitors. You have an advantage if you are not plagued with the same issues as your competitors.

How did you foresee the land mines of 2008 and react in time?

It comes down to market experience, having traded through past crises over the last 20 years. This time, we began seeing signs and issues popping up in 2007, and we really started to get nervous about the economic situation globally. We were especially nervous about some financial instruments getting out of control, such as LIBOR basis blowing out and ABX (asset-backed securities index) and other credit spreads widening dramatically. We concluded that it was inappropriate to have a large gross derivative book which was something we had been thinking about for some time, at least a year in advance. So we made the decision to drastically reduce our leverage and then Bear Stearns happened, which caused a lot of volatility. After Bear was sold in a fire sale, there was a lot of excess trading due to the unwinding of positions, and we used that period of high liquidity to get out of our derivatives quicker than we had originally planned. It was a great opportunity for us to unwind things at minimal costs.

Although we always have leverage, it is mostly with government bonds so there was no real reason to get out of those highly liquid positions. It was mainly the gross derivative book we took down out of fear of counterparty risk and more banks going down. Regardless, we still took our government bond leverage down slightly after Bear Stearns and we reduced it further in the weeks after Lehmans went under. We deemed it inappropriate to have such leverage, relatively speaking, given what was going on in the financial system at the time. We reduced our balance sheet even further for the last quarter of 2008 just to be safe. If the problems worsened, even cash markets could, in theory, suffer mark-to-market problems. So the right thing to do was drastically reduce the gross leverage and have all remaining positions primarily in liquid G3 bonds. We followed this course over a period of nine months so that we would minimize the cost of bid–offer spreads. Having said that, it still cost a lot of money but it cost less than it could have because we did it over a period of time rather than in the space of a day. Half of it was done in the first few weeks after Bear and the rest was done over the course of nine months.

When you see land mines ahead, is reducing the size of your portfolio your primary risk management tactic?

It is one of them, but it may be that the environment at the time is inappropriate for this kind of action. It depends on what is going on in the markets. It may be that you want to add to your portfolio through hedges. In 2008, we deemed reducing the portfolio as the appropriate course of action as we were concerned about the viability of the banks and overall financial system.

You mentioned being invested in illiquids as one of the things that caused losses in 2008. Does a large asset base push an investor towards illiquids?

No, I don't think so. What pushes people into less liquid trades is their belief that they can make more money and that they will be less volatile over time giving them a smoother P&L (profit and loss) profile either because bid–offer spreads are wide or due to a low number of transactions.

We saw illiquidity show up in strange places during 2008. The gates and side pockets that hedge funds imposed at the end of 2008 definitely surprised me. I don't understand the gates and side pockets—the use of them is not right. Managers should know the liquidity of the instruments they are trading and understand that liquidity changes over time. Changing liquidity is not an excuse for putting up a gate. If you raised money from investors, charging them hedge fund fees and offering certain liquidity terms, then you should stick to what you sold.

How did you manage that issue in 2008?

The liquidity of our portfolio matches the liquidity we offer our investors.

Did you ever run into a point at the end of 2008 where redemptions were getting worrisome?

No. You should run your fund so that you are never put in such a position. That is bad management of the fund. You should work out how much unencumbered cash you need under worst case scenarios and be in a situation to manage liquidity for these scenarios, which can and do occur.

Has it become more difficult to manage the liquidity in your portfolio as banks have disappeared from the Street?

The markets are less liquid now but the volatility is higher, so the two roughly cancel each other out. You can make the same returns now with a fraction of the position sizes that you needed before 2008. You just have to regularly adjust for your asset size and the liquidity of the instruments you trade. It's a constant process.

Are you concerned about potential land mines right now?

We are always on the lookout for land mines, but given that we are running more liquid positions than we used to, and since we have sorted out most of the counterparty issues, I am less concerned.

Where do you get your trading ideas?

We generate most ideas internally through our own fundamental analysis. We develop our own analysis from reading the usual stuff like government reports, general press, and economic statistics, as well as from interpreting data from a host of primary sources. The key is solving the puzzle, forming your own economic view of the world and comparing that view with what is already priced into markets. There are no shortcuts. You have to do the work yourself.

It all comes down to honestly interpreting the data. If you have been watching data, markets, and prices for long enough, you can interpret data. Some data points are better than others as leading indicators, and you need to know which to use when, depending on what point of the economic cycle you are in. You cannot use the same economic data as your leading indicator, year in and year out. It depends on what is going on in the world at the time. Things change, and you have to change with them. After interpreting the data, it helps to talk to people in the markets and in business to know how they are thinking about the data and the environment. You need to understand what they are looking at so that you understand what they think is going on.

How do you filter all this information from business people, policy makers, banks, market participants, and others?

There is no specific way to filter information. You cannot just lay it all out on the table and use it to form some judgment. Your personal read on what is driving a particular economic cycle is the most important. You focus on these drivers and disregard the rest.

How do you find the driver of the next economic cycle?

We form our own view of what is causing the current situation and what will cause it to change. We look at the indicators or events that might cause a shift in the drivers. These days, this is more difficult than before to some extent because the current environment is more dependent on government action, so government policies have a larger effect on the future path.

In your fixed income trading, do you focus more on central banks or markets?

I focus on both of them—they are both important, but many other things are important in fixed income markets as well. As much as possible, you should focus on what is already priced into the market, weighing this against your own view of what you think will happen, which is based partly on economics.

Do you view central banks as a source of alpha given that they are noneconomic actors?

I have never thought about central banks as a source of alpha. I look at them as one group amongst many important actors in markets, and we have to think about how they will behave.

What is your view on the talent of central bankers?

Central bankers are very smart people and it is a mistake to belittle them in any way whatsoever. However, their reaction functions are different than ours.

Who are the most influential players in the markets today? Government? Politicians? Central banks? Hedge funds? Banks?

I am not sure there is one. The market goes through periods where one is more influential than the other. You have to be aware of shifts in market drivers at certain times, but I do not think you can really say one is more influential than another. It changes.

How do you stay ahead of the market? Is it insecurity? Paranoia? Working twice as hard as everyone else?

I don't think it is any of these things. I stay ahead of the market simply by correctly interpreting the next driver of the economic cycle.

Do you spend more time thinking about how you will be right or how you might be wrong?

Both, but I would say more right because we are doing this to make money.

When considering a new trade, how do you decide whether or not to put it on? How do you determine sizing? What is your time horizon?

I look at how a given trade fits into my portfolio based on the other trades that I have on. In terms of sizing, most of the time I look at the daily volume and volatility of the instrument, and I decide how much I am willing to lose on the bet. Again, it depends on what is happening in the markets, what the volatilities are, what the overall environment is like. We focus on the volatility of the instruments we trade, trying to work out how much we think a given position can move in a day, week, or other period. In terms of the time horizon, again, that all depends on the structure and the transaction. So some of them are short-dated and some of them go out a few years.

Is market positioning an important factor?

It is very difficult to know how others are positioned. Because we are a more fundamentally based fund, we do not spend much time worrying about positioning, although it is one of the inputs that we look at. We do ask the investment banks about the common themes and trades. But positioning is just not a major part of our thought process.

Would it worry you if one of your core positions shows up as the top positions at all the banks?

It might worry me, but it might also be confirmation that it is a good trade, that we are on the right path. It would depend on how we structured the trade and also on the fundamental reason as to why everyone has it on.

How do you measure the liquidity of the instruments you trade?

We measure the liquidity of our positions based on how much we think it will cost to get out during a certain period of time. Because this changes over time, even as you are getting out, it is a constantly evolving process. We spend a lot of time thinking about liquidity.

Do you use options?

We do use options, but it all depends on the prevailing volatility. Our process for putting on options trades is the same as for other instruments: there is a price component and a view component, and we can be either long or short options depending on the opportunity set.

How do you decide to take profits?

There is no fixed formula for taking profits; it comes down to the pricing in the market. Likewise, there is also no fixed formula for scaling out on the way down. It all comes down to how far I think the market can go at a particular point in time.

Do you scale into and out of positions? Or is it full on, full off?

This changes depending on the strength of the conviction. Sometimes it is full on, full off, and sometimes it is much more scaling because my strength of conviction is slightly different, or I am not convinced that the market is at the bottom or top. Here, again, there is no fixed formula.

How do you manage risk at the firm level? Do you roll up all the traders' positions and then overlay the whole book? Or do you let each manage risk independently?

We do both, although the degree of each depends on the situation. There is no hard rule that one works or the other one doesn't, so you should not discount either of these approaches.

Do you diversify across traders, styles, time horizons, instruments, or asset classes?

All of these.

In hiring traders, is being a moneymaker the most important attribute?

Well, traders have to be moneymakers—especially so after they are hired. After that I would look at their trading style, the instruments they have traded, and how that fits into what we already have. There are many issues involved with hiring traders, and different characteristics are required for different kinds of trading. A macro trader does not have the same characteristics as a relative value trader, a long/short equity trader, or a statistical arbitrage trader. You need to look at the characteristics that are appropriate for a given strategy.

In addition to track record, how do you determine how much capital to allocate to your traders?

It depends on the market they are trading—what the level of the market is and if there is an opportunity in that market. It depends how they have been doing over the past few years and also how long they have been with us.

For younger traders—say, those hired after 2003—did you keep a tighter leash on them before 2008, knowing that they had never been through a crisis?

Yes, and I closed them all down straightaway after Lehman went bust. Within a week.

Are there any personality characteristics that predetermine whether a trader is going to be successful?

There are not really any particular characteristics. You need to hire people who you think will fit in with the people already around you. For example, argumentative natures can be fine, but you have to think about how one person will get on with the rest.

Do you like to hear counterfeedback to your views?

Yes, I do.

If everyone tells you that you are wrong, does it embolden you or does it make you think twice?

Again, it is case by case. It depends on my level of conviction and others' levels of conviction, and what reasons they provide for their arguments. We have a lot of that and I encourage it.

Have you ever interviewed someone and thought: "This person is going to be a star"?

I have thought that with certain people, but not all have become stars. On the contrary, I have never seen someone who I thought would become a star turn out to be a failure. I did see one or two that I had pegged as potential superstars actually become superstars, but I would not use that as proof that I can pick them.

Is there a common characteristic for the traders that you have seen flop?

Lack of risk control is the most common reason for failure.

What is the worst trade of your career?

I have never had one big blow-up trade, but a variety of trades have worked out poorly, specifically certain FX (foreign exchange) bets. In the summer of 2008, I was caught off-guard by the sell-off in interest rate markets, when the ECB and BoE were voicing fears about inflation while the global economy was rolling over a cliff. When the President of the ECB, Jean-Claude Trichet, warned of the potential for inflation to explode, I almost fell off my chair as I realized how much money I lost. It was very unpleasant. (See Figure 6.1.)

What about early in your career, was there ever a trade that taught you a lesson that made you say, "I'll never do that again!"?

The dramatic sell-off in the bond market at the beginning of 1994 taught me a lesson. Fortunately, that lesson was useful for the rest of

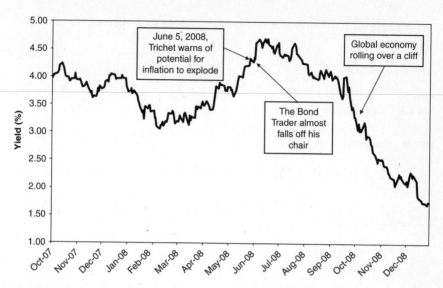

Figure 6.1   Generic Two-Year Euro Interest Rates, 2008–2009
SOURCE: Bloomberg.

the year. The velocity and ferocity of the sell-off was an indication that things could get much worse than anyone thought at the time. Upon recognition of that fact, I flipped my long position into a short and ended up having a reasonable year. It was not as good as 1993, but not the disaster it was for most macro traders. The bond market rout of '94, like the crisis of 2008, is a good example that market prices can go to silly levels.

Is the ability to change your mind and go the other way a positive attribute that makes you unique?

Sometimes it is useful; other times it is a hindrance. Most traders do not change their views that often but it is always interesting to hear when they do and why.

It is similar with academics. There are a lot of them I admire and there are some great academics that I enjoy reading. What I find most interesting with academics and research people is when they shift their view. When they go from bearish to bullish, for example. And understanding why they are shifting their views is of interest.

Do you try to have strong views about markets or do you try to be open-minded?

Sometimes I have strong views on the markets, at which point I don't care what other people think and I am not so open-minded. Other times, I don't have any strong convictions and I am more open-minded.

Were you trading in 1987?

Yes. 1987 was an amazing time to be trading and I really enjoyed the experience.

Were you long bonds?

I was both short and long bonds that year. Being long would not have been very good at certain times during 1987. The whole year, yields went up and then crashed. I was not long bonds before the crash, but was able to get long just after, which worked. (See Figure 6.2.)

What about 1998 when both LTCM (Long-Term Capital Management) and Russia blew up?

That was also a very interesting time to be running a prop desk. We definitely saw accidents coming as the sizes transacting and liquidity

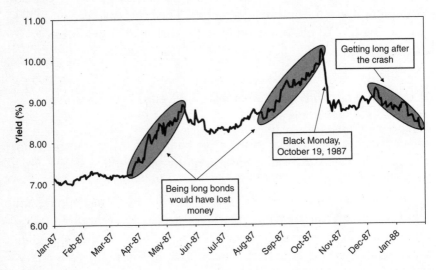

Figure 6.2   Ten-Year U.S. Treasury Bonds, 1987–1988
SOURCE: Bloomberg.

being offered across most markets was extremely high compared to prior years. I felt there was a possibility that liquidity would come off at some point. Early in the summer of 1998 I unwound most of our positions and dramatically cut those that either relied on liquidity or were common positions held by other big players.

How did you know they were common positions?

You don't know for sure that positions are common or crowded, but if you watch the market long enough, you can see something brewing from price action and liquidity levels. In this particular case, price action and market liquidity were the leading indicators, but again, these indicators are always changing. In 1998, we cut our risk before LTCM became an issue. The fact that other investment bank prop desks were being told to reduce their positions at the same time was also useful information.

Was trading through 1998 helpful for navigating 2008?

I found 1987 more useful. At one point in 1987, the bid–offer spreads on bonds blew out very wide, making things very difficult to navigate. We didn't have that in 1998. Nonetheless, 1998 was still useful as a crisis benchmark insofar as it taught us how quickly things can normalize.

What about the dot-com final rally and bust?

I struggled until December 2000, and then made all my profits for the year in the last month. I was flat in 1999, but that was after a big '98, so it was okay. I have never had a down year, and 1999 was the only flat year, so I consider myself fortunate. That doesn't mean it won't happen or that I don't go through down periods. I do.

What was your best trade of your career?

There hasn't been one best trade, but rather many good trades. I don't really remember individual trades. I am not preoccupied by individual trades, thinking any one was particularly good or bad. Each is just another trade, and I always move on to the next one.

Do you ever think about the big trades you missed?

Only for a short period of time. I definitely remember the ones that I missed earlier in 2009, although I don't remember the trades I missed a year ago. There is no point. Success is not about being right or getting the big trades. Rather, we measure success based on how well our fund does. What matters is our track record over time, regardless of what the competition does. If we do well over several years and another fund does better over one year, that is fine. I wish them luck and am happy for them. Medium-term, not short-term performance is most important to us because our own money is invested in the fund.

Is all of your money in your fund?

Not all, but enough to make a difference. Having all your own money in the fund could change your behavior for the worse.

What is the difference between running a hedge fund and running a prop desk?

They are completely different. Managing a fund is infinitely harder than managing a prop desk. On a prop desk you are only concerned about making money; volatility is irrelevant. As a prop trader, you don't have to worry about monthly return, capital usage, or anything else—you just have to stay within your risk limits.

With a fund, you have to worry about monthly returns, drawdowns, and the volatility of the portfolio, in addition to a host of other things. There are just more elements involved with running the firm, including cash management, counterparties, credit, investors, and employees. You have to look after the collateral, the unencumbered cash, and other things related to the business side, all of which are vitally important. Look at the many funds that got knocked out in 2008 due to business issues, as opposed to market issues. There is no excuse for that.

Was it difficult to make the adjustment?

I am not sure it was difficult; it just took time. As with anything, if you are competing with extremely talented people, you have to come up the curve as quickly as possible, but it cannot be done overnight.

How do you manage your time among markets, business issues, and family?

The market comes first. Everything else is second. There is no other way to do it. At least, it is very difficult any other way. That does not mean that you don't spend time on the other things, but that becomes a function of the markets. When the markets are quiet, you naturally have time to focus on other issues, such as the business side of the fund. In the fall of 2008, however, if you were doing your job, you were 100 percent focused on the markets. There was just too much going on.

How much has the market changed since you started trading?

The markets always change. They change every year. Just look at 2009 compared to 2008. You have to constantly be aware that markets are changing, in terms of participants, asset classes, instruments. I never want to get caught feeling that I have to behave as I always have. You have to evolve as a trader. If there is one constant, however, it is that I prefer to stick to simple, liquid instruments. That has not changed.

Some people listen to the market by watching the tape. They only care about price. Others don't care about daily price action. They just do what they think they should be doing. Each style has its advantages and disadvantages, and at different times one or the other might be optimal. Being aware of different trading styles and deciding when to use one or another is very important.

We try to be as flexible as possible, being open to all these different approaches without getting married to any one thing—absolutely nothing. We may have biases, but I think you are beginning to understand from this conversation that we don't have just one way of doing things. There are times when I listen to the market. Absolutely. Of course. And there are other times when it's a load of rubbish, when I don't agree with the market. It is case by case. And deciding on one case versus another depends on a variety of issues, such as the strength of your conviction, the data, the environment, and a number of other factors. You have to take everything into account.

Do you try to instill this flexibility into your traders, or do you let them be themselves?

I let them be themselves. Each has different characteristics. Some listen to the market; others don't. Each has strengths and weaknesses that are better suited to various points in a cycle, and some are much stronger overall than others. I try to listen to them all at all times and knowing them well enough as individuals helps to discern when I should follow one more than another.

When you see that one of your traders has "got it," do you lever up his trades?

No, it is not just a blind following. You have to know their trading history over the last so many years, how they have behaved at different times. You have to know the individual's strengths and weaknesses, as well as how they have evolved over time. Once you know roughly what is going on in their head, you have an anchor from which point you can weigh information. You take all of this into account, in the context of the prevailing cycle and price levels, all of which can lead to an "ah-ha moment" that helps you figure something out. But you cannot do this just by watching a trader's P&L. You have to know the individuals you are working with for many years and you have to have a methodology for extracting this kind of information. Regular communication with my traders is both formal and ad hoc.

If I put you on a desert island with a billion dollars to manage, what do you need to make money?

A Bloomberg terminal.

What other inputs do you use? Do you read The Economist? The Financial Times? Wall Street research?

I read all of them at different times. Sometimes I read more newspapers, other times I read *The Economist*. There is no one thing that I read every day or every week. Sometimes I may focus on specific research in a certain area based on an idea born out of reading or watching the markets. For example, in 2008 I focused on credit and did a lot of reading in this area, but right now I am less focused on credit given what is going on in the markets.

At what point in your career did you know you were a good trader?

I am not sure I can answer that question. There was never a moment when I made money or did something whereby I thought I had this game figured out.

What keeps you energized, focused on markets? You have done well; presumably you don't need anything material at this point.

I do not understand that question. I mean, it is not that I don't understand what you are asking. I just don't think about these things.

If someone wants to be you in 25 years, what is your advice to them?

It comes down to working hard. You have to believe in your ability, but you also have to adapt to the marketplace. It is a very difficult question to answer. I am not sure that someone wants to be in financial markets now, actually. Is finance the right field to go into now? I am not sure.

What about your next career? Would you like to be a central banker or prime minister?

I am not sure I will have a second career. I hope I don't, but if I do I would like to be a university lecturer.

If Harvard asked you to teach and run the endowment, could you do it?

Sure—I *could* do it. There is no reason why managing a hedge fund cannot be transported to running an endowment. But that does not mean that I want to do it. The skill set is the same. But I don't think about it because I cannot realistically see myself doing that.

You meet with many real money managers who are potential investors in your fund. What do they miss when allocating to a global macro hedge fund?

We tell our investors what we think is important to look at, which includes the risk management processes, the trading processes, cash management, and all the issues around the business side. Once they understand these elements, they should then look at the track record of the individuals at the fund, asking themselves if the managers can deliver what they say they can, based on their trading strategy and what instruments they use to express trades.

Anyone can see that the results of macro fund managers over the last whatever time period have been better than most other strategies and indices, although within macro itself, some managers have done better than others. Assuming that by macro you mean trading more liquid instruments, over time the strategy seems to have been a good place for real money managers to have had exposure.

Can investors make a decision based solely on a manager's track record?

No, absolutely not. A track record is very important, but you have to understand why the manager made the money they made. What was the market environment? What level of risk was being taken? What kind of risks? Many funds had solid track records until 2008, then suffered during the crisis. Again, it comes down to liquidity in the instruments someone is trading and the volatility. If a manager's volatility is too low, you may want to think about why it is so low, what type of instruments the manager is using. You always need context.

What should investors be looking for on the risk management side?

The risk management process should be appropriate for a given manager's style. It all depends on the style and the liquidity of the underlying instruments. If an investor is considering a macro firm that takes longer term bets and markets itself that way, then the risk management has to be appropriate to such a strategy. If it is a firm that focuses heavily on short-term trading, then again, the risk management process should reflect this style of high frequency trading.

What is the time horizon of the overall fund?

My time horizon changes with the market environment, but it always depends on pricing in the market. A few years ago, you could take a very long-term view because that was what the market was doing. Today, the market does not care about something six months from now—more market participants tend to be shortsighted. It does not mean that they are wrong—not at all. And this may change as market participants get more confident. If you had on a one-year bet before Lehmans went bust, it may have been completely wrong or it may have been right, depending on which way your bet was. The time horizon that the market uses to look at things changes dramatically over time, depending on the market participants and the prevailing environment. You have to decide for yourself: Do you want to trade against this prevailing environment? Why do you want to trade against it? You have to have a flexible approach to all of these things. My whole point is that there is no clear answer. We do not have a magic formula. That is just the way it is.

So are the following questions irrelevant to you: is the dollar's reserve currency status on the decline? Will China be the next superpower? Will the world run out of oil?

They are not irrelevant. They are very interesting questions, but they may or may not come into play at certain points. We may or may not run out of oil—I don't know. And what I think may be wrong anyway. There may well be periods when there is a shortage of oil for whatever reason. I can think of many reasons why that could become an issue, so I have to take that into account but I would not want to buy oil based on my view that we are going to run out of oil.

Are we headed towards inflation or deflation?

I don't think anybody knows the answer to that question. Everyone should be open-minded about this one, regardless of the strength of his opinions.

Are the markets a zero sum game?

No.

Are they efficient?

No.

If you took 10 years off and were forced to put all your money in one trade, what would it be?

Cash.

Dollars? Pounds? Euros? Swiss francs?

Probably euros but the question is difficult because it depends if my 10-year goal is to preserve my capital or maximize my wealth.

Let us assume it is to maximize your wealth.

In that case putting it in cash is a very bad bet because it is a bet that inflation will be contained. I would not want to make that bet because I do not know if there will be inflation or not in the next 10 years. I do not think we will have inflation, but I don't know. I hope the policy makers can generate inflation as deflation is a very bad outcome for a world awash with debt. I have a hard time picking one instrument that I would want to own for the next 10 years.

Are you worried about the potential for the European Union to break apart?

Anything can happen, but I very much doubt it will. With the European Union, the second 10 years will clearly be trickier than the first 10 as the first 10 years were a freebie period due to the high level of liquidity in the world. Although it does depend to a certain extent on who is in power in those countries and what the market environment is at that point, I would be extremely surprised if anything like that were to happen.

Where is the next bubble?

Many people think the next bubble will be inflation, real assets, or Chinese equities. I don't know. They are all possibilities, but possibilities that people have already been thinking about for some time. Like many other predicted bubbles, they happen or they don't, and the possibilities do not go into my trading thinking. All I really care about is working through the issues that matter at any given moment and trading accordingly.

Chapter 7

The Professor

"The Professor" is a modern adventurer who built his business by scouring the world for trade ideas. He quite simply wants to understand everything. Having landed in the financial markets by accident, he is as well-versed addressing the development challenges of certain sub-Saharan African countries as he is pontificating about the likely path of Swiss interest rates. But make no mistake, he is a competitor at core, a classic type-A personality who takes his fundamental understanding of textbook macroeconomics and translates it into compelling risk/reward trades, literally anywhere in the world.

Sourcing trades is not enough, however. The Professor is a portfolio optimizer, using his friends in academia to help build rigorous processes driven by a complex array of leading-edge quantitative and qualitative inputs. Although big game hunter might be a tempting analogy, mad scientist might be more apt: mad because he is not afraid of stretching his brain to envision the impossible, and scientist because his every move is calculating, particularly in measuring his downside risk.

The Professor practices what he refers to as "real macro," which involves identifying structural, country-specific issues and complex interlinkages in the global economy, all of which take time to work their way through the system. For this reason, he is not looking for short-term moves, but rather constructs trades around the medium-term. With the almost 30-year tail wind for risk assets arguably behind us and with policy makers becoming relevant to market prices once again, having a real macro approach is critical for navigating the road ahead. Although the Professor is focused on the risks and potential rewards of policy errors in the future, his social conscience laments the choice that he says policy makers have clearly made in the wake of 2008: protecting the current generation by roasting the next generation.

How did you get into the markets?

I got into markets because I strayed from an early idealistic goal of becoming a bureaucrat. I always aspired to public service because I found the subject matter fascinating and the work is substantive; improving people's lives and effectuating real change in the world just seemed like an incredibly important thing to do. My first job, a summer internship during university, was a research assistant role at an international organization in a developing country. Although I found this initial experience fascinating, I wanted to explore other opportunities, so I subsequently accepted a research assistant position with a macro hedge fund. The experience was eye-opening because the portfolio managers not only included former elite bureaucrats in some cases, but all were talented analysts charged with interpreting the same issues as policy makers, albeit with different agendas. They were using the same analysis but in a much more direct way: making large, educated, directional bets on their policy opinions. I had two choices after graduating from university: I could either continue on to graduate school, which was my original plan, or I could learn more about finance and save some funds for graduate school. I opted for the latter, ending up as a prop trader in the macro group within an investment bank.

How soon after starting were you managing capital?

Four months and I basically got lucky. I started off in a bank training program, then spent another few months in the economic research
area, after which I landed a role on the macro prop desk as a junior
portfolio manager. I was fortunate that so many fixed exchange rate
regimes were blowing up at the time, which buoyed my career. My
idea generation process was extremely research-driven due to my past
work experiences. Although I did not really have an instinct for markets, I was very lucky to be getting into my stride as a portfolio manager
when research mattered. Markets were questioning the valuations of
Asian currencies: the Thai peg, the Indonesian peg, and other regimes.
My style of analysis was well-suited to a research-driven trading approach, and networks from prior experiences were of immense value.
It is unclear if my initial approach would have been suited to a freely
floating market and today I would not consider hiring a portfolio manager with no experience. As with many success stories, I benefited in
part from being the right person in the right place at the right time.
(See Figure 7.1.)

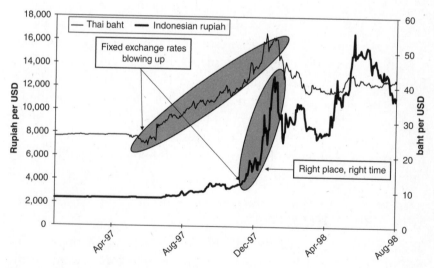

Figure 7.1 Asia Crisis, 1997–1998
SOURCE: Bloomberg.

What was your first setback as a trader?

The market always teaches you a lesson, and the first setback that I recall was due to concerns about a Chinese devaluation in 1997. After much research, one of my trades was fading risk premium in Chinese currency forwards on the thesis that China would not adjust its fixed currency peg. I was fading probably 1 to 2 percent annualized risk premium in the renminbi forward market when the Thai baht devalued. Frankly, it was a very sound thesis. But suddenly there was speculation of a Chinese devaluation, which I found confounding and astonishing because a large, sudden move occurred in the forward points of something that had been pegged for a long time. Since I sized the position as a low volatility trade, it was very painful. You could call it a baptism by fire for how markets can do silly things in phases of contagion and risk aversion.

At what point did you realize you were good at managing money and not just in the right place at the right time?

That is not something that ever explicitly dawned on me. I have been perhaps a little too idealistic and apolitical in managing my career—I generally trusted others to judge me, and I used their vote of confidence as a guide. I was also lucky that, with one exception, all of my managers were very talented, not only as investors but also as managers and mentors. As is always the case, trading success begot additional capital and better roles at extremely competitive and selective places until people just started showing up out of nowhere offering to invest in my fund if I set one up. Despite my accidental beginnings in this business, I have really enjoyed it along the way, and I always try to improve my investment process. Although I now have the funds for grad school, I have no immediate plans to attend.

Can you discuss your process?

My process has changed considerably in recent years. During the first half of my career, I had a singular focus on stop losses, which is the traditional macro way of thinking and managing money. The whole risk management process was anchored by trade-by-trade stop losses where the ultimate anchor was the year-to-date stop loss level. It is too easy to get caught up in the year-to-date stop loss and lose sight of aggregate volatility, the portfolio level stop loss, and correlations between trades, which are much more important. Over time, as my assets under management have grown, rendering a stop-loss approach futile, I have been focusing on developing more robust risk management factors. Contact with former classmates who are now in finance academia has helped greatly with this process.

To use an actual example from my past, buying a stock with an annual volatility of 30 percent with a plan to risk 1 percent and a goal of making 10 percent in a week is madness. Statistically, it is almost guaranteed to get stopped out. Yet, this kind of logic is very prevalent in macro, and admittedly I was guilty of it as well. You leave pennies on the table by overusing stops without understanding the implied volatility required to keep you in the trade.

My approach has evolved such that I am now more concerned about how my overall portfolio does in what I call "the Titanic scenario," where everything goes down, fundamental logic escapes the market, and risk aversion rules. I am concerned with how much I lose at the organization level if there is a repeat of the Asian crisis, if the bond market sells off like it did in 1994, or if the dot-com boom/bust or other cathartic experiences reproduce themselves. I set a hard number for the amount of money I am willing to lose in a variety of cataclysms given the return parameters that I have promised my investors. Because managing money means taking risk, I tend to focus most on limiting how much I lose if the world ends—this is my instinctive bias. I assess each investment based on how it will perform in various negative scenarios. What matters to the overall organization is: (1) research and expected return for each trade; and (2) how the overall fund performs in Armageddon. Thinking of both the individual position and portfolio level risks allows proper evaluation of trades, and by not overusing stop losses, I avoid leaving pennies on the table for others to collect.

When analyzing cataclysms, do you only look at historical events or do you try to imagine new potential scenarios?

Because I was actively invested in the Asian crisis, the Russian crisis, and the dot-com bubble, I refer to these and other past events. Going forward I will include the 2008 crisis. It is important to be cognizant that history will never allow you to perfectly predict the future, but history does rhyme, and historical events are all we really have for real-world case studies. As for new scenarios, this may sound odd, but I like to think about what would happen in financial markets and technology stocks if aliens landed in central Geneva tomorrow. Confirmation of alien life would have all kinds of implications. Although it might seem outlandish, this scenario really forces you to imagine the impossible. For scenario stress testing, we combine the analysis of hypothetical madness with our more straightforward analysis of historical events. One part of me cannot believe I devote time to hypothetical madness, but stretching your mind in a myriad of ways is important when looking into the future. In this case, if they were friendly aliens, opportunities for technology transfers would exist, so it might be very bullish. On the other hand, if they were evil, that would be bad for global growth.

How do you build out your portfolio?

I scale into trades. I know many non-macro hedge funds that simply go to a target risk level from day one, where that measure is a function of the portfolio's target volatility. Risk measures outside of volatility—factors such as entry and timing—really do not matter for them. I disagree with the narrowness of that approach because it camouflages a lack of short-term trading skill. It is no surprise that these types of funds come close to failing once every decade or so. Instead, I try to incorporate portfolio volatility measures with the instinctive, discretionary skill of vintage macro, which includes scaling into trades, amongst other things.

Structuring the portfolio for returns is easy once you have your "Titanic loss" number. For example, I might have a fantastic trade, but when I run it through my "Titanic funnel," one of my scenarios shows the trade will lose ten times the hard cash number limit I have set for the overall fund. That is not a trade that will wind up in the portfolio. Another example is a trade that, net of all adjustments, has considerable expected return based on my estimates, and in negative scenarios, actually makes 10 times my return estimate. This trade will make it into the portfolio and get sized up considerably, relatively speaking, due to the non-correlation benefits. The Titanic funnel, by definition, forces you to think about correlations between trades and what you are really doing in a portfolio context. It forces you to recognize that by going long some emerging market stock, you may be implicitly selling some insurance. If that is the case, and the return does not justify its probability-adjusted Titanic loss, it will force me to do some uncorrelated, antirisk trade if I really want to keep the position.

What is your Titanic scenario threshold?

It varies from year to year, but I am currently running it so that my maximum loss should be limited to 20 percent. Although this may seem high, I am talking about once-in-a-lifetime events, and this figure is commensurate with my target volatility and my target return. I would not be willing to risk losing that amount if my expected return is 5 percent.

To sum up your risk management process, it has shifted from individual idiosyncratic trade focus to portfolio level expected alpha and cross-correlation risk management, but retained some overlay of vintage macro risk management, which you still consider to be best of breed. Is this accurate?

Yes, but there are many intricacies and important details therein. Having studied the very intuitive, trade-by-trade stop loss world and other quantitative environments, I incorporate best practices from both worlds. I try to bridge the vintage macro world, where sizing and timing matters, with newer non-macro worlds, where these measures are less relevant. Again, the quantitative non-macro world attempts to go to target risk right after the research, where risk is based on historical volatilities, correlations, and returns. I am not a fan of that approach.

How do you generate returns?

My overarching thesis is that the presence of noneconomic actors, market change, and structural shifts are three of the main factors that generate recurrent high-quality risk-versus-reward opportunities. You can look for these in a global search of diverse macro inputs and factors. Genuine macro investing focuses primarily on policy and the underlying economic fundamentals. Hence, the sieve we use focuses on disequilibrium conditions in equities, currencies, interest rates, and derivatives thereof, as well as policy-generated situations. We look for situations where asset prices do not correctly reflect macro fundamentals or do not identify and anticipate structural shifts in the economy.

This approach is to be distinguished from more systematic approaches, which rely heavily on quantitative models based on historical data to take diversified positions in a large number of markets (commodity trading advisors, for example). Although these quantitative strategies may trade the same markets (currencies, fixed income, equity indices, etc.), the emphasis is on extracting technical signals rather than developing and expressing fundamental macro views.

Our process essentially commences with a detailed and thorough analysis of the data, an analysis that can be either quantitative or qualitative. Quantitative filtering takes guidance from theory and our own internal research. For example, there is a lengthy list of macroeconomic priors—which we call "Basic Principles"—and known patterns for the evolution of macroeconomic variables. Some examples are the behavior and persistence of inflation in convergence economies, the trend for exchange rates in small, open economies, the relationship between price/earnings (P/E) multiples and exchange rate valuation in economies with large net trade surpluses, and the behavior of the central bank credibility premium after an inflationary bust. Financial markets invariably lag structural developments in the real economy, which is itself another of my Basic Principles. Our proprietary tools extrapolate estimates of fair value from Basic Principles, where any significant divergence of forward market pricing from our estimates immediately highlights something worth exploring. Qualitative screening is also crucially important and can lead to viewpoints and trade ideas originated either in-house or from our external network of other portfolio managers, independent researchers, and academics. Like most of our respected competitors, we tend to ignore sell-side research for independence and quality reasons.

Although various quantitative models are important inputs to our investment process, they are typically used in combination with other factors that allow us to sidestep the naivety of black box applications. We are always cognizant, in our somewhat systematic global search for opportunities, that: (1) Since models of economic and financial time series are often found to be unstable through time, forecasting models are best viewed as approximations or tracking devices. Consequently, we do not expect that the same forecasting model will continue to dominate in different historical or future periods, and we try to use the appropriate model for a given paradigm; (2) The choice of sample period used to estimate the forecasting model parameters is important given model instability due to institutional shifts, changes in government policy, large technology or supply shocks, and other factors (i.e., the Great Moderation that began in the mid-1980s and ended recently); and (3) Forecast combinations can sometimes be better than trying to select one "best" model.

The point is that we always have an economic prior, even before data enters the equation. As such, using guidance from economic theory for quantitative and qualitative searches, we identify possible trade opportunities that can be researched further. This process is theoretically robust and intellectually honest—most of the trades result from a macroeconomic screen, and hence are genuine macro bets, not something ad hoc. This is in contrast to both data mining techniques applied to large, high frequency, or cross-sectional data sets, and instinctive trading that fits a story around what is really momentum or chart-based technical trading in macro instruments.

I tend to look for situations where reality diverges from theory, focusing on disconnects between P/E ratios and growth in transition economies, currency valuation, central bank rate path forecasts, and macro special situations such as the persistence of inflation or the inflation risk premium in the long end not conforming to theory (where theory is very anchoring). I will always have an underlying forecast for currency values, rate paths, or special situations.

After identifying the opportunities, I would do the following, in order of priority: First, conduct my own research; second, converse with researchers and other specialists in the field; third, expand the conversations to include portfolio managers and others in our field; fourth, reach out to the public sector, including central banks, ministries of finance, and their research departments; and fifth, see what others, particularly locals, are saying. This process will either coalesce the idea into a trade or render it null and void.

How do you measure the attractiveness of a trade?

After the global search and research scrub, the next input is our estimate of fair value, whereby attractiveness is the difference between our
estimate and current market pricing. One aspect of the portfolio construction process is how I determine the attractiveness of our trades. Our
tools take our estimate of expected return and adjust it to account for the
fact that different types of trades have different levels of uncertainty in
their return forecasts. Pure equity trades, interest rate trades, and directional currency bets (to name just three examples of many categories we
adjust for) have different adjustments. The intellectual property anchoring these adjustments is proprietary, but we developed these adjustments
largely from historical experience and they greatly enhance our ability
to scale trades appropriately.

This approach is anchored by Bayesian methods (see box). We know
that our own expected raw returns for trades can be more or less precise
depending on the type of trade. We shrink my expected returns towards
zero rather than towards some equilibrium model forecast, the latter of
which is more appropriate given our macro focus. We then input that
adjusted expected return into the Titanic funnel, which assesses how
much it will lose in a variety of cataclysms, giving me the recommended
position. It is important to note that I am not putting trades on just to
achieve the Titanic loss number. I am just looking for mispricings.

Bayesian Methods

The term *Bayesian* refers to the work Thomas Bayes, who proved
a specific case of the now eponymous theorem, published after
his death in 1761. The Bayesian interpretation of probability can
be seen as a form of logic that allows for analysis of uncertain
statements. To evaluate the probability of a hypothesis, Bayes'
theorem compares probabilities before and after the existence
of new data. Unlike other methods for analyzing hypotheses,
which attempt to reject or accept a statement, the Bayesian
view seeks to assign dynamic probabilities that depend on the
existence of relevant information.

Clearly you do not believe in efficient markets.

Some markets are very efficient. Deep, liquid short-dated interest rate markets can be very efficient. In money markets, for example, there is no possible arbitrage between central bank funding bills, interest rate futures, or FX forwards anymore. At the peak of the crisis in 2008, when there was a dollar shortage, there was obviously an arbitrage. But this was a very special situation where the financial system almost went bust. That aside, there is really no arbitrage opportunity in G3 and G7 liquid rate and FX markets—they are completely efficient.

But outside of these markets, the presence of noneconomic actors is very large, creating inefficiencies. These noneconomic actors dwarf the leveraged footprint of hedge funds, creating a significant source of alpha. Many other people are economic actors in the usual sense of the term, but their objective function is somewhat different, perhaps due to a different time horizon or some other constraint. Corporate hedgers, for example, do not really care about daily movements in FX or interest rates—they are primarily concerned that FX does not generate a large swing in their quarterly report. Governments have generational time horizons when they plan and execute currency regimes. The different time horizons of various agents are a big source of alpha when you have so many players involved in a large, liquid market.

What is your time horizon?

Because I have a macro thesis for each individual trade, my holding period is somewhat longer than that of my peers. For lack of a better term, I like to call what I do "real macro." It takes time for macro factors to evolve. The minimum horizon for a trade is about three months, and the longest is pretty open. As a hedge fund with leveraged money and annual returns to generate, I am not going to have endowment-level holding periods so my horizon is constrained such that a trade should start performing within a 12-month window, though longer periods can and do occur.

Real macro involves understanding macroeconomic developments at a fundamental level and then expressing these viewpoints using the appropriate instruments. Frequently this involves identifying disequilibrium situations in which asset prices do not correctly reflect macro fundamentals or identifying or anticipating structural shifts in the economy. Real macro always comes back to the true underlying macroeconomic fundamentals, which serve as primary inputs to your macro forecast, which, in turn, drives your risk allocation decision. All investors should take a real macro approach but few do.

Do you concentrate a few big positions or do you diversify across many small bets?

I try to have more bets because I do not like concentration risk. I tend to have 8 to 10 different trades on, which at least ex ante I hope are idiosyncratic, although it is difficult to find something truly idiosyncratic these days. I tend to get about 55 to 65 percent of trades right and my winners tend to make three or four times what the losers cost me.

Do you express your trades through options?

I used to, but I hardly ever do now. The Titanic funnel is an attempt to generate option-like payoff profiles in the portfolio by scoring and hammering everything down to my chosen loss number in absolute hard cash terms. You can never be fully hedged if you intend to make money—it is impossible, you have to take some risk. I do, however, try to generate option-like payoff streams from the various trades in my fund.

What was the best trade of your career?

I have one in a fixed exchange rate regime and one in a floating regime.

The best trade in the history of macro was in the final quarter of 1998, when the ECU (European Currency Unit) basket blew out less than three months before the euro went live, offering everyone in the world 3 to 4 percent free money with no capacity constraints. LTCM had blown up and the Russian crisis aftermath was still present, but this trade was a sure thing. You could even hedge the minute probability that EMU (European Monetary Union) would not happen almost for free, given that EMU was essentially a done deal. It was literally free money with no tail risk.

The key to this trade was that you knew the loser: the source of the alpha was deleveraging born of two gigantic crises. Although today it seems like small potatoes, at that time LTCM looked unimaginably horrible and the Russian default was even crazier. The coincidence of these outlandish events was a source of alpha. It is very important to know who is on the other side of trades and in this case, you knew. It was simply an enormous opportunity born out of an unimaginable scenario, where in theory you could go long the entire M2 of the country with the smallest M2 outstanding and make a sure 3 to 5 percent in a matter of weeks (see box). Of course, counterparty issues and other agency problems introduced an element of friction to the process, but still, this was money you could see and collect easily.

M2

M0 to M3 delineate different measurements of the money supply in an economy. M2 is a measure of money supply that includes a broader set of financial assets held principally by households than M1. M2 consists of M1 plus: (1) savings deposits (which include money market deposit accounts); (2) small-denomination time deposits (amounts less than $100,000); and (3) balances in retail money market mutual funds.

- **M0**: The total of all physical currency, plus accounts at the central bank that can be exchanged for physical currency.
- **M1**: The total of all physical currency part of bank reserves plus the amount in demand accounts ("checking" or "current" accounts).
- **M2**: M1 + most savings accounts, money market accounts, retail money market mutual funds, and small denomination time deposits (certificates of deposit of under $100,000).
- **M3**: M2 + all other CDs (large time deposits, institutional money market mutual fund balances), deposits of Eurodollars and repurchase agreements.

SOURCE: St. Louis Federal Reserve Bank.

In free floating markets without a nominal anchor, my most satisfying trade came out of the trip you arranged to Turkey in 1999, which Jim Leitner talked about in *Inside the House of Money*. This marked the penultimate inflection point in the emergence of Turkey. We were with a small group of macro hedge fund managers doing on-the-ground research, looking at the fiscal policies, getting a sense for how soundly reform packages were being implemented, and kicking the tires more generally on the Republic of Turkey. It became very clear that the conditions needed for Turkey to secure an IMF standby program would be met very easily. The fiscal and political reality on the ground implied that this was the central case forecast.

Anecdotally, as a sanity check, the consensus amongst the Turkish political and corporate leaders we met on the trip was orthogonal to the consensus in London and New York. With one-year yields above 100 percent, there was a lot of potential alpha in the trade and you had a massive cushion.

Turkey is a very large economy where the population has understood the time value of money since Ottoman rule. The country has never had capital controls. Financially speaking, the Turkish population today is much more sophisticated than that of the United States, the United Kingdom, or even Switzerland. Persistent high inflation has forced the merchant class to develop a certain financial knowledge; cab drivers wax lyrically about simple and compounded yield, and the average bank managers are familiar with Treasury funding and supply schedules.

At the time the size of the domestic T-bill market was around $40 billion, significantly larger than microstates where you might get a 100 percent return but can only do a small position size. It was a serious mispricing in a liquid emerging market, where equilibrium was egregiously far from fair value, and where the trigger to bring it back to equilibrium was clear, imminent, and led by an international organization. It really was one of those complete no-brainers. Just after the trip, the IMF announced a package based largely on the reasons we expected, and lo and behold, yields quickly went from more than 100 percent to, at one point, 30 percent. (See Figure 7.2.) This story was easily identifiable from genuine, focused, on-the-ground, fundamental macroeconomic research. It remains to this day the best emerging markets trade that I have ever done. On a side note, it also shows the power of genuine

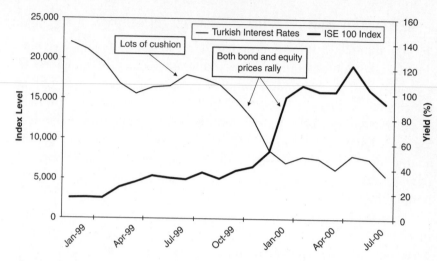

Figure 7.2 Turkish Investment Rates + Equities, 1999–2000
SOURCE: Bloomberg.

macro focus: Investment processes, without a macro focus or awareness of policy nuance, did not, and still would not, capture such trades.

If you took 10 years off to get your Ph.D. and had to put all your personal capital in one trade right now, what would it be?

Equities in sub-Saharan Africa, currency unhedged. The trend towards good governance in the region is glacial but irreversible, as the benefits of even marginally improved governance are evident. Mozambique is a good example. Africa has an abundance of commodities, particularly softs, which I am very bullish medium-term. Population growth rates in Africa are strong and the distribution for productivity growth going forward is highly skewed to the upside. The region's initial conditions—capital markets depth/development, market capitalization/GDP ratios, banking sector penetration, credit depth—remain, however, prehistoric. Hence, the region will soon enter the growth phase of maximum convexity, where these factors normalize with development and growth. Returns in equity markets and currencies will be particularly outsized as the risk profile of many countries in the region reprices completely whereby risk premiums will fall. However, this is really a generational trade, and a 10-year holding period is about right.

Do you travel to places like Africa to generate such ideas?

Yes, I find immense value in traveling. Ultimately, genuine macro comes down to a country opinion—the soundness or lack of soundness of a country and its economics, institutions, path, and transparency, all of which affect its long-term trend and are reflected in its equities, currency, or other macro instruments. My view on the instruments is a function of the underlying macroeconomic forecast. I hone this forecast by getting a sense for what policy makers in that country think, by understanding their sensitivity, by comparing their outlook to mine. It is all about honing the forecast.

People often mistake country travel for seeking inside information—that bit of granular detail you only uncover from being on the ground. That game used to be played in the 1980s and early 1990s by a select few who were powerful enough to call the president of a country to receive advanced notice of certain events. This kind of stuff never happens on the ground. Additionally, and much more importantly, on principle, that is not my game. I do not like it when people have an unfair advantage. Travel for research, sanity checking, or increasing the resolution of your forecast, however, is very valuable. I never go to a country without first trying to understand as much as I can from the outside, so that I have preconceived notions, which are either reinforced or proven false once I am on the ground.

In visiting a country, is part of your process talking to taxi drivers and hotel concierges?

That is only a very small part of it. Those types of conversations tend to provide marginal benefit only in very small, very transparent countries with highly developed institutional frameworks. Iceland is a great example. Iceland was a very good place to collect anecdotes because there are only around 300,000 people. If you collect 100 anecdotes, you have a decent sense of what is going on. In China, on the other hand, it would be impossible to make any sense of such anecdotes. Visiting a few big cities and seeing some empty buildings does not give you any texture. Likewise, visiting only Shanghai and seeing that it is booming with cranes everywhere is also meaningless. China's size and complexity renders this kind of concierge and taxi driver chatter absolutely useless.

How do you get a handle on what is happening in China?

China is a very tricky one and I struggle with it. I tend to rely on data, and the cleanest data I have is NGO data. Chinese national data is rightly criticized, but it does have some valuable information for macro investors because we are as concerned with rates of change as we are with levels.

One thing that is very clear, however, is that the China story is the result of a massive investment boom. Because we have seen investment booms before, we have a framework. This thought process drives my "back of the envelope" thematic view on China. West Germany, Japan, and Korea all had investment booms in the post–World War II period, and investment booms behave in distinct ways. Although I am not a very big fan of the Austrian School of economic thought, one statistic often cited by Austrians who do not buy the China story is that every country in history with sustained investment-to-GDP ratios of more than 50 percent has eventually blown up. By "blown up" they mean experienced a big investment bust. Others try to use the West German model as a counterargument, although I am not sure this is applicable to China because of both the vast cultural differences between the two and the difference in peak levels of investment-to-GDP ratios (Germany never approached the current levels in China). If we assume that the Japanese model is a better comparison, then in the medium-term, I can make a case for being very concerned about the likely path of Chinese growth. But, while I can see the value in this thesis, the opposing thesis that size matters also has merit. Even using very conservative assumptions, the Chinese middle class will grow dramatically, and it will want to consume. For argument's sake, even if we assume that the Chinese already have all the bicycles, trains, and infrastructure they need, people change their consumption behavior when they move up the income chain. It is a fact of life. They will want more brown goods, such as iPods, DVD players, video game consoles, and others. They will change their diet. Behavior changes with income, and although it is not clear how it all plays out, the numbers behind China make it difficult to want to bet against it longer term. But it is very complicated. While it is true that every example of a country with an investment-to-GDP ratio of greater than 50 percent has led to a bust, I am leaning towards the angle that maybe this time it is different, whilst being mindful of the downsides.

Let us assume that you agree with the thesis that China will blow up.
Since an investment boom means it will go up before it goes down, how
would you play it?

If that were the case, I would play it by being long the currency but instead of talking about China, I would like to answer your question by posing another example: India. India has had an investment-to-GDP ratio of around 25 percent, which has risen recently to a bit under 30 percent. For half the investment-to-GDP ratio of China, it has generated growth roughly 1 percent lower than China during the boom. India's return on investment is superb, which points to its prowess in financial management. India is coming from a lower base with a lower rate of change in investment—because it has horrible infrastructure but superior financial management, India has the potential to squeeze a lot more out of investment going forward. We forecast that India will embark on an investment boom at some point in the future. The gap between its current level of investment and where it needs to be is large, and the marginal return on investment is high. Taken together with their reserves and other factors, pessimists would say this boom would probably not be sustainable in the very long term. But as Keynes said, in the long run, we are all dead. Since the marginal return on investment (in terms of GDP) is so high right now, even if you doubt its longer term sustainability, you would probably get involved. Besides, at this stage of development, an investment boom can extend for a generation (see Figure 7.3).

The point I am making is that I look at the marginal return that investment generates in terms of growth. If it is very high, it is probably worth getting involved in the equity markets. If, on the other hand, it is very low, but sentiment is still very high—near euphoric—you probably still want to get involved but through the currency. The currencies of countries that experience investment booms typically do well, during both boom and bust. Deflation often sets in after an investment boom goes bust, and historically the currencies of countries that have gone bust have done very well. During the boom, you have foreign direct

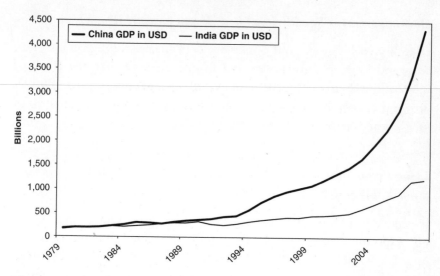

Figure 7.3 GDP, 1979–2008
SOURCE: Bloomberg.

investment (FDI) and potentially portfolio diversification flows going overseas if capital accounts are open and financial liberalization is part of the boom. At the end of the investment boom, if the country experiences a deflationary bust, you tend to get a rally in the currency, especially if the initial condition was one of currency undervaluation. Note, this is not a necessary condition to generate a currency rally, and after the bust you tend to have supportive real rates because of deflation.

How much does positioning and crowding factor into your process?

It should factor in more. Positioning remains much more instinctive thing for me. On one hand, if a trade is highly crowded, unanchored, not in some huge liquid market like EUR/USD, and people are involved for macroeconomic reasons, it is probably close to fair value, so my guess of expected return would be low. On the other hand, if a trade is very crowded because people are looking at the same instrument through non-macro goggles, it could be driven far from fair value, which to me is an ideal situation to think about going the other way.

How important is liquidity, and how do you measure it?

Liquidity is important and I measure it primarily through transaction costs and looking at turnover data from authorities like the Bank of International Settlements (BIS), or exchanges and counterparties. It will show up in volatility. Cost and volatility are two of the factors that I use to adjust my sense of a trade's attractiveness.

Liquidity conditions changed drastically in 2008. How did you manage through this period?

It was very difficult. I look at 2008 in two ways. One is that, given our exposures, our organization should have failed, but we were still up small, a testament to the risk management system we built. Another way of looking at it is that whilst the system did its job in preventing a blow-up, it probably lost focus on how liquidity evaporates in these scenarios. Taken to an extreme, losses are clearly amplified if average daily volume goes to zero.

I did not put enough weight on that in 2008—it is something I should have been aware of *ex-ante*. Further, I was not prepared for how much things can change. In 2008, the financial system almost collapsed. As part of my risk management methodology, I owned a lot of LIBOR futures all over the world. When LIBOR-OIS basis blew out in the G3 because the global financial system appeared to be on the brink of collapse, my hedge did not work, and that is not something I accounted for (see Figure 7.4). Going forward, if there is a requirement for insurance from short-end interest rates, I would probably look at exchange-traded futures on central bank rates themselves rather than LIBOR futures, the latter of which have a credit element.

In 2008, my risky trades sold off much more than they should have due to illiquidity, while my hedges did not work as much as expected. My front-end rates trades should have performed, which would have turned my small up year into a big up year. Otherwise, what saved us was being long interest rates in peripheral economies that had very steep yield curves. Regardless, I learned a lot in 2008, and you can put both a positive and negative spin on it.

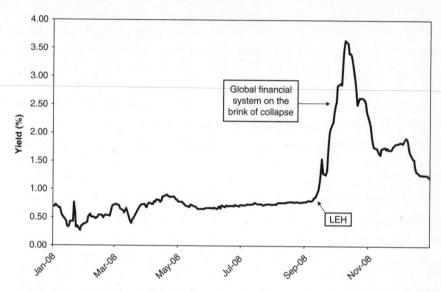

Figure 7.4   LIBOR-OIS Basis, 2008
Source: Bloomberg.

OIS

An overnight indexed swap (OIS) is an interest rate swap where
the periodic floating rate of the swap is equal to the geometric
average of an overnight index (e.g., a published interest rate)
during the course of the payment period. OIS rates are an indication of market expectations of the effective federal funds rate
over the term of the swap. The spread between OIS rates and
LIBOR rates reflects credit risk and the expectation of future
overnight rates. The LIBOR–OIS spread is an important measure of risk and liquidity in the money market and is considered
by many to be a strong indicator for relative stress. A higher
spread is typically interpreted as indication of a decreased willingness to lend by major banks, while a lower spread indicates
higher liquidity in the market.

What were the positive things you learned?

What I learned was subtle more than new or significant. After 2008, my process of focusing on the essence of the trade—each trade's riskiness—whether you are really implicitly selling insurance or not, has become more amplified. Because each risky trade was put through the Titanic funnel, there were many positions that, in a normal macro, ad hoc sense, would not have been there. A normal macro approach would have been: I am long "x," which is very risky, and my stop is here. But the stop would not have been possible. There was no stop in 2008 as markets gapped. 2008 reminded me of the importance of trade deconstruction, which I focus on more than ever.

I also learned that I need to focus more on liquidity, particularly on scenarios where the world does not blow up, everything performs essentially the way you want, except there is no liquidity, so you cannot actually get out. Continually evolving and learning is one of the positives that come out of every crisis, and if you are still around you can only benefit from these experiences.

During crises, incredible opportunities present themselves because there is no capital to take advantage of them. How would you compare the events of 1998, which you capitalized on, versus 2008, which you did not?

1998 and 2008 are very different. The ECU basket conformed to what I consider the ideal trade in macro: one with a nominal anchor. There were many opportunities in 2008, but none had a nominal anchor. Much of the blowout in spreads reflected genuine concerns about the banking system, which looked potentially insolvent. With the ECU trade, you had a nominal anchor not only in interest rates, which obviously always have a nominal anchor, but also in currencies, which are the largest, most liquid market in the world. Those factors did not apply in 2008.

The financial system almost went under but now global governments have backstopped them and flooded the world with liquidity. Everyone is feeling good again. What is your view of the world right now?

I am relatively frustrated because although I can see reasons for optimism, the extraordinary measures appear temporary. While there is a lot of liquidity out there, from governments to corporates, the money is not really being used for capital expenditures or hiring, whether you are looking at top-down or bottom-up data. Putting myself in the shoes of a corporate planner, I am not sure this behavior will change any time soon, either. After an asset bubble, the labor market flips from a lagging indicator to a leading indicator, and it is not looking good at present.

So, if this rally in risk assets is really just a search for yield, I don't see how that ignites something sustainable. The present situation is not like the past, where a country or region experienced a big asset bubble that subsequently deflated while the rest of the world continued to grow, helping the troubled country recover. Now, everyone is in it together. All these IOU papers and obligations cannot be exported to Mars. Someone has to pay. The basic but very difficult choice that policy makers face is: Do you roast the current generation or the future generation? In order to protect the current generation, they are trying to keep nominal asset values steady so that banks remain solvent and everyone who saved and owns a house is okay in nominal terms. But the cost of this policy is tremendous debt and very low potential growth, which screws my children and other youngsters with their lives ahead of them.

The other choice is to step back and let everything clear. I am curious whether this was actually ever discussed during the crisis. Obviously, asset values would completely deflate, house prices would deflate, and it would be painful, but this would give tremendous opportunities to those who have their lives ahead of them. So it is a very tough choice, but that is what the choice is. Some massive technological innovation could change things on the margin, but it will not eliminate the intertemporal cost allocation entirely.

It is now clear that the bias of policy makers is very much towards protecting the current generation. If you look at policy makers' instincts in the crisis, never once was the option of just letting the system figure it out on the table. But that makes sense given policy makers' short-term horizon, which is a function of the election cycle.

My medium-term theme projects a world with very high nominal growth and very low real growth, with increasing dispersion of growth and prosperity across regions of the world. Within that, we should see a rebalancing of growth models: rebalancing of extremely low consumption rates in Asia and rebalancing of the low U.S. savings rate. By rebalancing, I am talking about a normalization of the U.S. fiscal balance, U.S. household saving rates, Asian consumption, Asian saving rates, Asian exchange rates, and many other things that this crisis has kick-started. If the Asians strengthen their currencies and grow domestically, their buying power increases to a much larger percentage of global GDP.

Again, everyone is in this one together, even though as a first pass, certain countries stand out as having had no crisis and no subprime issues at all domestically. Brazilian, Australian, and Canadian banks look fine. Ultimately, however, much of global growth is still driven by G7 final demand. Hence, it may appear on the surface that Brazil is somewhat insulated from the rest of the world because its largest trading partner is China, but China, in turn, remains heavily reliant on G7 final demand. Any country that ultimately provides inputs into the Chinese supply chain is still reliant on G7 final demand, and it is an open question whether that will change or not. So far, policy makers in Asia are clinging to the old world. By that I mean they will maintain an export-led growth model despite the lack of export demand, thereby accumulating an increasing stock of dollars with no real tangible resultant growth. Ultimately, it seems that they will be forced to embrace change, either because they are smart and proactive, or because they are forced into it.

To summarize, I am bearish in the medium-term, but my bearishness is concentrated in G3. I do not believe in the robustness of anything that is liquidity-driven when there is no second-order multiplier into the real economy. But I can see this whole scenario being quite favorable for select emerging markets in the medium-term.

Where is the next bubble?

Whilst I remain bullish on select emerging markets, it is a very consensus view, implying that at some point emerging markets themselves will become bubbles—though I do not think we are there yet. Within the emerging markets, I like India, China, Brazil, Argentina, Chile, Turkey, Iran, Indonesia, Central Asia (especially Azerbaijan and Turkmenistan), most of the Gulf, North Africa, and Sub-Saharan Africa.

The next bubble could be due to both peak oil and the end of fiat money. There is much hysteria around commodities, not only because of peak oil and similar theories, but also because people wish to diversify into "real" assets that governments cannot manipulate. Disruptive processes always trigger a variety of bubbles. It is difficult to project which asset or technology will initially dominate as a replacement for something like oil and capital rushes into anything with even some probability of success. I cannot help thinking that one of the bubbles will be something related not only to gold, oil, natural gas, and traditional commodities, but also to windmills, solar power, and other related areas. Technology is very disruptive. Everyone is convinced about peak oil, and the rise of the BRICs has additional demand consequences that imply extremely bullish scenarios for oil. However, this also makes alternatives more attractive. I am sure that one of these alternatives will indeed become very important fundamentally, but many will be bubbles.

When you mention the end of fiat money, what do you mean?

Regarding the end of fiat money, there is understandable concern about that concept. The global response to this crisis is massive reflation. Quantitative easing is now ubiquitous enough to be on CNN Headline News, whereas just two years ago, it was an arcane economics term. Quantitative easing is the budgetization of monetary policy—essentially printing money—and the examination of global central bank balance sheets confirms that it is global in scope and massive in scale. We all know that (1) money is ultimately a confidence trick, so policy credibility is very important; and (2) inflation unequivocally erodes savings and capital in the long term, which is one of the main reasons that price stability became such a focal point the past two decades and one of the standards for judging convergence. The credibility and store of value anchors to fiat money are being questioned because the forces known to erode a currency's purchasing power and confidence are being enacted on such a large scale globally. At the margin, a rational investor would be right to seek out alternative, nonmanipulable real assets. Whilst I am not a fan of gold, it is the one real asset that also has a history as a currency, so its recent popularity is understandable.

So is the U.S. dollar's role as the world's reserve currency in question?

I have conflicting views on the dollar. On one hand, I can see the fundamental arguments for its status to erode gradually over time, and for people who have large stocks of dollars to start diversifying not only their flow—which pretty much all reserve managers have been doing—but also their stock.

My counter to that focuses on something very basic: you hold a reserve currency ultimately for precautionary reasons, i.e., safety. One source of safety is obviously economic fundamentals, institutional credibility, and all that. Another underreported source, however, is something very primal: power. The U.S. is likely to remain the world's sole hyperpower for the foreseeable future. We all talk about China aspiring to superpower status, and it very well may evolve into one in the fullness of time. However, in terms of projecting power and military dominance, no country will come close to the U.S. in the near future, and this fact plays heavily into the dollar's role as a reserve asset. A historical parallel is the British Empire in the mid-1800s, which ran a very large balance of payments deficit with China from the opium trade. They ultimately resorted to military action, not entirely but largely to address this situation. I am not saying that will happen today, but the reality is that when you are a superpower, you can do what you like, and this should have some positive demand implications for the liabilities you issue as a sovereign entity.

What are your views on the current inflation versus deflation debate?

I have no real opinion on the path of prices in the short-term. In the medium-term, however, I cannot help but agree with what seems to be consensus, which is that policy makers in the most wounded industrialized countries are effectively targeting 4 to 8 percent inflation. Inflating out of this debt problem is just such a powerful dynamic. Economists say, objectively, that the man on the street will realize that real values are falling, but I disagree. Psychologically, the man on the street will feel much less pain if debt is inflated away, if house prices remain stable in nominal terms despite underperforming in real terms.

This is the path of least resistance and the easiest way out of this mess. It is not the optimal path, but rather the easiest one, psychologically "electorate-adjusted." That being said, even if it is the goal of policy makers, it remains to be seen whether or not it can actually be achieved.

If you were running an unlevered portfolio like a university endowment, what is the best way to hedge high inflation and potentially hyperinflation?

It goes without saying that in the very long-term, which is the horizon you are talking about for endowments, there will always be a bid for real assets. The duration of equities is infinite and they, too, are real assets. I can see many sectors in developed country equity markets that would be a great hedge for inflation. Energy should do well, as should general consumer conglomerates, the latter of which can adjust prices to keep up with inflation. Real estate could do well, but because it is the bubble that just burst, it is unlikely to outperform. The Nasdaq is a great example of how a sector can underperform for the several consecutive business cycles that follow a bubble bursting.

Shorting the currency of inflationary countries would be an obvious trade as economic history clearly shows that sustained high inflation erodes currency values. It does not have to be hyperinflation either, just sustained high inflation. Assuming endowments are allowed to have large currency biases, I would diversify away from the G3. With respect to hyperinflation, the Zimbabwe example is instructive. The Zimbabwe equity market—a few large companies, not the index—after all the devaluation performed far better than you would have expected.

In summary, I would focus my exposure on liquid, real assets in countries that will likely emerge into being transparently or professionally regulated. My starting point would be countries that are or very soon will be signatories to IMF Article VIII, score highly on both the Human Development Index (HDI; see box on page 196) and Transparency International's Corruption Perceptions Index (CPI; see box on page 196), have high potential growth, and sound social policies.

Human Development Index (HDI)

The United Nations Human Development Index (HDI) is a statistical measure that gauges a country's level of human development in three principal areas: (1) life expectancy at birth; (2) knowledge and education, as measured by the adult literacy rating and enrollments at various levels of formal education; and (3) standard of living, measured principally by GDP per capita at purchasing power parity (PPP). While there is a strong correlation between having a high HDI score and a prosperous economy, the UN points out that the HDI accounts for more than income or productivity.

SOURCE: United Nations Development Program.

Corruption Perceptions Index (CPI)

Since 1995, Transparency International has published an annual Corruption Perceptions Index ordering the countries of the world according to "the degree to which corruption is perceived to exist among public officials and politicians." The organization defines corruption as "the abuse of entrusted power for private gain."

SOURCE: Transparency International.

Is your experience as a global macro fund manager transportable to the real money world? For example, if Harvard called and wanted you to run their endowment, could you do it?

If your question is specific to me, then yes, I could do it. I say this because of the various things that I outlined before: the way I identify and scale trades, and the way I generate forecasts. I invest based on macroeconomic forecasts for a variety of things, all of which have very long holding periods. That said, most macro hedge fund managers would not be particularly well-suited to running a real money fund because they have a more tactical approach. Conversely, however, many institutional hedge funds—the big, diversified hedge funds with multiple strategies—would probably be able to make the transition more easily because their general approach can be extended to much longer time periods with considerable value added.

If CalPERS, a $200 billion unlevered pension fund, hired you as CIO and required an 8 percent real annual return, could you construct a portfolio to achieve this?

At risk of sounding glib, I could do it. My edge, as with other macro-hedge fund managers, is firstly my personal background, and secondly, training that leverages that personal background, the combination of which allows me to look for optimal investment opportunities globally. Personal background is extremely important in having a global scope and view, which large pensions funds such as CalPERS must have in this day and age. In terms of investment decisions, the main driver of returns will be the asset allocation mix, and I believe CalPERS is not really constrained in optimizing that. Other than some ethical guidelines, there are no obstacles. At the same time, it is not really an alluring seat, even to those who believe they could run it. Few would want to, largely because of financial reasons. In a business as Darwinian as finance, unless you are pursuing something noble—like serving the state or contributing to the field in academia—money signals ability. You get what you pay for.

As for the specific target of 8 percent real annual returns, that is challenging but achievable. First, this is a long-term average return, not year-to-year. Second, the demographics of the State of California are well known, so the risk of long-term structural shocks is low. With a global, unconstrained mandate, you could take advantage of the risk premia in markets with underdeveloped capital markets and large populations—notably sub-Saharan Africa and the BRICs. The outlook for growth in most of the world is sufficiently positive to meet this hurdle. You would need to look to aggressively increase currency exposures and long equity exposures to emerging markets and frontier markets as capacity evolves. The initial condition of market capitalization-to-GDP in most of the world is so low that over the very long term—which is what CalPERS is focused on—with the right asset allocation and currency calls, this is an achievable target.

Essentially, to get to this target for CalPERS, I would have to significantly boost allocations to the higher expected return categories like equity, as well as intelligently take more risk within the equity category. But in taking this approach, you significantly increase your odds of being underfunded relative to liabilities. However, my sense is that CalPERS' level of awareness and exposure to high-risk, high-return equity opportunities in the BRIC and frontier markets currency unhedged is low. This should allow them to boost expected returns without a corresponding increase in risk. It sounds like a strong statement, but if you look at their track record over the past decade, compared to macro hedge fund managers and skilled unleveraged money managers, they are clearly not on the efficient frontier.

What do most investors miss when approaching portfolio management?

Most investors miss the implicit risks they are taking. Many very skilled investors insufficiently deconstruct their trades down to their core bets. In keeping with my earlier example of Turkish T-bills, let us illustrate what I mean by this. A trader may believe that yields on Turkish T-bills are too high for a variety of fundamental reasons, leading to a decision to buy bills in anticipation of lower yields. However, doing this actually gives you exposure not only to Turkish interest rates, but also to foreign exchange and government default risk. Hedging out the currency reduces a large portion of the yield, which may then make the trade unattractive.

In other words, the question to always ask is: After making all the necessary adjustments, what are you actually betting on? A surprisingly large number of people miss this point. Further, even after you have extracted all the extraneous factors and think you are left with your core bet, other implicit risks may still exist. All assets have some embedded probability of the unfavorable. With a risky asset, it is possible that, even after extracting alpha, you are really only selling some kind of put on an unfavorable state of the world. You should be cognizant of this fact, and not many people are. Those who are aware of it but still do the trade without tail hedges are quite possibly just gaming an annual compensation system or worse, they are fooling themselves.

If a friend who wins $1 billion in the lottery approaches you and says: "Tell me what to do. I just want to make sure that I have sufficient income to live large. I don't want to lose capital." What strategy would you employ? He wants to never worry about buying the next Lamborghini, but does not want to wake up one day and find his balance at zero.

The key risk is inflation. To take your question literally, the income on $1 billion of capital invested in a global portfolio of credible, G20, sovereign, inflation-linked bonds would be so large that he could buy 20 Lamborghinis a year. Assuming that he does not want to compete with Abramovich by spending $1 billion dollars on a new yacht, achieving his motoring ambitions would be rather easy. Because inflation is the main enemy of savings in the long term, 70 percent of the capital should be invested in a global portfolio of inflation-linked bonds, currency unhedged. My recommendation would be Norway, Sweden, Euroland, U.S., and U.K. inflation-linked bonds—countries with credible inflation indices and institutions. The remaining 30 percent should be in other real assets in emerging markets, which, if they go to zero, the coupon instruments would compensate. Thus, I would invest half of the remainder in some weighted basket of BRIC inflation-linked bonds and the other half in BRIC equities, currency unhedged.

If everything is currency unhedged and your friend is based in the U.S., then a large dollar rally is a big risk, no?

It is and it isn't. Because such a large percentage of the portfolio is in linkers, a massive U.S. dollar rally means that other currencies have depreciated. Many of the countries I mentioned will actually start producing a higher inflation coupon from the pass-through of currency to CPI. A dollar rally would be a bigger risk if you were holding nominal bonds.

What are your thoughts on the hedge fund space?

The business is returning to what it was generation ago, and it will be better off. For most of my career, hedge funds meant global macro.

From the collapse of the Bretton Woods system, to the appointment of Fed chairman Paul Volcker, until the dot-com bust, governments, policy makers, and central banks dominated financial markets. Many different things affect prices, but the weight ascribed to policy maker conduct and analysis—estimating their intentions, analyzing their speeches, reviewing their published research, etc.—was crucial to investing. There was also a wide dispersion in official actions across the globe and we are now reverting to that paradigm because of the crisis in 2008. Many banks are nationalized, market regulation is increasing, and the G-7 economies are permanently wounded. Central banks are talking about limiting risk taking and talk of rebalancing implies some kind of change in the Asian growth model. All of this makes the world an interesting place for macro again.

The point is governments, monetary authorities, and noneconomic agents matter again, and these agents will provide much more alpha to markets going forward than they have for years. When you have volatility in times of flux, you have increased probability of a policy error, and that is one of the greatest sources of alpha for macro managers.

How does policy error provide alpha or at least opportunities for alpha?

Policy makers intervene in markets by directly affecting the prices of instruments or by providing a framework or nominal anchor to conduct policy, around which opportunities arise. Managed exchange rate regimes and short end interest rate trading are two ubiquitous examples.

Another example is policy change. Central banks changing the manner in which they conduct policy can be a source of alpha. People think of inflation targeting as the Holy Grail, but that cachet has applied for less than a decade. For example, the National Bank Act in Switzerland formalized the Swiss National Bank's (SNB) independence and mandate in the constitution only in 2003, which is frankly like yesterday in the big picture. You could argue that inflation targeting has worked as planned, but that it also led to the crisis of 2008. Because people thought that price stability was here forever, they started levering up, and asset prices exploded.

An example where alpha may result from policy change going forward is central banks moving away from inflation targeting, whereby they perhaps target inflation and credit growth. That would generate volatility and change how risk premia are valued. Another source of alpha from policy makers is when there is some kind of regime in place that is at odds with valuation, whether it is a managed exchange rate regime or artificially low interest rates. These regimes tend to work until the world changes. During structural breaks and regime shifts, financial markets tend to lag the real economy, generating opportunities for macro investors.

What personality traits or characteristics are required for success in real macro?

That is a very interesting question, and something I think about often here in my own business. My thoughts over the years have evolved into a collection of some basic views, which have very successfully guided our hiring and business. Taking intellectual ability and IQ as a given for any role, we tend to filter for some key traits. Foremost, to be successful in real macro, you need to be a type-A personality. The nature of macro is highly centered on individual competitiveness and individual success compared to collaborative strategies. The Darwinian, competitive nature of macro investing is why successful macro money managers sustain or even expand their competitive edge over time—the skill set being honed is one of defeating the person on the other side of the trade. Certainly, some macro trades have similarities to collaborative strategies, where the investing community is taking on a country with a fixed exchange rate, for example. But those trades are not all of what macro is about and even in those situations there is an element of zero-sumness and a competitive, performance-driven spirit. Tactical trading, macro special situations, and other strategies within broader macro that constitute the bulk of the strategy have a winner-take-all flavor. That is a very competitive, type-A kind of trait and we will only hire people who have that. It is a telling signal that most successful money management firms are generally run by type-A personalities with high ability and individual, performance-driven cultures.

Personal background is also very important. We almost never hire people who have not had global careers or led global lives, due either to their upbringing or previous global professional experiences in investment banks, academia, or the public sector. The ideal candidate is someone who has a combination of these experiences. We have found that the best managers are those who have a macro perspective even before they were aware of what money management was. Those with a latent sense of awareness about the world, an understanding of how things operate in different places, and cultural awareness, tend to be best at macro investing. Without these personal characteristics, people simply have no context and are unable to judge macro value. That lack of knowledge base means that a person will constantly be behind the game.

Experience is another filter. Although this may sound hypocritical given that I got into the business with zero experience, I would never hire someone with zero experience—I acknowledge the flukiness of my career path. Macro money management is a strategy where people generally improve with age, where experience is accretive. I do not think that this dynamic applies so powerfully to other strategies. Arguably, in some systematic strategies experience is a negative because the basic principles that may have guided your systematic investing become widely known over time, making you increasingly redundant. Managing the investors' capital entrusted to us is a serious proposition, and like most of our macro competitors, we do not hire trainees. We only hire fully formed portfolio managers with a track record, former public sector officials, or people from academia. And experience, knowledge base, skepticism, and thoughtfulness tend to form a key thread in all three types of candidates.

What advice do you have for a college kid who wants to be in your seat in 20 years?

It sounds like a cliché, but my first recommendation would be to see the world. Global life experience really does give you an edge in macro investing. I am not talking about investing experience per se, just personal life experience. Most successful macro managers seem to have this common thread. Second, since macro ultimately means global equities, currencies, and rates, it would be helpful to start in a bank, a top institution known for being a school for macro and macro products or a high-quality public sector organization. Last, have opinions. Start having opinions on which countries are good or bad, even if these opinions are completely incorrect. "I think this country sucks and this culture sucks. I think that person sucks because he likes this government." It could be very politically incorrect, even very narrow-minded. However, such opinions, coupled with information and experience, will broaden into a sense of what kind of cultures or countries are sound or not. This is always good input for macro, particularly if it is real macro.

Chapter 8

The Commodity Trader

Massive inflows into passive commodity investment vehicles, increased volatility, new markets and products, and important new players from the East lead us to "The Commodity Trader," who says that given the volatility and cyclicality of financial markets in the last decade, real money managers will have to increasingly think and act like traders in order to thrive. All investors should pay close attention, as the Commodity Trader forms a rare breed of those able to post strong returns in both 2008 and 2009, a function of his ability to continually find good asymmetric bets.

Although the Commodity Trader remains a trader at his core, he constructs fundamental views for the entire range of commodity complexes, analyzing interest rate markets, currencies, and a host of other macroeconomic variables in the process. He remains above all a trade structure specialist. Where other commodity players might go long the front end contract in, say, wheat or crude, the Commodity Trader will decide where on those curves are the best places to express the trades, often constructing spread trades with a significant use of both derivative financial products and derivative commodity products (e.g., crack spreads).

I first met the Commodity Trader on a dreary winter day, when we sat by the fire in a hotel lobby to discuss plans for his new fund launch, a short time after he had left a major hedge fund. Polite and polished, he is a far cry from the rough-edged stereotype that permeates in the aggressive, bare-knuckled commodity trading worlds of the Chicago Mercantile Exchange or the London Metals Exchange. I knew from that initial conversation that he understood how to construct great risk-versus-reward trades and would be a moneymaker, which has proven correct.

Nearly two years later, I sat down with the Commodity Trader again at a mahogany table in an art-adorned conference room in his high tech offices, where currently he presides over one of the largest commodity hedge funds in the world. He is a firm believer in the commodity super cycle, and spends a great deal of time thinking about the second-order effects on other markets and products. He says that pension funds and other real money investors have an economic reason to invest in commodities as an inflation hedge, but the devil is in the details. It's all about how you construct the trade.

How did you get into the markets?

I had family working in finance and in The City so I had always been fascinated by that world. My first job was with a small brokerage house that did business with a broad range of clients from very small retail to institutional, but trading was what really interested me. Eventually, I landed a role as a junior trader on an energy desk.

Did you know you wanted to be in commodities?

When I started out in the business, I just wanted to trade. It didn't make much difference to me whether I was trading oil, copper, stocks, dollar/yen, or bonds. It could have been anything.

What did you study in school?

I studied business but my real education came directly from the markets. I started off prop trading in the front end of the oil market—trading Brent, WTI, and the front spreads and arbitrages (see box). Being the junior on the desk, I also initially took care of the accounts for the senior traders as well as executing customer business further out the curves. Within two years, I was running the global crude oil derivative book.

Brent and WTI

Brent crude is a light, intermediate-grade oil sourced from the North Sea in the United Kingdom. Brent crude futures are traded on the Intercontinental Exchange (ICE) and New York Mercantile Exchange (NYMEX).

WTI or West Texas Intermediate crude is a light, sweet-grade crude oil produced in Oklahoma and Texas and traded on the NYMEX. WTI typically trades at a premium to Brent crude.

That was quite a quick transition from leaving university to retail brokerage to running a global book at a major trading house.

I became one of the prominent traders in the market at a young age. At the time, there weren't many players of any size in the forward energy markets so margins in the OTC market were pretty high. Not many people would quote the size and tenor that I would, so I quickly became the go-to guy for customers looking to put on large trades or hedges. It wasn't until the mid-1990s that a large number of banks came into the commodity markets, which drove margins through the floor and erased the easy profitability from the customer side.

Did the customer flow help your prop trading?

In part, but more importantly, it gave me a tremendous early education in managing risk and learning what drives the longer dated pricing of commodity curves. The customer book was primarily comprised of corporate hedging activity at least six months forward, whereas my prop trading at the time was mostly focused in the front months. However, as a result of running the customer book and providing forward delta hedges for the options book, I would end up with large longer dated spread positions, since one customer would need to hedge 6 months forward, another 15 months forward, and another five years forward. This mismatch in client requirements meant that I had to take in long-dated spread positions, where I felt comfortable being long or short the curve, which I then had to try to exit with some margin left over. The forward markets had virtually no liquidity at that time, so sometimes I had to warehouse long-dated curve risk for weeks or months before being able to liquidate it. Today, the markets are so liquid all the way along the curve that one would be able to offset similar positions in minutes or hours. The majority of my time was spent prop trading in the spot and front months of the energy markets, although the customer business brought in substantial, steady, low-risk income.

How were you able to take strong views and run such large positions in global energy markets at such a young age?

When you focus on one market, you spend your entire day speaking to all the dealers, brokers, and hedgers in that market, and very soon you begin to build a picture of the flow in all the various component parts of the curve. Watching the data, positioning, and news, second by second, for just that one market, day in and day out, gives you the ability to anticipate market pricing and volatility. You literally start to live and breathe that market.

Being so focused on only energy at that point in my career helped tremendously for my current role as a hedge fund manager with a much broader investment mandate, because I was able to focus and become an expert in the most complicated and diverse area of commodity trading. The energy markets are extremely complex, comprising many different grades of crude and a number of different oil products, which later made the analysis of other commodity markets more straightforward by comparison. Also, trading derivatives at such an early stage, particularly long-dated derivatives, taught me a great deal about the pricing structure of commodity markets. Derivatives in the commodity markets were very new when I started, which forced me to be creative in my analyses and positioning. Having said that, this doesn't make other areas of commodities, such as metals and agriculture, easier to trade, it just makes them easier to follow, as there are fewer inputs to the analysis. Also, economic, political, and particularly weather events are always a wild card when it comes to the trading of any commodity. However, the main point is that it's a lot easier to analyze and trade soybeans after having traded energy, than trying to trade energy with experience only in the soybean markets.

What drives your view on commodities?

All market prices are a function of supply and demand. Exogenous events aside, with most commodities the supply side of the equation tends to trend, especially in energy and metals. In most cases, supply up to 18 months forward is relatively predictable. However, it's the demand side of the equation that has proven to be volatile in the last 20 years, so our forward macro outlook drives our demand assumptions. Understanding the demand side requires an enormous amount of micro analysis of global industrial production (IP) and global GDP, as well as having a view on the potential for U.S. dollar movements. GDP, IP, and the dollar have seen extraordinary moves of late. When structuring a trade in an industrial commodity, you can make reasonable assumptions on supply, but the economic cycles have been so violent in recent years that they have been an even bigger driver of commodity prices than the underlying supply cycles for example.

The volatility during 2008 and 2009 reminds me of the 1997–1998 period (see Figure 8.1). Back then, the Asia crisis and the collapse of emerging markets caused a massive sell-off in commodities. It looked like the commodity super cycle that people *even back then* had been talking about for so long was off the table. It looked as if it was going to take years for some of the emerging market countries to pay back the IMF for their loans, creating a strong headwind to a commodity price recovery and an environment of extreme bearishness. What transpired instead was commodity markets, and particularly oil, bounced back very quickly on the heels of a quicker and stronger than expected global recovery, largely

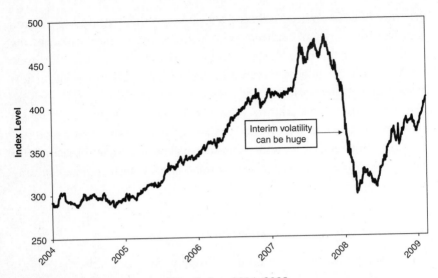

Figure 8.1 CRB Commodities Index, 2004–2009
SOURCE: Bloomberg.

created by a reduction in interest rates by global central banks. A similar story played out following the Nasdaq crash and September 11.

What is interesting about the macro picture in the current environment is how emerging markets are driving an exponential shift in the demand for commodities. Granted this is coming off a very low base in some emerging market countries, but this phenomenon is now having a huge impact on the demand balances of virtually all commodities. In the G7 countries, on the other hand, commodity demand is trailing off after a decade of strong growth, which in hindsight was fueled by overly easy credit expansion. In fact, due to the more efficient use of natural resources and the mature nature of several of these economies, some areas of their commodity demand are actually in structural decline. The cross currents of these two opposing forces—slowing G7 demand coupled with strongly expanding emerging market demand—is creating massive volatility, which means understanding the macroeconomic picture is more important than ever.

Does the heightened volatility force you to be more tactical in your trading?

Although we are definitely more tactical in this environment, we are also confident that we are in the midst of an ongoing super cycle in commodity demand, so we tend to be long biased (see box). Confirmation of the super cycle can be seen in the strong upward trajectory of demand for home wares and autos in emerging markets. Emerging markets have an enormous and ever-expanding middle-class population that is striving to better its standard of living, which is the overreaching trend dominating commodity markets. Demand is going to grow exponentially from emerging markets, but against this trend you can still have cyclical troughs. Anytime that demand drops suddenly and initiates a sharp rise in storage levels, commodity prices crash. As a trader or a portfolio manager you have to retain a reasonable level of flexibility in your view and have the ability to be extremely nimble in your trading, so as to avoid or even benefit from those movements. Even though we are in a general strong upward trend in commodity prices, interim volatility can be huge, as we saw in the second half of 2008.

Commodity Super Cycle

The *Commodity Super Cycle* is an economic theory based on demographic trends and the resultant effect on demand for basic commodities. According to the theory, it is generally believed that by 2050, the global population is expected to number 9.1 billion people, assuming declining fertility rates. Finite raw materials, coupled with an increasing population base, will translate into higher prices. Over the past decade, Jim Rogers (*Inside the House of Money*, Chapter 11) has become one of the best-known advocates of the "Commodity Super Cycle" theory. According to Rogers, the twentieth century has seen three secular bull markets in commodities (1906–1923, 1933–1955, 1968–1982). Each of those secular bull markets lasted a little more than 17 years. Rogers believes that we are currently in the middle of another secular bull market in commodities, which began in 1999.

When did the commodity super cycle start?

From a macro perspective, the underlying effects started showing up as far back as the 1980s, but because there was so much spare capacity in the production of most commodities, and because emerging market demand was increasing from such a low base, the larger trends went unnoticed for a long time. Technological advances in the production of many commodities have also helped prevent prices from spiking out of control. Extraction processes in mining and drilling have made huge advances in the past 20 years. In agriculture, the use of genetically modified seeds in the U.S. in the late 1990s and early 2000s meaningfully expanded crop yields per acre in a way that few people predicted. More recently, new techniques in extracting natural gas in the U.S. have increased gas production in a way that many would have considered unlikely just a few years ago. Prices of some of the agricultural commodities have not moved that much over the last 30 or 40 years because the agricultural markets have done a good job of producing extra supply through expanded global acreage and better farming technology. These advances created extra supply which offset an upward sloping demand curve. This balance may well be shifting into a more bullish phase for several agricultural commodities, particularly those which emerging markets are in short supply and those now being used to produce bio-fuels. Soybeans fall into both of these categories so I am extremely bullish soybean prices for the foreseeable future. (See Figure 8.2–8.5.)

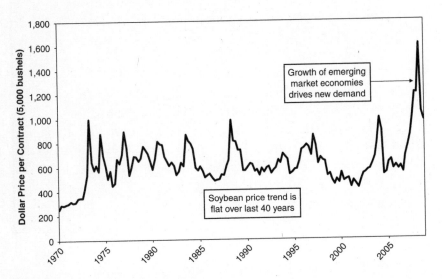

Figure 8.2   Soybeans, 1970–2009
SOURCE: Bloomberg.

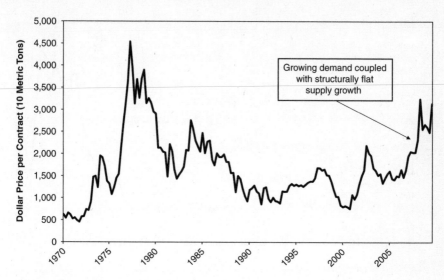

Figure 8.3 Cocoa, 1970–2009
SOURCE: Bloomberg.

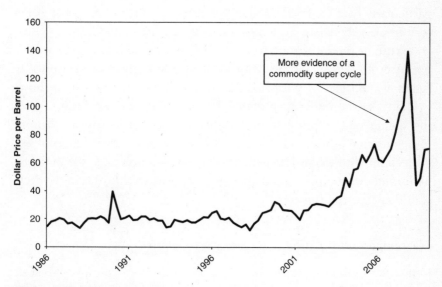

Figure 8.4 Oil, 1986–2009
SOURCE: Bloomberg.

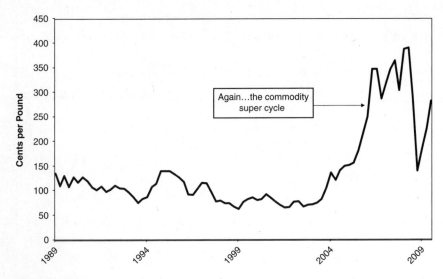

Figure 8.5   Copper, 1989–2009
SOURCE: Bloomberg.

As emerging markets get richer and a growing middle class acquires a taste for richer foods, commodities like cocoa will rise in price. This is particularly true for cocoa, as supply seems to be structurally flat going forward, largely due to the constrained geographical conditions in which cocoa can be produced and the age of the trees in the Ivory Coast, which produces 40 percent of the world's cocoa. Meanwhile, crude oil today trades at multiples of what it did a decade ago, which not only shows evidence of the underlying demand super cycle but also demonstrates the higher cost of production created from having to source oil from more difficult locations or using more expensive extraction processes just to keep up with expanding demand. In general, looking at the numbers behind demographics, population growth, and wealth, the super cycle is difficult to argue against.

How important is China to the super cycle thesis?

China is absolutely critical, and car data alone paints the picture of its importance. It is estimated that there are currently around 30 million passenger vehicles on the road in China, which has a population of approximately 1.35 billion. The passenger component of vehicle sales is running at over 800,000 per month, sales have been growing at around 40–90 percent year over year, and vehicle sales overall (including light trucks, etc.) are growing at about 25 percent year over year. Compare this to the U.S., where 240 million passenger cars service a population of about 300 million people and you can get a sense for the extraordinary growth potential of vehicle sales in China, which translates into extraordinary demand for motor fuels and metals.

Although the gigantic population situation in India is similar, they are much further behind China with respect to infrastructure and consumer income. But, on current trends, it is estimated that India's population will overtake China's in around 25 years. Interestingly, the new Tata car, which sells for US$2,500 in its lowest specification form in India, had an initial production run of 100,000 units, but orders were for over twice that amount. From an infrastructure expansion standpoint, India will be over the next 30 years what China has been over the last 30.

The bearish view on commodities and emerging markets suggests that it will take a long time for large portions of the population in China and India to be able to afford cars. The bears point to GDP per capita, which in China is around US$4,000 and in India around US$1,200, which compares to the U.S. at about US$47,000. Hidden in these figures, however, is the fact that there are around 100 million Chinese whose annual income is over US$10,000. That equates to 100 million people who can almost certainly afford a cheap car or a mortgage, especially as consumer financing becomes more widespread. There is also enormous pent-up savings in most emerging market countries, particularly China, where it is often the case that several family members will group years of savings together to buy a house for a young couple. The one-child policy also leads in many cases to two sets of parents plus two individuals being responsible for buying one new family home, thus making seemingly expensive properties, much more affordable.

Interestingly, in nominal terms the reduction in U.S. retail sales since the beginning of the recent crisis has been more than offset by the rise in retail sales in China alone, a reassuring statistic for those that believe that growth in the wider global economy is decoupling from that of the mature G3. This is consistent with the nature of human economic history going back 3,000 years.

Do you spend much time thinking about the second-order effects of such strong auto sales? For example, the effect of all that incremental CO_2 on global warming and the impact of pollution on crop yields. Or the circularity of more drivers buying more fuel pushing up prices and ultimately pricing future drivers out of the market.

Absolutely. Oil, like all commodities, will rise to a point where the price reduces demand and drives technological changes. Such inflection points are an integral part of our analyses. We are currently a long way off from any such inflection point, but the additional drive to move away from hydrocarbons for environmental reasons has become an additional factor in our long-term predictions for oil demand.

There is a strong political impetus in the world to address carbon emissions and political efforts have been aggressively expanded in the last few years with the carbon trading system in Europe and emissions trading in the U.S. In recent years there have been a large number of clean-energy companies listing on the global stock exchanges, and while some of these may have taken a form similar to the 1990s tech boom/bust, the essence of their eco-friendly technological developments will continue. There is a real incentive right now to make money by improving the world through developing new, cleaner, and cheaper ways to produce energy. We think about that a lot not only because we want our children to live in a better world, but also because these developments are very relevant to the price of commodities. For example, the moves toward greater engine fuel efficiency and increased use of bio-fuels leads us to believe that gasoline demand in the U.S. has already peaked.

Do you travel to China to try to get a sense of what is going on there?

Since China is essentially a continent in itself, it is quite difficult for me personally to gauge what is going on there after spending a week visiting two or three different cities, although I do make one or two fact-finding trips a year to one region or another, be it China or elsewhere. We have an analyst on our team who is from Shanghai and focuses full time on the Chinese macro picture. She also visits there frequently and spends considerable time researching Chinese government Web sites, talking to businesses and people on the ground, all over the country. Her father runs a construction company in Shanghai and that has also proven to be a good primary source of information. Meanwhile, most of the major banks now have offices in China so the flow of information from there is greatly increasing all the time. Having said all this, we do intend to open an office in the Far East in the coming year, mainly to cover analysis of the Chinese and Indian economies, and their respective natural resource requirements.

Are the commodity markets manipulated by the Chinese government as the conspiracy theorists say?

The Chinese government does a good job of restocking when prices are low. They also appear to try to keep a lid on prices when things are getting frothy by releasing supply onto the market or by canceling purchase orders for cargoes of certain commodities at times when they know that it will have a bearish impact on market sentiment. For the most part they seem to manage their reserves reasonably well.

The collapse in commodity prices during the second half of 2008 was a major get out of jail free card for the Chinese government. During the summer of 2008, when agricultural prices were strong and the price of crude was approaching $150 a barrel, they were facing 8 percent inflation and were building out more storage capacity for their crude oil strategic reserve. They must have been quite distressed thinking about the prices they were going to be forced to pay to fill that reserve. So while 2008 was disastrous for Chinese exports, the silver lining for them was that they have been able to restock things such as copper, soybeans, and crude oil at levels they probably never thought they would see again. The Chinese authorities are clearly very nervous about commodity supply in general. You can see evidence of this not only in their recent restocking activities, but also in their buying up of various mining and energy companies as well as their extensive investment forays into politically challenging areas of the world such as Central Africa and some the more politically risky parts of the Middle East.

Do financial flows drive commodity prices?

Speculators or investors can drive prices for very short periods of time, but fundamentals always win out in the long run. Over the last seven years in particular, we have seen an influx of pension fund and other long-only money-buying commodities. Initially, these flows came into the market fairly predictably with bursts of buying at month-end or quarter-end, sometimes driving up market prices for these brief periods. But commodity prices ultimately trade to their fundamental value, regardless of the prevailing money flows, and long-only investors have become a bit more subtle in recent years as to how they execute their commodity length. In fact, despite the massive amount of length held in the commodity markets during the summer 2008 peak, and despite the commodity markets being hit by the largest drop in global GDP and IP since World War II, the fall in commodity prices that ensued was actually incredibly orderly. And while the fall was understandably large given the sudden and extreme shift in fundamentals and positioning, there was never a panic in any of the commodity markets, and they continued to trade in a very robust fashion compared to many other financial markets. Commodity markets have just gone through the ultimate stress test, and one can safely say that they have traded extremely well. Also, it is interesting to note that during the rally up to mid-2008, many commodities that were not investible by nonspecialists, such as coal, steel, and many of the minor metals, also rallied at least as much as the other commodities that the pension funds and speculators were supposedly driving higher.

It is important to recognize that pension funds and other real money investors have a real economic reason to invest in commodities. A pension fund's main risk is inflation because it debases the value of the long-term money their pensioners receive when they retire. The pension fund manager has to make sure that his retirees can afford clothes, put food on the table, heat their homes and fuel their cars. That is a pension fund manager's job and it's a monstrously difficult one. The need for pension funds to hedge against rising food and energy prices is therefore clear and I believe the financial demand for commodities will continue if for no other reason.

What's your view on inflation going forward?

Core inflation is clearly contained in the medium-term because of the predominant output gap and the significant spare capacity characterizing labor markets. Growth will continue to be challenged in the mature markets such as the UK, Japan, and the U.S., so any inflation will be driven by emerging markets and will be more related to headline inflation than core (see box). The numbers behind car demand in China are an obvious indicator. I hate to keep mentioning it, but this really symbolizes what is going on in the world. It is a trend that can be extrapolated into many other emerging market countries, whether they are of similar proportions such as India or smaller but still very large places like Russia and Brazil. Ultimately, the long-term picture is inflationary, driven by commodity prices and growth as people grow wealthier and buy more homes, autos, and household and lifestyle goods. Given the low growth in the G7, this may well lead to a more stagflationary environment, particularly for those with a substantial trade deficit and a weakening currency as import-led inflation will be greatly aggravated. Add to that all the printing of money by the G7 governments and you could see a substantial stagflationary problem for the mature economies.

Headline versus Core Inflation

Headline inflation, or the Consumer Price Index (CPI) released monthly by the Bureau of Labor Statistics (BLS), calculates the cost to purchase a fixed basket of goods as a way of monitoring inflation in the U.S. economy. The CPI components are: (1) food and beverages; (2) housing; (3) apparel; (4) transportation; (5) medical care; (6) recreation; (7) education and communication; and (8) other goods and services. CPI uses a base year and indexes current year prices to the base year's values. This measure is also known as "top-line inflation."

Core inflation is a measure of inflation that excludes certain items from the CPI measure that face volatile price movements. Core inflation eliminates products that can have temporary price shocks because these shocks can diverge from the overall trend of inflation and give a false measure of inflation. Core inflation is most often calculated by taking the CPI and excluding certain items from the index, usually energy and food products.

SOURCE: U.S. Bureau of Labor Statistics.

Does it makes sense for real money investors to get exposure to
commodities via an index?

The problem with commodity indices is that when commodity markets are well supplied, they can be very negative yielding (see box). If you own a commodity, you pay to insure, store, and secure it. Then you pay to ship it so you can move it to a location where it might be sold more easily. Owning a commodity costs money, which is exactly the opposite of keeping money in equities, bonds, a bank deposit, or property, where you get paid a dividend or receive a yield. An investment vehicle that optimizes for roll yields would be a better investment, such as an enhanced index that is not just long the front contract. Better still, investing with active commodity managers who tend to hold a long bias but actively manage downside risk is the most attractive option.

Roll Yield, Backwardation and Contango

Roll Yield—The amount of return generated in a backwardated futures market that is achieved by rolling a futures contract into the higher-priced spot market. As time passes and the futures contract appreciates, traders will take profits in the near-dated positions and purchase less-expensive futures contracts. Backwardation allows the trader to consistently profit from the rise in a futures' price as it nears expiration or the spot price. The biggest risk to this strategy is that the market will shift, resulting in a futures price above the spot price, a condition is known as *contango*.

Backwardation—The market condition in which the spot price is above the futures price. This is also known an inverted sloping forward curve. This is said to occur due to the convenience yield being higher than the prevailing risk-free rate. The phenomenon of backwardation in commodity futures contracts was originally called "normal backwardation" by economist John Maynard Keynes. Keynes believed that commodity producers are more prone to hedge their price risk than consumers, creating additional demand to sell forward commodities.

Contango—The market condition in which the futures price is above the spot price. As time passes, the futures price will decline to the spot price before the delivery date. Contango describes an upward-sloping, or normal, forward curve.

But is an active commodity manager a good hedge to inflation?

If you are invested with a commodity manager who turns bearish halfway through a bull cycle, the result will be disappointing. Losing money when inflation is soaring could doubly hurt, so manager selection is key. That being said, if the goal is simply to hedge against inflation, then I would advocate a mix of active management and enhanced indexing.

In the same vein, does it make sense for real money investors to gain exposure to commodities via commodity equities?

Buying an equity stake in a commodity producer will not properly hedge against headline inflation because you then become reliant on one of the contributory problems of inflation: supply. Buying a mine or an oil company, which subsequently has supply issues or even management issues could simultaneously drive down the stock price and drive up the commodity price. So, while there is strategic merit to having part of your portfolio invested in the major oil companies and the miners, it is not a clean inflation hedge. Thus, the decision about which companies to buy is again critical. Many of the major oil companies, for example, are experiencing long-term difficulties in identifying new areas of exploration because the producing countries are exploiting the new fields themselves through their own national oil companies. If you look at the production profiles of the major old-fashioned "seven sisters"–type companies, several of them are actually pretty flat and some are even in decline (see box on page 222).

Seven Sisters

The Seven Sisters of the petroleum industry is a term coined by Enrico Mattei, an Italian entrepreneur, which refers to seven oil companies that dominated mid-twentieth-century oil production, refining, and distribution. On March 11, 2007, the *Financial Times* identified the "New Seven Sisters," the most influential and mainly state-owned national oil and gas companies from countries outside the OECD. The terms "Big Oil" and "Super Major" are now often used to describe the biggest and richest nonstate owned companies: ExxonMobil, Shell, British Petroleum, Chevron, Total, and ConocoPhillips.

As an active commodity fund manager, how do you approach commodity markets?

We are fundamental traders and take directional views on various commodity markets. We structure the trades in our portfolio to have an asymmetric payout whereby there are a series of scenarios where the odds are in our favor. If you can consistently structure trades with a positive mathematical reward-versus-risk skew and combine that with a minimum 30 to 40 percent target rate of winning trades versus losers, this will translate over time into profitability without the need to be consistently correct on market predictions.

We use a lot of optionality when structuring our trades and are big buyers of volatility when we think it's cheap, allowing us to get that asymmetric payoff profile. The past five years have seen a lot of shocks in the commodities markets whereby prices moved to levels unimaginable to most. Using options in such an environment means that we put ourselves in a position to receive outsized returns relative to our risk. Option structures also allow us to ignore a lot of the noise in the price action. But reducing the noise through options is only part of the challenge; you still have to be right on the fundamentals. As fundamental traders we have a view that a certain market might go from "A" to "B" over a period of six months or a year or longer. But we never really know the trajectory that price action will take on its way from "A" to "B," nor exactly when "B" will be achieved. So using options gives us longevity as long as we are careful about our entry point from a volatility/price perspective. You can use options to produce great leverage with limited risk, to buy time and eradicate market noise, and to help manage positions and portfolio risk, but if you are not right about the fundamentals a reasonable amount of the time, option price decay will bleed you to death. Strong fundamental research allows a balance between the option premia spent on the trades and the probability that the trades end up being right.

So you only have to be right 30 to 40 percent of the time to make money as long as you structure good asymmetric bets?

At my last company, I compounded at almost 40 percent annually over nearly four years and statistically slightly more than half of the trades made money. At my current fund we've been right around 60 percent of the time and returns have continued to be consistently high. The danger of investing with us is that if our hit rate goes down to, say, 25 percent and the markets are not moving enough to provide those 5-to-1 winners from time to time, then we'll be lucky to be flat on the year. Like any strategy, if you rarely make a winning trade, you'll lose money ad infinitum unless you have one major blowout trade that makes up for everything else, but that is not our style as we tend to run a very diverse portfolio made up of 20 to 30 positions. Over time, we've proven that we can make very good returns while only being right a little more than half the time.

Trade design, portfolio diversity, and risk management are just as important as being right about the markets, if not more so. At least that is how it has worked for me. Having said that, the commodities markets have been conducive to this approach in recent years. Still, I believe the key is running a fairly diverse portfolio of good risk-versus-reward trades coupled with very careful risk management on a portfolio level. It is important to have limits on VaR (value at risk), on margin-to-equity, portfolio P&L volatility, sector risk, individual position risk, vega, theta and premium spent if you trade a lot of options. It is also extremely important to deliver the portfolio when you're losing money in order to preserve capital.

What's the difference between being a prop trader and being a hedge fund manager?

A prop trader is someone who speculates by taking a lot of risk, without necessarily thinking about capital preservation as rule number one. A prop trader at a bank is incentivized to take the most risk possible while utilizing limited amounts of cash. If a prop trader has a very bad year and loses a lot of money, they may well retain their job and start the subsequent year in the same position as if they had had a good year. A fund manager doesn't have the luxury of starting with a fresh track record every 12 months and therefore has to be consistently profitable. In actuality, a fund manager is trying to create a relatively steady return stream with moderate drawdowns, where the expectation of returns is a lot less and the preservation of capital is paramount. We are actually competing with the yields of other assets and trying to beat those consistently on a risk-adjusted basis. A fund manager should be focused on continually knocking up against the high-water mark, so it is crucial to always run tight risk management to avoid straying too far from this barrier. There is little incentive for a fund manager who intends to be in the business for many years to try to hit the ball out of the park and have a 200 percent year. It's a very different risk profile when compared with a prop trader.

Do you prefer trading for a prop shop or running your own fund?

Combining strong fundamental research with consistently favorable risk/reward trade structures is a more compelling model to me than arbitraging, swinging for the fences, spending all day trading one group of markets, and/or pricing customer business. The first part of my approach is getting the fundamentals right and understanding the supply and demand dynamics of the market. The second part is structuring trades in such a way that I limit my downside and capture any upside skew. On this latter point, understanding the probability of a complex stream of possible outcomes is key. We are in the game of trying to predict the future, but because the future is inherently unpredictable, capital preservation is the most important. In commodities, there are too many moving parts between supply, demand, weather, politics, U.S. dollar, and other factors. I have to be an economist, a foreign exchange analyst, a commodities expert, and a meteorologist. But first and foremost, I have to be a risk manager in a portfolio context. Fund management is the ultimate test of a trader's ability.

Are there any lessons from your career where you learned the importance of risk management?

My first important lesson was to never discuss gains and losses and absolute cash amounts, but rather to speak in percentage terms. Percentages are all that matter, which is another key difference between a fund manager and a prop trader. I've also learned never to focus on a maximum drawdown limit but rather to target a drawdown level much smaller than the stipulated level. I then try to think about how many positions I have in the portfolio and what my risk factors are, always measuring these against a fraction of this drawdown limit.

I also work very hard to take the emotion out of trading, instead focusing on doing my best on the research side and carefully managing the risk side. Emotionally living and breathing every move in the markets can be a distraction from my main job, which is one of hard analysis and trying to figure out where markets are heading over an extended period of time. It is a marathon, not a 100-meter race. If things are going well, I don't get excited because a drawdown could be around the corner. Equally, if things are going poorly, I'll be disappointed, but I'll try not to beat myself up too much, as every fund manager is in the business of predicting the future and you can't be expected to get it right all the time.

What mistakes or risk management failings have you seen in other traders or fund managers?

A sign of a weak manager is one that describes their portfolio by saying that there are certain trades they really like and others that are more marginal. I have never understood that. Why would you ever put a marginal trade in your portfolio? Over time I have learned that it doesn't make sense to get overly positioned in any one trade. I normally have over 20 positions in my portfolio at any one time with none being particularly larger than the other on a daily volatility and liquidity-adjusted basis. The only exception to this is when an option position has run deep into the money and premium risk rises accordingly for that position.

Oversizing positions is what kills most traders. It is so easy to get excited about a theme that in actuality may take months or years to play out. I've seen traders have perfectly good fundamental views, get extremely excited, put on a big trade that requires a tight stop, and then get stopped-out of the position almost immediately. It's absurd, but excitement and thoughtlessness kill 80 percent of would-be traders who never end up getting off the ground. Oversizing a position versus the expected longevity of a theme prohibits traders from making money even when they might have otherwise had perfectly reasonable assumptions about the markets.

Does using options help mitigate these issues?

Options help with sizing issues, allowing me to remain with a position during periods of noisy price-action where short-term moves are disconnected from the long-term fundamental drivers of the market. Options aid risk management greatly by helping to reduce the timing of position entry as well as helping to define the risk-versus-reward characteristics of the trade.

What is liquidity like in the commodity options markets?

We have been positively surprised at the day-to-day liquidity in the options markets, even through the commodity crash of 2008. Although overall open interest has dropped when compared with early 2008, daily volumes in commodities have remained quite high. As buyers of options, our main concern is capturing profit or hedging them should they run into the money. If an option runs very deep into the money, the ability to delta hedge the option is often more important than the liquidity of getting out of it, so we always make sure that there is enough liquidity to be able to trade around a position. Also, because we are always long options and tend to be directionally long, our potential profit is unlimited and can grow exponentially during times when both price and volatility explode higher. The traders who are short options in this situation usually panic and try to source the traders that are long the options to get them out. These situations provide nice opportunities to liquidate or reduce positions without the need to delta hedge.

Is it easier to be long commodities than short?

In recent years, it has generally been easier to be long because emerging market growth and dollar weakness have driven many commodity prices to new highs. So, for the foreseeable future, macro forces greatly favor being long commodities. From a trading perspective, I personally find it just as easy to be bullish as bearish, and going long or short depending on the prevailing macro environment and micro fundamentals of each commodity that we trade. In fact, my two most profitable years as a fund manager were 1998 and 2008, which were years when commodities crashed.

How many markets do you cover?

We cover about 50 different commodity markets, including energy, base metals, precious metals, soft commodities, and agriculture; but there are synergies across many of these. Using energy as an example, we look at gasoline, gas oil, heating oil, fuel oil, jet fuel, WTI crude, North Sea crude, Dubai crude, natural gas, and coal. We also look at different grades of crude oil and different grades of the underlying crude oil products. Then we look at spread relationships such as gasoline in the Gulf Coast versus gasoline in Europe or coal in South Africa versus coal in Australia. In the agricultural space for example, we trade European wheat, Minneapolis wheat, Kansas wheat, and Chicago wheat. Although these are really four distinct markets and four different types of wheat, there are obvious synergies and interrelationships.

In addition, we also have a small weighting in the portfolio to trade currencies and interest rates. Sometimes we use this area of the portfolio to hedge macroeconomic or currency exposure in the commodity portfolio; and sometimes we use it to take risk. We tend to be more active in the currencies of countries that have a large commodity component to their trade balance, such as Brazil, Russia, Norway, South Africa, Australia, etc.

We hope and expect that there will be new tradable commodity contracts in the future. Some of the contracts on the Shanghai futures exchange are becoming very liquid but are not easily traded without a presence in China. Some of the Brazilian agricultural contracts are also becoming more liquid, and we are monitoring these for opportunities. The commodity markets seem to be developing globally in a way that should attract more participants and more volume over time. On the flipside, there have been contracts launched over the last 20 years in various parts of the world that have ceased to trade. But overall there is an increased awareness about commodity trading around the world today, which should fuel the development of the markets in Asia, South America, and elsewhere, creating all sorts of new trading opportunities.

What factors are specific to the commodity markets that do not come into play in other markets such as equities and fixed income?

The price curves are what really differentiate commodities from other markets such as interest rates and foreign exchange. Commodity curves are often negative yielding and can experience violent, whippy reactions more regularly than other markets. Because of this whippiness, we often try to avoid the front months of commodities, which are often driven by short-term physical factors. We don't participate in the physical markets so do not have an edge there but we can make just as reasonable assumptions as anybody else on where prices might be in six months and beyond. We build out our portfolio by trying to take advantage of our analysis of medium- to long-term fundamentals rather than predicting short-term physical market movements, preferring to structure our trades further out the curve.

Can you explain how physical commodities players have an advantage in the front contracts?

If you are one of the major storers or shippers of a commodity that is deliverable into the futures contract, then you have an advantage because you have firsthand knowledge of the quantity stored, the locations of storage, and the quality of the commodity. You already know whether you are going to take some of the commodity off the exchange or if you are going to make a delivery into it, so you know how much the stock level is going to change from your activity. Physical participants are also much more focused day-to-day on where the cash is actually trading versus the exchange traded future.

To take an extreme example, there have been circumstances in the past where a small number of players have controlled a significant portion of the stock in a particular futures contract whereby they were able to control the front spreads and even the overall commodity price for brief periods. If prices move against the way the rest of the market is positioned or if that commodity is in short supply, a lot of money can be made controlling that front spread or even the entire price via a classic commodity squeeze. However, greater regulatory oversight has all but killed this form of extreme activity in commodities trading, and most attempts to squeeze commodity markets in the past didn't actually work anyway.

Given that we sit in an office away from the exchanges and cover a broad number of markets with a limited amount of intraday physical information flow, we don't really have any edge in trying to make a call on where the front spreads are going to trade, so we stay out of that part of the market. Trading physical commodities also limits your flexibility and liquidity, and as a fund management company, we prefer to keep our positioning as liquid as possible.

Why are commodity curves more susceptible to violent swings than, say, yield curves?

Fairly small differences in the daily global supply of a commodity can have quite a large effect on the open stock on the exchange, which can create a major change in the overall forward curve. These moves often appear in the front months, which can then cause a reaction in the front spreads, causing a reverberation down the curve. However, movements tend to diminish further out the curve such that after two or three years the movements might be negligible. Thus, the curves can swing around quite a bit from steep backwardation into big contango or vice versa if there is a meaningful structural shift in the supply/demand situation of that commodity.

Given your super cycle view, what would be your favorite trade for the next 10 years?

Long crude oil and soybeans. China and India are both short of physical crude oil and their imports are only heading higher over time. Greater engine efficiencies and greater use of new automotive fuel technologies, including bio-fuels and electric and hybrid cars, will still not be enough to offset their increasing needs. Outside of pure commodities, I would buy the Russian ruble as a bullish play on energy and metals prices, which will lead to an improvement in the Russian economy and trade balance and ultimately to a virtuous cycle over time.

What about on the short side?

I can't think of a single commodity that I would want to be short with a long-term time horizon. I would be very cautious about UK commercial property priced in sterling. I'm very bearish the pound, which has a massive problem long term. The UK is running out of North Sea oil and natural gas, and its manufacturing has been moving east for 30 years. Heavy industries such as oil refining, steel refining, and car manufacturing are all also moving east. The City of London and services sector have been the main drivers for maintaining a reasonable current account balance against a big trade deficit in the UK in recent years. But now, with heightened regulation, more restrictions on the banks, and rising taxes, headwinds will be brought to the financial and services sectors of the economy. The UK is a very mature economy with high levels of home, vehicle, and household goods ownership and a leveraged consumer, which will make growth challenging at the best of times. The UK current account will continue to deteriorate significantly over time, which will greatly weaken the pound and probably force sterling into the euro currency at some point in the future. That is, assuming that the euro remains in its present form as the world's second reserve currency.

What was the worst trade of your career?

The worst trade of my career was not a commodity trade but an equity trade. I lost a lot of money shorting the NASDAQ during the second half of 1999. This was at a time when I drifted away from purely trading commodities into trading more financial futures. The lesson learned from that is never short a market that's skyrocketing because, even if you think it's doing something completely and utterly irrational, financial flows can keep it behaving irrationally for some time for no other reason than just pure momentum. Risk management is often learned the hard way, and this was one of those occasions. I finally stopped out of my short and gave up when the AOL–Time Warner deal happened. The fact that emerging tech companies like AOL could merge with an established old world company like Time Warner made me reconsider my bearish

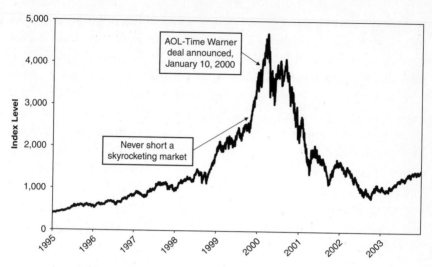

Figure 8.6   NASDAQ Index, 1995–2003
SOURCE: Bloomberg.

view. I thought, wow, maybe the NASDAQ can go to 7,000 or 10,000 if transactions like this become a new trend. Of course, that deal turned out to be close to the top of the market. (See Figure 8.6.)

I lost about a third of my capital that year on a broad range of trades, and it was my first and only large annual loss. I cut risk and was flat the next year. I had been compounding at 50 percent per annum for several years prior and then had drifted into trading broader financial markets, branching out from my more narrow commodity focus. Looking back, the bigger picture issue was that I had grown a bit overconfident because of my run of strong returns. Of course, the markets tend to have a habit of humbling you very badly. When the day comes in your career where you think, "I'm really good at this," you are clearly in trouble. That's one reason to think twice before investing a lot of money with someone that has never had a significant drawdown. Despite having fantastic returns in previous years including making over 100 percent in 1998, that drawdown caused a significant setback in my career.

What was your worst commodity trade?

My worst commodity trade was also in 1999, so it was a bad year across the board. In 1998, I shorted oil from $23 down to $11 and made a killing. I was playing for a big macro downturn during 1998 and had many fixed income, currency, and commodity positions to reflect this view. I nailed it when LTCM and Russia went bust and covered everything pretty well at the beginning of 1999 when I thought that things had gone down about as far as they could. I thought that it would take years for some of the emerging market countries to recover, and I never really believed in the meteoric rise of the NASDAQ. So, after watching a relief rally from the sidelines at the beginning of 1999, I put my bearish macro bets back on, which proved way too premature. The current macro environment feels similar to 1999; but this time I am not betting against the bounce because the super cycle and the growth from emerging markets are just too strong with no signs of slowing. There was evidence of the super cycle back in the 1990s, but today we know for sure it is here.

What is your view of the hedge fund money management business over the next 5 to 10 years?

Hedge funds will remain a stable and necessary part of the financial system and assets will continue to accumulate gradually. The industry started to look overinvested in 2007 with large amounts of capital chasing marginal strategies and managers, but the recent crisis has taken the bubble elements out of the industry for now. Weaker managers are gone and investors are focusing on a smaller number of better managers. For the most part, hedge funds held up very well through the crisis. Minus a $65 billion Ponzi scheme masquerading as a hedge fund, there weren't any major hedge fund blow ups of note. You cannot say that about the banks or even the governments that are supposed to be monitoring them. The hedge fund industry can say to any critics that it actually aided liquidity during the recent crisis, helping to keep the whole financial system together in a way that the commercial banks certainly could not. In fact, the banks and lack of regulatory attention in the banking system is really what caused it.

Is what you do as a hedge fund manager transportable to the real money world?

Definitely. Most hedge fund managers are equipped with a broad range of investing skills and experience as a hedge fund manager enhances the way that one looks at risk. Many pension funds move glacially through the markets and while that is essentially their *raison d'être*, during times like financial crises, there should probably be a more tactical element to their management in order to hedge at least part of their long asset price risk, which hedge fund managers should be able to do.

What would you do if British Telecom's pension fund hired you to run it? How would you do it?

I would put together a strong investment team experienced at investing in some of the areas that aren't my strong suit. Running a large endowment or any real money operation of size requires a strong synergy between a good team of people with very diverse backgrounds, ranging from commercial and retail property, to private equity, to commodities and currencies, as well as equities and bonds. Then I would spend a lot of time defining our objectives: What are we trying to achieve? What are we indexing our returns against? Is it inflation? It is interest rates?

I would tend to have a significant weighting to long commodities because inflation is a pension fund's real risk. I would also have a heavy weighting to the emerging market economies because that is where the drivers of overall global growth will continue to be. A large weighting to property is also important, since it is a physical asset with a positive yield and if well chosen, it should hedge the rising costs of home ownership for the fund's pensioners over time.

Let's take another example. Assume a friend of yours sells his company for $10 billion and now has that balance in cash, which he wants you to manage. His goal is to stay wealthy, but have decent capital appreciation to fund an extravagant lifestyle while not getting destroyed by inflation.

Ah, the Holy Grail! There are ways of creating a reasonable yield from the corporate bond market but you need a very diversified portfolio to be able to withstand some bankruptcies over time. Again, a weighting to real assets would be important for the same reasons as a pension fund. To hedge against inflation and growth, I would put money into some combination of long commodity indices, active commodity and macro managers, and selective emerging market equities. Finally, I would have a large portion of it in cash at stable banks, spread across deposits with different maturities to generate some yield. In terms of what currency to denominate it in, I would keep it simple, placing most of it in the currency or currencies where the friend plans on spending his time.

How important is liquidity for a real money manager?

Liquidity is less important for real money managers than it is for hedge fund managers who must manage to a relatively flexible liquidity schedule offered to their underlying investors. That said, a good proportion of a real money portfolio should be kept relatively liquid in case an extreme event occurs such as the recent credit crisis. If the vast majority of your investments are completely illiquid, or you are so big in any market that you risk moving that market, the process of getting out of an investment can be painful. Because you are talking about managing other people's money over decades, you are going to have a major event in there at some point so the ability to preserve capital in such circumstances should be a priority. There are no easy answers. But given the massive cyclicality of the financial markets in the last decade, it's as if real money managers have to become traders themselves.

Chapter 9

The Commodity Investor

I met "The Commodity Investor" in his nondescript conference room in a nondescript office building on a nondescript street that could have been anywhere in the world. It was amidst this backdrop that he discussed his very descriptive view of global balance sheets across the commodity complexes.

Depth personified, the Commodity Investor can cite the numbers driving global supply and demand conditions across a dizzying array of commodities, synthesizing this data into coherent medium-term views backed by significant capital. What distinguishes him is not necessarily the depth of analysis, but his willingness to put on risk across the entire commodity supply chain, expressing themes in commodity and equity markets all over the world.

He is a long-term structural commodity bull; as such, his views on the inter-linkages between East and West, the true drivers of supply chains, and the importance of timing trades offer tremendous insights about not only the various commodity complexes he trades, but also other asset classes, politics, policy, and higher-level, fast-moving changes in the world order.

The Commodity Investor combines bottom-up, fundamental analysis with rigorous macro analysis, and he has worked with some of the best in the business for each of these disciplines. His biggest lesson from 2008 was that risk management is everything as it applies to both core portfolio risks, such as hedging the inherently large tail risks in commodity markets, and to more peripheral but no less important pitfalls, such as counterparty risk, which dominated last year.

He says that real money should be invested predominantly in commodities, and he worries about hyperinflation, stagflation, and a sovereign default in the G3.

How did you get into the business?

My earliest interest in markets was sparked by an after-school job during high school in a local brokerage office, where I did basic things such as filing Value Line investment surveys, studying charts, learning the basics of corporate financial metrics, and performing cut-and-paste type research for the head of the office. While cold calling to drum up interest in a financial planning seminar that the broker was about to hold, I learned a lesson about myself: I am not a particularly adept salesman.

In college in the late 1980s and early 1990s, I majored in monetary finance and international economics and minored in Japanese. During my summers, I worked in equity research in New York, landing a job in the asset management division of a sell-side shop upon graduation. I worked for a fantastic guy who became a mentor and spent all my time looking at company balance sheets and income statements—a very bottom-up, nonmacro approach where I learned the financial modeling process and tried to understand what drives stock prices.

After a few years, in a bout of exceptional good luck, I was approached by a large global macro hedge fund looking for someone to do cyclicals and commodities on the research side. They said, "Look, you're young and you're obviously hungry, so we'll give you a chance for six months. The worst thing that can happen is you lose your job, but someone else will hire you after this experience. If it works, however, we'll try for another six months." That job lasted for seven years.

Working at a hedge fund was a full-time job in every respect. I worked the grueling hours typical of an investment banking associate and had an extraordinary trial by fire learning how to integrate the macro context with the micro fundamentals, using equity, commodity, or other supply chains to assess which primary macro themes prevailed as market bias at the time. We used to call it "thinking about the matrix." It was just after the Asian crisis, which was an amazing period for macro; I was very fortunate to be working closely with some of the finest people in the business. It is where I began to learn that good macro investing is never easy, and is often brutal, but it can be simple—simple in the expression and implementation of a core theme. The firm had an extraordinary capability for taking a very simple theme and looking across the matrix of assets—equities, commodities, fixed income, currencies—to figure out where to get optimal leverage from the trade. The fund held very few positions and maintained that risk management meant you only play in real size when you have a triangulated conviction. The team not only had great skill for selecting trade entry and exit points, but they would also endure extended periods with no market exposure, which is a skill in itself.

What do you mean by triangulated conviction?

Before putting a trade on, we would triangulate our conviction level among the prevailing macro and micro factors, as well as across the various asset classes—commodities, equities, currencies, and bonds—and only really ever participate in a trade when we had very strong conviction on all fronts.

Do you have the same philosophy now?

To a significant degree, I still have the same philosophy, especially with regards to having no risk on when there is no triangulated conviction. I completely disagree with the notion that you have to be invested all the time because it gives you some kind of theoretical feel or pulse. In my current role, I go through periods with very little exposure until a thesis first starts to show confirmation signals and these signals are verifiable across the different supply chains. Only then do I increase risk levels. While this kind of patience is always important, it is crucial in the current environment.

How did you come to focus on commodities and commodity equities?

When I started out in this business, my first mentor was primarily a technology investor, but for some reason predicting product cycles was both challenging and unnatural for me. I found the macro and micro dynamic inherent in analyzing supply and demand in the context of business cycles extraordinarily interesting. And the modeling, from an intellectual standpoint, fit within a very straightforward framework. Dismantling the component parts of a commodity process—from upstream to downstream—was pretty exciting.

Can your process be modeled?

My overall process cannot be modeled in the strictest sense. The process of trying to ascertain the macro themes involves a variety of inputs, both qualitative and quantitative. This makes modeling the macro "algorithm" more challenging. However, we adhere to a very strict and logical process of modeling commodity market variables and the dynamics of equity supply chains. So the heavy modeling process really gets underway once the primary macro themes are determined. It is more a business process with a specific investment discipline and framework for assessing the fundamentals that drive our markets. Where many people think commodities have discrete supply and demand components, we have always tried to look at supply in the context of demand. The real goal is to figure out when a market will break out of the range of a balanced convenience yield for a given product, where a "convenience yield" is the benefit or detriment that accrues to the holder of a physical commodity as a function of relative inventory levels (see box on page 239).

If I told you that crude oil inventory was a hundred million barrels, this number is meaningless without a demand context—what is demand growth: One percent? Three percent? Five percent? The methodology of putting supply in a demand context is essential when we think about stocks-to-use curves and convenience yields, and this really applies to any market: coffee, crude, cocoa, sugar—any commodity market. Surpassing the threshold level of supply in the context of demand is when you get a nonlinear fundamental event: a squeeze, or an oversupply that leads to a collapse in the term structure of the forward curve. These types of extreme events or fat tails produce a markedly different outcome than when a market's convenience yield is in balance.

Convenience yield is the premium a buyer is willing to pay for prompt physical delivery of a commodity. Conditions of reasonably balanced supply tend to prevail in the commodity markets, and in such cases there is no convenience yield of any consequence. When you surpass a certain threshold, however, a nonlinear fundamental event will lead to a corresponding nonlinear price event, or a spike. Our process is figuring out how to narrow down the universe of 80 deep, liquid commodity products across energy, metals, agriculture, even freight, trying to first identify that threshold level and then determine when that level might be breached.

Convenience Yield

The *convenience yield* is the premium associated with holding an underlying product or physical good instead of a futures contract or other derivative product. The convenience yield is typically inversely related to the inventory levels of a particular commodity. In the event of a supply shock, the convenience yield will likely spike in anticipation of pressure on future inventory levels.

Do you try to capture a few events like this per year to make your annual returns?

Exactly. Out of the 80 products we trade, at any given time there are probably 5 that are close to this threshold, either from a bullish or bearish perspective. It then becomes a question of how long it will take for a shock to come to fruition and does this particular product fit within our macro view and qualitative feedback from meetings with company managements. This is why our commodity positions tend to be reasonably concentrated. There is a natural filtering mechanism for positions: Do they fit the macro view? Is there a stocks-to-use constraint? Does the qualitative information support it? Has it been discounted or not in the forward market?

We combine this fundamental but rather quantitative analysis with the more qualitative information we receive from meeting company managements, which is where the triangulation comes into play. This is where we combine the macro context with the micro fundamentals—it's an integrative process.

Traditionally, investors participate in commodities by taking either a macro approach or a micro approach, but rarely do they effectively combine the two. An example of the macro approach would be where a macro hedge fund sells copper on the view that global growth is slowing. Although this approach can work, it has its faults. For example, many years ago, everyone became wild about corn because of the whole ethanol story. The macro hedge fund community thought ethanol would usher in a structural demand change in the grain markets. But all these macro funds bought the front month corn contract, and corn turned out to have a bumper crop that year, causing prices to fall. Meanwhile, the ethanol story would take another one to two years to have any material impact on the supply and demand balances. So ethanol did induce a structural change in the corn market, but the micro did not justify a front-end position at the time ethanol was introduced. Combining the macro backdrop with micro expertise allows an investor to more optimally position a trade on the term structure of the forward curve. (See Figure 9.1.)

Conversely, being too micro-oriented has its downside as well. A year ago, many thought that copper was cheap based on stocks, use, and other micro fundamentals, but they missed the macroeconomic expertise that signaled a massive collapse in credit, which caused epic destocking. We believe that integrating the macro and micro is really the only way to go in the commodity markets.

Do you find that one tends to dominate—either the macro or the micro?

It is important to first try to ascertain the prevailing bias in the market then determine if the macro and micro are in concert or in conflict. Cyclical analysis is all about microeconomic imbalances, whereas

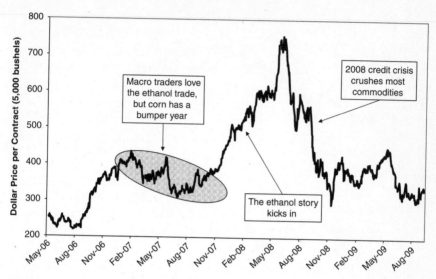

Figure 9.1 Corn Futures, 2006–2009
SOURCE: Bloomberg.

secular is all about macroeconomic imbalances. The prevailing bias will determine which is more important at any given time.

Looking back on 2008, the cyclical and secular were very much in alignment during the first half of the year. But then crude spiked, and the cyclical process of demand destruction, commodity reversion, then substitution or incremental supply, led to a negative trigger. Emerging market countries went from current account surpluses to current account deficits as U.S. demand collapsed with the destocking trend. The trend in the broader macro bias then turned negative quite quickly.

So you tend to go through these interesting cyclical and secular phases and at the extremes, people tend to confuse the two, mistaking cyclical for secular and vice versa. At the end of the first quarter of 2009, for example, most market participants extrapolated an Armageddon scenario indefinitely. Fear blinds market participants to the self-correcting mechanisms at the extremes.

Because such an important part of what we do is deciphering the cyclical and the secular, after extensive research, we recognized that what people perceived as a secular cost increase in oil in 2008 was actually a cyclical phenomenon. Strangely enough, a significant degree of the

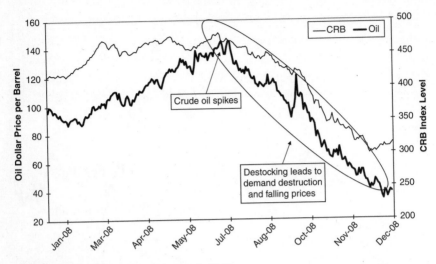

Figure 9.2   Commodities and Oil, 2008
SOURCE: Bloomberg.

cost of oil production has an oil price component as a key variable of
influence. As we became more concerned about demand destruction
and the possible price reversion that could result, it became clearer that
an oil price decline could have a pervasive effect across most of the key
commodity markets. We shorted commodities when many of our peers
remained long. (See Figure 9.2.)

This cyclical/secular, macro/micro thought process is very important. Sometimes one leads, sometimes the other leads. I would argue
that although we are in an important cyclical phase in the deleveraging process—restocking depleted inventories—the structural or secular
macro theme of deleveraging remains in place. Currently, the cyclical
and secular are in conflict, which is a much more challenging environment than when they are in concert. It is prudent to keep risk low at
these times.

Besides running low risk at times of uncertainty, how else do you
manage risk in your portfolio?

Our risk system has evolved quite dramatically in recent years. As a product of trial, error, and experience, we have built a scalable, custom risk
model that fits our investment methodology, essentially comprising both

the macro and micro components we discussed, as well as incorporating unique aspects in both commodity futures and commodity equities.

Most people have their biggest drawdowns, myself included, when cross-correlations are misunderstood. Whether the correlations are a function of macro factors or between macro and micro factors, it doesn't matter. Failing to adjust for correlations and changes in volatility often carries people out of our markets. Every day we measure the portfolio against various macro factors across different time frames, mapping a broad risk matrix. If we can more intelligently assess correlations among these primary macro factors and have some clue as to when and how these correlations are changing, we can actively reduce unintended consequences in the portfolio.

Examining all these macro factors daily allows me to calculate my dollar beta to these components of risk. For example, let us assume that I am running a pure commodity fund, leaving aside the equity component for a moment. If I am 60 percent long commodities, I am really just a currency fund in drag because commodities have a high correlation to the U.S. dollar at the moment. In this sense, I am essentially running a 50 percent dollar short position.

Much of what we do seeks to mitigate unintended consequences, enabling us to do more with less from a volatility standpoint, which should increase our Sharpe ratio over time (see box on page 244). Our risk system functions as a toolkit with two discrete parts, one of which is defensive, the other offensive. The defensive component tries to understand macro factor exposures, throwing up flags when unintended exposures creep into the portfolio. The offensive component is where we look at data for different rates of change in core factors, to see if the macro matrix is beginning to cross-correlate. There is very powerful information in this latter analysis because cross-correlation will translate into higher volatility. When that happens, we adjust our gross and net exposures to compensate for the higher volatility environment. Most managers, however, would add hedges, which actually increase gross exposures and add basis risk precisely when overall portfolio risk should be reduced.

So stage one is the macro factor risk and stage two is the diversification risk in the portfolio. After these two primary analyses, we then look at our top 10 strategies by exposure, compiling a similar correlation matrix. For example, is a deferred grain position highly correlated with an energy equity position? If for some reason it is, then I want to know about it and understand why. Basically, our risk process mimics our investment process in that we work down from macro factor diversification to micro factor risk, allowing us to integrate the equity and commodity strategies that comprise our overall portfolio.

Sharpe Ratio

The *Sharpe*, or *reward-to-variability*, *ratio* is a measure of the excess return (or risk premium) per unit of risk in an investment asset or a trading strategy. The Sharpe ratio is used to measure the return of an asset relative to the level of risk taken. When comparing two assets, an investor can compare the expected returns $E[R]$ against the relative benchmarks with return R_f. The asset with the higher Sharpe ratio gives more return for the same risk.

How do you deal with the closet dollar exposure?

We hedge our dollar factor exposure actively. For example, we are currently running pretty heavy overall risk, but because our dollar factor started to go to 50 percent of the portfolio, we cut this risk materially by selling a basket of currencies versus the dollar. In this case, although we increased gross exposure, we reduced positions elsewhere, cutting exposures to base metals, where our conviction was lower.

We also pay a significant amount of attention to position sizing relative to changes in the volatility regime. Assuming that I had equal conviction in natural gas and gold, running equal dollar-sized positions would be completely inappropriate given the drastically different levels of volatility in these two commodities. We have another matrix that analyzes risk units, examining different time factors and calculating the appropriate position size for a given commodity according to how much daily swing we can tolerate in the portfolio. This provides us with a common denominator to ensure that trades are sized appropriately not only in the context of the portfolio, but also relative to one another. Last year, for example, equity volatility, as measured by the VIX index, in

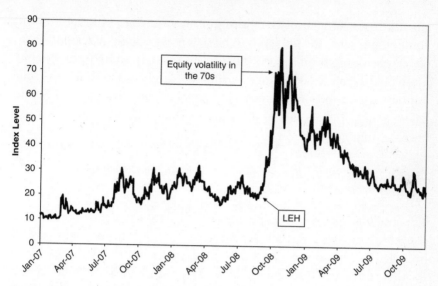

Figure 9.3   VIX Index, 2007–2009
SOURCE: Bloomberg.

the 70s meant that my stock positions were probably a quarter of what I would normally run (see Figure 9.3).

How do you measure liquidity, a notoriously slippery concept to nail down?

Liquidity is measured according to a proprietary equation. We generally look at liquidity by measuring volumes on a 30-day and 60-day basis, and also relative to the comparable 180-day and 360-day figures in order to capture the rate of change, which is the most important element.

Are there risks specific to commodity markets that do not exist in equities?

Commodity markets have much larger tail risk because spot shortages and outages can occur in the face of rather inelastic demand. Heating oil or natural gas especially can exhibit this phenomenon at times. Significant changes in the demand profile of a commodity rarely occur, unless there is some step change, similar to the one in the corn market when ethanol was introduced as an energy option. On the supply side, though, tail risk is inherent, usually resulting from an outage of some kind. In equities, however, the tail tends to be different because incremental supply can be brought online via issuance. In the very short-term, because it can be difficult to create incremental supply in commodities, the only solution is demand destruction, which occurs at higher prices. So we have a general belief that the distribution of an inelastic commodity can become pretty extended when these diffusions occur.

Does it follow, then, that commodities are inherently riskier than equities?

This really comes down to how you define riskier. If the distributions are more non-normal, then according to that qualification, the answer is clearly yes. However, given how much the commodity markets have evolved in the last five years in terms of product breadth, volume, and other factors, it is difficult to give a precise answer because these distributions are changing along with changes in the types of players in the market. The increased speculative flows in recent years have definitely changed the level of volatility, both from long-only players entering the market through indices and other means, and from the growing size and influence of CTA's (commodity trading advisors).

While some question whether speculative flows are fundamental to the functioning of the market, for me, it is clear that such flows have had a major impact. Speculative flows change the term structure of a market, which, in turn, changes the reaction function of a producer or storage operator. Commodity markets now tend to gap more quickly, showing evidence of what I call "single point volatility." And there is some evidence of a greater prevalence of serial correlation in pricing, so trends are established much more quickly. This doesn't necessarily mean commodities are riskier, but it is a change in the market microstructure that you have to stay on top of.

As a result of spot shortages and outages, is it easier to be long commodities than short?

Although none of this could be described as "easy," each manager may have a different comfort zone, which is a function of how trades are structured, what the asymmetry is, the risk versus reward, etc. However, because of the index component in the marketplace, recently it appears that bull trend moves tend to be much more exaggerated over time than bear trend moves. But a single manager can be agnostic to playing the market from the short or long side, and this is definitely the case for me.

What do you consider more important, coming up with trade ideas or mitigating downside risk?

Both capturing the upside and limiting the downside are essential. I know some people who are phenomenal on the idea side but cannot make money. There are three types of people in our business: those who are great analysts, those who are great portfolio managers, and those who can do both. This last category is very rare. Closing the gap between having a high Sharpe ratio on your ideas and the translation of those ideas into profits is a never-ending quest for all of us. It is really what this business is all about.

Risk-taking ability has a lot to do with emotional discipline. I find that people who have significant personal discipline tend to be reasonably good risk takers. Their emotional control allows them to remain detached from the vicissitudes of the markets. This might be innate. Then there is what I call "time on the water," meaning experience builds psychological capital. The more time you spend in the markets, the broader variety of different market environments you have to trade through. Not only did 2008 wreck people's accounts, it also destroyed some people psychologically. On the other hand, surviving such an event can build enormous psychological strength.

What lessons did you learn in 2008?

Risk management, risk management, risk management. My frustration with 2008, despite having had a solid absolute and quite robust relative year, was the reasonable gap between our analytical Sharpe and our trading Sharpe. But when I look back on 2008 and read our monthly investor letters, we could have had a much better year had franchise risk not been so pervasive across the financial services industry. Fiduciary responsibility to our investors was paramount—we simply had to ensure that we would not lose all their money because of counterparties going bust. Counterparty risk was a massive game changer in 2008. The idea that your collateral could get locked up and disappear overnight superseded all portfolio management responsibilities. Many funds lost a

lot of money with Lehman. Reducing exposures and focusing on counterparty risk was more of a fiduciary responsibility call, and in 2008 this
superseded the goal of maximizing profits.

*Where do you get your trade ideas—travel, research, network,
company visits?*

I use all of these to source and generate ideas. Running a fund, you are
trying to make four judgments, and these four judgments affect how you
acquire, assimilate, and analyze information as part of your investment
process:

1. What is your direction? Long or short.
2. What is your duration? Commodities versus equities—commodities
   tend to be slightly longer duration.
3. What is the diffusion of an idea? Pervasiveness of a fundamental
   event across the supply chain.
4. What is your expected value? Our own estimates versus both intrinsic value and consensus estimates.

We develop our macro framework from a very diverse array of
research, interaction with policy makers, interaction with other areas
of our firm, and interaction with our broader network of consultants.
Interestingly, our big macro themes often come out of very specific
microeconomic conversations. We bring this process together in the idea
flow from the quantitative information in commodity markets—price
differentials, regional arbitrages, rates of change in demand—and then in
equity markets. The cycle of ideas in the equity universe revolves around
cash flow, capital expenditure, and the operating margin cycle.

In commodities, the core of the process is driven by spending a
lot of time with our physical market contacts, which requires getting
out in the field, spending time with the physical market participants,
doing crop tours, visiting mines or oil fields, etc. These trips are often
done in conjunction with our consultant universe. Our focus is on the
translation of these inputs into our investment process. It is important
to know what you are not: I am not a trained geologist or petroleum
engineer, for example. However, fortunately we have relationships with

and access to experts in these core disciplines across energy, metals, and agriculture. Incorporating their expertise and interpretation of the microeconomic factors is an essential part of what we do. We use this information to have a much more qualified discussion when we sit down with corporate managements.

What kind of information do you acquire during a crop field visit or oil field tour?

In fall 2008, our macro thesis was anchored around collapsing cash flow and capital expenditure, and we wanted to see how this broader view manifested itself in different sectors. We sent our in-house agronomist to Brazil with one of our consultants, who only focuses on Brazilian agriculture, for a two-week crop tour of the key crops in that region. What came back was very important real-time feedback that the major agricultural companies were all cutting a combined $40 to $50 billion of fertilizer and crop financing to Brazilian farmers due to the credit crisis. As a result, the farmers were becoming much more pessimistic about both acreage and yield, which we then incorporated into our modeling process. This kind of primary research in commodities is very important for us; you cannot acquire this kind of information sitting in your office. Rather, it is a function of diligence.

Can you give me an example of a big macro theme that came from a specific micro conversation?

We are playing the current economic bounce, which has come off the back of the broader inventory restocking theme. Our understanding of this theme crystallized during a dinner conversation in the beginning of 2009 with the CEO of one of the largest metals companies in the world.

For some time, we have held a very high-level macro view that the move to just-in-time inventory management would at some point be destabilizing for the commodity markets. There is an exceptional book on this called *The End of the Line* by Barry Lynn, a manufacturing specialist. Its simple premise is that the move to just-in-time inventory and global outsourcing forced all of the volatility of output and debt associated with production onto a much less well-capitalized supply chain. Although our global system of production is the most efficient in history, it is perfectly calibrated to a world where nothing goes wrong. The credit crisis gave the supply chain a massive shock, which caused a shock to commodity distribution and production. Going forward, the whip in the data is going to be extraordinary. The down 30 percent, up 30 percent industrial production numbers we are seeing in Asia are setting up for something very interesting in broader data numbers. Just-in-time was all about running minimal inventory, but as activity picks up, we are just as likely to have a binary event on the way up as we did on the way down. A squeeze can occur in a low-growth environment because the supply chain cannot adapt fast enough—it's counterintuitive, but very powerful.

When I presented this high-level macro theme to the CEO of the metals company, he replied that in a delevered world of lower trend growth, achieving pricing power will be much more difficult, so competition will take place on market share, not price. Therefore, following destocking, once activity starts to turn, credit becomes available once again, and the issues of liquidity, velocity, and confidence return to stabilize asset prices, there will be a huge rush of demand to restock because the only way to compete is on volume. He confirmed that this was already starting to happen; he saw evidence in his order book and in the supply chain, the latter of which had been essentially bled dry as everyone minimized working capital.

This discussion with the CEO basically confirmed our higher-order macro theme. Because producers had depleted inventories out of a need for cash to delever, a pick-up in activity at a time when the system was sized for Armageddon would have a huge near-term impact on price. That is a phenomenal opportunity if you can spot it early. (See Figure 9.4.)

Getting back to ideas and how they translate into the portfolio, we form a macro view based on primary research and from visiting company management and asking ourselves if the information we are receiving makes any practical sense in the context of the equity and commodity supply chain. Then we take this information and look for verification in the physical market. Is there truly no inventory? What is the location of the inventory? Is there evidence of distortions being expressed through regional arbitrages or through physical market differentials? Is it a commodity manifestation or an equity manifestation? If

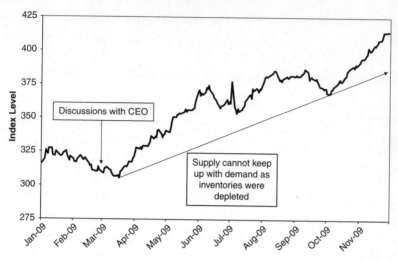

Figure 9.4 CRB Commodities Index, 2009
SOURCE: Bloomberg.

it's an equity manifestation, where is it in the supply chain: upstream, midstream, or downstream? Where will value be created or destroyed? Lastly, we look at value on an absolute and relative basis in what is a rather complex process.

These field trips or dinners with management seem somewhat fortuitous—could they just be giving you false confidence?

Our research process is a kind of triage. Where we might have 3 or 4 big themes in the portfolio at any one time, we always have another 5 or 10 themes in the hopper ready to go. As we triage, we ask: (1) what is our macro context for the world and (2) what do we think about the direction, duration, and diffusion of these different ideas? We try to push our limited bandwidth in these different directions. For example, if the focus is within grains, and we are trying to understand the effect on yield and acreage from collapsing cash flow and capital expenditure, then we will go to Brazil. If the focus is within metals, and we are digging into this restocking phenomenon as it concerns China or the U.S., then we go to these regions and dig into more primary information. Many times it does end up being fortuitous, but I find it tends to be more fortuitous when resources are allocated to an idea that is on the cusp of coming to fruition.

How important is China in the commodity world?

Quantitatively, China is dramatically more important than it was before 2000. It is worth broadening the answer to the growing importance of the emerging markets and especially the BRICs (Brazil, Russia, India, and China), but with China as the cornerstone. Before 2000, metals demand in the developed economies was roughly equivalent to that in the emerging economies, whereas after 2000, emerging markets demand for metals grew at 8 percent, while developed world demand was flat. As you can see, the Asian influence is very important. Emerging markets now contribute more to nominal GDP growth globally than developed markets. This is a pivotal structural transition, and China's entry into the WTO in the fall of 2001 was the big structural change that coincided with the beginning of the bottoming of the tech-led recession. There was an incredible inflection point where commodity-producing nations went from running current account deficits to current account surpluses. At the time, we were at the higher end of the risk premium spectrum. Then, suddenly, China's WTO entry prompted a deluge of investment, which sparked a six- to seven-year run of current account surpluses that were reinvested domestically, generating a monetary and growth boom and additional consumption of commodities as a result.

Do you see this trend continuing?

I would separate this trend into two phases, where phase one was the post-WTO entry and the build-out of Chinese infrastructure to create commodity supply. During this time, China was importing steel to make steel mills, whereas now they run a substantial domestic steel surplus. Phase two—the present—is something very different, characterized by the diversification of China's foreign exchange reserves and a global resource grab. The Chinese will spend half a trillion dollars in the next six years acquiring resources through diverse means, such as buying an iron ore mine in Australia, developing port infrastructure in Brazil in exchange for off-take rights, or taking direct control of a company like

Rio Tinto. The net effect of China's push for resource security will be a lower tradable float of commodity supply going forward, which is a very important and underappreciated factor impacting the commodity markets. Spending $500 billion will allow China to exercise monopolistic control of the supply in certain markets. Perhaps the most extreme example will be in the rare earth metals, which are the components that go into magnets, lasers, and high-tech strategic production.

This is part of a much more important thesis that some have termed "resource nationalism." Resource nationalism means if you have it, you are going to keep it. Countries will keep commodities to control domestic inflation, a phenomenon we saw in the grain markets in early 2008 when dozens of countries put tariffs on exports. Also, instead of exporting raw material and giving the production benefits away to another country, raw materials and their value-added processing will increasingly be kept at home in efforts to bolster job growth. It's a strategic decision. Russia and certain African countries have already begun to do it, and the Chinese will start to do it as well. Again, due to the emergence of China, the tradable float of commodity supply will be lower over the next three to five years.

Does the emergence of China and commodity hoarding lead to higher inflation globally?

The rise of China and emerging markets really matters with respect to inflation. Commodity price inflation is now being achieved at a much lower level of global output than what we witnessed over the past 50 years, showing up at 2.3 percent of global GDP growth, compared to over 4 percent in prior cycles. Much of that has to do with the rise of emerging markets, but the greater concern now is that cash flow and capital expenditure have been collapsing as well. In the past year, we have seen $250 billion in cancellations or delays in metals and mining spend, which is equivalent to 25 percent of forward copper capacity. Meanwhile, 2.3 percent global growth means China is growing at 9 percent and the rest of the world at only 1.3 percent. We are now getting commodity price inflation at a rate of global growth below the level that generates employment gains, and this is especially true in the U.S. This is a real paradox for policy makers.

Another factor enhancing this trend is that commodity producers are becoming more vigorous consumers of their internal production. One of our oil consultants calls this the "export land model," and we see great evidence of it in the Middle East. Since 2000, Middle East oil production is up 11 percent, but net exports are only up 5 percent because domestic demand has risen 40 percent. As base demand in emerging markets continues to expand with rising incomes and value-added manufacturing, this trend will only grow stronger.

With commodity price inflation now occurring at a much lower level of economic growth relative to its potential, and with this trend of commodity producers becoming key consumers as well, a key structural change is evolving in markets. When you consider these phenomena in the context of U.S. unemployment at 10 percent, or 500 basis points over NAIRU, we have stagflation in the making (see box). And stagflation is an extraordinarily difficult environment for policy makers to navigate.

NAIRU

NAIRU, or *Non-Accelerating Inflation Rate of Unemployment*, is an economic theory that suggests inflation will rise or fall relative to an equilibrium rate of unemployment. It is widely used in mainstream economics, but is rejected, most notably, by Keynesian economists, who argue that full employment—the rate at which all persons willing to work for the prevailing wages are actually employed, and the unemployment rate is close to zero—is natural and attainable.

From an inflationary standpoint, China is the cornerstone of this thesis. China will create more boom–bust cycles in commodities than we have had in the past because the volatility of their growth and output is so much higher than that of the developed world. Furthermore, their motives for economic output do not necessarily have profit as the cornerstone. That will create more volatility in both commodity markets and broader financial markets going forward.

Will China and the emerging markets decouple from the developed world?

On a secular basis, emerging markets will continue to grow because these economies do not have the structural financing issues that exist in the developed world and they have much more active central bank management. China is a great example. It is extraordinarily rare that an economy of that order of magnitude can grow money and credit simultaneously. Normally, money supply growth would have to precede credit growth. Although growing the two simultaneously is extremely stimulative, it is only possible in a semicommand economy where the People's Bank of China can order the regional banks to lend.

The bigger question is whether China can achieve the same growth rates now that it did prior to 2008. The answer is likely no because the U.S. current account deficits had become Chinese current account surpluses and the U.S. is now in a three- to five-year process of structural deleveraging. The deleveraging process will continue, but the main question for emerging markets will be how quickly these economies can transition from being export-led to domestic-led. Currently, the composition of Chinese stimulus is much more focused domestically than on the export sector, but sustainable domestic growth is more of a 5- to 10-year phenomenon. The whole point of global outsourcing was to more closely link the producer and consumer. Until this process formally breaks, it will be difficult to have Asia decouple. China is the vendor financing mechanism for the U.S. and this is another factor that will prevent decoupling. The two countries may experience different relative rates of growth and inflation, but the links between them are still profound.

Where could it all go wrong for China?

China's story is centered on inflation and limited commodity supply. Structurally, China will have significant inflation at some point, considering the intensity of use per unit of GDP and all those S curves that show incredible commodity demand growth relative to increasing per capita income. China is still in the lower third of demand intensity for most of these commodities. Once the Chinese consumer actually kicks in, the numbers do not add up. For example, China is going to be the largest auto market in the world in the next few years, which means oil supply would have to grow at a million barrels a day just to fulfill Chinese demand.

The next big structural shift for the world will occur when China goes to a convertible currency. It will create a final, extraordinary parabolic move in asset prices because it will unleash dramatic consumption in Asia—but it may take considerable time for convertibility to happen. It potentially all goes wrong for China in the transition zone. How quickly China handles the transition to free float with regards to monetary and fiscal policy adjustments will be key.

The other key risk for the Chinese is that economic output at the corporate level is not driven exclusively by the profit motive. Employment stability, inflation control, and a slow transition to a domestic-led economy are the apparent policy goals. Therefore, at some point, excess production will be significant. We already see evidence of this in markets such as steel. If U.S. demand remains stagnant for several years, this could drive a destabilizing deflationary impulse, considering how fast lending growth and debt has been over the past year.

China also presents a clear challenge to the U.S. dollar as the world's reserve currency for the first time since World War II. Although the Chinese renminbi will not become the sole reserve currency, it will become a major tradable currency and could eventually become an important part of a world reserve currency basket. A clear concern is the structural flaw in the global monetary system, whereby the U.S. deficit is everyone else's surplus. As such, everyone else is simply wed to the level of U.S. debt and implicitly to the U.S. economy's growth rate. Nevertheless, regardless of the rhetoric, it would be impossible to move to an SDR model (see box) within the immediate investment horizon.

Special Drawing Rights (SDR)

The *SDR* is an international reserve asset created by the International Monetary Fund (IMF) in 1969 to supplement member country reserves and to support the Bretton Woods fixed exchange rate system. The SDR is a potential claim on the freely usable currencies of IMF members. Holders of SDRs can obtain currencies in exchange for their SDRs in two ways: first, through the arrangement of voluntary exchanges between members; and second, through the IMF, which designates members with strong external positions to purchase SDRs from members with weak external positions.

The value of the SDR was initially defined as equivalent to 0.888671 grams of fine gold, which at the time was equivalent to one U.S. dollar. After the collapse of the Bretton Woods system, the SDR was redefined as a basket of currencies. Today the basket consists of specific amounts of the euro, Japanese yen, British pound, and U.S. dollar. The U.S. dollar-value of the SDR is posted daily on the IMF's Web site.

SOURCE: International Monetary Fund (www.imf.org).

With a long-term investment horizon, if you had to put all your liquid net worth in one trade for 10 years, what would it be?

I would be torn between the deferred gold trade and the deferred oil trade. I do believe in the debasement of fiat currency thesis. When I think about the transfer of risk from the private sector to the public sector, the numbers just don't work. At some point, the debts will have to be paid or restructured. If you look at the assets and liabilities of the U.S. government in the same way that I look at a company, we would all be short shares of the U.S. government even though they can print money. U.S. dollars are those shares, and in such a scenario, gold becomes interesting as a true reserve asset to replace currencies. The challenge becomes distinguishing between the intrinsic and extrinsic values of gold. If gold were valued on supply and demand, it would probably be trading at $42 an ounce. But as a reserve asset, I would argue it is clearly worth more than $42, maybe even more than $2,000. Gold is worth whatever people think it's worth. I know that sounds trite, but gold is unique in this regard. If the extrinsic value is being determined based on gold's worth as a store of value, there is another dimension. The more the price goes up, the more people believe in its worth as a store of value, particularly when it is appreciating relative

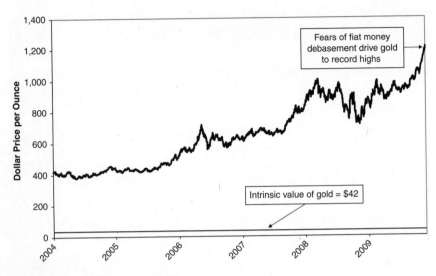

Figure 9.5   Gold, 2004–2009
SOURCE: Bloomberg.

to the major currencies of the world. There is a common belief that the gold market cannot be squeezed because there is about 50 years of above-ground supply available. However, in that rare scenario where people's faith in fiat currency is truly shaken, there may be a shortage of gold that will be lent to the market. Since supply growth is actually negative, lending is a clear balancing mechanism, and its absence would have enormous impact on the gold price. That is potentially a truly asymmetric outcome. (See Figure 9.5.)

And what about the deferred oil trade?

In Drobny parlance, this would be my "favorite trade." I would express it by owning oil via 10-year futures contracts. Structural impediments to oil supply are dramatic and in certain cases even irreversible, while the demand trajectory is increasingly driven by emerging markets. In emerging markets, the elasticity of demand is different than in developed markets due to variation in tax regimes, substantial government subsidies, and currency strength. If my China thesis comes to fruition and they do move to a convertible currency, unleashing the incredible savings of the Asian consumer, the oil market will become extraordinarily difficult to balance.

What about increased supply from alternative energy sources?

If the spike in energy prices during the last two or three years proved anything, the ability for renewables to impact the market will remain limited, leaving only a small volume of high-cost marginal alternatives. We learned at $140 crude that the market could only supply an additional 400,000 to 500,000 barrels a day of ethanol to an 86 million barrel-a-day market.

What was the worst trade of your career?

There have been so many bad trades. It really comes down to discipline. It's similar to what Vince Lombardi said about winning: "Winning is not a sometime thing; it's an all-the-time thing. You don't win once in a while; you don't do things right once in a while; you do them right all the time. Winning is a habit. Unfortunately, so is losing." It is a quotation my father gave me and I keep it on my desk as a clear reminder. The same should be said of trading discipline. My biggest losing trades were when we were not only obviously wrong, but also failed to stick to our process and discipline—we allowed fear or denial to take over. That cannot become a habit. However, sometimes the worst trades are the ones that you miss. If you are properly managing risk, no one trade can put you out of business. But the ones you miss, where you could have been up 30, 40, 50 percent in a year, those are the ones that really hurt, because those are the returns that build longevity into a franchise.

There was one particular corn trade that taught me some valuable lessons. We were premature in establishing a big grain position in August 2007 when the USDA came out and increased yield expectations. Although we thought the announcement was completely unrealistic relative to our primary research, the grain market had its largest one-day decline since 1994, costing us almost 3 percent on the fund. Six weeks later, as prices were going down even further, the USDA revised down their yield estimates in line with our internal models, sending the grain price soaring. (See Figure 9.6.) It proved to be a great lesson in

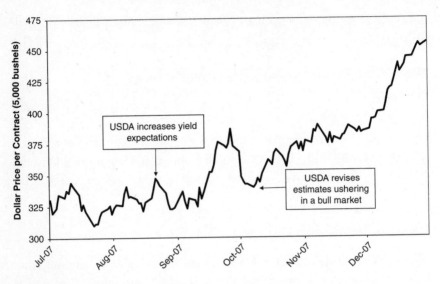

Figure 9.6   Corn Futures, 2007
SOURCE: Bloomberg.

timing and scaling, teaching me to build into positions and showing me that a disconnect can persist between the information farmers are providing in the physical market and the data the USDA is reporting and revising on its end. Assimilation of information—either qualitative or quantitative—into the price structure is one of the most challenging aspects of what we do.

Do you always scale into positions?

I always scale into the large core positions, and that grain trade reminded me why this is so important. Scaling into positions is just basic risk management. We also have internal stops on all positions so that no one trade or commodity can completely take us out.

If you were a real money manager who wanted to get exposure to commodities, how would you get it? Would you select an index product or an actively managed fund?

I would employ a combination of active and passive management. First, I find the more efficient passive indices or enhanced roll yield products to be pretty solid. They attempt to mitigate the negative consequences of contango when it exists, and they optimize for backwardation. These types of indices would serve a long-duration investor quite well and are reasonably scalable. However, because index products are exposed to significant drawdowns, I would complement any index strategy with an actively managed strategy, which should be flat to up when commodity markets sell off dramatically. There are scale issues with actively managed strategies, though, so a combination of the two would be optimal for investors with a large capital base. A third option is to invest in physical commodity assets, which is what many of the large real money investors do. This aligns well with the duration of the investment capital and provides both cash flow and capital appreciation.

If you were conducting a search for an active manager in the commodity space, what would you look for?

The most important criteria would be an integrative process, discipline, and an adaptive risk management framework. Too many risk management systems are overly regimented and do not adapt to the environment; they fail to adapt to volatility and do not adjust position sizes accordingly. Again, the biggest issue in commodity investing is the fat tails, so it is crucial that a manager thinks about how to deal with this inherent feature of the market ahead of time. This means putting a premium on process, making sure someone has the discipline to implement that process, and making sure the process is both integrative and reasonably unique. Ensuring that the proper risk measurement and risk management framework are in place is also crucial. I would argue that the risk management function either has to be shared or be independent of the CIO so that it is strictly enforced, preventing the manager from blowing up.

If you were running a new sovereign wealth fund, where several hundred billion dollars in cash was deposited in a new account, how would you approach asset allocation?

The first step would be currency diversification. Most of the large sovereign wealth funds are in business now because they are running large current account surpluses that are largely dollar based. I would first focus on how that U.S. dollar risk can be mitigated through a currency or commodity strategy. Next, it would be important to define the goals of this particular sovereign wealth fund. Is the goal long-term capital appreciation, strategic acquisition of foreign interests, or protection of a nation's savings? Regardless, considering our belief in debasement of fiat currency, we believe hard assets will outperform many other financial assets over the coming years. Therefore, hard assets would be a cornerstone of the allocation, and if structured properly, would provide cash flow and capital appreciation.

How about a state pension fund where you have an 8 percent annual return target as a result of retiree liabilities?

In that case, I would have very low exposure to both developed market sovereign fixed income and equities. I would put the majority of assets in a commodity allocation because that is where the greatest asymmetry is, and trades in the physical and paper market can be created to achieve this return hurdle with acceptable levels of risk.

Being heavily weighted in commodities would really make you stand out from your pension fund peers.

Let me put it this way, my exposure to commodities would be far greater than the 3 percent recommended by most real money consultants. I would be focused more than ever on that left tail of the commodity risk, and on the arbitrage opportunity between hard assets and financial assets that will continue to take place. I would pursue the direct acquisition of producing assets in the resource space, providing a different liquidity and cash flow profile as well. I would orient the portfolio toward more liquid manifestations of a hard asset strategy by simultaneously implementing an actively managed segment and an index segment, which we discussed earlier. The actively managed portion is what will provide the alpha, diversification, and protection during volatile markets.

Would you buy oil fields and mines for your pensioner constituents?

I would buy long duration assets or off-take agreements. By off-take agreement I mean building a port in some country in exchange for, say, 10 percent of that country's soybean output, or some similar arrangement. This is effectively what the Chinese are doing with their own global version of the U.S.'s Marshall Plan, enacted after World War II. The key issue is that financial market players are not operators of commodity assets. Therefore, a growing trend will be more joint ventures between the pension funds, sovereign wealth funds, and other real money players, and the great operators of commodity assets globally.

I would keep a very sharp eye on liquidity, so all this would depend on the size of my portfolio and my ability to keep the majority of my assets in liquid investments. The lesson of 2008 is that liquidity is all that matters when it ceases to exist. Therefore, real money managers need to reorient their portfolios to avoid large tail risks.

Looking ahead at potential tail risks, I believe that a developed market sovereign debt crisis looms stemming from the inability of a major sovereign to completely fulfill its commitments. I am talking about a G3 nation.

Wow, that would be a shock! In keeping with the pension discussion, what would be your base currency?

Physical gold and then oil and grains. In that scenario, I do not want to hold my store of value in a mechanism where value is defined by a politician's judgment or conscience.

If your pension fund's base currency is gold and gold falls out of favor reverting to its supply and demand price of $42 an ounce, will your pension fund be down 95 percent?

I would be an active user of options if I were running a real money portfolio. We have had a significant retrenchment in implied volatility, creating opportunities to manage exposures using option premium. The direction depends on the skews in the volatility market at any given time. Having a hard asset base exposure provides a potential natural hedge because people will still need the basic elements that drive economic existence.

So you envision being a very active and tactical pension fund manager?

In this day and age, you have to be tactical. Until this process of deleveraging is complete—on a consumer, corporate, and sovereign level—holding large public market positions will be more challenging.

Would the structure of pensions, with trustee and board meetings, inhibit the ability to be tactical?

Quarterly adjusting would be active enough. The big risk to liability managers is inflation, so it is crucial to stay ahead of it. What matters is a mandate with significant degrees of freedom for the investment process. People have to be able to adapt to market conditions either offensively or defensively.

A number of the broader themes that we discussed can translate into inflation. There is the commodity scenario we have described. There is resource nationalism, where in certain markets oligopolistic price structures are going to emerge. Because of the collapse in capital expenditure, the small producer has essentially been taken out of the equation, creating greater concentration with greater pricing pressure. You have China acquiring global reserves and the impact that will have on commodities. You have this whole just-in-time inventory management/supply chain dislocation that is taking place. You have the public risk that is now taking all of the private risk. You have commodity inflation at a lower threshold. And you have the inversion of the demographic pyramid, meaning dependency ratios are going to rise (see box).

Dependency Ratio

Also referred to as the *total dependency ratio, the dependency ratio* is a measure showing the number of dependents (aged 0–14 and over the age of 65) to the total population (aged 15–64), which is calculated by Number of dependents ÷ Population (ages 15–64) × 100%.

This indicator gives insight into the amount of people of nonworking age compared to the number of those of working age. A high ratio means those of working age—and the overall economy—face a greater burden in supporting the aging population.

SOURCE: *Forbes Investopedia.*

All of these issues and themes indicate upward pressure on inflation, which, in turn, means upward pressure on forward interest rates. So there are probably six or seven reasons why interest rates can rise. Higher interest rates change the discount rate used to calculate the present value of long duration liabilities. This alleviates some of the burden, but other crises will emerge because bubbles beget bubbles. This monetary bubble that has been created amidst the first coordinated global central bank quantitative easing has to have consequences. It is all untested and unproven. As a manager, regardless of the asset class, you need to be thinking more about the next potential tail risk. If I am a pension fund manager, I am going to be worried about interest rates going up on a forward basis and inflation in a low-growth world, which does not necessarily lead me to equities.

The challenge with investment committees or boards is not that they only meet quarterly but that they tend to drive portfolios to the things that have performed well recently—the things that are in vogue. The focus is too oriented on "survivorship bias." At these extremes, on the upside or the downside, people do not interpolate based on the current data set but rather extrapolate based on recent past experience. Said another way, they chase returns, and that is a big problem. Good macro investors try to do the inverse: at extremes they interpolate based on small data points and do not necessarily try to extrapolate Armageddon or euphoria. That is a key difference. But another problem in the real money world results from mandates being too rigid in terms of rules of engagement and implementation.

How would you fix that?

The problem can be fixed by bringing in people with more tactical experience who can synthesize the macro and micro. It is a structural business model issue, but also a question of power concentration versus power diffusion. The environment going forward will be governed by the secular process of deleveraging and the private-to-public sector risk transfer, meaning liquidity and flexibility will command a huge premium for all investors. A rethinking of the business model could result in a separation of functions into a capital preservation unit and an alpha unit, with the former mandated by inflationary protection. Any reorienting of the business model would have to deal with the structural changes taking place in liquidity and credit.

Are your skills as a hedge fund manager transportable to the real money world?

The transportable skills are the ability to identify opportunities across the matrix of asset classes and in liquid market trade structures. Where does the opportunity set reside? Is it equities or commodities? Is it fixed income? Currencies? That type of skill is likely transportable but the perception of duration in the real money context might not be. Because I have a liquid markets mentality, I have a different interpretation or appreciation of liquidity, which might not necessarily serve a long-duration capital type of mentality. I am wired to think about risk in a hedge fund liquidity structure, which is all about maximizing returns for my investors based on the duration of our capital, which is much shorter than real money. The most important issue on this point is that if we really are at the end of what many people have called "the Great Moderation," a reference to the moderation in interest rates and economic volatility, then tactical positioning in a portfolio will become even more important for all of us. As business cycles become more truncated, economic volatility will rise and markets will reflect this. This tactical ability is the most important skill a liquid markets hedge fund manager could offer to a long-duration pension fund. Tactical expertise associated with the knowledge of flows and asset allocation expertise could be quite a robust combination for "real money" businesses.

What if all the real money managers take your advice and increase their commodity and real asset allocations from 3 percent, to say, 50 percent— is there enough capacity in the commodity markets to handle that size?

There are different manifestations of capacity, depending on where you are in the matrix. Do you express a view via commodity currencies, via the term structure of fixed income, or in the actual physical commodities? I may have a strong commodity view but only have a small allocation directly to commodities. I can be expressing an inflationary view through the ownership of physical commodities, cash flow generating assets, forward fixed income, TIPs, or other asset classes or instruments.

There are many different ways to express the same trade idea or theme. If everyone decided to allocate 50 percent to the paper market, there would be a problem. However, we would advocate a broader application of the definition of "commodity exposure."

How worried are you about hyperinflation?

We have some of the preconditions for a hyperinflation scenario in the sense that we could have a sovereign crisis that drives a massive dislocation in asset prices. The minute someone believes that a sovereign entity will not fulfill its obligations, he will start voting by purchasing resources and diversifying out of the currency. The first mover advantage from game theory is essential here. A lot of people are very long dollars, and there is evidence on the margin that some of these actions are beginning to occur in scale.

In Weimar Germany, hyperinflation occurred in about 18 months between 1922 and 1923, where it suddenly took the entire circulation of Reichsmarks to purchase a newspaper. People forget, however, that it took about six years to get to that final period of dislocation. Foreign holders of Reichsmarks during that period started to acquire hard assets denominated in Reichsmarks in a very aggressive manner—farmland, oil assets, other hard assets. This might be occurring now with the Chinese voting with their foreign exchange reserves by buying assets and diversifying out the dollar. Another example is the recent acceleration in gold buying by the central bank community. The world's central banks are now net buyers of gold for the first time since the 1960s. This is all part of an antidollar diversification strategy.

When we talk about the preconditions required for hyperinflation, think about the liquidity base that has just been created. The current stimulus that has been provided, if you account for everything, is 100 percent of GDP, which is equal to the sum of the last 13 recessionary stimulus packages in aggregate. It is six times what was provided during the Great Depression for one-fifteenth of the economic impact. What happens when velocity picks up on this extraordinary base of liquidity? Inflation accompanies velocity. Prices start to go up but wages do not follow. People spend, buying and borrowing today what they need for tomorrow, thus creating velocity.

But does transmission into wages occur? That is my one issue with why I don't think we see hyperinflation. Because of the rapid decline in the influence of unions and the strong tendency now of corporations to substitute capital for labor, it will be very difficult to achieve the wage price spiral that is a hallmark of any hyperinflationary period. The question then becomes: does Bernanke try to prevent the 1930s and wind up getting the 1970s? That is probably the more central case. I don't think we are there yet, but policy navigation will have to be intensely successful to avoid a problem. If you talk to policy makers off the record about the ultimate impact of all this stimulus and how it will manifest itself in terms of the economic impacts over time, no one can actually provide a clear and decisive answer. When the liquidity base is so large, no one truly knows how the translation mechanism between velocity and liquidity actually occurs. For an idea of magnitude, $13 trillion has been printed or injected globally, including asset purchases. If we believe that we can achieve the typical money multiplier of four times once again, this would mean $52 trillion, or roughly 60 percent of global GDP. But can a money multiplier of four times be achieved? I don't know. No one knows. You cannot model it because there is no historical precedent. That is the real challenge for us all. These situations are never a perfect analog, which is why we focus on scenarios and plan, structure, and trade accordingly.

Chapter 10

The Commodity Hedger

"The Commodity Hedger" has had a long and varied career in both commodities and broader financial markets, having traded most products available to investors today. From feed lots to grain elevators to barges on the Mississippi to trading desks in the Midwestern United States, Asia, Switzerland, and New York, she places good risk/reward bets in energy, metals, and agricultural commodities, as well as currencies, interest rates, and equities.

She is the Commodity Hedger because of her ruthless attention to risk management, which she implements through the consistent use of risk collars on all large trades, a practice that would have saved real money players a considerable amount of money in 2008. She thinks she might be well-suited to run a real money fund because of her natural long-term investment horizon, and she says real money players should pay much more attention to cutting off their downside tail risk.

Her hardscrabble Midwestern American roots have given the Commodity Hedger as much general business acumen as trading skill, enabling her to launch her own proprietary trading group inside of Cargill, one of the most powerful players in global commodity markets, and more recently her own hedge fund. She has had about 20 different addresses in the last 30 years, and her extreme versatility and flexibility are partly what allow her to express trades in a multitude of ways. She runs her current hedge fund out of a loft in downtown Manhattan, the result of having launched amidst considerable personal debt. Despite the initial struggle, her conservative, risk-focused style has proven attractive over time, enabling her to grow to what is now the largest female-owned global macro-hedge fund firm in the world.

The Commodity Hedger says that commodities and real assets drive all other markets, so she tends to view all markets through her commodity lens. She is particularly bullish Latin America, believing that the region will outperform Asia, and would advocate owning agricultural land around the world for those with the ability to take a long-term view.

How did you get into markets?

My dad was the sheriff of a small town in southeastern Minnesota, and he flew a small private aircraft. We had a parcel of land outside of town where he planted corn. When I was five years old, he took me up in the plane to survey the corn crops—he was looking to see the quality. Then we flew into Iowa and he continued to check out the corn quality, to compare it. I asked, "Dad, why are you looking at the corn here in Iowa?" He replied, "Well, there's this thing called the futures exchange," and he went on to explain the basics of supply and demand, and how you can sell corn in the future. I was perplexed and fascinated, asking, "Do you mean to tell me you can sell this guy's corn without owning it?" I have been following markets ever since.

What was your first trading job, and how did you get there?

It was a circuitous route, which is perhaps analogous to my thought process. I wanted a career in business but did not want to get a business degree—I felt business school could contaminate my "out of the box" thinking, much like a chef who has never been to culinary school or an artist who has not been to art school. This was absolutely clear to me from a young age. I also wanted a degree in science and math, but did not want to touch, so I settled on forestry based on my love for the outdoors. It was perfectly logical, really.

Politics was my second love. I actually ran for state representative when I was 22 years old, but that is another story—I lost, but it proved a great experience. After college, I lined up a job with the Minnesota State Legislature on the Natural Resources Committee. I graduated in December, and the job did not start until January. I really needed some money to buy Christmas presents, so I decided to work at a temp agency. My thinking was that it could kill two birds with one stone by giving me a chance see how different large companies worked from the inside while generating some cash.

One of the temp jobs was at Cargill, where I was doing filing for country grain elevators. After a few days, I asked the person next to me, "What does this company do?" She replied, "They trade things." A few days later I asked, "How do you become president of this company?" She answered, "You need to be a merchant."

I immediately went home and tried to learn what a grain merchant was, and I was totally blown away by what I read. The job comprised many things I loved to do: monitor the weather, examine supply and demand, travel—and you had to understand all markets, from currencies to commodities to interest rates and equities. I thought I had struck gold, finding exactly what I wanted to do. I contacted the HR Department, telling them I had just graduated from university and wanted work as a merchant, neglecting of course to say that I had been temping for them. After more than six months of tenacity, I finally got an interview, convinced them to hire me, and stayed at Cargill for 13 years.

What did you do at Cargill?

My first job was a grain originator in Kansas City, which meant buying grain for the traders' books from country elevators and farmers. The wheat trader, the corn trader, the bean trader, the sorghum trader, and others would post bids and offers and have trading positions, and I would buy for the traders' programs. I would call up any producer, any country elevator, anyone who had grain, and give them bids, tell them why they should sell their grain to us.

So you were basically doing information arbitrage. Because there was no listed price, you would do price discovery, trying to get the best price from these different physical holders.

Yes. I would travel and develop relationships with all these guys because everyone was calling them. Continental, Bunge, Dreyfus—we were all calling the same people and it was very competitive. There were two ways that I could buy grain for Cargill: either our trader had the best price, or someone else had a better price and I was forced to use another angle, such as loyalty, relationship, or my own market analysis. I believe I increased origination by 200 or 300 percent in that first year, which is basically how you earned your stripes to become a trader. I knew I wanted to become a trader on my second day in origination.

When did you become a trader, and what did you trade?

I spent two years in origination before I finally became a trader. The first thing I traded was multi-car corn, each unit representing a three-car train. It was a small program that included a logistics book and other interesting aspects. Everyone started small at Cargill and you had to work your way up. I traded corn and continued to originate until one day someone called the Kansas City office asking for a bid on "sunnies," or sunflower seeds.

After asking around, I learned that no one in our Cargill regional office traded sunnies. It seemed logical to me that the largest grain company in the world should be trading sunnies, so I pitched the idea to management and they let me run it as my own desk inside Cargill. My first order was from a guy wanting to sell three barges of sunnies.

I really didn't know anything about sunnies, but I learned everything I could in a very short time—those barges were on the river, just waiting for a buyer. Sunnies had both an export market, which was primarily for seeds with high oil content (the higher the oil content, the better the price), and a domestic market, for seeds with low oil content, which typically became birdseed. Birdseed was a labor-intensive market requiring bagging and trucking. Export was done by rail, and there were good bids for sunnies in Mexico. I figured three barges would be enough to establish a market if I got the right price. I asked our transportation manager to get me a quote on rail rates to Mexico, while I researched trucking rates to the northeast for birdseed, as well as options for getting the birdseed bagged, a function that Cargill did not perform in-house. He came back to me with a rail rate of approximately $3.05/hundred-weight (cwt). I was disappointed, as I figured I needed $1.20/cwt or lower, in case the seeds had low oil content and went for less. Then I remembered that new legislation had just passed, allowing rail rates to be negotiated instead of remaining fixed. I had the transport manager ask again if they would lower their rate to $1.10/cwt. He laughed, incredulous: "Why would they do that?" Then I had an idea. I told him to guarantee the railroad the entire volume of the three barges, and to tell them that they could set a deadline, making the rate available for only three months on that volume. It was win-win: I would have enough time to work out how to buy the seeds competitively and to find a profitable end-market, until which time the railroad hadn't officially changed any rate, so it would not be a big deal to them if I couldn't execute my transaction. He still didn't think the railroad would lower their rate so dramatically. I remember pleading with him: "Just try. Just ask, see what they say." The next day he came back to my desk with a very serious look. Then he broke out into a smile: "We got it even better—I got you $1.05/cwt. Go get 'em." Even he couldn't believe that just by asking, we achieved everything we wanted on our price, no matter how out of reach it had seemed. That was a major lesson for me: always ask.

I negotiated the rest of the deal, much of which hinged upon pricing the sunnies' potential oil content, and upon the arbitrage to the domestic birdseed market. It also entailed negotiation for storage with Cargill's elevators in Houston. They initially balked at my idea because sunnies typically clogged the elevation equipment and were difficult to aerate because they are more prone to combustion than other grains. Long story short, the trade worked out great: the seeds went for high oil content and we shipped to Mexico for profits north of $20/ton, when typical trading margins were $1–3/ton. From there I never looked back.

After that sunnies experience, I was more convinced than ever that I had found my calling. I wanted to know everything about every department and every aspect of Cargill's business. In 1985, I moved to Cargill's foreign exchange desk in Geneva, Switzerland. I started at the bottom, rolling currency positions and taking some small risk of my own. I honed my trading skills and eventually became desk manager.

From there I moved into fixed income back in Minneapolis, where I again started at the bottom of the desk: rolling fixed income positions for the financial division (repo and reverse repo), concomitantly trading fixed income and currency exposures. I view these housekeeping trading roles—rolling currency positions, repo/reverse repo, stock borrow/lend, and futures rolls—as integral to the process of learning the pulse of any market. My next position took me to Australia, where I managed our branch office in Melbourne, a position that entailed overseeing portfolios in currency, fixed income, and equities markets, as well as responsibility for accounting functions. Eventually, I pitched management a business plan to start a proprietary risk-taking desk based on my profile and theme approach. They agreed, and my Structural Trading Department was formed, where I was basically running an internal macro hedge fund—the forerunner of my current hedge fund.

Was it difficult leaving Cargill?

Working at Cargill was not easy. I was the wrong gender, the wrong political persuasion, and very opinionated. I often look back and marvel that I actually survived and excelled in spite of myself. It was difficult to leave, but I knew it was time. When I announced my departure, my boss and mentor was very disappointed but he told me something I will never forget, something very uncharacteristic for Cargill management. He said, "I actually think you will flourish on your own without the rules and structure here. You have got what it takes to be very successful."

I still revel in the feeling and excitement of these old Cargill experiences. Cargill is a great company and it was an incredible training ground for me. I was very lucky to have extremely smart and talented managers during my time there. Cargill gave me the opportunity and foundation to build my firm, not to mention the fact that my former boss saved me by making a substantial investment in my hedge fund while other investors were still "watching" after five years of positive returns. That gave me the validation I needed, and it was just in time.

Without the information flow that comes from being inside Cargill, how do you generate trade ideas for your hedge fund?

That is one area where I am very different, almost New Age. I don't think you can chase trades or even seek out trades. Rather, I stay aware, stay informed, understand relationships, and wait for trades to come to me. Then, when I can't fight it any longer, I put the trade on. I use my experience to develop themes and identify signals to tell me when a trade is ripe. My background is unique because I've lived and traded in all three principal time zones and I have had probably 20 addresses in the last 30 years, all around the globe. In addition to having traded every single asset class—commodities, fixed income, foreign exchange, high yield, equities, and private equity—I have traded these asset classes from both the bottom of the trading desk totem pole to the head of the desk. I love to look at intra-asset class relationships and then wait for themes, trades, and ideas to develop. I form the themes from an awareness of a wide-range of information—everything from demographics to migration patterns to the impact of currency movements on other asset classes. In particular, I place a lot of emphasis on how commodities and other real assets affect all other asset classes. I believe commodities and other real assets drive movements in other markets more so than vice versa. Real assets have been and will continue to be a major source of opportunity going forward.

I have a very philosophical view about how to define a commodity. Globalization means almost everything is becoming commoditized. My definition of commodities is broad, not only including real assets but currency and even culture. If you look through the real asset lens first, you can have an advantage.

Can you explain how looking through the real asset lens gives you an advantage?

Looking at real assets first entails major supply and demand analysis of all goods, services, and commodities, rather than just focusing on boilerplate economic analysis. Using this lens has given me an edge. For example, we were ahead of the game in predicting that the yield curve would invert during the Greenspan conundrum era (see box on page 276). We realized that the world had switched from one of supply constriction in commodities to one of demand pull, and that a bull market in commodities (with the associated switch from backwardation into contango in commodity futures curves) would be reflected in an inverted yield curve. In a deflationary consumer environment with an inflationary real asset environment, the real asset inflationary aspects

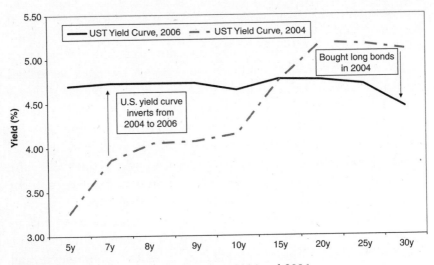

Figure 10.1 U.S. Treasury Yield Curve, 2004 and 2006
SOURCE: Bloomberg.

affect the short end of the curve, but the long end remains locked down. With productivity gains and no real inflation feeding through to core CPI—because core excludes food and energy—we bought bonds on the long end and put on yield curve inversion trades, which practically everyone scoffed at. We caught that move not by being smarter than everyone else, but by interpreting events through a commodity lens and being able to predict their effect on interest rate curves. (See Figure 10.1.)

The Greenspan Conundrum Speech, 2005

There is little doubt that, with the breakup of the Soviet Union and the integration of China and India into the global trading market, more of the world's productive capacity is being tapped to satisfy global demands for goods and services. Concurrently, greater integration of financial markets has meant that a larger share of the world's pool of savings is being deployed in cross-border financing of investment. The favorable inflation performance across a broad range of countries, resulting from enlarged global goods, services, and financial capacity has doubtless contributed to expectations of lower inflation in the years ahead and lower inflation risk premiums. But none of this is new and hence it is difficult to attribute the long-term interest rate declines of the last nine months to glacially increasing globalization. For the moment, the broadly unanticipated behavior of world bond markets remains a conundrum. Bond price movements may be a short-term aberration, but it will be some time before we are able to better judge the forces underlying recent experience.

SOURCE: Federal Reserve System, www.federalreserve.gov, February 17, 2005.

Can you give me an example of a trade coming to you?

One example is the Philippine peso. I used to go to Hong Kong regularly and on Sundays I would see all the Filipino housekeepers and nannies in Central and was interested to learn that they systematically send their earnings home via remittances. In 1994, everyone was bearish the Philippine peso despite interest rates of 14 to 15 percent. I dug more into the story about the Filipino diaspora and found that remittances remained strong and persistent—yet no one was looking at that flow of funds. We had also peaked out on USD/PHP at 30 in late 1993, after which time it started strengthening, much to everyone's surprise. In addition to our positive in-house economic analysis, this peripheral and persistent demand for the currency gave me the courage to get long the Philippine peso at 27.50 (see Figure 10.2). Where the market community was short the peso because of the inflation concerns, I thought interest rates were way too high relative to the inflation risk; and with the positive carry, you were being more than compensated. I also bought very short-term local paper at 13 to 14 percent and it was a great trade. I find most of the time a good trade comes from identifying something that most other people miss and may even consider insignificant. Everything quantitative, everything related to economics, everything numerical that can be number-crunched and is widely available is all in the rear-view mirror. The key is finding a piece of information that people are missing that is relevant for the future.

Many trades begin with basic observations of changes in supply and demand trends that I subsequently dig into. A good example of this

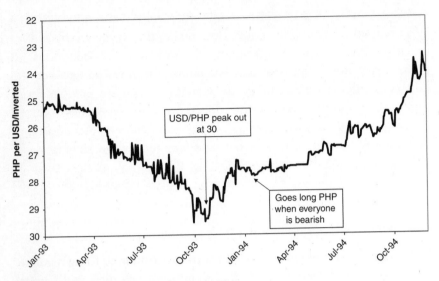

Figure 10.2 Philippine Peso, 1993–1994
SOURCE: Bloomberg.

would be when I identified bullish aspects of the natural gas market after learning that my small hometown in Minnesota switched over from 100 percent electricity to 100 percent natural gas. This led me to dig in further and I found some great trades related to energy switching. I tend to develop a macro theme, which I then analyze on a micro basis to verify or disprove it by some kind of quantitative construct. If my hypothesis becomes validated, whereby the numbers move in the direction of my theme, I will have more conviction to put on the trade. I often put a trade on small, and then as my further digging confirms my underlying hypotheses, I add. But if my underlying hypotheses are invalidated, I will take the trade off, even if I am making money.

With millions of people looking at financial markets and everyone inundated by data, how do you still find things that others miss?

There is an adage that says: The science of trading ponders the past, the art of trading focuses on the future—a good hedge fund needs a reasonable mix of both. I would argue that most hedge funds overweight the importance of past correlations. I catch things that others miss because I focus equally on the art and science of trading.

I have a unique methodology of looking around the world and developing themes that are not based on asset classes or geographies, but rather on bigger picture trends in the world. We distill down from a given trend, identifying trading opportunities that might develop because of the trend. I am looking for themes and ways to express these themes in specific trades. Instead of deciding if I am bullish or bearish currencies, equities, or China, I prefer to look for trades that catch important thematic developments. If my theme is a demographic theme of remittances, I will start from the top down to identify all the countries impacted by a significant diaspora community sending money home, then find out who sends what home, what the underlying economics are. If the theme is climate volatility, I will focus on any country, any market in the world that will be impacted by either short-term climate events or new alternative fuels. This top-down theme of new fuels or technologies then drives my bottom up process where I will work from companies back up to sectors in this new space.

So trade ideas just come to you as a result of your experience and awareness?

Yes, both experience and awareness help me source trade ideas. Some would refer to awareness as intuition, but it's not. Our brain only synthesizes about 5 to 8 percent of what's going on around us, though we are really analyzing everything, even if 92 percent is not on a conscious level. There is something that enables an astute trader to have a feel for certain trades, certain relationships, even if she cannot fully articulate why. Currently, I cannot yet articulate why I am very bearish dollar/yen all of a sudden. I have not been bearish dollar/yen in 20 years. I have always bought dips. I cannot articulate a reason, but my awareness from having traded currencies and having been in the markets for years is definitely picking something up. (*Note:* dollar/yen was at 94 when this interview was conducted; six weeks later it was at 86.)

I will give you another example. One of my best trades ever was in 1993, my highest return year, on three instruments that I had never traded before: gold, Canadian provincial bonds, and small cap gold equities in Australia. I borrowed gold at $410, using it as a funding currency since it was even cheaper to borrow than yen at a yield less than 1 percent. I deposited the proceeds and using a bit of leverage bought Saskatchewan, Alberta and British Columbia one year bonds at 9 to 12 percent. As a hedge to my short gold position, besides being in commodity rich province credits, I looked around for undervalued small cap mining equities in either South Africa, Australia, or Canada that had large margins and low cost of production, below $250 per ounce. I felt these would hold their value even if gold went down, and would outperform if gold rallied. Though my initial long-term bear target on gold was $250 for various supply and demand reasons including central bank sales, currency depreciation, and new low cost producers in emerging markets. When gold fell from $410 to my interim target, $350, I added another leg to my trade. I bought cheap small-cap mining producers in Australia that got pummeled by more than 50 percent as bullion lost $60 on the thesis that they now represented great value even if gold continued to decline. And that was it—I sat back and basically did nothing for the rest of the year. It was a fun and lazy year as all three legs worked.

What event or news triggered you to look at this trade?

Actually, it was very simple. I was reading *The Economist*—I love to look at the back two pages of statistics—searching extreme values for a number of relationships: the highest and lowest nominal interest rates in the world, the strongest and weakest currencies, the highest and lowest stock markets and commodities. In commodities, I look at cost of production, noting which are trading the most over and the most under their cost of production. Then I ask myself if these extreme levels are justified. I'm just looking at the extremes first. In this instance, gold caught my eye because it had the lowest nominal interest rate in the world and was the most expensive commodity, trading some 30 to 40 percent above the highest global cost of production and I had a view that global cost of production levels would be coming down rapidly. Canadian provincial bonds also caught my eye, as they had some of the highest nominal interest rates in the developed world, and they were provinces rich in commodities and real assets, which provided a floor. Eureka! I could buy these provincials by shorting the most expensive commodity in the world to use as a funding currency, thereby paying the lowest interest rate in the world. And I only needed a credit line to borrow it—no cash was required for margin. I knew this would be a great trade. After that initial "*Economist* moment," I did several weeks of both macro and micro analysis to make sure I wasn't missing anything. Again, once I put the trade on I was constantly reassessing my hypothesis to make sure everything unfolded according to plan.

How do you construct your portfolio around these themes, and how do you manage risk?

I'll start with risk, which is what I focus on in the fund. I believe simple is smart, so I manage risk on absolute dollar stops. I have all my liquid assets in the fund, so I never rely exclusively on quantitative formulas, although I use VaR and quantitative analysis as tools to monitor risk. I want to know how many dollars I can lose at all times, which then translates into a percentage loss that must remain within our fund guidelines.

I have a hard-coded discipline, comprised of the following: a hard stop of 2 percent of portfolio assets per trade; a delevering of a theme down 5 percent; and a delevering of the whole portfolio at down 10 percent, at which point I clearly need to review my analysis. I also always cut off the tails to protect the portfolio in a disaster scenario. I protect all full positions with risk collars, which for longs are structured by selling out-of-the-money call options to buy out-of-the-money puts and the inverse for shorts (see box on page 282). If something unpredictable happens, my risk collars kick in and take me out of the trade. These collars produced amazing results in both 2007 and 2008.

How many trades and themes do you typically run?

I have a maximum of five themes, and within each, I run 5 to 15 trades. Typically our portfolio has around 35 trades, and I have two criteria for how a trade gets into the portfolio. First, composition and direction of the portfolio is fundamental, discretionary, and economically driven. I crunch the numbers, estimate supply and demand, and formulate an economic value for a trade. Fundamental reasons can be purely economic, contain some artistic or psychological elements, or represent the identification of a new trend. They are everything from quantitative to qualitative, but driven by my fundamental estimate for economic value. At core, I am a value trader, not a momentum trader. Once the fundamental economic value criteria are met, I then plug the trade into my price analysis model, which is a proprietary technical model I developed. Because I am not a momentum trader, I needed a technical model that identifies undervalued and overvalued technical pricing, basically trying to find bull traps, bear traps, and zones of value. The model helps me find overvalued zones to go short or undervalued zones to go long, and then the economic fundamentals must support the position before I invest.

Risk Collars

Risk collars are an investment strategy that employs options to limit both the potential gain and loss of a position to a specific range. This strategy is employed by writing (selling) a covered call option on an owned asset and using the premium earned from the sale to buy a put option on the same asset; vice versa for assets sold short. Portfolio managers will attempt to employ this strategy at no cost by matching the cash flows of the call options and the put options.

Do the risk collars and tail hedging end up truncating your returns or just dampening your volatility?

They dampen volatility but do not truncate returns because I use them dynamically. Their main purpose is to protect the downside from the unexpected. I started using them opportunistically years ago, when I was on vacation, when we were at an important technical level, or when there was an important data release and I was running a big position. I decided to make it a mandatory part of my process after 9/11, an event that made me realize the importance of protecting the portfolio from unexpected extreme events that cannot be predicted.

On 9/11, I didn't have risk collars on, and I stopped out of most of my trades as they hit their 2 percent levels, taking a 10 percent hit across the portfolio. Although I stuck to my risk rules, I felt as if I was making a mistake in getting out of many of those positions. Several of the trades

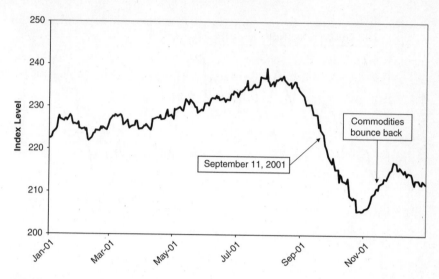

Figure 10.3 CRB Commodity Index, 2001
SOURCE: Bloomberg.

we were involved in bounced back pretty quickly, and I realized if I had the risk collars on, I would have held my position because of the positive convexity they add to the portfolio. (See Figure 10.3.)

Now risk collars are mandatory on all my full-risk positions. I determine levels for my risk collars the same way I enter positions: I plug them into my price analysis model. Instead of using a one-year time horizon, which I use for individual trades, I look at two-week overvaluation and undervaluation zones, then structure my risk collars around those bands using two-week to two-month options. The majority of our risk collars expire worthless, which is exactly what I would like them to do. They are close to zero cost and act as insurance, and they help me sleep at night, which is valuable.

Can you give me an example of when the risk collars saved you?

In August 2007, I was running average leverage when markets started to roll over, due to the start of the credit crisis and issues in the quant fund space. We went through the collars' protective strikes on the majority of our 35 positions, which completely protected us without taking us out of the positions. If things worsened, we were protected, but within

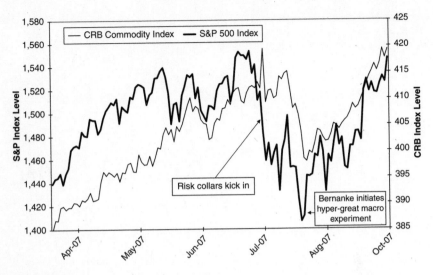

Figure 10.4   CRB and S&P 500, 2007
Source: Bloomberg.

two weeks, our positions bounced back above our collars and we were making money. I went from a few billion dollars of positions to minimal exposure with no trading, no slippage, no dealing with banks, no emotional turmoil; yet because of the positive convexity in the collars, we had the entire position on again as markets rebounded. I was soon making money again, thanks in no small part to Fed Chairman Bernanke cutting the discount rate. That is really the crucial point: unexpected things can happen on both the downside and the upside. If we hit our upside collar, it means we are taking profit where we want to, so it's a luxury problem. But if we hit the downside collar, we are not only hedged, preventing a blow-up, but we also stay in the trade giving it a chance to come back. The fourth quarter of 2007 ended up making our year, after having been essentially stopped out of our positions in August. The collars made all the difference between a mediocre year and a great year. (See Figure 10.4.)

Do the risk collars allow you to safely lever up your portfolio?

Yes, the lower volatility and known downside allow us to run decent-sized leverage. Although we normally run gross leverage of 3 to 5 times, it has been as high as 11—but that was only for a brief moment one time (see box).

Eleven

Nigel Tufnel:	The numbers all go to 11. Look, right across the board, 11, 11, 11 and ...
Marty DiBergi:	Oh, I see. And most amps go up to 10?
Nigel Tufnel:	Exactly.
Marty DiBergi:	Does that mean it's louder? Is it any louder?
Nigel Tufnel:	Well, it's one louder, isn't it? It's not 10. You see, most blokes, you know, will be playing at 10. You're on 10 here, all the way up, all the way up, all the way up, you're on 10 on your guitar. Where can you go from there? Where?
Marty DiBergi:	I don't know.
Nigel Tufnel:	Nowhere. Exactly. What we do is, if we need that extra push over the cliff, you know what we do?
Marty DiBergi:	Put it up to 11.
Nigel Tufnel:	Eleven. Exactly. One louder.
Marty DiBergi:	Why don't you just make 10 louder and make ten be the top number and make that a little louder?
Nigel Tufnel:	[pause] These go to 11.

SOURCE: *This is Spinal Tap*, 1984.

Do you use leverage because you are playing for small moves in various markets?

No. We are very directional and play for large moves. We don't trade for two or three basis points. We typically look for at least a 20 to 30 percent move, but can have situations where we think 100 percent or more is possible. Risk versus reward is everything. We will not put on a trade unless we can make about three times what we risk. On a negative carry trade, the return target is often five times the risk. We don't basis trade, spread trade, calendar trade, or relative value trade. We always want to be right for the right reasons. We believe simplicity is the best way to approach this and we look for major moves, not minor moves.

When we talk about leverage, we are talking about the notional value of our positions, not the cash value. For currency and futures trades, you're putting up cash margin of 3 to 5 percent of the notional value. And the risk collars require little initial margin because they are a zero cost option structure. So it's a conservative measure of leverage and we always have cash on hand. We would never go negative cash, nor would we ever borrow to lever. Even when I was levered 11 times, I still had the cash on hand to support the positions. If I got to the point where I didn't have cash, I would not put any more trades on. It's highly unlikely that we'd ever have less than 20 to 30 percent of cash on hand, even when the portfolio is 5 to 10 times leveraged.

Given that you are looking for big moves, how often are you right?

We have a pretty high hit ratio whereby we're right a majority of the time. We have very wide zones that we scale into, so we aren't putting on a trade and stopping out multiple times before we finally catch the move. Also, we do not predict the timing of a price move—price is the ultimate variable, so many times a trade may sit there longer than we would like. But given our opportunistic pricing, even if our assumptions do not pan out, our downside risk is minimal. The reason we have a high hit ratio is the way we exit trades. We spend several months vetting the trade on fundamentals, after which time we plug it into our price analysis model to get a technical valuation. So we have two significant valuation hurdles before we put a trade on. Even if we are wrong on our underlying premises, we usually break even because we have entered at optimum pricing. And if the underlying hypotheses do not materialize, we get out, even if the trade is making money. Making money for the wrong reasons means you are rolling the dice, not trading. We are not here to gamble. Trades have to be making money for the reasons that we have identified and have the proper risk versus reward.

The Asian financial crisis theme in 1998–1999 is a good example. The underlying premise was that a lack of transparency would stop the flow of funds into Asia, and we shorted the Hang Seng. The trade started working in our favor, but funds did not stop flowing into Asia, even though transparency did not increase, so we got out of the trade.

With such a high hurdle for trades to get into your portfolio, do you sometimes find that you have a shortage of trades in the book?

We never have a shortage of trades in the portfolio. We draw from the entire global macro universe of instruments: any asset class, any instrument, anywhere in the world. I cannot recall an instance where we did not find at least five trades in a given theme that met our valuation criteria. By having a diverse menu of potential trades, we have many options at our disposal. We never want to be limited or restricted in our instrument choice.

I'll give you an example: If you have a view that gold is overvalued, you can express it by shorting the South African rand or the Aussie dollar, selling a gold-related equity, or doing a structured note. There are a myriad of ways to express themes. We are very good at looking out at the periphery for trade ideas, not getting stuck at the center of a view or theme.

You mentioned you have a one-year time horizon for trades. How far ahead do you look in developing your themes?

Time horizons on themes vary considerably, from maybe six months to five years. We look at trends. For example, the Asian financial crisis theme lasted about six months, whereas the theme around commodity inelasticity of demand and supply has been on since inception. But the trades within a theme are all structured around a one-year investment horizon, both economically and technically. We look at valuations and targets based on one-year economic values, and our technical price model is also based on a one-year horizon. We might have two-, three-, five-year economic targets, but trades are one year. Another example was buying gold at $250 in 1999. We had a big-picture economic target of $500 to $600 a few years down the road, but because our target for the year was $320—based on the price analysis model—we took profit at this level. (See Figure 10.5.)

Did your time horizon shorten during the 2008 financial crisis?

Our horizon didn't change, although we did incorporate three- to six-month time frames in our technical analysis alongside the one-year time horizon. Because of the extreme flux in the market, the shutdown of

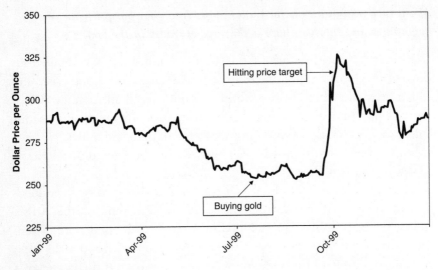

Figure 10.5   Gold, 1999
SOURCE: Bloomberg.

credit, and the lack of liquidity, we focused more on tactical trades with three-month value zones instead of one-year zones. We tightened up risk management with closer stops and took profits more quickly because of the treacherous environment.

The risk collars worked exactly the way they were supposed to: We closed the year flat even though the portfolio leverage had reached almost four times and our core positions moved against us 30 to 60 percent in a two-month time period. Preservation of capital, risk management, and avoiding tail risk are of the utmost importance to us—our collars kicked in automatically, so we didn't have to get caught up in trading wide spreads and illiquid markets.

What lessons did you learn in 2008?

There are two important parts to running a hedge fund: the business part and the trading and investment part. It is very important that the two are in sync with each other. You may have a great trade with great valuation, but if you are running a business on quarterly liquidity, it's crucial that your portfolio liquidity matches the liquidity offered to your investors. Although 2008 was a difficult, frustrating time, we managed liquidity well, honoring all redemption requests without putting up a gate or creating a side pocket. We saw all kinds of trades that presented tremendous opportunities, but because their time horizon and liquidity didn't match what we offered our investors, we couldn't put them in our fund.

The importance of certain factors comes and goes based on the broader environment, and right now liquidity is overvalued. People are paying way too much for liquidity. Liquidity was needed in 2008, but no longer. The need for liquidity is often inversely related to valuation. Valuations are so low now that you can buy and hold certain illiquid instruments if you have both the cash and a long enough horizon. You always need some base level of liquidity, and you always have to match it with what you offer investors.

I recently saw an opportunity to capitalize on some of these mispricings. I started a new strategy with a three-year lockup to take advantage of some of the incredible opportunities created in the wake of 2008. But this strategy is not for the faint of heart, as most investors don't have high tolerance for downside risk that is 5 to 10 times higher than our main fund. Farmland offers great opportunities, as do private deals in the commodity and real asset space. Knowing that you can scale into two-year and three-year value zones in these wild markets gives you a clear edge if you have the stomach for it.

How do you value liquidity?

Quantitative models can value liquidity, but I tend to look at the risk versus reward of a specific opportunity. Right now, for example, opportunities abound in highly liquid instruments that you can trade short-term, and the liquidity premium attached to longer term illiquid trades offers really attractive valuations for those with a longer horizon.

We are in a lower return environment going forward—returns around the world will come down. The risk-free rate is close to zero and long end interest rates around the world are converging toward levels significantly lower than historical norms. Going forward, everyone will be forced to accept lower returns on all assets, from stocks to bonds to businesses. We will also have slower growth stabilizing somewhere between 0 and 3 percent globally. In a lower return environment, it makes sense to do higher yielding, longer-term trades, which you hold to maturity.

Illiquid investments, however, require a solid understanding of the supply and demand of the supply and demand. In other words, fast and fickle global capital flows make it important to identify the number and type of investors involved in all trades, as well as any negative carry or other specific features. I value a crowded illiquid instrument completely differently than I do an opportunity that no one is talking about. More factors go into assessing illiquids than liquids, but although the bar is much higher for the former, the returns can be much greater as well.

Looking through your commodity lens, did you foresee the collapse in commodities in the second half of 2008?

I was on CNBC *Squawk Box* in August 2008 when oil was at $115 a barrel, and I said it was going down to $80. I really thought it was going to $50, but I played it conservatively, since everyone thought it was going back up to $200. And I still took a lot of heat for that call. We didn't have the position on because the risk/reward was not there. We had just come off an all-time high of $147 the prior month, and any geopolitical event could have taken it right back up. Even if such a geopolitical shock was unlikely, it skewed the risk/reward and we didn't like it as a trade. So yes, the fall in the oil price was predictable, and I definitely felt oil was a bubble due to index flows in GSCI and other commodity indices. We did actually get short around $140, but only in small size and we took profit quickly, which became our modus operandi in the second half of 2008 and early 2009.

I did not foresee the more comprehensive commodity meltdown, however. I expected some decoupling within the commodity complex because food and agricultural commodities were underinvested relative to oil and others. Food and ags were up a bit on passive commodity index flows, but I underestimated how quickly that money would come out of the market and take prices down. Passive money rushed into the ags and the softs late, and exited en masse soon thereafter. Although I underestimated the strength of the move down, our collars and risk management kicked in to take us out of the positions. Without the index money, the extent of decoupling would have been more significant, and going forward we will see intracommodity complex decoupling as a major trend. We are currently bearish base metals and energy, but bullish agricultural commodities on a five-year view. We are seeing a big shift of wealth from the developed world to the developing economies, whereby people in emerging markets are moving up the food chain and demanding different types of food as their wealth grows. This is one of the best long-term opportunities out there.

Further, although food and grains are being considered for alternative energy, the current pricing of food does not factor in water, although people are starting to realize that water will be priced drastically differently in the future. For example, certain places in the Middle East stopped growing their own wheat and grains last year because water was too expensive, making it more advantageous to import food. Others will follow suit, which will only serve to further reduce the supply of agricultural commodities while demand remains constant or rising. Increased demand with less supply creates an opportunity for prices to shoot substantially higher.

What was the worst trade of your career, and what lessons did you learn from it?

I hate to admit it, but sadly my worst trade was shorting the S&P at slightly over 400 a few years after the 1987 crash. I sold on a major rally in late 1991, so it wasn't the low, but in the big picture it wasn't far from it. At that time, I was convinced that the equity market was overvalued based on a historical perspective.

That event really clarified my thinking, and it forced me to look at historical events in the proper context. I learned to think in the future and not get caught up in the past. I had been analyzing markets from a backward-looking perspective, holding relationships and correlations constant but markets can move in unexpected ways. I learned that things do not necessarily act logically in the future and this new way of thinking helped me later on. Around 1992–1993, for example, I thought bonds would go up at the same time that equity markets were going up, yet my peers thought I was crazy since historically those markets are inversely

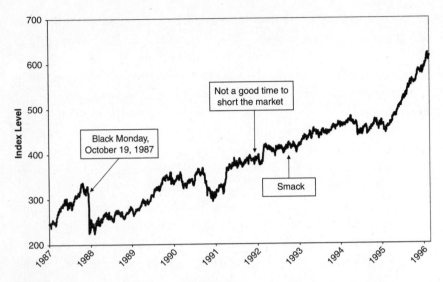

Figure 10.6　S&P 500 Index, 1987–1996
SOURCE: Bloomberg.

correlated. I had begun to see productivity gains around the world in many of the businesses that I was familiar with, especially in the U.S. I thought that business restructuring, productivity gains, and the decrease in overall expensed costs would offset any inflationary aspect to growth. I really think that my ability to figure that out came from being wrong about equities from the crash right up until my short position smacked me in 1991. (See Figure 10.6.)

Investing according to future expectations, rather than in a rear-view mirror, is difficult for most investors. How do you overcome that human bias?

I definitely look at the rear-view mirror to define the past, which gives me a sense for return and correlation relationships under "normal" conditions. Then, however, I think about what could make things happen differently. I fight the urge to look backwards by focusing on the ingredients of the current situation and on the ranges of potential outcomes rather than absolute outcomes. People get caught up thinking that certain inputs produce certain outputs, but they forget to qualify the environment into which the inputs were introduced.

For example, we make mistakes when we look backwards at events like 1929, 1973, or 1998 and try to compare them to today. Different monetary and fiscal policies produce different growth rates, which, in turn, produce different results in the "market." You have to understand the nuances of the environment into which the input was introduced. Similarly, the impact of monetary or fiscal stimulus is completely different today given the important demographic shifts of the baby boom generation. We are all now in our peak earning years, which compares to the 1970s, when we were in our peak indebtedness. I always ask myself: "What characterizes the current environment today?" and, "How is today's picture the same as or different from the past?" Then I look at the inputs and outputs. If you focus on what is different today, it's easier to fight the urge to assume that the same inputs will produce the same outputs as prior periods.

What do most investors miss when analyzing your fund or investment opportunities more generally?

Investors focus on asset class, geography, and strategy way too much. To me, it's manager, manager, manager. Finding someone that regularly makes money and runs a good business is much more important than what instruments she trades, what strategy she employs, or what regions of the world she specializes in. The key is to find someone that could make money trading nuts and bolts in a hardware store if she were forced to. Investing based on some quantitative analysis of a strategy, asset class, or geography is imperfect. Again, it's the rear-view mirror. It really does not make any difference what you invest in; the key is with whom you invest. Try to understand a manager's ability to make money, and don't focus on the specific assets or instruments traded. It is more important to focus on how someone manages risk, whether she has the ability to preserve capital.

You need to recognize the different styles of managers in order to be able to assess their talent. Some managers produce return streams from long-term directional investments while other managers produce returns from short-term trades. It is important that investors recognize what they are evaluating in the first place. The quant stuff matters, but the intangibles matter as well. It's art versus science again. It is very important that the manager shows the willingness and ability to evolve. Managers who are content with their process, believing it will continue to work because it has always worked, will run into trouble at some point.

If you were running a large endowment with a long-term time horizon and without redemptions, how would you go about it?

At the moment, my biggest position—about a third of the portfolio— would be in farmland and agricultural land around the world. China will slowly transition their reserves into real assets around the world, and that will drive valuations. Next, I would have a big chunk, around 20 to 30 percent, in selective, high-yield fixed income. Because of my view that interest rates will converge at low levels, I would be in higher yielding sovereign bonds in places like Brazil. I would not be in any equity indices, but I would get involved in select individual equities and select businesses opportunistically; my preference would be to avoid listed equities, instead opting for private equity stakes in businesses. But this is right now, based on the current environment. I would be very tactical and opportunistic at all times. The remaining 20 to 30 percent would be with good risk managers, regardless of their strategy: short term, long term, systematic, whatever. I wouldn't care whether it was commodities, fixed income, or equities. I would just find good traders that offered me good risk/reward.

It is almost conventional wisdom in the real money world and among the consultants who advise them that market timing doesn't work; instead they suggest setting strategy allocation at a policy level and then sticking with it.

That is wrong, particularly with respect to equities. When a market is in a bubble or overvaluation like equities were—and I believe are again now—why have any exposure to them at all? Let's face it, owning equities since 2000 has not worked unless you got in at precisely the right time, which is being tactical. And it's going to be worse for the next 5 to 10 years because developed-country equities are the most overinvested, overvalued, mismanaged asset class in the world.

Select emerging market equities are a different story, though. Just this past year we began to see evidence of emerging markets decoupling from developed markets. The September 2009 *Boston Consulting Group Report on Global Wealth* said the average wealth of Americans decreased by 21 percent in 2008, whereas Europe was down 5.8 percent, Asia Pacific 6.2 percent, the Middle East 6.9 percent, and Latin America actually up 3 percent. We think this is significant. Global wealth has decoupled while global equity markets have been synchronized, which has masked the economic decoupling. Decoupling will eventually be recognized and emerging market equities will outperform. I am particularly bullish Latin America, which I think will outperform Asia.

Why do you think Latin America will outperform Asia?

Demographics are one reason. Because of its aging population, Asia has a bigger demographic problem than Latin America. Even China's population will be in decline in the next 20 years due to the one child policy. Latin America is quite young, however, and the importance of commodities and natural resources, which they have, will provide a strong tailwind to the region relative to Asia. North and South America are the breadbasket of real commodity assets—particularly food and feed—and will remain so in the future.

Could you run a real money fund?

Absolutely, I would love to run a real money fund. It would be easier than what I do now because a longer-term approach fits my investment style; my natural investment time frame is very long term. Ideas and themes tend to be clearer over longer time periods, and one of our strengths is identifying major price dislocation. Timing the market consistently can be frustrating, even if you have obtained the perfect price, and real money funds can afford the patience to let trends unfold at their own pace. What you may lose in short-term opportunity costs, you will typically more than make up in absolute return.

I would not be invested in passive commodity indices. Rather, I would gain exposure to commodities in the same way that I currently do in my hedge fund. There was a run on all assets in 2008 and we were wrong on everything, but we cut off the downside tail with our risk collars, allowing us to maintain longer-term positions in the face of short-term volatility. Even in longer-term portfolios with illiquid investments like farmland, I always look to find an uncorrelated trade or a hedge. I look at my portfolio in the context of different market environments, identifying where I will make money and make sure I am protected if everything falls. I always focus first and foremost on the preservation of capital because compounding works—if you can avoid the steep losses, you will generate solid returns over time.

Right now, real money accounts are too focused on long-only investments; they do not use the full financial spectrum of global instruments to properly structure their investment portfolios, especially with respect to currencies and interest rates. The U.S. dollar is not the only currency in the world. Over the next 5 to 10 years, the dollar should depreciate by 30 to 50 percent because it's politically expedient and economically prudent. Meanwhile, investors here in the U.S. will think they performed relatively well as long as equities and bonds don't crash, despite losing 50 percent of their global purchasing power. If I were running a real money portfolio, I would be out of the dollar completely, as I am now.

Real money should cut off the tails. By this I am speaking less about employing efficient stops and more about constructing a safety net. Wait and buy value. Don't allocate to an asset class just because you feel the need to diversify, to be involved in every asset bucket. I believe it was Warren Buffett who once said, "Diversification, diworsification." Trying to create a recipe for managing a portfolio is like trying to create a recipe for making someone laugh: it's impossible. Diversification has evolved such that people use it to absolve themselves of any blame. Because everything is spread around, they don't have to commit to anything. Rational and purposeful concentration makes sense, but not dogmatic concentration, such as everything in one stock market. In general, being more concentrated while adhering to your investment goals makes sense. And of course, the liquidity profile should match the annual needs for cash.

Why are indices the wrong way to gain exposure to commodities, and what is the right way?

The right route is either investing in commodities directly if you have the expertise, or allocating to an active commodity manager if you do not. I would not recommend quantitative systematic commodity funds. My preference is always for value-oriented, risk managers. Current commodity index structures, because of how they manage the roll yield, practically guarantee that you overpay for exposure. Further, weightings are based on past correlations and flows, rather than dynamically investing as markets evolve.

I believe in being tactical. I don't believe that you get into equities, bonds, or commodities and stay there forever. Yet this latter scenario is precisely what the passive commodity indices offer, and they got big at the wrong time. People were piling into the indices with no concept of value: the indices were going up so they had to get in, yet as they got in, they went up more. Had that supply come in over the course of 5 or 10 years, it would not have had the same impact. But it came in all at once, all at the wrong time. I chastise myself for not realizing the importance of this flow at the time, but every single real money manager we talked to said they were in for the long term. I would ask, "If commodities are down 30 percent, are you going to get out?" And they would say no. Yet when commodities fell along with everything else, they all got out. Everyone sold.

Do you believe in peak oil whereby crude goes to several hundred dollars, and all other commodities are dragged up with it?

No. I believe that over time oil will go back down. $50 to $80 is a reasonable range for oil, but I wouldn't be surprised to see it below these levels. There is serious demand destruction in fossil fuels, and a strong movement in favor of bio and alternative fuels. Again, there is going to be a decoupling within the commodity spectrum, with food and ags leading the way.

Is the world headed towards inflation or deflation?

We have huge overcapacity in everything from cars to consumables. We will see inflation in real assets but not in consumer prices, the latter of which impact bonds. China cannot stop buying Treasuries because China is the one with the problem. They will do anything to help us because they are the ones holding all that worthless paper. The U.S. is too big to fail.

Will U.S. Treasuries become worthless?

Global GDP is approximately $60 trillion, and that is during a high-growth period. The U.S. has unfunded liabilities of around $125 trillion, which includes counties, states, federal, Medicare/Medicaid, Social Security, and off-balance-sheet expenditures like Katrina and Iraq. Officially, our current deficit is $11 trillion, but if you add the off-balance-sheet items and exclude the unfunded liabilities, we believe it's closer to $25 trillion. If that is true, we are running a deficit of 200 percent of GDP. In some ironic way, we are already too big to fail, so the more debt we issue, the safer we are. This is the real conundrum, and the next few years will be exciting, at the very least.

Chapter 11

The Equity Trader

"The Equity Trader" started trading in middle school and has been passionate about markets ever since. A soft-spoken but aggressive trader, his first forays in the markets were with mutual funds, after which time he joined an equity-focused prop desk before finally starting his own hedge fund. Although he primarily trades individual stocks, he also trades futures, currencies, credit, commodities, and options.

The Equity Trader has evolved from a priced-based, technical trader to a more fundamental, theme-based trader as his business has grown and matured. Nevertheless, he can aggressively trade around core positions, which remains one of his hallmarks. Being in the markets all the time keeps him sharp, he says.

When I met the Equity Trader, he told me that he was worried about the interview. A few years earlier, he explained, he had done an interview and proceeded to get killed in the subsequent months. Superstition seemed incongruous with the analytical, risk-obsessed process he employs in the markets.

Although he remains a stock trader, the Equity Trader combines his bottom-up fundamental work with a robust understanding of the macro environment, something that he implements to change the shape of his book aggressively in various environments. He now employs a large team of risk takers, and interviews hundreds of people a year for a small number of slots, preferring to take on people with specific traits that he can mold over time rather than those with particular specialties.

He says the biggest mistake from the institutional side of the investing world is bucketing by type of investment, as opposed to by correlation or risk factors. By taking a more risk-based approach when managing a real money portfolio, large drawdowns could be mitigated, protecting longer term compounded returns. And evolving your processes is something this manager should know about, as continually striving to improve his processes—particularly on the risk management side—has become a career-long obsession.

***

How did you get into the business?

I was introduced to the market when I was about 13 years old. My junior high school held a stock picking contest, and I bought some bankrupt stock that doubled on paper. After that, I began investing in mutual funds, using the money that I made in part-time jobs. I started reading markets books, following the market as best I could, trying to learn. During college, I worked as a stockbroker, pitching people different investment ideas even though I really didn't know what I was doing. I would take my earnings from that job and use them to trade for myself, which I also was terrible at.

Did you get blown out in your trading account?

Indeed, after a couple of years of trading for myself, I lost everything and was broke. I had no idea what I was doing and was essentially just chasing stuff around, trading momentum. I had no method, no discipline, no money management. I had nothing to anchor me amidst the madness.

Do you occasionally see the old you in your traders or traders you interview?

I definitely recognize my unformed self in some of the young people I see in the business. Even good traders tend to revert to chasing momentum when they get frustrated or are in a slump. It is easy to lose confidence when this happens because whatever you are doing is not working, and just randomly doing things does not solve the problem. With no method, trading winds up being more emotional.

Do you preplan all your trading?

My trading is definitely preplanned when I am looking for certain scenarios to develop around clear catalysts, where my views on a particular company are based on fundamental information. At other times my trading can be more reactionary to what's going on in the market. I try to react in a disciplined way to what's happening in the market on a given day—adjusting positions as the odds change.

How did you learn discipline?

Losing money definitely helped. Also, I changed jobs to become a trader at a proprietary trading firm, which had a very disciplined risk management system that was drilled into us. This new trading role meant a fixed capital allocation with clear stop-loss levels on every trade, as well as a predefined universe of the names we were allowed to trade. It was a very good place for someone new to the business to learn.

Everyone was forced to operate under the same basic rules, which were then adapted over time to fit individual personalities and trading styles. The more experienced guys at the firm would spend time with the more junior guys, going over trades and offering critiques. Between learning from your own experience and learning from mentors, you gradually pick up the craft. And trading better meant more capital, wider mandates, and higher limits, so you were incentivized to learn quickly. Not to mention that base compensation was zero.

How much time did you spend there?

I was there for about seven years. I went sideways for the first 9 or 10 months but then I got the hang of it and started making money pretty consistently. I define consistency based on annual performance, but I was profitable most months and my best months were significantly bigger than my worst. Performance per day is more random, but there are definitely streaks where you make money daily for even two or three weeks at a stretch, and other streaks where you lose money daily for the same amount of time. The key is managing position size so that you cut when you are losing and maximize profits when you are really in a groove.

How did you find the transition from a risk framework imposed on you to developing your own rules for your own fund?

The development of my risk systems took a gradual path as my own trading style evolved. When I started trading, I was primarily focused on price action, so my trading was very short-term and very technical. There was little fundamental input, with the exception of observing how stocks reacted to news. After three or four years, however, I started hiring analysts to help us become more fundamental in our approach so that we could manage more capital. More capital meant running bigger position sizes for longer periods, which required a fundamental understanding of companies.

Every year since inception, we have become increasingly more fundamental in our investment approach. Our average holding periods have lengthened but we still trade very actively around positions based on price action. We might have a core position that we hold for six months, but at times it will represent 5 percent of the portfolio, while other times it will be only 50 basis points, depending on our assessment of the fundamental risk/reward and how the stock is behaving at that moment. Volatility also plays a part in how we size and trade around positions. During the second half of 2008, when volatility was crazy and fundamentals were not really impacting price action, we were very active, with an average holding period of only a few days. Regardless of environment, we stick to disciplined drawdowns and stop-out limits for every portfolio manager we employ, which definitely helped in a year like 2008.

Do you use indices or options to trade around core positions?

I use everything available to me. Although I primarily trade individual stocks outright, I also trade futures, currencies, credit, commodities, and

options. Having the ability to trade all these different instruments is both
a strength and a weakness. For example, it can be beneficial when you get
a bank shot trade where you can see a relationship in how information in
"Company A" or "Instrument A" will affect the trading in "Instrument
B," and you can be there quicker than the next guy. But other times such
breadth just complicates things because you think that such a relationship
will hold and it doesn't. Thus, rather than concentrating your trade in the
original instrument where you had the information and strong view, you
wind up structuring it through a derivative that nobody else cares about
at that particular moment in time. You have to be careful not to make
things too complex in this business. However, because the markets today
are so interconnected, you have to be very aware of what is happening
in all these asset classes even if you don't actively trade them.

*You mentioned that understanding fundamentals allows you to run a
bigger position, yet you also mentioned the importance of being faster
than the next guy. How much of the market is fundamental and how
much is behavioral?*

Markets go up and down because people buy and sell. This is the most
important thing to understand. We run into problems with our analysts when they become too concerned about being right on some
fundamental data point and forget that it's only an input to a trading
decision. It is really about understanding how that data point is going to
cause people to change their positions and how aggressively. This second
derivative is much harder to figure out. We spend a lot of time trying
to get the fundamentals right while also trying to understand how the
holders of a particular stock will behave. This latter exercise can be quite
difficult, but it is necessary in order to have good predictive trades.

*How do you get an understanding of how other holders of a given stock
are thinking?*

We talk to as many people as possible in the market. All of our teams
of analysts and portfolio managers in different sectors attend dinners,
conferences, and company meetings. In addition, each tends to have
a network of 20 or so people at other funds which, combined with
the network of players on the sell side, can help to form an idea of

expectations in the market. We are primarily trying to understand how people are positioning, and how bullish and bearish they are in particular sectors and individual names.

Sometimes understanding positioning is obvious. For example, if a stock got upgraded by several banks before the company reports earnings, chances are that expectations are fairly high. Before earnings results, we call around and compile the whisper numbers, what analysts are really looking for beyond the published estimates. Sometimes you can get a feel just from price action by watching how things react to news. If you are short a stock and a bearish piece of information comes out—numbers get cut or the stock is downgraded or whatever—and the thing is up, that tells you that expectations are probably somewhat low and a significant number of people are short. While that doesn't mean if results are even worse the stock won't go down, it does give you a sense of how people are positioned at that moment.

Do you feel that you are competing with other traders and other funds?

I am definitely in competition with other traders, but most importantly, I am constantly in competition with myself, to get better, to improve my skills and add to my repertoire as a trader. Constantly improving against your own benchmarks is far more important than beating a competitor, although this latter type of competition is intense in this business.

Given how active you are, how do you stay sharp trading so much day in, day out, year in, year out?

Activity keeps me sharp. I am always fighting a battle of how many trades or ideas to be involved with, always feeling that I have either too many or too few. If I am trading well and things are working, I tend to get preoccupied with thinking that I could have done something bigger, maybe been more offensive. When things are not working, I am always trying to cut back, asking myself why I have a given position, why it is a certain size, etc.

But this keeps me sharp. Having many different balls in the air, even if they are only small positions, enables me to be tangentially aware of what is going on across many different sectors and companies. Such breadth might jog a different idea, allowing me to connect a few different data points, giving me more conviction on something else. For me, the biggest and best trades tend to develop over time. I start small on an idea, using initial research and initial data points, and then as I get more confirming research and data points, I grow the position. Observing the price action of a stock against its sector, how it reacts with news, should hopefully give more or less conviction in an idea. The best trades usually develop when confirmation comes from both price action and additional research, enabling me to increase the position size maybe five- or tenfold from the initial level.

Are you always looking for confirming evidence, or do you focus on how you might be wrong?

I am always trying to figure out both of them. It is impossible to have complete information on something, so my process is iterative. I am constantly doing research, talking to my team, making sure I am thinking about the whole picture as best I can, thinking about everything that could influence an idea while simultaneously asking myself where I could be wrong, what I could be missing. Decisions are always made on partial information and waiting for over-confirmation on a trade is a sure way to miss a big part of the move.

What worries you most in running a hedge fund?

I am constantly worried about both the existing portfolio and the next big theme or idea. I do not usually have super-concentrated portfolios, but I worry about whether I will be right on some of the bigger positions in the book. These days, I particularly worry about missing one of the next themes or ideas.

Worries change over time. I remember one day early on in my trading, when my average daily swing was $5,000 or $10,000, I lost $50,000 on Hewlett-Packard after they preannounced a bad earnings number. The stock was down $10 at the open, when normally it would not move more than a dollar a day. After the close, I went home and lay on the floor for several hours wondering how I was ever going to make up that kind of money. It seemed like an impossible task.

A few weeks ago my wife asked how I was doing and I replied, "It was a boring, nothing type of day." She asked, "Oh, you were up?" I replied,

"Yeah, a couple million dollars." It sounds funny saying that but it's all relative to what you are managing, which is now a few billion dollars. Your emotions correlate with the significance of the amount compared to both your capital and your typical daily swing. Fifty thousand back then was much more painful than significantly larger numbers now. Speaking of which, it is extraordinarily important to have supportive people behind you to help deal with drawdowns. You need people who will stand behind you—your spouse, boss, partners, investors, parents, coworkers, etc. I have been fortunate to have a great team—especially my wife—who is stuck watching me mope around the house after bad trading days but still manages to help me keep things in perspective.

What was the best big trade of your career?

We do so many trades that it is difficult to think of one that really stands out from the rest, winning or losing. Talking about missing a trade, the most frustrating one that I missed was the subprime short a few years ago. Although we looked at it and did a decent amount of research, we ultimately passed because it was not our area of expertise. We had never traded mortgages or mortgage derivatives before so I did not feel comfortable doing it in the fund. Since then, the index went down from 99 to 5 so we missed a home run. (See Figure 11.1.)

I learned a valuable lesson missing this trade. Even if you are not the foremost expert on something, it pays to put on something even in small size as long as you can get comfortable with the downside and believe that there is clear risk-versus-reward asymmetry, which was definitely the case in this trade. Adding to the position once you are involved is much easier and you learn a lot about a position just by having it on.

You've never had any trading disasters?

Yahoo! was one trade that I tend to remember from about 10 years ago, back when internet stocks were going to the moon. I came in one morning short the stock and some positive news came out, taking it up 20 points. Then it went up 30, 40, 50, and I was scaling out of the short, cutting losses as others were initiating shorts or adding to their losing short position. When the stock held at +50 points, I actually reversed my short and went long. By the close that day Yahoo! was up 100 points

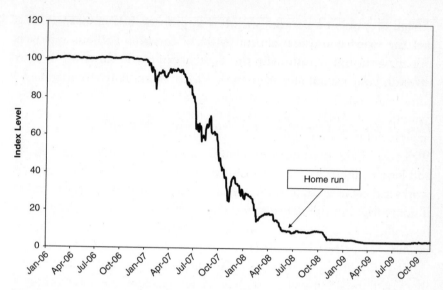

Figure 11.1 Subprime Index (ABX.HE.BBB 6–1), 2007–2009
SOURCE: Markit.

and I had made back my losses. I always remember this one because it beautifully illustrates that stocks are driven by supply and demand, and can go absolutely anywhere regardless of what you think the business might be worth.

What lessons did you learn during 2008?

You cannot get complacent during easy periods. Things such as counterparty risk and portfolio liquidity have to be worked on when things are good because once markets turn it's too late.

During 2008, what separated the winners and losers was risk management. It is important to clearly define your job and your mandate. Because I came from a trading background, I always defined my job as doing whatever was necessary to generate good quality P&L. I have never said that I have to stay in a particular exposure range or that I have to be invested in the market by a certain amount, to be net long or whatever. People from a more fundamental background have a higher tendency to fall into that trap, where they start defining their job or business as, "I am a long biased long/short manager where I keep an exposure between

20 and 80 percent long and my job is to pick the best companies long and the worst companies short." Most of the time such an approach might work, but occasionally this type of approach blows up. For an investor, blowing up once every 5 or 10 years is more than enough.

How do you avoid the once-every-5-to-10-year blow-up?

We concentrate on fundamental work. We have a huge team of analysts and have really strong research, but there are times when this approach works and other times when it does not. When your P&L tells you that it is not working, you have to adapt, stop betting as much on fundamental research, reduce exposures, and stick to stops. Many people do not do that.

It is important to match fundamental investing and research with the time frames that you are trading. If, for example, you have a process like Warren Buffett's where you try to find the greatest business with the best long-term potential, you need to have a long holding period which requires long-term capital. If you cannot hold positions for 5, 10, 15 years through various volatility regimes or your investors are not comfortable dealing with that kind of interim volatility, you cannot have this kind of investment process. Instead, perhaps you should be more focused on shorter-term catalysts, stocks that might outperform in the next few months or quarters, etc.

Long-term stories do not really change that much. If you were long energy in 2008, whether it's crude or mining companies or oil companies, on the theory of emerging markets growth, peak oil, and all that good stuff, you can make the same arguments today that you could have made a year ago, even five years ago. In the meantime, however, crude has gone up a few times, then down 80 percent and back up 50 percent, while many equities doubled and tripled and then went down 90 percent. As things get cheaper, people tend to want to buy more of them because the value seems better; but they are often trying to fit long-term judgment onto a shorter-term mandate. We try hard to match our research process to our holding periods, using stop losses on every subportfolio. Once we hit those stops, we cut, regardless if we think it is the greatest company for the next 10 years or not. And if we lose enough, we take the portfolio to cash.

Is trading your P&L part of your risk management process?

Trading our P&L is one part of the risk management process. Each portfolio manager, myself included, has a stop loss of 7 percent, at which point we shut down the book. We reduce risk as a trader is losing money to avoid blowing through stops on an extreme move. Sometimes the reduction is permanent, while other times it serves as a pause to revisit a theme or position, whether it makes sense to keep it or not.

The start of the risk management process is running a very diverse portfolio while having drawdown limits on every decision maker, every allocation. Then, of course, we have a host of more granular rules and limits, depending on the specific strategy, such as VaR limits, stress test limits, net exposure limits, concentration limits, and liquidity limits.

How do you decide to take profits on your winners?

How we manage the upside depends on the specific situation. When we get into a trade, we try to have an idea of the risk versus reward, and what type of trade it is. For a short-term tactical trade, we are trying to get a base hit because something seems out of line for a day or a few days. When we have more conviction on a particular theme, we will run a bigger position, going for a double or a triple. In either case, we look for asymmetric risk/return profiles, risking, say, 5 percent to make 10 or 15 percent, or risking 25 percent to make 50 to 100 percent. In general, we always sell winners "too soon" because we are scaling out into strength. It's more art than science on the upside. We try to balance how consensus our idea has become, what kind of price target makes sense for our time horizon and the market action.

And then, of course, we are trading around positions as well. If we have a long that is working and receive a piece of positive news that confirms our thesis causing the stock to gap in our favor, we will usually take some profits. We are constantly watching price action in the market, examining how a stock is trading and how the overall market is trading at any given time. If we sense that a trade is running out of steam due to technicals or if it reacts unfavorably to some information, we try to lighten up. We take profits into strength and momentum and cut when momentum is waning. In more volatile stocks, we might put on a part of the position through options to better manage the volatility. Although it costs more to use options, many times it keeps you in the trade because you have defined risk at the outset. We also try to be open minded enough to buy back a stock at a higher price. Sometimes, although the price is higher, the risk/reward can be even better.

Where do you get your trade ideas?

We start with the fundamentals. I have a lot of analysts and sector portfolio managers who travel everywhere, do thousands of company meetings a year and attend every industry conference for the sectors we follow. Having the same people talking to the same companies all the time allows us to gauge changes and shifts in tone. We also do a lot of proprietary checks, speaking to private companies, distributors, suppliers, basically everybody in the supply chain so that our analysts can model everything out, looking for out-of-consensus ideas and points of inflection.

Then we try to understand how we differ from the consensus view and how surprising it would be if we were right. Many times, situations arise where we might think we have something different because our model is spitting out significantly different numbers than sell side consensus, but those consensus figures could be stale, or too many players on the buy side could already be involved, thus making it a crowded position. It is important to figure out how you are different from both the Street and the buy side.

We also generate ideas watching the behavior of stocks and sectors, following that up with fundamental work. Often a stock or sector will change character prior to a fundamental shift—especially at major turning points.

If you didn't have your team and all your analysts, could you still do what you do?

I could still do my job without my vast research team, but not on the same scale. I learned to trade by going into a dark room by myself with only a screen. Although I think that I could do that today, my performance would depend on the type of market. In a volatile, trading market, I could definitely do very well. But in a more range-bound, stock selection market, the role of the fundamental research team becomes much more important to really differentiate between names. Trading off screens also becomes a little less interesting because it's only about price action, whereas focusing on the fundamentals is more intellectually engaging. Being intellectually engaged, being up to date with what is going on with different sectors, companies, and industries, is a positive for my trading in the long term.

It seems that an important part of what you do is identifying the prevailing market environment and then implementing the appropriate trading style.

That is certainly a big part of our process. There are periods when the fundamental research is really important and very helpful, and then other periods where it can be damaging. In fall 2008, when the markets were falling apart and correlations were going to one, I did not spend a tremendous amount of time talking to the analysts and going in-depth on different ideas because it didn't really matter. I was much more focused on price action and trading the daily flow, trying to identify short-term trading opportunities and really managing risk to make sure I did not get caught out in the large moves. Because companies had no visibility in this type of extreme market environment, distinguishing between two different stocks on a fundamental basis became impossible. During 2006 or the first half of 2007, however, when markets were much more range-bound, almost everything we did was fundamentally driven. In such periods, we make money on fundamental ideas and get chopped up trading because the market just slowly grinds up.

What is your current view of the world?

It has been really difficult lately. I was worried before doing this interview because I always felt that interviews wind up jinxing people. A few years ago, we had a big year in the markets and were the cover story for a hedge fund magazine, then proceeded to get killed over the next six months. Since I have not made any money in the past few months, I thought maybe this interview wouldn't hurt. All traders are a bit superstitious. I used to work with a guy who would never walk into his office through the front door because he once had a bad day trading following such an entry.

Big picture, we are in a liquidity driven rally. Companies are beating numbers due to aggressive cost cutting, some business stabilization, and easy comparisons. There has been very little differentiation between stocks as everything has gone up, making it difficult to generate alpha. We think this is starting to change.

How much more important have policy makers become in your trading decisions?

Policy makers have become much more important. Most of the big moves in 2008 were based off policy changes, making the environment difficult to predict. Policy makers themselves often do not know what they are going to do, and issues are constantly getting debated, rehashed, and nuanced, depending on the particular issue. We have had better luck reacting to policy changes than predicting them. Being small and nimble is an advantage in these circumstances because we can get in and out of positions much faster than a company like Fidelity, which has to rebalance its giant portfolios.

We try to avoid making significant bets in front of things where we cannot quantify the risk. You can be right about the broader path but be off on the timing and get killed. For example, we went virtually flat before the first TARP vote in September 2008 following the Lehman debacle. We had no idea what was going to happen, but felt there was a good chance of a very large market move that would be impossible to control. Plus, we had no idea if any counterparties were going to be left in a month. It was a bad risk-taking environment. (See Figure 11.2.) Whenever things move more towards gambling than investing or trading, we cut risk and then react to what winds up happening.

At the end of 2008, you said that socialism was your biggest concern. Does that still worry you?

Yes, although it is another one of those things that is difficult to predict. I could see policy action that is negative in the short-term but positive in the long term. In the short-term, government intervention and regulation across many different industries initially looks unproductive. In the long term, however, the pendulum can swing the other way, making it ultimately beneficial by discrediting that initial approach.

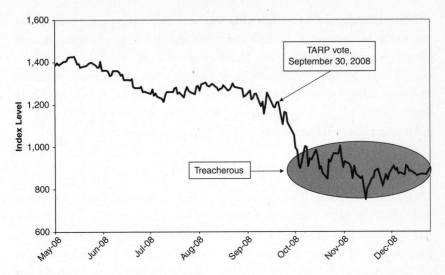

Figure 11.2 S&P 500 Index, 2008
SOURCE: Bloomberg.

I can also see a situation where policy makers' medicine does not work, leading to yet more ineffective medicine and prolonging a cycle of higher regulation, higher taxation, and higher government interference. I definitely think that we are heading in this direction, but I wonder how long it will take the public to realize it is not working. It seems that every 20, 30, or 40 years we go through this process. I don't know if we will be wiser this time and figure out more quickly that it does not work. The long-term trends that worry me are (A) an ever-growing portion of global spending being driven by governments; (B) incredibly large or off balance sheet government debt burdens in the U.S., Japan, and many European countries; and (C) ever larger "one time stimulus" programs to counter declines without any corresponding spending cuts. These trends are clearly not sustainable and, if they are not reversed fairly soon, will lead to massive inflation or government defaults down the road.

The one major problem with democratic society is the ability to vote yourself a share of your neighbor's wallet. It is a virus that hurts the most productive in the short-term, but especially damages the most in need in the long term. The recent subprime debacle is a textbook example, whereby Fannie Mae and Freddie Mac approved loans based on a political mandate to broaden home ownership.

Meanwhile, the U.S. more broadly and the hedge fund industry in particular are among the most charitable on Earth. Look at the Robin Hood Foundation, Math for America, or Teach for America, where over 10 percent of graduating Ivy League seniors apply to teach in the most impoverished inner-city schools. Contrast the voluntary drive, results, and dedication people bring to these programs versus the various government welfare programs.

Is there any way to hedge higher taxes?

You can try to make more money but it will be an uphill battle. Congress is talking about putting a 5 percent tax on the "wealthy" to pay for healthcare reform. But when their reform ends up driving up healthcare prices, they will raise taxes again, driving up prices again. Who will want to go to school for years to become a doctor when income levels and geographic location will eventually be bureaucratic decisions? Personally, I would like to be treated by the most expensive surgeon around, not one everyone could afford. What corporation is going to invest billions in R&D with no clarity on its ability to monetize the investment? Do we really believe that after countless examples, from the post office to public education, that the government is better at allocating and managing resources?

Policy makers are enacting legislation without fully comprehending how the change in incentives will flow through and impact society. Would someone really want to start a business in California or New York City if 60 or 70 percent of what they make is going to disappear in taxes? And then when they sell the business, they will be taxed again. And when they pass the wealth on to their kids, yet again. All this taxation definitely changes people's incentives. But because politicians are operating under two- to four-year time horizons, they are focused on short-term cash instead of longer-term incentives.

Where did hedge funds go wrong in 2008?

George Soros's theory on self-reinforcing cycles addresses this, and it makes a lot of sense because inevitably you get money flowing to the winners. Whether it's individuals buying houses or mutual funds buying stocks, as people make money, they get a self-reinforcing effect where they reinvest it in the same things.

Hedge funds experienced a similar phenomenon in recent years. Looking through 13-F filings has revealed that a lot of hedge funds owned the same stocks, whether the funds were called long/short equity, global macro, event-driven, special situations, multi-strat, whatever. Everybody was long the same big NASDAQ names and the same big commodity and energy names. Crowding was pervasive. As these funds posted good performance and raised more money, they plowed it back into the same positions, driving them even higher.

Betting against an unwind is tricky because the timing has to be perfect. With any extended trend—the Internet, housing, etc.—you can be totally right on the long-term view but go broke because your timing is off. Crowding in a particular thesis or strategy means that when things start breaking, the break tends to be much sharper, much faster, and much bigger than expected. Our biggest mistake in 2008 was covering shorts too early. We had shorts in the summer of 2008 that were down 30, 40, 50 percent, yet they ended up down 80 or 90 percent because the positions were so crowded. When people were finally forced to throw in the towels, the names completely imploded.

Is it better to go after momentum trades with options or to chase something after it cracks?

You have to do both because timing a big position before something turns is difficult. It's important to have on some position, whether it's a small short or a small put option, to force you to keep an eye on it. Then once it turns, get more aggressive and try to stay with the trend. This is what happened when dot-coms finally popped in 2000. The initial moves were huge, with some stocks falling from 300 to 150 in a month. But while catching these initial moves proved to be great trades, the key was recognizing that the game was over for many of these companies and staying short until they went to one or zero.

The difficulty in that example is that once something is halved, the risk/reward of the trade changes drastically. Using your example, the stock could have rebounded from 150 to 200 before ultimately going to 1. How do you manage this kind of risk?

This is something that I am trying to get better at. The more bubble situations you experience over time, the more confident you can be in staying with a core position and trading around it. Staying with some sort of core position is important because the moves on that second or third leg can be huge. Maintaining exposure in these situations is critical because catching these moves is when you turn good performance into outstanding performance.

Is it more difficult to short stocks than to own them?

I have never really found shorting more difficult, it just depends on the market environment. For example, the first half of 2007 was a very difficult environment for shorting because of the private equity buyouts, restructurings, buybacks, mergers, and corporate actions. Everyone on the sell side was trying to predict the next one, which affected price action. Not only could you potentially get hurt on the short if a real event occurred, but you also ran the risk of getting hurt by expectations of some corporate action. It was like walking through a minefield.

Other periods, like the second half 2008, are the opposite. Almost anything you shorted on a bounce would have worked out, yet being long anything was a minefield. We try to adjust our bar for long or short ideas based on the type of market we think we're in, how things are reacting, and how the portfolio is structured. If I already have six long semiconductor ideas where we think each will beat numbers and raise guidance, the bar for adding a seventh will be very high given what we would need it to add in a portfolio context. Conversely, if the seventh semiconductor idea turned out to be related and correlated, but expected to surprise on the downside, the bar might not be that high to adding it as a short position. We are always looking for ideas that are not only good risk/reward in themselves, but also improve the portfolio.

What are you looking for in the traders you hire?

In 2008, we interviewed several hundred traders and hired three. There is no perfect formula, although we have become more selective over the years. Rather than hiring 50 people to do the same thing, putting them all in competition with each other, we try to have a collaborative culture where people work together and specialize in different things. But similar to a portfolio, we are looking for somebody that adds something that we don't currently have. Over time, I have come to recognize just how difficult it is to hire someone that winds up having a very consistent long-term career. We look for a certain risk-taking psychology, a certain consistency, not people who are going to come in and try to blast home runs every day. We look for discipline, people that are comfortable operating with stops, drawdown limits, and net exposure limits, and who are happy to try to grind it out every month. At the same time, we hope they have enough of a risk-taking mentality to put on a meaningful enough position to move the needle in those rare instances when they have strong conviction.

There is a fine line between too aggressive and too defensive, and finding people that fit this profile can be very difficult. We interview zillions of people, maintain vast networks at different funds, which hopefully, over time, lead us to a few in each area that are really top notch. Identifying someone who is not only top notch today, but also has the potential to evolve and get better over time is something generally overlooked in our business. We always ask candidates, "What have you done to get better?" "How do you differ today versus a few years ago?" We always want to see evidence of continual improvement.

Another thing that we look for is passion for and commitment to the business, a conviction that this is really what they want to do. Trading is very hard, and if someone is getting involved because they heard it was a great way to make lots of money they will wind up washing out.

When you meet investors evaluating you and your fund, what do they miss?

Investors focus too much on the basic parameters. They try to assign managers into particular buckets. Much time is spent on very basic things such as your typical gross or net exposure, concentrations, etc. But the best managers wind up shifting quite significantly over time as the markets change, as their strategies change, and as opportunities change. That focus or bucketing is one of the reasons for poor hedge fund performance last year. A lot of managers wound up defining themselves and their business in strict ranges. If you tell your investor, "I do X, Y, Z, within the following exposure ranges," it becomes very difficult to change that. If you look at some of the best managers, they change significantly over time as the opportunity set changes. John Paulson started out as a risk arbitrage manager. If you forced him to stay in that bucket, you would have missed a multihundred percent return from his shorting subprime.

Another thing we often hear is, "How do you manage all these different traders and strategies?" Investors are inherently more comfortable with something easy to wrap their arms around. A firm with one PM and a few concentrated positions is significantly easier to understand—but also a much less consistent business. I am more comfortable having lots of uncorrelated return streams and a diverse portfolio even though it is more complex and difficult. If it were easy, there would be hundreds of similar firms and none of us would make any money.

The ability to adapt to different environments is probably the most important thing in the markets. If I look back at the guys with whom I traded over the years and compare the guys who are still around today and doing well to those that have dropped out, the ones that drop out typically are much more focused. They had a particular style, a particular strategy, something that worked for a period of time, but when it stopped working, they did not adapt their style and their strategies. If I am an investor looking at someone to invest with for the next 5 or 10 years, I want to know that the person is capable of adapting.

Future adaptability is inherently unpredictable. How do you recommend allocators go about it?

It starts with how a manager defines their mandate. It's okay to invest with somebody that defines their approach narrowly, but you have to recognize that you're investing in a particular strategy as a trade for as long as it works. If, for example, you think there is an inefficiency in convertible bonds, and you think a certain manager is good at exploiting that inefficiency, then as soon as that inefficiency is gone, you're out. And that's okay. Part of it is how people define themselves and their business and part of it is a track record of adapting to different markets and changing strategies over time.

But let's go back to the Paulson example. He has gone from a risk arbitrage manager to a credit fund, and now he is long gold and financials and even doing some private equity. In advance of the first shift, how do you make that adaptability call?

First, it helps to look at how they have changed their approach and the amount of risk they take in the original strategy over time—do they adjust their approach to market changes? Understanding a trader's risk management process is essential to understanding their ability to adapt to different environments. If someone is more of a generalist portfolio manager with a "go anywhere do anything" type of mandate, you just have to make sure that you are on the same wavelength with how they will manage risk in the event that their trading goes against them. This type of approach contrasts with a manager who is very fundamentally driven, more of a value investor. This latter type of manager will probably be more long term, and as things get cheaper they will want to buy more, so the risk management framework is completely different and much less defined. These types of valuation managers are more difficult bets in the long term because even if they are eventually right, there can be huge drawdowns in the interim. It is much easier to make long-term bets on a disciplined manager who has a well-defined risk management framework which they can adapt to different strategies over time.

How much does the investor base affect a manager?

Managers should make sure that their investor base is somewhat aligned with their own objectives. It will never be perfectly aligned, and everybody would love to have permanent capital, so there is a give and take with the investor base. You have to be consistent and transparent on things such as volatility and liquidity in your portfolio such that they match investor liquidity. The very existence of investors in your fund psychologically influences your decision making, so it is important to be cognizant of this as well.

Investors in your fund tend to exaggerate emotional states and psychological swings. When you are just trading your own money or one firm's money, the responsibility that you feel in a drawdown is limited to one person. Explaining to a few hundred people why you lost a portion of their money can really diminish your confidence. Likewise, when you are really doing well and people are sending you more money every month, it makes it easier to believe that you really know what you are doing, a state of mind that usually precedes a big drawdown.

Choosing your investors wisely can help mitigate this problem. Emotional, momentum investors can really exacerbate the psychological issues. Very good investors who understand your process and believe in what you are doing can be a countercyclical influence. When you are having a drawdown and you speak to them, they encourage you in such a way that you walk away from the conversation with confidence. These are the best investor relationships to have.

If you were managing a large, real money fund like a state pension fund, how would you go about it?

I have always wondered about the thought process behind these plans. What is the primary objective? One objective might be to have the most efficient beta possible, with a high correlation to global stock markets, while keeping costs low. This certainly seems to be the model that many subscribe to. But if the objective is how someone might manage their own long-term personal money, then such a mandate should be much more about absolute return, regardless of what the markets are doing. My approach would be to structure the portfolio to have the highest probability of achieving 10 to 15 percent annual returns over the next 10 to 20 years or more.

The bet that Warren Buffett made at the beginning of 2008 with one of the fund-of-hedge funds is case in point. Buffett bet that a simple S&P index would outperform a basket of funds-of-hedge funds over the next 10 years. He might be right, and he might be wrong. Who the hell knows what the S&P is going to do over the next 10 years? Maybe it will be up a lot; maybe it will be down a lot. Many investors want absolute uncorrelated returns, but they also want to beat the stock market at all times (see box). If you are slightly positive in a year like 2008, your investors are very excited. But then you have a period like the second quarter of 2009, when the market is up a lot and you are flat, and the same investors are very disappointed. We are constantly chastised during investor meetings for underperforming the S&P, and I often ask myself if investors listen when I explain what we do. Everyone wants noncorrelation, but only when markets are down. In conversations with my parents, they still assume I've had a good day if the market is up.

Stocks versus Hedge Funds

In the fall of 2007, Warren Buffett and Protégé Partners, a money management firm that runs funds-of-hedge funds, placed a bet on the following question: Will a representative collection of hedge funds, selected by experts, return more to investors over the next 10 years than the return on the S&P 500? Protégé bet on the performance of five funds-of-hedge funds—specifically, the averaged returns that those vehicles deliver net of all fees, costs, and expenses. Buffett bet on the performance of the Vanguard S&P 500 Admiral Fund. The time frame is January 1, 2008 to December 31, 2017. Each side committed roughly $320,000. The total funds of about $640,000 were used to buy a zero-coupon Treasury bond that will deliver $1 million at the bet's conclusion, which will be given to charity regardless of who wins. If Protégé wins, the money is to be given to Absolute Return for Kids (ARK), an international philanthropy based in London. If Buffett wins, the intended recipient is Girls Inc. of Omaha. To see more information about the bet, go to www.longbets.org. During the course of 2008, the Vanguard S&P 500 fund was down 37 percent and on average (net of all fees, costs, and expenses) the five funds-of-funds selected by Protégé were down 23.9 percent. At year-end 2009, the Vanguard 500 Index Fund's (VFINX) return was 26.5 percent while the HFRI Fund of Funds Composite Index (a proxy for the five funds-of-hedge-funds) was up 11.2 percent for the year. After two years of performance, the approximate BAV (Bet Asset Value) is: Protégé 84.6; Buffett 79.7.

You cannot have it both ways. Either you take an absolute return approach regardless of the market environment, or you just go for efficient beta and be happy with the outcome. I use the former approach when managing my personal money. I have the vast majority of my wealth in my own fund and with other hedge fund managers whom I respect, where I am confident in their ability to make money year in and year out. Some years might be up a lot, while others only up a little, but there is a very high probability that each year will at least be positive. And as a group, there is an even higher probability that they will be positive every year. I also have on more tactical trades when credit or emerging markets or something else is cheap after a big sell-off. These are beta trades and I don't need to pay a hedge fund to put on that kind of trade. If you think credit is cheap, go buy a credit index. If you think emerging markets are cheap, go buy an ETF on emerging markets and define your risk at some predetermined stop loss level. There is no need to deal with all the complexities involved in picking the best manager, dealing with less liquidity, and addressing all of the other issues required in executing that strategy through a hedge fund. Many hedge funds perpetuated this problem by pitching themselves as absolute returns when they were really just disguised beta plays.

Should real money investors, such as state pension funds, take an absolute return approach?

Yes, I have less than 1 or 2 percent of my net worth invested in long-only strategies. When I try to pick mutual funds for my kids, I cannot find any that I want to own. If I were managing a real money fund, I would dedicate the vast majority of my capital to true, absolute return type strategies, diversifying across 15 to 25 managers in different strategies, each with solid long-term, uncorrelated performance, and robust risk management frameworks. I would select managers whom I believe in and can stick with for 5 or 10 years. A small portion of capital would be devoted to more tactical, opportunistic trades when those come around.

If you were running CalPERS with assets of $200 billion, could you find enough good managers that would or could take $5–10 billion each?

You could allocate this kind of sum if you got creative and locked up the money with managers for a long period. Taken to the extreme, however, if every pension fund in the world followed my advice, then it would obviously no longer be possible. We are far from such a scenario right now.

If you were asked to run a new sovereign wealth fund, how would you approach it?

Sovereign wealth funds are a little bit trickier because I am not sure that they have a returns focused mandate. Much of what they are looking at concerns the strategic interests of a given country. If you are managing the country's money, you should think about the country's interests, beyond just earning a percentage return on capital. So if you are running China's fund and crude drops 80 percent, I can see how putting on a big crude position would make sense. Beyond the strategic investments, I do think they have too much money in long-only strategies.

Investments in the financial space (banks, fund management companies, etc.) by some sovereign wealth funds in the Middle East and China have been ones where there is a strategic benefit to furthering their knowledge and expertise in a particular industry. Sure, they ideally want a good return on their capital, or at least want to ensure they do not lose money on the transaction. But they also want to become smarter in the financial space so they can duplicate some of the activities in their own countries, and this makes sense.

What are real money investors missing with respect to diversification?

Again, the biggest mistake from the institutional side of the investing world is bucketing by type of investment, as opposed to by correlation or risk factors. If you get a job running some pension or endowment fund, your predecessor probably hands you the keys and says, here's your bucket for private equity, your bucket for real estate, your bucket for hedge funds, long only, credit, etc.

Instead of deciding how much risk should be taken overall, which is the ideal way to approach investing, the allocator begins by deciding how much capital to allocate into each bucket. Not nearly enough focus is spent on the overall correlations and overall risk levels. Rather, bucket allocations are tweaked by a few percent up or down, but the most fundamental question of how much overall risk should be taken is largely ignored.

In 2008, many investors got caught with funds that were supposed to be absolute return, but in reality had very high correlations with stock markets. Over time, you essentially wind up with much more of a diversified beta portfolio. And when the markets really roll over, all these asset classes correlate, whether you are long credit, long emerging markets, long equities, long private equity, long real estate, or long commodities. You are just long, and everything is rolling over.

This is why drawdowns were much larger than anyone expected. If you ask how much overall risk you should take, you are essentially asking how much you can stand to lose if everything goes against you, which is what no one in these seats seemed to do. The opportunity cost of an absolute return/risk focused approach, however, is that you might not be up big when markets rally. If you take a big chunk of the portfolio and allocate it to true absolute return hedge fund strategies and global stock markets rally 50 percent, you will not be up the same amount. You have to be comfortable giving that up for the consistency of the returns over time.

Let's say you are a very large pension fund and your board of trustees agrees that you don't want to be down more than, say, 15 percent a year. How do you structure your portfolio to make sure you do not lose more than that amount?

You need certain things in your portfolio that should benefit from riskier markets. Maybe you have a global macro allocation, where although you do not have a guarantee that the manager will make money in a down market, you definitely have a much higher chance than you do in a long equity portfolio or a long credit portfolio. You need managers that have shown over time that they can change their exposures and make money in down markets. Again, you are not guaranteed that they will make money, but your odds are much better with such a manager than with one who keeps significant net long exposure. You can also have dedicated short funds, but they are a difficult strategy to make money in over time.

With large buying power, you could structure all sorts of customized accounts with managers, especially now. If a large investor asked us to run a $5 billion long-term account with a 15 percent stop loss, I would do it, and I think most managers would do it. You can get creative and customize things if you are a large enough investor. If you cannot find enough managers or are constrained by rules or a board, you could have a program of regularly buying long volatility exposure, or run a sizable cash or government bond allocation. What you cannot do is have a big chunk in LBO's, which are levered long bets, a big chunk in long only-equities, and then a "portable alpha" allocation that goes to long biased long/short managers.

Many real money funds ran into trouble with illiquid private deals. Do you do privates in your fund?

We did a few small private deals, but like anything else, what you do or don't do is less important than the size of the transaction relative to your capital base and how much you are risking. Doing different things allows you to learn from the process, fueling idea generation and enabling you to grow over time. We never had a significant amount of money in privates because our primary business is trading. Our strength is evaluating risk/reward and managing risk, and an important component of managing risk is being able to get out of things. Risk/reward profiles tend to change over time, and you can get stuck in a trade as the liquidity regime changes. It was really the illiquidity in these types of transactions that kept us from doing anything significant in the space. There are definitely opportunities in privates if you have the manpower, but these transactions are very labor intensive. The bar is very high for us to get involved in something with limited liquidity, much higher than a more typical investment. I know I can go buy $50 million of stock in "X, Y, Z" and if I don't like how it's acting I can sell it. If I know my holding period in an illiquid is at least three years, it changes the risk/reward profile of the trade knowing you are locked in. A lot can change in three years.

CalPERS recently announced they plan to create, seed, and run hedge funds in-house. What do you think of this idea?

That will be difficult. You can see from the experience of private equity firms the last couple of years that it is difficult to seed and develop hedge funds in-house. The private equity firms have great infrastructure, they have really smart guys, really experienced investors, a huge marketing infrastructure, great recruiting ability, and a vast network where creating funds is their business. Yet I don't think they produced any successful hedge funds. Similarly, look at Bear Stearns or Citibank and their internal hedge funds as another example of institutions failing in the hedge fund space. A hedge fund is a very entrepreneurial business. Very talented managers and risk takers will typically want to run their own business their own way, or work in a small group with like-minded partners. They do not want to work for big, bureaucratic institutions, even if they are able to start with much larger amounts of capital. Because of this, institutions have a huge negative selection bias on hiring and trying to build out hedge fund platforms. Further, if you are successful, you will have the Harvard compensation problem of portfolio managers making multiples of what the president makes.

What is your outlook for the hedge fund business over the next 5 to 10 years?

Although we are in the midst of a necessary shakeout in the broader hedge fund industry, the returns for hedge funds as a whole were better than most other investing categories during 2008. And if you picked funds with good track records and good risk management, the returns were substantially better than almost everything else available.

The hedge fund industry should become much less homogenous than it has been. The fee structures and the operating models that everyone more or less duplicated will become much more varied. There will be small groups that trade a particular sector, a particular niche strategy where a manager has an edge in what they do but with limited capacity. There will also be big institutional hedge fund firms offering a variety of different products and different customized mandates for different types of investors. The people in the middle—a generalist manager with a small team and a standard structure, not particularly differentiated—will have a hard time. Overall, the industry is very entrepreneurial and if it doesn't get over-regulated, it will continue to attract very bright people who will figure out how to adapt and generate good returns for their clients.

More generally, the world will increasingly be split between pure alpha and efficient beta.

Chapter 12

The Predator

"The Predator" is the quintessential gentleman. He warmly invites me inside his corner office, overlooking both his trading floor and the city outside, the latter a more peaceful financial center than most. A burning cigar lay half-smoked in an ashtray, and he promptly asks me if I would like one, or if I mind if he smokes.

The Predator is candid about what he calls the "wealth transfer" in markets: the transfer of capital from his competitors to him. Conditions must be right for this to happen; if they are not, The Predator—like a lion after a good meal—could merely laze around with not much to do.

He claims to change his style every six months or so, in order to never be figured out, to remain a step ahead of the competition. Although he expresses most ideas in the equity markets, he is not afraid to look elsewhere in the capital structure, again a function of the environment in which he is trading. He survived 2008 by abandoning valuation considerations, reducing gross exposure, and ultimately going to cash, as he says that cash is the only thing that can save you in a liquidity crisis.

The Predator makes the big bucks from the long side and uses the short side to manage risk, but being a stock picker is not good enough over time. To survive in the long term, he insists you have to have a macro overlay to be able to manage the downside risk; otherwise, you become the prey.

Why did so many institutional investors, including hedge funds, lose money in 2008?

Although many people in our industry read the market correctly and were bearish, they still did poorly. There were two types of people who got it wrong in 2008. First, you have the value managers who kept buying as prices fell. They were buying Fannie Mae, Freddie Mac, AIG, Lehman, and others because these companies looked cheap according to their models. For example, during the summer of 2007, there was a mutual fund guy who was buying millions and millions of shares of Countrywide as we were shorting. We kept shorting and he kept buying—it was crazy. This type of value investor is a function of the environment; they had been playing the rally from 1980 to 2008 beautifully, making a lot of money buying the dips. But they did not see the dislocation, the fracture. What derailed them in 2008 was the fracture, which resulted from the break in liquidity. (See Figure 12.1.)

The second type of investor was bearish and saw the difficulties in advance, but his hedges did not work, also because of the liquidity break. These investors did not expect the liquidity crisis to be so severe. Markets broke down to such an extent that things that normally work in a crash did not work this time. Credit issues rendered many hedges null and void.

How do you value liquidity?

Liquidity is hugely important in this business—it is everything for me. Liquidity is how quickly I can liquidate my portfolio and how quickly I can reduce my leverage on no notice. Since every long-term investment you make goes through a period where it is tested, you have to be prepared for these times. Liquidity enables you to get rid of something

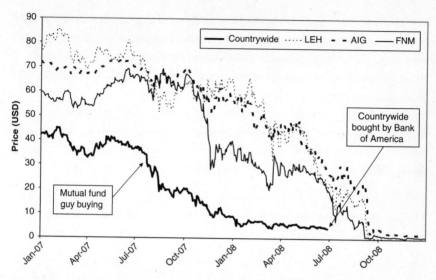

Figure 12.1   Select Financial Stocks, 2007–2008
SOURCE: Bloomberg.

before you are forced to. Quantitatively, I define liquidity as the number of days it takes to sell out of a position or the whole portfolio. But liquidity is also a function of the number of people involved in the name you own. I want to know who will be the buyer of last resort. If you are the buyer of last resort, then there is no liquidity.

Over the past two years, I have focused on getting rid of all trades that are even partially illiquid. Presently, we focus on major, big-cap, investment grade names. We are running smaller position sizes and are more diversified.

When did you start becoming bearish?

I started becoming bearish in the summer of 2007, but I was too early—a final bull run ensued, driven by all the players who still had cash to deploy. The equity markets had their final bull run, peaking in October 2007, but that was an aberration. Aberration or not, you still have to play the game because there is a big difference between being bearish and being right. There is always a lag. Sometimes it takes up to three years before one of my shorts finally collapses, which often comes after management has exhausted all of its ammunition dressing up the company.

With respect to the big crash in 2008, the real trigger came in June of that year, when Lehman Brothers released its horrible second-quarter earnings. Citigroup, Merrill, and others came out with bad results at the same time. The magnitude of the bad results was not as informative as their consistency and trajectory—they continued and worsened. At that point, we retrenched the fund violently, reducing leverage and increasing cash. We sold relentlessly and started to get out a few months before everyone else. We just continued selling securities, driving them down. We didn't care—we just wanted out.

Do you typically manage risk by going to cash when you are concerned about the environment?

Yes. Cash is the only thing that saves you in a liquidity crisis—cash or government bonds. There is no other way. You can never hedge a liquidity crisis.

Why did investors continue buying the dips despite the looming crisis?

They bought the dips because this is what has worked for the past 20 or 30 years. Most value managers active today have always made money this way. Because of the success of people like Warren Buffett, many believe Graham and Dodd is the only way. They just do not know any better.

Different fund managers have different dimensions of thinking, different levels. Many investors have one, maybe two dimensions, although the best probably have five. Managers with five dimensions will still buy, but they will have a hedge to save them if they are wrong. The basic value funds are one-dimensional managers, and they lost 50 or 60 percent in 2008 because they only know how to buy stock and buy more as it gets cheaper. The worst one-dimensional managers, however, were the hedge funds that exploded early in the crisis, due to leverage, counterparty risk, liquidity risk, prime broker risk, and client risk. Their clients wanted their money back, and they were unprepared for that. Because they had never experienced such a series of events, they thought: "My assets are cheap, so I will hold onto them." They never imagined that clients would want their money back or that the whole system could come close to collapse.

A bear market is one in which everything tests zero then bounces back. That is what happened in 2008, and people were completely unprepared. To prepare for such extreme environments, you have to value every asset in your fund at an absurdly low price and make sure that you can still survive. If you can survive without being forced to liquidate, then you will benefit from being around when the environment and market pricing comes back to reality.

The liquidity crisis of 2008 was created by leverage, by everyone unwinding their leverage. There was simply too much leverage in the system. We knew it. We knew Lehman was too leveraged. If you looked at Lehman's balance sheet, you could see that management actually increased the leverage in 2007, and again in March 2008. They spent a billion dollars buying back their stock in January 2008. That is almost criminal! Clearly they failed to see the liquidity crisis coming and their lack of vision sent the firm and asset markets in general into another dimension.

We are all inundated by information today. How do you sift through the vast amount of publicly available information and still find things that others miss?

We focus on the actors. Half the money we make is at the expense of other market participants. Knowing something is good or bad is only part of the process. Each situation depends on who is involved. Is long-only coming in to buy the dip? Is levered money getting involved? What are the insiders doing? Is retail involved? It is important to know the types of actors involved in a trade—the buyers and sellers—in order to understand what motivates them and identify the points at which they might let go or not.

But even when you take a position, and especially when you are short, you have to make sure you are properly hedged. Dick Fuld had many opportunities to save Lehman, to do something like Merrill Lynch did. So the Lehman short was not such an obvious short. If Dick Fuld was not such an egomaniac, Lehman could have been saved and we probably would not have gone through the liquidity crisis as fast as we did. Of course, we would still be managing losses, but we would not have had that break, that fracture in the markets that we had in the fall of 2008.

The so-called great stock pickers all tried to hedge with equity index futures, but they do not know how to hedge by using derivatives. They assumed the futures would hedge their individual stock positions, but they misunderstood the risks. They were long some stocks that they found very cheap, and they hedged sporadically with futures. They hated the market, yet they got whipsawed every time they put on a hedge with futures, so they lost money on that bit, too. Then, these stock market gurus sold everything at the bottom in early 2009 and went short the market. They got it totally, totally wrong.

To be an effective stock picker over time, you must have a macro overlay component. Looking at equities alone is not enough. Last year, I recognized that the macro elements of the market were horrible, and I did something about it. Stocks can look cheap, but they can continue getting cheaper until you are bust. Last year, I just stepped back and let the market find its balance. I reduced the size of the portfolio, got out of all my financials, and bought puts on everything else. In September 2008, the news of Lehman going bust was clearly very bad, so we retrenched further and went fully to cash. I was in cash until the end of November, at which point I started buying bonds—corporate bonds, investment grade bonds, any credit I could because good companies had gone to absurdly cheap prices.

Do you make more money from your stock picking or your macro overlay?

You make the real money from stocks on the long side, whereas the shorts and the macro overlay protect the money you made on the way up. You cannot separate the two. In general, we outperform on the way down, which gives us ammunition to buy cheaply and take advantage of a subsequent rally. Our fund did not get destroyed in 2008, so we had the firepower available to be full long, which is where we have been since March 2009.

What made you go long stocks in March 2009?

My worst two weeks ever were the second half of March 2009. When Lehman went bust in September 2008, I told my investors that the markets would suffer two horrible quarters before rebounding around

May or June '09. The fourth quarter of '08 was horrible; then in January '09 numbers came in with negative guidance, driving the market down further. February and early March '09 marked the final selling by all the equity greats. Yet it was in early March that JPMorgan, Citigroup, and a few other banks began saying business was not that bad, that they were making money again. This was the first signal of some stability.

Further, the figures for the broader economy suggested a slowing of the deterioration, what people now call the second derivative. I did not know the term at the time, but that leveling off was very important and it was due to the extraordinary stimulus injected by the major governments of the world. I calculated that the sum of all the government interventions—fiscal stimulus plans, interest rate cuts, and other emergency government programs—amounted to multiples of the contraction in global GDP. Although global GDP contracted 6 percent, something like 20 percent was being thrown at the problem, much of which had not yet been deployed at the time.

I also looked at the swap rate and credit default swap levels. The swap rate is the inter-bank interest rate—the rate that banks use to lend to other banks. In November 2008, it reached a high of 5 percent amidst a total breakdown in confidence in the financial system. By March 2009, it came back to 2 percent and it is now at a quarter of a percent, which is the long-term trend. Credit default swaps, which are indications of credit deterioration, were also improving. Meanwhile, every corporate bond that I bought in November '08 was up 10 to 15 points. So you could see liquidity back in the market, the monetary aggregates returning to normal, the flow of money being guaranteed by governments; a colossal amount of money had been thrown at the problem and the rate of deterioration of the economy was beginning to slow.

By mid-March 2009, I had covered my S&P shorts at 670, but at 730 I was happily shorting again. At 820, I became really worried, but luckily for me, there was one day where Obama said he would let GM go bankrupt, and the market opened down to 780. With two days before the close of the quarter and people still very depressed, I flipped my book, closing every one of my shorts, and I have been full long ever since. (See Figure 12.2.)

I had been looking for the moment to turn and go long ever since the fracture. I read every article possible looking for a reason, a catalyst,

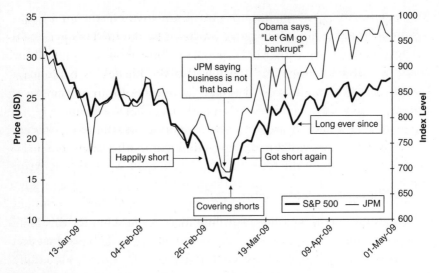

Figure 12.2 S&P 500 and JPMorgan (JPM), 2009
SOURCE: Bloomberg.

the right time, and I finally found it in valuations. Certain stocks were trading at a discount to book value. I reasoned that any slowing of the economic deterioration would send these stocks back to book value. Around the same time, many investors came to see us unexpectedly, saying, "How have you been making money? What is your secret? What is your recipe? You should be in cash! It's the end of the world!" The overwhelming panic and fear we saw in investors, combined with everything else, helped push me to make the turn and go long.

Do you consider yourself an optimist?

Every fund manager has to be an optimist in order to survive in the long term. In the short-term, however, people like me survive by becoming a different fund manager every six months. I was a short seller a year-and-a-half ago, so at that time I was a pessimist. Speaking at a conference in the spring of 2008, I said there is a good chance the market goes to hell because the system needs to be cleaned and we have to pay for an orgy of credit. People thought I was crazy.

A year ago I was a cash manager. Then I became a corporate bond buyer—I did not care about stocks. Six months ago I became a value stock buyer, buying all the deep value I could find. Now I am a long-only index fund, trying not to get whipsawed by the market's gyrations and trying not to get distracted by people talking about the end of the rally. I am working from the principle that the big fear is behind us. Because people are only as good as their last six months in our industry, those who were negative and have not participated in the recent rally are looking for an excuse. In markets, you cannot be one thing or another; rather, you have to evolve according to different market environments.

Who will you be six months from now?

In six months, I will be a free cash flow manager looking for dividend yield. I will still be in stocks, but I will be a dividend yield buyer looking to extract value by picking up yield and running a low gross book. We will have more regulation, companies will be overcapitalized, and governments will be raising taxes. So markets will be boring and I will still be long stocks. I will be a bored fund manager, but it will be the right strategy to have for the environment.

You say that you make half your money at the expense of other people. What do you mean by that?

Someone has to be on the other side of your trades. You need buyers to short against at the top of a market and sellers to buy from at the bottom. You have to identify the type of person who shorts at the bottom or the one who leverages on the way up and use the liquidity they provide to do your trades. You need to understand where other people get it wrong in order to see if their errors create an opportunity for you. The liquidity they provide allows for a transfer of wealth.

For example, all the big pension funds and endowments were selling equities and had their lowest allocation ever to stocks at the end of first quarter, 2009. I was buying the stocks that they were selling—they should have been buying like me. A liquidity crisis occurs only every 20 or 30 years, and we had just had one. It looks clear up ahead, and that is what you have to extrapolate. Along the way, some will be right and some will be wrong, and you have to identify who will be wrong in order to profit from their mistakes.

If the crisis is behind us, will we pay for the tremendous government stimulus thrown at the problem in the form of high inflation or the hyperinflation scenario that some predict?

No. Inflation needs excess money, and at the moment money is contracting. The quantity of money injected by governments remains a fraction of the shrinkage of bank balance sheets and personal balance sheets. Everyone is raising cash levels now, which means foregoing buying property, foregoing capital investments, foregoing speculation. If you run a company, you are not building a new plant right now. If you are running a bank, you are sitting in government bonds. The whole money supply of the economy is shrinking. You need capital expenditure, lending, and speculation to have inflation. Of course, it is still too early to tell and it could happen further down the road. But right now we are still in a worldwide deflation scenario. If this were not the case, interest rates would not still be at zero.

Where do you get your trading ideas?

Level one is the newspaper—everyone can read it, and all the important information is there. What you make of what you read, however, depends on whether you are interested, whether you care to dig deeper. Beyond the papers, we have three types of sources for ideas. One is meeting with companies. We have around 2000 office visits a year, half from companies, half from analysts or strategists. Another is reaching out to analysts or strategists to see what is happening in their sector or specific stocks. The last is talking to the Street to better understand flow dynamics. The three have had an equal weight in our decision-making process over time but there are times when one or the other dominates.

Similarly, I break my trading down to either stock picking or tactical trading. In 2008, my stock picking was horrible because we were in a down market. Instead, I relied on my macro overlay and market timing, which luckily were very good, allowing us to preserve capital. In 2009, conversely, it has been the other way around. The environment is all about stock picking; market timing does not matter. Over time the relative contribution between stock picking and market timing is roughly equal.

How much of markets are a function of fundamentals versus psychology?

I would say half-half, which places a considerable weight on psychology. Knowing the psychology of the market is as important as knowing your stock. I use psychology to try to understand why markets are not reflecting what I think they should. But knowing the fundamentals of a stock is very important because that is what ultimately bails you out if you are wrong on timing, scenario, or position sizing.

How do you get an understanding of market psychology?

I talk to people and I read the tape. Why is the stock up? Why is the stock down? What types of buyers are out there? What type of sellers? Who is reporting earnings? You try to take ownership of a stock's move, to understand why it is at a certain price level and where it should be trading. But the big moves come from fundamentals. Although inflection points are very fundamental, they are basic ideas that people miss. People do not read the paper every day; they rely on other people to provide them with news. They do not look for the news themselves. They are very busy. And most people are specialists and not generalists. I am a generalist who sometimes recognizes an opportunity and goes very deeply into it. So my edge is to be everything at the same time and focus on a specific period where I can seize an opportunity. Sometimes you just want to avoid an asset class because it is too rich, so you move to another one. Having the capacity to identify this is key. For example, we are currently in a low-volatility market, so the stock specialists are back in favor. The oil guy will make more money on oil stocks than I will make. But this year I probably made 10 times more money in bank stocks than a traditional mutual fund financial specialist made over the last few years because financials were completely wiped out. Identifying a new subject and having the flexibility and the skill to go trade it is what is required.

So you read the papers and watch the tape all day, every day, in markets around the world?

At times like the present, I do nothing—again, I am an index fund right now. I do not want to watch the tape—I do not care about the tape. Sometimes it is very important to look at the tape, but not right now.

Sometimes, as a fund manager, it is very important to escape from the markets in order to avoid getting disturbed by the noise. I try to stay out of the office now. Every time the market has a wobble my traders get nervous and say it looks very bad—they want to sell everything, yet I tell them to buy. Your focus changes depending on the fundamentals of the prevailing environment.

During 2008, were you watching the tape constantly?

Yes—24 hours a day, every day. I gained a lot of weight because I never went to the gym. There were too many things moving at the same time, demanding an immense intellectual effort to understand what was going on. I was losing money on everything I owned, so it was a struggle to understand the dynamics of why and how and who and where. It took some time, but by the summer and especially into the fall, I finally understood the dynamics of the game. I could see a pattern setting in, which eventually allowed me to get ahead of things.

Did 2008 force everyone to become more tactical?

Sure, but now everyone wants to be tactical, and it is too late. Now it is time to be an index fund or a long-only guy—tactical is no longer feasible. People will tell you market timing is not possible, and they will be right at this moment. But when you need to be tactical, very few people have that skill and there are times when you need to be tactical to stay out of trouble.

Has your style evolved through lessons from bad trades, bad years, or other experiences?

My style has definitely evolved. In order to learn in this business, you need to lose a lot of money and survive it. You also need to have a good memory to ensure that you learn from all your mistakes. The bear market in 2008 was a sum of all the bear markets since 1987. We took something from each of the prior crises—the Russian crisis, the LTCM crisis, the 1987 crash, the Gulf War, everything—to guide us in 2008, so having a good memory is important.

Of course, it is easy to say that having lived through crises gives you the ability to recognize the next one, but it is very difficult to identify what is happening as you are going through a particular crisis. People always forget how violent crises are on both the downside and the upside. Nevertheless, ironically, crises have elements that are always the same, even if each has unique elements as well. For example, the exponential liquidity that governments provided to the market in 2008 was an exception, not the norm.

In general, you try to take your cues from little things because even if you have great ideas, you still need a trigger. Identifying the trigger is as difficult as having the idea. Also, never try to be too clever; instead, just analyze, trying to see why certain things are happening and behaving in a certain way. Sometimes the name of the game is just common sense. If you cannot see why things are happening, if you do not understand what is going on, just get out. Again, liquidity is vitally important because it enables you to get out if you change your mind. There is nothing I sell that I cannot buy back the next day.

What is the worst trade of your career?

During the crash of '87, I was buying all the way down. When the Dow was down 300, then 400, then 500, I thought, "Well, it's cheap." (See Figure 12.3.) I was doing exactly what some of my competitors were

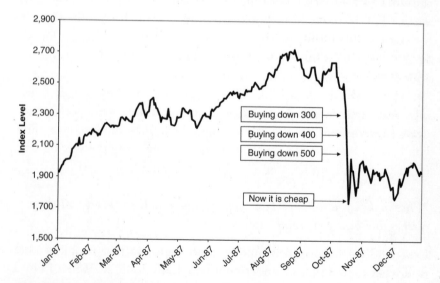

Figure 12.3 Dow Jones Industrial Average, 1987
SOURCE: Bloomberg.

doing in the second half of '08. I was young, I didn't know any better, and I kept buying as the market fell apart. Now, because I am older and have some battle scars, I get out when a trade is going against me. I can always buy back in when things are safer, when the environment stabilizes. And if levels are higher or lower, it's really irrelevant. The crash of '87 cost me a lot of money. I managed to survive because I had made a lot of money before and had management support, but that was a big lesson. Nevertheless, that lesson has made me a lot of money over time.

And your best trade ever?

My best trade was long Softbank of Japan in 2005. That was extraordinary. In that particular case, the stock dropped and dropped during 18 months of slow deterioration, then exploded up. It was trading at a discount to book value and the valuation on tech stocks tends to go from discount to premium rather quickly. You never know what the trigger will be, but you know that something, someday, will happen. That something came in the summer of 2005, and over the next six months the stock went up more than fourfold. I owned half a billion dollars of converts, which doubled in price. After the stock exploded up, I began to short it, and found myself short over a billion dollars of the stock in December '05, when it crashed by 30 or 40 percent. That was a fabulous trade, but it took two years. People have to be shorting for you to get a sizable position on and they have to be buying for you to get out. It takes time. You do not build into a trade like that to make a lot of money instantly. (See Figure 12.4.)

The best trades always take time. They happen when you are building something, losing money on it, building more—whether through derivatives, options, or convertible bonds. To build something over time, you have to have staying power. You lose money along the way but you never get wiped out because you don't overextend.

What makes you unique? How have you been able to survive all these crashes and beat your competitors over time?

I try hard to make myself unique. I do things so that people cannot read what I am doing or understand why I am doing it. When I buy a stock, people don't know if I am buying for the long term or for the

Figure 12.4 Softbank (9984:JP), 2006
SOURCE: Bloomberg.

short-term, to close a short or to trade it. I do not want other people to make money off me. I do not want to be guessed—but if people do guess, I want them to be wrong. Sometimes I put trades on just to test the markets, in which case there is nothing to read in the trade. I also cannot be copied because I am a different person every six months. Because I am always changing, it is impossible to predict my motivations in a trade or to anticipate my next move.

Markets are a competition and I take pleasure out of beating my competitors. It is an intellectual challenge. Winning the intellectual war is what I love about markets. At one stage, when I was between jobs for a period of about nine months, my wife and close friends all said that I was miserable and bored—I had lost the adrenaline. Adrenaline comes from getting winning trades ahead of others, from being ahead of the game.

Some of my investors have told me that when I read a newspaper, I can read between the lines. They say I have a capacity of judgment. For a stock, a bond, a currency, you may have 10 things that could precipitate a move, but you don't know which one of the 10 will be the trigger. My skill is to be able to identify the trigger ahead of others.

Let us talk about the real money world. If you were asked to run CalPERs, a $200 billion pension fund, could you run it successfully?

I could but it would not be easy. I could, however, make a difference at the fringes. Someone like me would be very helpful when equity market valuations are peaking or bottoming. During normal market recoveries, such as the present, someone like me is probably less valuable. But the knowledge and experience I bring to inflection points are very valuable.

The difficulty of having me in such a position would be that, given my versatile style, I would need to have sole decision-making power to be effective. And that is just not feasible in a large, bureaucratic organization like a pension fund, with its boards and trustees and committees. So although I would be able to help, it would be impossible under the current structure. The liability is too big for any institution. This is why I have a hedge fund. Even my own hedge fund clients thought I was crazy buying the market in March. They said, "What if you're wrong?" I said, "If I'm wrong, I will sell." And then for three months they kept on screaming at me. Even now six months into the rally, people scream at me for being long and not taking profit. If a committee determined my trades, I would still be in cash.

Does it embolden you when people tell you you're wrong?

Absolutely. I love it. But it cannot be the only point in your analysis because sometimes they are right. It depends on who is telling you and what is going on in the markets. Sometimes I take others' views, sometimes I don't. It is similar with pundits like Nouriel Roubini; sometimes you incorporate his view, sometimes you dismiss it.

What did the big endowments get wrong in 2008?

The endowments made a lot of money, and it gave them a certain false comfort level. Also, they relied on one individual in many cases. Where pensions have decision-making boards, endowments have more moderating boards. Because of this difference, endowments are quite flexible and had made good money up until 2008. But flexibility is not enough in fund management—you need other skills. One day or another you need a sanity check, someone to tell you that you're wrong.

And who will be that person? I don't know. In my case, my investors tell me that I am wrong; when they all leave, I know I am wrong. But endowment managers say, "I am investing for the long term." In that model, who is going to tell them that they are wrong? It is impossible.

Making a lot of money leads to hubris. In fund management, if you continue to make money the same way, sooner or later you will collapse, not because you are wrong, but because you failed to understand that everyone else had copied you. This was the primary mistake of the endowment model. After making a lot of money for 10 years, even if you believe the outlook for the next 10 years looks great, you should still take 50 percent and do something different. Put it in Treasuries. Buy an index fund and some put options. Do something very basic, but at least something different. Success brings emulation, emulation brings leverage, and leverage eventually brings disaster. Disaster comes not because the idea is wrong, but rather because there are too many people in it.

What advice do you have for Jane Mendillo, who just took over Harvard Management?

Try to understand what went wrong. In America, people are very good at that. Don't make it public, but quietly really try to understand first what went right for 15 years, then what went wrong after Jack Meyer left. Understand what went wrong in the asset allocation process. Mendillo inherited a very difficult situation. She had a fracture of the market, something with one chance in a thousand, yet it occurred just as she took over. Although she is not responsible for it, she had to deal with it, and that must have been a horrible position to be in. Harvard is a bit like UBS: They sinned because of arrogance; they thought nothing bad could happen to them. They were the smartest in the world. But markets will humble you.

What went wrong at Harvard?

Illiquidity. They made a lot of money in their illiquid trades: private equity, real estate, etc. The proportion of their illiquid trades was too big exactly because these assets had done so well in the past. Well, they had performed well because they were the most under-priced asset class precisely because nobody wanted them. A small cap always looks cheap because people like me don't want to buy it—there is no liquidity. But when the small cap does well, it outperforms the large cap, and then everyone says that you should you put more money into small caps. Suddenly, everyone is involved and small caps go from cheap to expensive and then crash. The problem feeds on itself, and consultants exacerbate the problem. Consultants are people who don't understand managing money yet try to tell you how to manage money.

Fund management is a skill—you cannot run money through consultants or committees. If you have a committee, you should buy an index fund and stop trying. Committees settle to the lowest common denominator, which is the lowest risk. A committee will not take risk. By the time a committee decides to buy tech, it is already March 2000.

Fund management is like cooking, whereby 10 chefs have the same ingredients but make 10 different things. You have great chefs who get three stars and lousy chefs who make horrible food. Fund management is similar in that what is important is what you make out of the mix, how you interpret information, how you structure trades and build portfolios. But with committees somehow the results are always the same. When you have a committee, you cannot be the only guy making the decision because, at some stage, you will be wrong in the short-term and everyone will get fired. So the whole groupthink model makes things very difficult, as does the visibility of these posts. Making or losing a lot of money always makes headlines—there is no upside or solution for that.

To what do you attribute your ability to see inflection points? Luck? Mental flexibility? The fact that you are always liquid and can change your mind?

Luck is a term that people attribute to other people's talents. Luck does not happen regularly or consistently; rather, it happens only once. For example, David Swensen, head of Yale University's endowment, says that market timing is luck (see box). I can prove that market timing is not luck, but am I here to contradict him? I don't care what others think about that. I had a meeting with a professor from Princeton who contends that markets are perfect. I said, "No, they are not because people like me are able to steal money from the markets." He said, "It's impossible over the long term." I said, "Okay. I'm not saying over the long term. Over a certain period, however, I can apply my theories to find overvaluation and undervaluation, allowing me to make money out of a situation that you think has incorporated all the available information."

Lunch with the *FT*: David Swensen

The larger point, Swensen believes, is that even though moments of radical disruption, such as the 2007 financial crisis, reward investors who make a big bet on major change, "ultimately, market timing is an exercise in futility. When you've got dramatic movements in the markets you can identify after the fact a handful of investors that succeeded in the short run. But making big, aggressive asset allocation moves isn't a strategy that's likely to prove successful in the long run."

SOURCE: *Financial Times*, October 8, 2009.

Coming out of business school, I was very puzzled by the CAPM model, which says there is no imperfection in the market. I asked my first boss in the markets, "What am I doing here if markets are perfect?" He said, "No, no. Don't worry. There are lots of opportunities. Just do your homework and stay ahead of others. Have an edge. See where your edge is and profit from it." My edge is that I am a global investor and I am flexible. I look for inflection points. Take Japan now—it's a dull, horrible market. Everyone is leaving the Japanese market—no one cares. Should things change in Japan, I could be earlier there, which is what I did in 2005. I was much earlier than the competition, and the market went up. Then I took my huge profits and left. So you can identify a situation where size, lack of flexibility, or lack of attention becomes the enemy of performance, and you can go there, profit from it, and leave. It is difficult to do consistently over time, but at moments it is definitely possible.

What is your time horizon—how far ahead do you think?

I am able to think far ahead, provided the unexpected does not occur. For now, the unexpected has a very small probability. Over the next three years things look relatively okay. All the elements are in place for a nice, slow recovery and I have plenty of ammunition to stop my trades if I am wrong. Big cycle inflection points happen every five to seven years and we just had one, so I am relaxed.

If you had to put on one trade right now and go sailing for the next 10 years, what would it be?

Nothing. I cannot think of anything I would have on for 10 years. When I said I am able think far ahead, I was not talking about a decade ahead—that is too far in the future. Things change and evolve; nothing remains good for 10 years. If I became incapacitated, I would have to give money to someone who would find the best trades for me. I would hire the best active manager, fund-of-hedge funds, or advisor to manage it. There isn't one trade or one style that always works for 10 years.

What other lessons did you take from 2008?

We learned that we have four principal risks as hedge fund managers, and focusing on each one is what saved us. First, because we concentrated on counterparty risk, we didn't get hurt when banks went under. Second, we focused on liquidity risk, and are even more focused on it now. Third, leverage can be pulled from prime brokers abruptly, making it significantly more expensive to access the same leverage. We expected this and had prepared for it because we saw it happen in 1998 during the LTCM crisis. Last, we paid a lot of attention to client risk—all clients wanting to leave at once because they are scared of all the other clients leaving—which became a problem for many hedge funds. I mitigated this risk by going to all of my clients, showing them the portfolio and convincing them to stay.

What have I learned? I learned that there is justice in the world because the incompetent get eliminated. It just takes time. I learned that capitalism worked. The system got cleansed. Finally, I learned that the good people stay and the bad people get eliminated. But does any of this knowledge make me wiser? Having survived 2008, I will be able to recognize certain problems the next time a big crisis comes along, but again, that will not happen for another five to seven years.

Will you get nervous here if the stock market hits new highs?

I will go to cash and force myself to go sailing. Indirectly, it will mean that I should be short, so I will have to start building up my shorts or be long puts. By then, it will also mean that my assets under management will be up 50 to 100 percent from performance and from new clients, which means that I have to be cautious if I want to protect that. We need both liquidity and volatility to do our jobs—they are our lifeblood. I am most bored when markets do nothing.

Chapter 13

The Plasticine Macro Trader

"The Plasticine Macro Trader" is an equity specialist who says he sources trade ideas from the voices in his head and manages risk by being a piece of plasticine—malleable and flexible, able to take down gross exposure aggressively to limit the downside risk. We sat down in his white-washed loft office in a leafy residential neighborhood in a major financial capital. You will not find this manager in the usual hedge fund haunts of midtown Manhattan or Mayfair, London. He is asocial by admission and thoroughly contrarian. He doesn't mix with his peers for information, have drinks with the guys, or seem to need confirmation of his theses by others. He does concede that he is trying to develop more vices over time.

During the course of a two-hour interview, he twice more refers to voices in his head, and I am never sure if he is serious. At times self-effacing, he can oscillate toward egocentrism, comparing himself to his hero, George Soros, when describing short positions in the Icelandic króna: "I want to be known as the man who bankrupted Iceland." Moments later he is self-deprecating once again, saying that he has no friends and often doubts his abilities. "No one wants to work with me. I'm a bit of a circus freak."

Having once worked for an asset manager for pensions, then run a long-only mutual fund, he is not afraid to offer scathing comments about those "arrogant people who think it's okay to lose 30 percent of their clients' money so long as the peer group loses 31." During the dot-com boom, he was punished by an industry association for not conforming to the mandate of his long-only mutual fund (i.e., being fully invested), a strategy that ultimately preserved client capital in the subsequent bust when all of his peers suffered tremendously.

The Plasticine Macro Trader notes that, even going back to the early 1700s, it is impossible to find another 30-year period as favorable for stocks as the last 30 years. In this vein, he tends to view even iconic names such as Warren Buffett as having dominated a zeitgeist that in itself was extraordinary because it was anomalous. His skepticism proved correct, and he made a lot of money in 2008, a time when most others were crushed.

When did you know you wanted to be in the markets?

I just wanted a job. I didn't even want to go to university but I saw sense in it. I am fantastically sensible, very working class. My father was a truck driver and my mother a receptionist. My dad was 21 when I was born, and he had ideas of us hanging out together in suburbia where I grew up. Instead, I was a shy and reclusive teenager listening to opera in my bedroom, and he thought I was gay, so he didn't really want to hang out. I have never been the master of detail, and to get into university you had to fill out this form with your top three choices. Because I filled it out wrong, I ended up being accepted for accountancy, something I didn't really want to study but which was nonetheless a very suitable middle class aspiration for a working class kid. I sublimated everything in studying and had no vices to speak of. I studied through summer holidays; I didn't drink, didn't smoke, and didn't have any girlfriends. As I get older, however, I am trying to create vices. I am the original Benjamin Button.

During my last year at university I started doing market based accounting research. I used a Datastream machine, which is like a very old predecessor to Bloomberg, to test how market data would react to, say, a change in depreciation policy. For example, reducing the depreciable life of an asset would reduce reported profits, but there would be no change in cash flow. Intrinsically, the equity price should only be affected by changes in cash flow, rather than changes in earnings, and I was trying to gauge the market impact of the release of such changes in accounting policy. I got quite hooked on it.

When I started to apply for jobs in the fund management industry, one particular firm had a policy of recruiting exclusively from Oxford and Cambridge as a filter to get the best people. When I was applying, the firm in question was trying to break into the American pension fund market and the consultants were expressing concern over the lack of gene diversity. They didn't want to take on a caste system where the fund managers were sitting around on deck chairs watching the cricket, eating cucumber sandwiches and talking stocks. So by a happy coincidence they were keen to meet local kids from all walks of life, and I got my chance.

How did you perform?

I've always had a good sense of the future, of change. When I write my market reports, I seem to be more often right than wrong. The difficulty that I had back then was in conforming to the devout scripture preached by orthodox long-only managers, and I was employed at the time by the most fundamental long-only house in the UK. Nevertheless, we used considerable rigor in our approach, ran very concentrated portfolios, and knew our businesses better than anyone; I am very grateful for the experience.

Once a month I had to present an economic paper, an intimidating practice that fomented the macro approach that I employ today. The firm rotated its new hires through different departments, and I started out in the Japanese team. I vividly recall presenting a report on the Japanese economy six weeks out of university. It was in a huge Georgian room, with the partners sitting around an imposing mahogany table and another 40 or so people standing and poised to tear my arguments apart; it was terrifying.

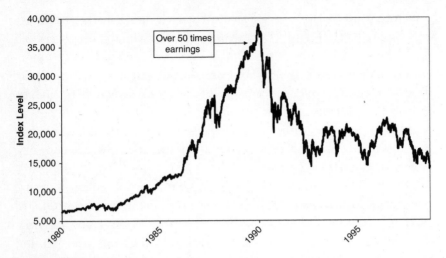

Figure 13.1   Nikkei, 1980–1998
SOURCE: Bloomberg.

Were you bullish Japan?

No, God no! This was 1991, and stocks were trading at over 50 times earnings (see Figure 13.1). Yet I had to present the view of the two key partners who, of course, were as horny as anything for Japan. I could not understand their bias, which obviously came from the very long bull market. That created some conflict between me and them.

Is the long-only real money world similarly deluded about equity and equity-like assets today?

Problems always change. Today's problems are unique to today, and essentially emanate from the fact that equity returns over the last 30 years have been exceptionally high and consistent. Stock market data goes back to 1720 and it is almost impossible to find a period comparable to the last 30 years. But this modern time period encapsulates the lifespan of people who have already amassed massive reputations and fortunes, and who are now often feted as having deployed cunning and individual wit, rather than having been swept up in a historically long period of sustained prosperity. In the long-only community, people such as Anthony Bolton in the UK, or Bill Miller and Warren Buffett in the U.S., have achieved extraordinary success. Perhaps uncharitably, I attribute some of this to

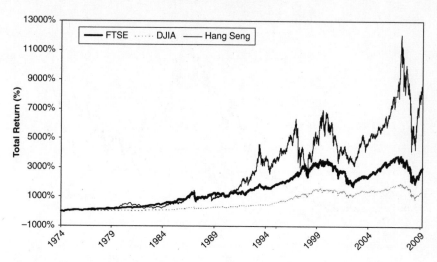

Figure 13.2   Stock Index Total Returns, 1974–2009
SOURCE: Bloomberg.

having dominated the zeitgeist of the age: with inflation, taxes and interest rates collapsing, returns on capital exploded. However, with the tremendous upheaval in the last year, people are beginning to question the sustainability of this long trend.

For some context on just how extraordinary the nominal dollar returns have been, the FTSE All Share is up 43 times from its 1970s low, the American markets are up 25 times and Hong Kong, with its fixed exchange rate, is up over 116 times. These are exceptional moves by any standard. (See Figure 13.2.)

We have, of course, had repeated crises since the 1970s, with, on occasion, stock markets falling precipitously. But it has always proven enormously profitable to buy the dips, creating a Pavlovian response whereby being contrarian has come to mean buying risk or at least holding on to long stock positions come what may. We have created an environment where the benchmark is everything. If something has gone up 43 times, it is difficult to ignore. We have institutionalized a behavior that defines risk taking as being a function of market deviations rather than the likelihood of losing clients' money.

Things may have changed, and the next 30 years will prove more challenging, especially when viewed through the prism of the last three decades. Today we are faced with the prospect of debt deflation, which we last experienced globally after the crash of 1929. My argument is that

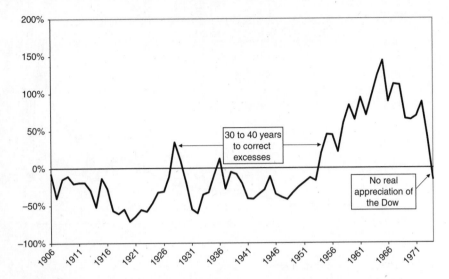

Figure 13.3   Dow Jones Industrial Average Real Returns, 1906–1974
SOURCE: Dow Jones, Bureau of Labor Statistics.

it took 30 to 40 years for society to correct for the previous financial excesses. For instance, did you know that in the absence of dividends, there was no real appreciation in the Dow Jones from 1906 to 1974 (see Figure 13.3)? This is what happens when society develops revulsion for debt and seeks to live in a nonleveraged world—asset prices take the brunt of it and it takes a long time to work off. Asset prices have gone up so much in part because the anchor was pitched so low. Again, market practitioners today have been rationalizing their risk behavior using returns measured off an absolute low point in the history of financial markets; can we really be surprised that their behavior is so out of kilter?

Are all the long-only stars today just a function of the environment for the past 30 years?

Today's long-only stars operated during a period of time where investors did not require a macro compass. Today your average long-only guy does not spend much time looking at interest rates, currencies, debt levels, and other key macro variables. I have even been to conferences where fund managers have boasted, "I don't know where oil prices are going; I don't know where interest rates are going; I don't know anything about the government." I, on the other hand, spend all my time trying to formulate views on these things and yet these guys brag that such factors are irrelevant. All they care about is that they own the best companies in the world. For the last 30 years they could get away with that nonsense, but now at a historic turning point they are being found out.

How will the long-only community adapt?

The long-only community will not adapt. The history of mutual funds in America could be a telling proxy. By the early 1990s, 80 percent of the money committed during the first era of the "gunslinger" fund manager, back in the late 1960s, was withdrawn from mutual funds out of a combination of boredom, confusion, and disgust; remember in real terms, and again ignoring dividends, the American stock market took 25 years to surpass its nominal price high of 1966. Something similar could happen again because the long-only industry will not change its ways. And the reason it won't change is that it perceives its biggest risk as franchise risk, whereby it is okay to lose money as long as everyone else is losing money; it's not their money after all. This benchmarked approach is hardwired into their portfolios, but it is an intellectual conceit that could jeopardize their clients' money.

Take the UK's Investment Management Association (IMA), a gaggle of long-only fund managers who masquerade as some kind of government regulator. During the savage TMT bust at the turn of the century, when the European stock market was down over 50 percent, I was running a long-only mutual fund and I was up small. However, the IMA threatened me with expulsion from my equity sector on the grounds that I was "cheating," which basically resulted from my refusal to obey their benchmark rules. The IMA insists that a fund should be at least 80 percent invested in the stock market of their categorization at all times, and there were brief moments when I was running 50 percent cash levels because the market rout was so severe.

At the time, the Saturday edition of the *Financial Times* featured a series of interviews with long-only managers, many of whom were bragging about how much money they lost. "We do what it says on the brochure, we invest in equities, and if they go down, we go down." Again, they were confident in making such claims because every decline in the preceding 30-year period was followed by a resumption of the bullish trend, as society was still yearning to further leverage its balance sheet. And they were right! But I thought it revealed a complacent attitude that was subsequently confirmed during the waterfall slide in stock prices since late 2007. My question to them is, "What happens if we exhaust the private sector's willingness to take on more leverage?"

Recently, I have begun to notice two distinct types of investors emerging. The people who manage other people's money think they are the "contrarians," and they are bullish and fully invested; but then they always are. And on the other side of the table sit the clients whose money is at risk. But having seen their capital so damaged by such "contrarians" they are more circumspect today and they are beginning to challenge the wisdom of such persistent long-term bullishness in the current environment.

What do you say to people who claim that 2008 was a one-in-a-hundred year storm, who defend their investment approach by citing that the storm has passed?

Strange things can happen. We all have to sit down and think long and hard about what transpired last year, and it's only right that you get different interpretations and conclusions. But remember I see last year in the context of the last 200 or 300 years where there have been long periods of time when the market did nothing. Last year has fulfilled part of this prophecy as the stock market is flat for 10 years so things are going according to plan. Markets are behaving in a manner that is predictable to anyone who is conversant on previous stock market movements and economic history.

If you see a coming storm but it's potentially a few years away, how do you manage capital in the short to medium term, when everyone is picking up pennies in front of a steam roller?

It is desperately important to identify and expose your own intellectual prejudice. The more that you can articulate this prejudice, the more you can control it. The great thing about 2006 and 2007 was the low price of options volatility. In our long-only portfolios, we used 1 percent of the assets to buy out-of-the-money put options on the stock market, which we rolled on a quarterly basis. This allowed us to adhere to our cockroach mandate, which I define as being a survivor no matter what; if something profoundly nasty were to occur, we would be insulated from a shocking loss. During 2006 and 2007, you almost could have your cake and eat it, too.

Of course, you would not blow the indices away under such a model, but you could pretty much match their performance, which is fine. After all, my grandmother could make money from the stock market when it's going up. But when the market goes down, especially when it goes down dramatically, you pray that your manager truly understands risk. It is not enough just to get the one big call right; there has to be some consistency.

The most powerful means of compounding returns is to not lose money in the first place. If you start off with 100 and lose 30 percent, you are left with 70. Before you are truly in the black you have to make back the 30 you lost, which represents a gain of 43 percent! So, if you can minimize your drawdowns, you stand a better chance of compounding money more effectively over time.

Again, remember, I believe there is a degree of predictability to what has been happening in markets for the last 10 years. I believe that our generation is embarking upon a long period of unwinding financial excesses. Stock market returns could be terrible for the foreseeable future. If you believe people like Niall Ferguson, debt deflation eliminates all of the gains from the preceding boom, it purges everything. By 1974, we had eliminated all of the real gains from the American stock market since 1906. If we consider Japan as an example, the Topix would have to trade at 300 (or one third its present level) to be comparable with the lows reached during the 1970s on Wall Street. At this point, all of the real gains since the index was reconfigured in 1969 would have been eliminated. (See Figure 13.4.)

Given the bounce in 2009, everyone is feeling good. Are people being too complacent?

Because markets are created and run by human beings, they are necessarily a psychological affair. Whilst I have misgivings about Warren Buffett these days, his tale about the oil tycoon is still the very best.

I tell it a slightly different way, using the cover of Pink Floyd's *Wish You Were Here* album as my visual.

The oil tycoon is ablaze, talking with St. Peter who is at the gates of heaven, which is really a Hollywood studio lot (I think stardom is the

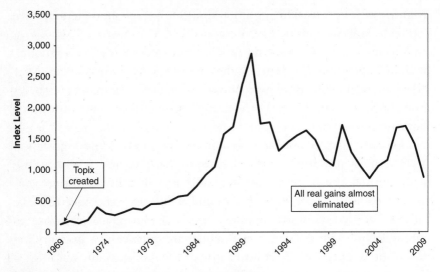

Figure 13.4   Topix Real Returns, 1969–2009
Source: Bloomberg.

new religion). St. Peter says to the oil tycoon, "My goodness, look at the mess you're in. I'm afraid that I can't let you in; the oil tycoon department is full." And the oil guy thinks, I've never had to wait for anything in my life, and asks, "Can I just say 'hi' to the old boys one last time?" St. Peter concedes, and the tycoon yells, "Oil found in hell!" After all the wildcatters have stampeded from heaven to hell, St. Peter says, "You're a clever guy, we've now got some space so you'd better come in." But the oil tycoon turns around and says, "You know what . . . there just might be some truth to that rumor after all," and he goes to hell. The clamor to reload on equities and commodities this year is kind of similar; investors are determined to go to hell.

Of course, last year was the closest incarnation of hell on earth that most professional investors have seen in their careers and yet, having beaten themselves up, saying, "I'm never going to make that mistake again," 2009 comes around and the benchmark rises and the green shoots say, "Oil found in hell." Will they ever learn?

Could it, in fact, be different this time? Real productivity gains, globalization, technology, trade, etc. . . .

There's a yin and yang, a reason markets behave as they do, and there are 300 years of historical context to help us understand that we have not changed. For instance, here I am in the internet age using Japanese candlestick techniques that were devised by rice traders in Japan in the eighteenth century. This type of chart analysis allows me to respect cyclicality, to remind me that certain patterns have arisen before. But it runs deeper than that. It exposes the conceit of our time. Our generation truly came to think of itself as different, that somehow we were better than our ancestors.

I'm practicing yoga now. I did a headstand in my class this morning. Yoga is all about passing on the wisdom of life from elders, making sure traditions continue. I see someone like Robert Prechter as a yogi and I practice some of his teaching. Although I'm not one for counting waves, I think his socioeconomics has an appealing logic and a certain yogic feeling to me. He says that fundamentals are quite useless because they just reinforce the trend. As an example, let's consider the summer of 2008, when oil moved from $100 to $150 in six to seven weeks. The fundamentals were reinforcing the moves, as peak oil theories abounded. Whilst I was taking off a lot of my fund's long oil futures positions in the interest of managing risk, I was still eager to recreate the exposure with a reasonably modest out-of-the-money call option. But I should have been buying out-of-the-money puts.

This reveals the challenge of running a portfolio that is more macro orientated. We are constantly trying to challenge ourselves by looking for opportunities in low delta, cheap trades that run in direct opposition to the consensus. Can you imagine how much oil you could have sold short at $50 in July 2008 for almost no premium and with such a spectacular return? Yet instead of buying puts, I was buying calls because the fundamentals just reinforced the trend. I got sucked in; lesson learned. This is why I try to listen to people like Prechter who say there are more than fundamentals at work.

Stepping back a bit, having run money for pensions via a long-only mutual fund and now running a hedge fund, what advice do you have for the people who are running more institutional real money mandates?

Have the courage to be different, the courage to risk the ire of others for the sake of being right; to fight rather than embrace compromises everywhere. We have to encourage rebellious notions such as playfulness and curiosity. There is no one correct way of doing things that is set in stone. Periodically managers should be open to trying different approaches.

If you read Edwin Lefèvre's book, *Reminiscences of a Stock Operator*, the fictionalized version of the early years of Jesse Livermore, he gives a great account of this kind of behavior. Livermore goes long before he goes short. That's genius. He would buy because he wanted to experience the thrill of owning something. Taking a position changes the chemical balance of the body and the brain and you start to understand what it is you were missing. Likewise being subject to the risk that it might go down opens up neuro passageways in the mind which you perhaps didn't see. So you begin to understand and articulate what you're fighting against, which you wouldn't have known had you just gone short straight away. It is like touching a hot plate; as the plate gets hotter, your sense of timing gets heightened by the fact that you have risk on.

George Soros explains a version of this phenomenon when he says, "Invest first, and investigate later." But this is heresy in the institutional money world. When I suggest stuff like that, the number crunchers and the box tickers write down, "crazy guy" and make their polite goodbyes. But every so often a heretic turns out to be a genius.

I was presenting at a conference for institutional investors recently on the topic of a safe haven. The whole conference was about safe havens, and clearly the event was conceived during the tumult of 2008. I argued that there is no such thing as the popular conception of a safe haven, and the closest they'll get to one is me. The very fact that no one in the room will give me money makes me safe.

Today, investors think gold is a safe haven. They are almost certainly correct at one level of abstraction. But there are all kinds of people buying gold who had never owned it historically, and they are gloating about the fact. In 2003, I enjoyed the good fortune of making a lot of money in gold, in both my hedge fund and my long-only funds. The funny thing, however, is that back then, I couldn't read the *Financial Times* or *The Economist* because every time I opened one of those newspapers, it said that owning gold was idiotic, gold had been falling for 25 years, Gordon Brown was selling, Keynes called it a barbaric relic, etc. So I ignored the papers, and gold went straight up for years. What has happened since the third quarter of 2007 has confirmed every dire warning of the gold bug community. Governments are basically printing paper money and

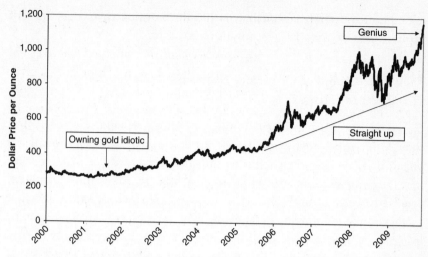

Figure 13.5 Gold, 2000–2009
SOURCE: Bloomberg.

bailing out weak institutions, fiat currencies are being debased, and so on. Atlas shrugged and thankfully for Ayn Rand's sake, she's dead. Yet the gold price today is not that much higher than it was at the end of 2007, and that's kind of a long time. Now, if you own gold today, the *Financial Times* says you're a genius. (See Figure 13.5.) Not only do you understand economics, you understand central banking, the quantity theory of money, and a host of other theories; there are even vending machines at German airports dispensing gold bars. But buying once things are popular is not how I try to make money. So the message to pension fund advisors and the like is that there is actually safety in disciplined, contrarian, heretical types of portfolio construction.

Imagine you are running a pension fund for British teachers. How would you manage that portfolio?

I do not believe I would ever be invited to run such a plan. With my business I have put together something that is intriguing and disciplined, that has massively outperformed, and yet I still cannot get enough people interested, which is frustrating but par for the course. At least I get to live an interesting life. The problem with pension funds is that they are designed to fail, so we should not be surprised when they do. It would take the brink of Armageddon to usher in change, to get rid of the pen pushers. But by then I fear it might be too late.

Should the Oxford or Cambridge Endowment give you 100 percent of their assets to manage?

Certainly not. Perhaps they should give me 1 percent. But of course they won't and I have come to accept that. As an asset allocator, I am engaged in the same exercises as the managers of these plans, except that I am marked-to-market daily and have to meet more stringent criteria because a good portion of my assets are absolute return vehicles. I cannot hide behind any benchmark. My decisions can make money or lose money. It is not a theoretical exercise. It's my money and my clients' money, and I am relieved to say that I have endured; that I have stood the test of time positively. Ironically, my heretical approach has fostered longevity and made money.

Hedge funds in the 1970s did not receive any money from the institutional world. The managers were fantastically interesting and entertaining, and you wanted to spend time with them, learn from them. But when it came down to giving them money, big allocators hesitated and probably spent the rest of their careers wishing they had given them money.

My complaint with hedge funds today is that they are a safe option. It feels good giving them money; no one demurs. Likewise, it feels good allocating money to gold. But if it feels so good and is easy to allocate to whatever strategy or instrument is in vogue, then maybe that is a signal to take a step back. The kind of investing that I do, that yields the really big returns, always involves fear and a sick feeling of the consequences of being wrong in isolation, away from the shelter of accepted opinion. Of course, you can't have hundreds of "I'm fearfuls" in the portfolio. But today I sense there is very little in institutional investors' portfolios where they're fearful of being wrong—zero. If pressed, they would say it's hedge funds because they are edgy and "alternative." Allocating to a large $10 billion hedge fund is like investing with a long-only manager; they are never going to bet their business franchise over such a trifling notion of being right. Investing with a multibillion-dollar hedge fund manager is the pinnacle of consensus. The guy who gave them the first $100 million, that was different; but not the last $100 million.

By investing in a more conservative, "safe way", does that mean real money ends up owning things at the top, once these things are popular?

Exactly. Case in point is the Church of England, whose commissioners became convinced by the cult of equity way back in the whimsical days of 1999 and went 100 percent long the stock market. Today the Church of England pension fund has assets of just £461 million against liabilities of £813 million. Austerity beckons for the clergymen. Investors today recant a new mantra of, "Anything but the dollar (A-B-D)." Inflation bets are all the rage. Some would insist that it is their fiduciary duty to protect their clients' capital and the spell cast by a contemporary cult is hard to resist.

Take another august body, the Harvard Endowment Fund (see box). Not typically renowned as a hotbed of reactionary fervor, the fund is nevertheless radical in its construction and has come to typify the A-B-D stance. Harvard's position could well be construed as a one-way bet. Almost half of the fund is invested in emerging market equities, commodities, real-estate, private equity, and junk bonds. It is as though the rap artist 50 Cent has taken over the advisory board. The fund is going to "get rich or die tryin'."

Harvard Endowment Portfolio (ABD), Fiscal Year 2010

Foreign Equities	11%
Domestic Equities	11%
Emerging Equities	11%
Private Equities	13%
Absolute Returns	16%
Commodities	14%
Real Estate	9%
High Yield Bonds	2%
Foreign Bonds	2%
Domestic Bonds	4%
Inflation Indexed Bonds	5%
Cash	2%

SOURCE: *Financial Times.*

This portfolio will work if the dollar keeps falling or the world has inflation. It is a hopeful portfolio, and it all depends on China. China in fact shares the same risk as the world's largest pension schemes—that an overleveraged American consumer does not return to their manic buying of old. As William White, former chief economist of the BIS, has argued: Many countries that relied heavily on exports as a growth strategy are now geared up to provide goods and services to heavily indebted countries that no longer have the will or the means to buy them.

We, on the other hand, approach risk by considering the worst possible outcome. For real money funds at present, the greatest torment would be a repeat of 2008's final quarter when 30-year Treasuries yielded just 2.5 percent. This would require an annual return of 20 percent or more from the fund's riskier assets at precisely the time that their future returns would seem most questionable; insolvency would beckon. And yet, they blithely run the risk of ruination.

So you say you are a contrarian through and through, genuinely horrified by anything of convention. Why do you do conferences and go on TV even though you claim you can't stand people in the industry? Is this a way of filtering information or understanding what the crowd is talking about, enabling you to go the other way?

That's a deep question, and one that I'm currently working through with my shrink. That's really hard.

Even a true contrarian is only really contrarian about 20 percent of the time; it's all about choosing the right moment to fight convention. The rest of the time is spent trend following. So I guess I am a trend-following contrarian. I come back to describing myself as a disciplined deviant. But every description that I have for myself is an oxymoron, and when I present my views, most people just think I'm a moron.

Everyone comes from a different walk of life. I don't think I am like other managers in this business. I have no social interaction. I don't have a drink with the guys. I've never done that. The only sport I ever pursued actively was rock and alpine climbing, which is a real, life-on-the-limb solo activity. I don't feel comfortable in groups, anywhere where I can be associated, categorized. I absolutely cower when I'm identified, when someone could say that's the group he fits into over there, they're such and such. That really sets off alarm bells in me. This is what creates the contrarian in me. I have Tourette's syndrome—I say "fuck" at all at the wrong times. One of my mentors taught me how to articulate that Tourette's and then play the odds, become trend following and recognize when the elasticity becomes so extreme that your Tourette's becomes valid and has the possibility of profits.

What else did you learn from your mentor?

One of the most important things is playfulness—the mind needs mischievousness. In trying to get a sense of the future, you have to play games with yourself. A nice example of playfulness is Paul Tudor Jones overlaying the stock market of 1987 on top of 1929 and predicting the crash (see *Inside the House of Money,* Chapter 2). And it worked. It was fortuitous that it worked, but it worked, he was lucky. In this business, being consistently lucky is fine—just stay lucky.

At the moment, I am being playful with my presumption that 2009 is following virtually the same path as 2008—it would be intriguing and fun, and if it came to pass I would make a lot of money, and people would call me a genius. But I would be the first to recognize that a lot of it was luck.

Is Paul Tudor Jones's success, or George Soros's success for that matter, due to luck?

No, I don't think their success is luck; they have become legends because they can be wrong about future events and yet they still make money. Take Soros and the insights he generously provides to the outside world in books such as *The Alchemy of Finance,* where he keeps a journal of his thoughts during a tumultuous period in the mid-1980s. With the benefit of hindsight, we know that he is often wrong and yet he always makes money. Having years with 100 percent returns while getting some trends wrong means there is an instinctive genius in his trading that I don't fully comprehend. I'm still trying to learn. Meanwhile, most of the things that I write actually do come to pass, yet I don't make the same returns as people such as Soros or Tudor Jones. I'm obviously missing something. The key is choosing your moments to fight with the market, and I'm beginning to learn when to avoid a fight. The wonderful thing about life and getting older is learning from your mistakes. If you don't learn from your mistakes, you get kicked out.

You once claimed that you made trading decisions based off of voices in your head, is that still the case?

I jokingly claim that my best investment decisions come from being a paranoid schizophrenic. I hear voices in my head. Subconsciously and explicitly I seek to create a macro prejudice. And so there's an ongoing debate by those voices in my head. But the scary thing is that I make investment decisions based on these voices. And so does everyone else. I just talk about it openly and honestly. When I make such decisions I become very fearful, paranoid like a schizophrenic, that these decisions may jeopardize my investors and my portfolio. I would contend that this fear makes me a better investor.

We generate our ideas from a global macro prejudice and then filter them through a global macro prism. Let me give you an example. I read research by people such as Mark Faber. Mark is wonderful, but I have to read him through the prism of sheet music. Charts are my sheet music; Faber is my Mozart. However, by putting his thoughts and prejudices through a different medium I can raise or lower the volume of Mark and the others. Right now I've got the volume on Mark and people like James Grant turned low; not because I disrespect them but because they are currently in conflict with my disciplines, my sheet music, and with my understanding of how to make money. Normally, these guys are contentious, but today I fear they are expressing everyone's fears. Mark Faber is saying the U.S. will end up with hyperinflation. I don't have to agree or disagree with that, but I have to recognize it's an extreme view that has become an acceptable currency. And his confidence in saying something so provocative, and not being strongly challenged, is a function of it seeming very likely at the present time. Typically such consensus arises when the majority of investors are tilting their portfolios in that direction. Clearly, my instincts are to go the other way. But I need the legitimacy of a positive price trend to confirm my prejudice; you won't find me buying things in a downtrend.

Can you tell me more about how you generate your ideas through a global macro prism?

I really struggle to be long any equity today. If you put a gun to my head, or even better, my macro prism, I might buy some agricultural names. Farming was the very worst place to be invested from its mid-1970s nominal price high. In real terms, the price of corn, wheat, and other agricultural commodities have fallen by 80 percent, whereas the American stock market has risen nine times from its real price low in 1982. Perhaps ags have a chance once more? (See Figure 13.6.)

Don Coxe, the strategist and now hedge fund manager in Canada, had this great saying that the best investment opportunities are presented in areas where the people who know it best love it least. If something has fallen 80 percent in real terms, you might be a farmer but still hate agriculture; persistently weak prices, year in and year out, change people's behavior. No one keeps any inventory because they want to sell the stuff fast before the price falls further. When economic behavior changes in such a way, big macro opportunities are created. This year we are likely to grow more corn than ever before and yet stocks will fall; the world is getting seriously short. Furthermore, whilst the rest of the economy has taken on unprecedented leverage in the past 30 years, agriculture

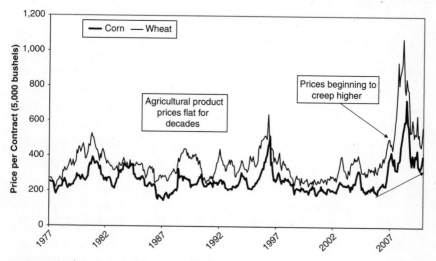

Figure 13.6 Agricultural Futures, 1977–2009
SOURCE: Bloomberg.

has actually deleveraged (debt and falling prices are untenable). When I look at monthly charts on agriculture, I find a profound nominal price drawdown, and then nothing for the longest time. In the last few years, however, prices have gradually begun to creep higher. That's the hook; it is one thing to create the intellectual color but it doesn't go into the portfolio until it starts to gain the attraction of relative momentum. I need the legitimacy of other curious strangers before I get involved.

Does going on TV or writing something in your monthly investor letter make it harder to change your mind?

I hope not. I go on CNBC not to give investment counsel, but rather to say, "This is me, this is what I'm doing." My wife says I'm the dullest person in the world because I have no secrets. I absolutely have no secrets in the portfolio. I go on TV to say I want you to challenge me, tell me I'm wrong; if I am wrong, it is better that I find out sooner rather than later. The difficulty a fund manager has is that he is king in his organization, so it's very hard to get people to take you on. On CNBC, I can invite people to take me on; it is completely unscripted and the need to respond with brevity is a real discipline.

Last summer I was on CNBC talking up Potash [Corporation of Saskatchewan], saying it was the best positioned company in the world when I suddenly realized everyone was agreeing with me. So I got out. Thank God I can reject my own advice because from July to October of 2008 its performance was diabolical. It had a perfect correlation with other risk assets, providing no safe harbor. I'd still make the same case today for Potash but in terms of the sphere that I occupy, the stock market and real-time mark-to-market, it has gone from $260 to $90. We occupy a world where fundamentals are on one side and an emotional landscape of human psychology and behavior is on another. Potash is a compelling investment based off fundamentals, but emotionally it was disastrous to have in the portfolio in late 2008. (See Figure 13.7.)

You once told me you hated the "Favorite Trade" format of the Drobny Conference. Can you explain?

The thing that I'm most fearful of is a focused fund, or a portfolio of 20 best ideas, which is a concept that marketed well a few years ago.

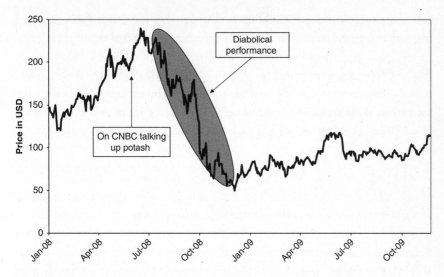

Figure 13.7 Potash Corporation of Saskatchewan (POT), 2008
SOURCE: Bloomberg.

The reason this idea can prove disastrous is that "best" is an emotionally charged word. Giving up on your best idea is the same as admitting that you're wrong, something crucially important but very difficult to do.

I create portfolios with many moving parts, literally hundreds of positions. We are like a centipede: we can lose a few legs but keep moving forward, and I have no reservations about hacking off a leg or two. A focused fund, on the other hand, is the antithesis of the centipede portfolio. A focused fund says I only have two legs and I don't want to lose them; they are my best legs, so running a two-stock portfolio is optimal. There was a climber in Utah who hacked off an arm to stay alive, but he's the exception. Most of us would be dead because we would dither and hesitate.

With my portfolios, we are constantly conducting thought experiments to keep our minds flexible and to keep moving. We are always doing something to test ourselves, the market, or a view. We're like the French Foreign Legion, if in doubt, move forward. I guess they don't mind losing a few volunteers. Our philosophy is, if in doubt, buy a third or sell a third. Put on one third of the position size you would normally have. If we're right, thank God we have a position on, albeit a smaller one than we would normally run. If we're wrong, thank God we only did a third, but always movement, movement, movement.

Do you have a different interpretation of diversification? Diversification traditionally means having positions that are theoretically or historically uncorrelated, whereas it sounds as if you diversify more as a function of position sizing to ensure that no one position can take you out of the game.

I don't believe that there is any real diversification left in the world today, at least not the kind of diversification to which you refer. And the shocking nature of the results in 2008 demonstrates this fact. We live in a world of binary events. Over the last 10 years, markets have oscillated between inflation and deflation, and people are either all in or all out. What we're trying to do is make sure that we're leaning at the right time, correctly anticipating the oscillation.

We don't run diversified portfolios. Rather, we are very direct, articulating our overarching prejudice through a series of smaller bets. But our prejudice is the thing that sits on our shoulders, forcing us to deal with it. Our prejudice will clearly shape our portfolios, so we have to acknowledge it and respect it. And living with this blasted thing on our shoulders is much easier if it is composed of lots of moving parts. That way, if the time comes when the prejudice is just wrong, I can get moving by cutting and reducing the component parts. Again, it gets me moving; action, lights, camera.

Should portfolio construction be completely rethought?

The industry traditionally judges investment opportunities and managers based on returns, volatility, and correlation, an approach premised on a view of the world that just isn't true. The binary world that I described earlier, one in which managers either have risk on or off and everything is highly correlated, is a world that cannot be correctly navigated by the old model. If I am right and this is a debt deflation, it will take 30 years to work through the system, and you do not want to be paying an active management fee for passive execution during that time because it will not be worth it. Rather, you just want to own cash, bonds, an ETF and then pay up for a good active manager. Right now, however, given the lack of diversification in the world, you need an active and contentious manager who is willing to take on your taboos. They will be your diversifier because their oscillations, behavior, and decisions will probably prove uncorrelated to movements in the rest of your fund. You can't get any diversification today from investing in Indian shares, technology shares, and agricultural shares, and certainly not from trying to diversify into other forms of equity, such as private equity, venture capital, and real estate; why sacrifice precious liquidity for correlated return streams?

What place will hedge funds have in this new paradigm that you describe?

Given the remuneration profile, hedge fund management offers the highest return on intellectual capital of any discipline known to man. Now, if you had never met a hedge fund manager, you might rationally assume that they are some of the brightest people on the planet. Again, it helps to form this opinion if you haven't met any. My take on it is that it is a waste of time to assume that I can outsmart the smartest people on the planet. Most hedge fund managers disagree. They present to pension funds saying, "We are the smartest people you could give your money to." My presentation, on the other hand, is, "How do smart people keep fucking it up?" And the answer is because orthodox intelligence is subject to the whims of irony and paradox: nonlinear distribution events catch these managers out time and time again. Recognizing that such events happen with a greater tendency than they are supposed to statistically, you get a chance to extract gains from them.

Nassim Taleb built a career off the premise that fat-tail events happen more frequently than people predict. How do you capture such events in a portfolio context? Can you give me an example?

My thesis going into 2006 was that the enthusiasm for commodities was correct and that we were in for a multiyear capital shift into the asset class. But for the super cycle to happen, we first needed a deflationary shock. If something profoundly bad could shock the system, then the behavior of the central banking community becomes predictable: They become heroic again and try to save the world. Typically this has been a function of reducing interest rates to zero and keeping them down there for a long time. Only then, I reasoned, could we see some absurdly high prices, like gold at $3,000 and oil at $500. So for the past three years our trading philosophy was, if you think the future is inflation, buy government bonds. This reasoning just blows fuses in people because bonds are normally not good when you have inflation. But I argued that the mechanism for getting to inflation is deflation and this would produce a new price high for government debt. And something like our scenario came to pass in 2008. We made money from interest rate contracts and government bonds.

According to this line of thinking, I should be making money right now owning commodities, which have bounced from the lows, but I am not. People are impatient at turning points and I think this turn will take longer. Some might say the opportunity was at the end of 2008, when 10-year U.S. Treasuries were yielding around 2.1 percent, but they stayed at those levels for such a short period that most people did not get involved. People are back to taking inflation risk right now and I don't think they get it. I think the death of leverage and its effect on the velocity of money gushing through the economy has initiated a debt deflation that continues to see a contraction in bank loans even in 2009.

The same "upside down" logic prevailed in 1979 when Volcker became chairman of the Fed. You had this new sheriff in town who was honest and tough. He was going to raise interest rates to make the economy very weak in order to parch the system of its inflation. He was a dream come true for a bond bull, and yet bonds got destroyed whilst gold doubled to $800 in three months. (See Figure 13.8.) The problem was that Volcker had to come clean on the Fed's dirty little secret. In order to have the legitimacy to be so hawkish, he had to admit that the problem was inflation; investors panicked and scrambled to protect themselves with gold. A hawk produced a melt-up in gold. Could the dovish Bernanke produce a similar melt-up at the long end of the bond market?

Does the Bernanke Fed understand the big picture in the way that the Volcker Fed did in the 1970s?

The Fed understands the gravity of the present situation and is fearful of a debt deflation. However, if I were to be super critical, I would contend

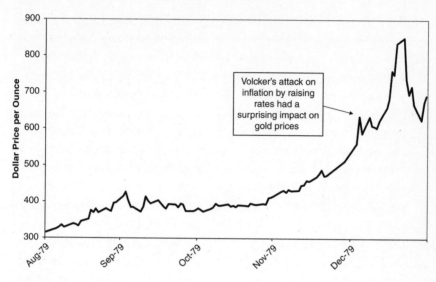

Figure 13.8   Gold, 1979–1980
SOURCE: Bloomberg.

that they are tackling a Minsky moment (see box) through the lens of Milton Friedman and that they may convince themselves that the worst is behind us too soon. But then I would also argue that stock market gurus, the government, and the Central Bank of China certainly don't get it either. Trichet doesn't get it. Angela Merkel certainly doesn't get it. The hysteria with Milton Friedman's notion that inflation is always and everywhere a monetary phenomenon places too little significance on the overleveraged nature of our society. It is of course orthodox thinking and it's hard to say it's wrong, but I believe it's wrong. But this is the prevailing mood in investing today.

Minsky Moment

A *Minsky moment* is a term coined after American economist Hyman Minsky (1919–1996), whose work was primarily focused on understanding the phenomena around financial crises. Minsky held that in good times, investors begin to take on

(continued)

excessive leverage when cash flows begin to cover debt payments, leading to a debt spiral and ultimately a crash. In essence, strong economic environments lead to a certain euphoria, fueling increased debt until levels of borrowing can no longer be supported. The point at which the debt-fueled speculation begins to come unraveled is the point at which no counterparty can be found to bid at the inflated asking prices prevailing in the market. This leads to a precipitous decline in prices and an evaporation of liquidity, as investors must sell even liquid securities in order to cover their debt payments. It is believed that the term "Minsky moment" was first employed by Paul McCulley of PIMCO in 1998, to describe the 1998 Russian financial crisis.

Wouldn't it be ironic if in 50 years time we look back on 2008 and the conventional wisdom becomes that the central banks should have done more? They should have printed more money and been more aggressive, yet they screwed up by taking baby steps because they were terrified of gold at $1,000, of the dollar collapsing, and of the Chinese pulling the money away. Yet they are creatures of habit, they don't like being unorthodox. When the Germans and the Chinese said this is wrong, they all listened. Wouldn't it be ironic if we find out later that there is only one chance against debt deflation and they all missed it? We are spending all of our time looking for inflation because the Fed will be slow in raising interest rates while the roof is caving in. The private sector's desire to unburden itself of debt is so great that debt deflation seems much more likely. And if it rolls over with everyone loaded up on risk again, playing commodities and inflation expectations, bonds could go parabolic. The bull market in government bonds is one of the greatest bull markets of all time, and bull markets of that magnitude do not end with a whimper. (See Figure 13.9.)

What was your worst trade ever?

Reader's Digest destroyed my career for a good five years. I had been brought up with all of that cheesy Warren Buffett franchise and value

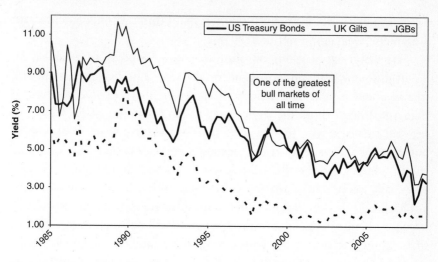

Figure 13.9 Government Bond Bull Market, 1985–2009
SOURCE: Bloomberg.

stuff. In my naive days, I thought I discovered Warren Buffett's next franchise—*Reader's Digest*. It has a dominant franchise with the older generation and when the walls to Eastern Europe were coming down, *Reader's Digest* was being embraced as an icon of the West. The problem was that I had a potent idea that wasn't subject to the scrutiny of the chart. Today, because of this error, I check all my ideas for the legitimacy of a positive trend. I am always late, I will never be early. But I never lose much money when I am wrong. I noticed recently that *Reader's Digest* had filed for bankruptcy, having been acquired by private equity last year; it's just a bad coin.

Tell me about a trade where you are waiting for the legitimacy of a trend.

Some of the voices in my head are quite stale because they've been in there for years. The events I foresaw are now coming to pass, and the more they come to pass, the more my confidence in the ideas increases and my willingness to take risk goes up. I have been talking about the Nikkei going back to 40,000 for some time now, and that's quite a convoluted tale. I wasn't bullish Japan when the Nikkei was trading at 40,000 back in 1990, and I am not now. But I can conceive of an extraordinary move in Japanese equities that I think would coincide with a dramatic weakening in the Yen.

Typically my work is all about creating context to establish an environment where I might want to take risk. The challenge with risk management is finding the appropriate moment to expose yourself to that risk. I don't think the right moment has come to pass for Japan just yet, but this is an idea that I have fermented for five years. Back then, I said that for the trade to work, we would need an extraneous economic shock which pushes dollar/yen down to around the 80s, and we have essentially been there. I am always in danger of wanting too much, but I am looking for those levels again in any subsequent round of global risk aversion. If that happens, I fear the Japanese will debauch their currency in an attempt to generate inflation to monetize their considerable public sector debts. With the majority of the private sector still invested in post office savings, such a step would cause a panic to buy equities and the Nikkei could go back to 40,000. Typically it requires 25 years to break a previous nominal price high in an asset class that has suffered a bubble. So who knows, maybe this is the trade for next decade? They have covered the place with kerosene, now all they have to do is light the match.

In developing these trade theses, do you travel to places such as Japan?

Yes, but it probably has a detrimental impact on the trade. For example, in July 2008, I was 3,000 feet under the soil in Saskatchewan seeing potash extracted. I generally try to shy away from travel, but I am an economic tourist. I have to get out of my office. When you are in the office, you are just bombarded with instant feedback on yourself, which gets crazy so I have to get away. It's like with children when you have them plant flower seeds into the soil and promise them that they will grow into beautiful plants. The children come out the first few days with the watering can, but after three days they forget about it.

How important is China in your thinking about the world right now?

I was very fortunate to receive an invitation recently to present to a Chinese bank. Yet I had the misfortune of them asking me my view of the world, which is not very bullish on China. My view on China is one of irony and paradox.

I jokingly suggest that it is as though we put Bernie Madoff in charge of America's GDP accounting. Of course he would overstate it. In a similar manner I believe that all the credit card and home-equity spending of the last decade served to overstate the true size of the American economy. And the surplus nations bought into the dream that American GDP was $15 trillion. Furthermore, in 10 years time they thought it might be $25 trillion and that the growth would continue uninterrupted. It is my fear, however, that American GDP will not be any greater than $20 trillion in 10 years as the process of working through the mountain of debt subdues spending in the economy. And without growth, the guys that own all the marginal capacity in the world are dead, just plain dead. This is certainly a contrarian thought, but I am actually amazed at how contrarian it is.

I am absolutely sick to death of people putting America down while putting China and other surplus nations on pedestals. It's a joke, and the whole theory of decoupling is a joke. The size of America is enormous compared to anything else, unless you look at the EU as a whole, which is comparable or even larger depending on what source you use. Otherwise Japan, China, and Germany are far behind, with about $5 trillion, $4.5 trillion, and just under $4 trillion, respectively. If you did a chart of U.S. debt to GDP from 2000, against a chart of MSCI Asia, i.e., China, it is a perfect fit. (See Figure 13.10.) I contend that the surplus nations are nothing but a leveraged play on the U.S. economy. China is a very deep out-of-the-money call option on the U.S. economy, and that is not something I am looking to buy right now. If America chooses to save more, then China has huge problems.

I have traveled into the deepest, darkest areas of China. The average GDP per head in China is something like $3,000, and yet they have the best infrastructure in the world. It's mismatched. With that GDP per head, you do not need the best infrastructure; you are not in any hurry and yet they have built an incredible train system that moves people around at over 200 kilometers per hour. I need it, but they don't and the pay-back on such schemes is simply untenable. And what more can China build?

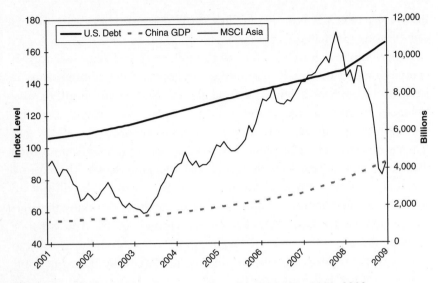

Figure 13.10 U.S. Debt, China GDP, and MSCI Asia, 2001–2009
SOURCE: Bloomberg.

What about the argument that China has all those foreign exchange reserves and is creating a domestic led economy, so it won't need the United States?

That is a joke. Being a creditor nation and running a current account surplus should not go together over the long term. What happens in an open global economy is that as I get richer from selling you more of my goods, my currency becomes more expensive while yours gets cheaper and more competitive, and so things eventually come back into balance and we can live happily side by side. However, spurred on by the Asian crisis of 1997–1998, the Asians have resisted this by not allowing their currencies to rise. Instead, their trade surpluses have been monetized into local currencies which have been leveraged by the international banking community and have created asset price bubbles from Shanghai to San Francisco.

America was guilty of the same practice in the 1920s. It was more competitive than Europe, but they prevented the dollar from rising by lending generously to the Germans and other debtor nations. Again, this is eerily similar to what China has been doing for the last 10 years. China is recirculating the money from its overseas trade and manipulating its currency to keep it from rising. The same thing also happened in the 1980s with Japan. These three events, when a creditor nation has run a persistent trade surplus, have come to define the global financial landscape of the last 100 years. Their legacy has been a cycle of stock market booms and busts. And the common attribute has been the decision to not allow their currency to rise, which funnels the resulting liquidity into rising asset prices, such as the stock market and real estate. This is the real quantitative easing, and over the past decade it sent oil from $10 a barrel to $150. Where were all the bond vigilantes then?

Now that everyone has whipped themselves up into a frenzy of inflation paranoia, the moment may have passed. The desire for Americans to save more will reduce Asian surpluses and therefore the Asian money printing will abate.

The interesting thing about today is that the renminbi is not rising; it has flat lined since the middle of 2008 just before everything fell apart (see Figure 13.11). An appreciating renminbi would tell me that the American economy and Chinese exports are doing well again, and that I might have to reject all of my contrarian risk aversion bias that favors owning government bonds. But here we are, almost a year after

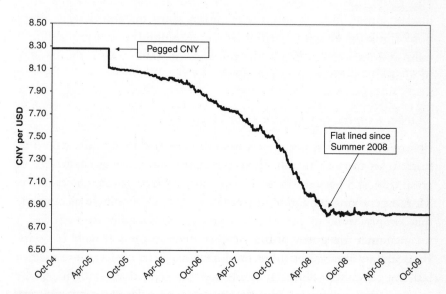

Figure 13.11   Chinese renminbi, 2005–2009
Source: Bloomberg.

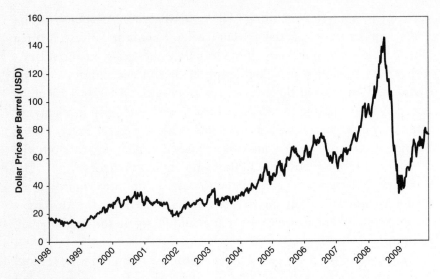

Figure 13.12   Oil, 1998–2009
SOURCE: Bloomberg.

the renminbi peaked in July 2008, and it has not changed. And yet the stock market and industrial commodities have rallied furiously from their post crash lows (see Figure 13.12). It is not inconsistent that the stock market should move before the economy gains traction. It's just that I don't think the economy can sustain a meaningful recovery; a glance at railroad container loading at the ports in the States reveals the fragility of such green shoots. (See Figure 13.13.)

So what happens to China in 10 or 20 years?

Before this year's fiscal surge I would have argued that China would be fine. Apart from their politics, which stink, they have an abundance of good things. Their goods are cheap and they have great infrastructure. Moreover, if one can ignore the politics, they are genuinely nice people that simply want to get ahead. However, this combination today is no guarantee that they will look very clever over the next 10 years. By doubling up on yet more productive capacity and yet more office buildings and yet more fast trains and the like, they have financially exposed themselves. For the first time in two decades they are very vulnerable. If I am right and the Western economies enjoy subdued

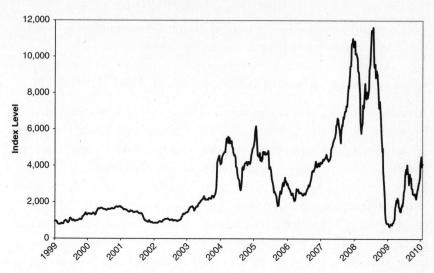

Figure 13.13   Baltic Dry Shipping Rate, 1999–2009
SOURCE: Bloomberg.

economic growth at best, then all of us will be swimming in deflation. The Chinese munificence of 2009 could be a legacy of yet more surplus industrial capacity. The price of Chinese and indeed all internationally traded goods like steel will need to come down to a level where, despite our misgivings and our collective desire to run down debt, their stuff is just so incredibly cheap that we will definitely consume more.

How important is liquidity to you?

Liquidity is very important. As I said earlier, changing my mind is in the nature of how I trade. I force myself to have the discipline to change my mind, to be flexible. I pride myself on the ability to reject everything that I said the day before. I can be long Potash, go on CNBC and say Potash is the greatest company in the world, then sell it the next day if something changes because I have that mental flexibility. How ironic would it be if, after having worked hard to develop this kind of flexibility over many years, I found out that I could not get out of a position because of lack of liquidity? My portfolio positions and sizing have to take into account the ability to change my mind, and it is very important to me that our portfolios can be liquidated immediately. We offer two weeks liquidity to investors in our hedge fund so we have to be liquid. I would offer daily liquidity if you told me I could raise billions of dollars as a result, but I don't think that is what investors care about.

What risk management lessons did you learn in 2008?

Actually, one of the big things that caught me was sitting with a hedged barbell book for the first half of 2008. On the one hand, I was long commodities as the prevailing and dominant economic trend. But, on the other hand, fearing a deflationary shock, I believed that the market's expectations for short-term interest rates were too high. So I had two positions: long commodities and long front-end rates. But something profoundly bad happened to my portfolio between the months of December 2007 and February 2008: I made a huge amount of money on both views. There was no hedge, after all. In effect, I had one position on top of the other, and it was all pointed in one direction. Then in March it all moved the other way and I had the biggest monthly drawdown since I started. Obviously, I should have recognized the correlation on the way up before the drawdown and brought down the gross on both sides. But, with interest rate expectations so out of proportion to the mounting economic storm, I guess I got greedy.

What is more important in your fund and money management in general—trade ideas and investment theses or risk management?

Clearly both are important. However, without a doubt my returns would be much better if I were a better risk manager, and this is something that I am working on. I always look back and think I could have done better, but that is exciting because that means there is always room for improvement. What it shows is that potent ideas can make you money, but disciplined risk management coupled with potent ideas can make you one of the richest people on the planet.

I live an interesting life. I made 50 percent in October 2008 and my biggest investor fired me. He said he had a manager that was down 30 percent on the year, but that manager "gets it," so he was going to stay invested with him. Meanwhile, I made 30 percent on the year and I get fired because I don't get it? This is the curse of my life. I seem to collect all sorts of witty dinner party anecdotes from my experiences, but I pray for a less interesting life.

Do you relate to the irrationality of markets, or does their rationality give you something to hold onto?

Markets are irrational but they are right at every moment. They are right until they are wrong. You have to marry the notion of being right or wrong with being right with the timing of a given proposition. This is not a business that indulges intellectual prejudice.

As part of your work on your evolving risk management, are you using more options?

Yes, but then of course, the problem today is that using options is more difficult because implied volatilities are high. The thing that I've morphed into over my career is a piece of plasticine. To me, risk management is all about manipulation of gross exposure. The very best risk procedure is moving your gross exposure up or down. If you're fearful, you could buy some put options, but the best strategy is to take the blasted exposure down. It's clear, it's clean, and it's very effective.

Plasticine™

Plasticine is a brand of modeling clay. The putty-like material is made from calcium salts, petroleum jelly, and aliphatic acids. It is soft, nontoxic, malleable, and does not dry on exposure to air. It melts when exposed to heat and is flammable at much higher temperatures. Plasticine is a registered trademark of Flair Leisure Products plc.

Meanwhile, for generating returns, we are always trying to create something asymmetric and that often leads us to options. In March 2003, I was buying a lot of out-of-the-money call options on gold. Before getting gold right via options and making 50 percent that year, we were down 12 percent by the end of the first quarter. So I brought down our gross exposure and converted a lot of my outright long gold position into an option to manage the downside risk. We have often reverted to using options when our timing is off, when we are coming under duress and are trying to find ways of retaining an idea without killing ourselves. My fear gene is far greater than my greed gene.

At what point in the future would you consider yourself successful?

I have this debate with my shrink all the time. He tells me to look at everything I have, that I am in the top tiny percentage of the entire population. He tells me that I am very successful and wonders why I have all of this mental baggage. What am I fearful of? Again, I'm a paranoid schizophrenic. Paranoia is what drives me. But the nicest thing is that I can see change and evolution over my career. I am getting better and I now have documented evidence that I can generate better ideas and make money. So there's a thrust and a great desire to be better.

Part Three

FINAL WORD

What if I am wrong? Any rational investment plan has to start with that question.

—Peter L. Bernstein

Chapter 14

The Pensioner

We thought it only fair to speak to a real money manager who did not lose money in 2008. Despite the difficulty in finding such a manager, I finally unearthed "The Pensioner," who runs a major portfolio for one of the largest pension funds in the world. He invests by seeking out risk premia in equities, commodities, fixed income and currencies, and uses quantitative tools and discretionary analysis to build a diversified basket of assets with a global focus.

His views on the business are timely and important. According to the Pensioner, portfolio construction needs to be revisited in its most basic forms, where Markowitz and CAPM might still be valid, but not in the way these theoretical concepts have been applied to pension fund management in recent years. In short, he challenges some of the most basic assumptions behind real money investment, but he does so from the vantage of someone who fully understands the complex web of constraints that pension managers face.

The Pensioner says real money investors, on average, are led astray at the beginning the portfolio construction process by focusing on a return

target. Managing to a stipulated return target means that the level of risk
assumed to achieve that target becomes secondary. Taken to an extreme,
"if the return requirement were 20 percent, then you would have to put
all your money in microcap stocks and just pray like hell." It is time to
begin a dialogue about how real money managers can construct more
effective portfolios, says the Pensioner, because the implications are far
too serious.

Less pioneering than rigorously disciplined, the Pensioner remains
grounded in the principles of Finance 101, principles that many have
abandoned. Although he advocates a back-to-basics mentality for real
money, along the way he raises some heretical concepts, such as the use
of leverage to construct truly efficient portfolios. Rooted in humility, the
Pensioner concedes that his performance is principally due to his ability
to get paid for the host of risk premia that he assumes, not for picking
the winning trades, the latter of which is not a strategy with long-term
staying power. Finance is boring—especially so when you are practicing
it effectively.

What lessons did you learn in 2008?

The single largest lesson that investors should take away from 2008 is
the importance of proper portfolio construction and risk control. This
means having a true understanding of all the risks being assumed in your
plan, sizing them correctly, and assembling them into an overall portfolio
optimally. The events of 2008 showed us that the following elements
are all very important: (1) passive asset mix; (2) active risk allocation;
(3) risk measurement techniques; and (4) risk control decisions. More
importantly, 2008 revealed that extremely few real money plans were
doing any of the four very well.

In terms of asset mix, 2008 demonstrated in dramatic form how truly
undiversified the classic 60–40 policy portfolio mix really is. Most plans
put too much faith in the equity risk premium, when this is but one of the
many risk premia that could be assumed. Further, the diversification that
managers thought they had in alternative assets was proven mostly a mi-
rage, as many of the "nonequity" assets included in asset mixes—private

capital, real estate, and infrastructure, for example—turned out to be very equity-like after all. In hindsight this makes sense, since all three are businesses packaged in an illiquid form, not securities or asset classes, per se.

The diversification that most plans had hoped for in their active programs turned out to be just as much of an illusion. Fixed income departments that had expanded their mandate into credit (which is really just a slice of the equity risk premium) also found their books looking suddenly very equity-like and surprisingly illiquid. In fact, 2008 helped confirm that the vast majority of managers had been generating their "alpha" over the preceding six years through a persistent exposure to the equity risk premium (beta), illiquidity risk premium, short volatility, and/or credit, all four of which are highly correlated for purely theoretical reasons. And plans' exposure to the illiquidity risk premium proved to be particularly pervasive. Diversification across asset classes and departments failed in large part because most had exposed themselves in some form to this risk premium; cross-asset and cross-department correlations went to one, and certain plans lost a staggering amount of money.

To be fair, for many plans, a large part of their exposure to the illiquidity risk premium was by design. In fact, one of the great, untold stories of the last 20 years of real money investing is the unprecedented reallocation of institutional risk into the illiquidity risk premium. Most private investments are simply equivalents of their public market counterparts wrapped up with an illiquidity risk premium. I am not aware of any plan that had an explicitly defined allocation to the illiquidity premium the way they had, for example, explicitly defined allocations to the equity premium or fixed income risk premium. Nevertheless, it was where they had chosen to allocate a great deal of their risk.

However, even after taking into account deliberate allocations to illiquid assets, most plans still had more illiquidity risk than they realized. More overlooked were investments in assets that were liquid in good times but became very illiquid in periods of stress, including external managers who threw up gates, credit derivatives whereby whole tranches became toxic, and even crowded trades such as single stocks chosen according to well-known quantitative screens. As a result, when the liquidity crisis hit, it hit everywhere all at once, creating devastating effects.

Finally, 2008 also exposed faults in the traditional methods of calculating risk. No matter how your plan went about calculating value at risk (VaR)—historical, parametric, Monte Carlo, or other—the statisticians claimed that the more data used to calculate the parameters (i.e., the further the look-back in time), the better. But 2008 showed that this is not necessarily correct, especially for the liquid portions of our investments. The result was that almost all real money funds got caught badly off-guard with the ferociousness and comprehensiveness of the market declines. Explaining away the volatility of 2008 by claiming that the market was nonnormal shows a true misunderstanding of tail risk; 2008 simply showed us for the first time in decades the true fatness of the tails. Claiming that 2008 was a nonnormal event simply seeks to abrogate responsibility. Rather than finding excuses for poorly constructed models, risk managers would be much better served by an examination of stochastic volatility (see box). Granted, it is a complicated topic, but when juxtaposed against the possibility of losing billions again, most plans would be well-served by making an investment to study it. It turns out that liquid markets and instruments, such as the S&P 500, were not exceedingly "fat" or nonnormal in 2008; rather, they exhibited nonconstant volatility, which is not the same thing. A risk system capable of capturing short-term changes in risk would have gone a long way to reducing losses in 2008.

Stochastic Volatility

Stochastic volatility models are used to evaluate various derivative securities, whereby—as their name implies—they treat the volatility of the underlying securities as a random process. Stochastic volatility models attempt to capture the changing nature of volatility over the life of a derivative contract, something that the traditional Black-Scholes model and other constant volatility models fail to address.

In summary, the damage in 2008 was caused by asset allocations being overexposed to equities, active management being overexposed to illiquidity, and risk systems that were unable to keep up with the rapidly changing short-term risks of all of these investments. Risk measurements further missed the mark because of a failure to recognize the pervasiveness with which the illiquidity premium was embedded in so many diverse alpha processes, therefore dramatically underestimating most correlations under stress.

There is an important comment I would like to make here: investing money, especially large pools of money, is very difficult. If pension plans hope to be able to learn from the lessons of 2008 and make changes in hopes of reducing the probability of a repeat, they will have to ensure that they have the talent to properly do so. This extends all the way from risk managers and portfolio managers right up to their boards. You get what you pay for in this world. And I can say with confidence that if 2008 taught us anything, it is that the costs of paying for talent are miniscule compared to the costs of not doing so.

How are your pension peers invested after the crash of 2008?

There are as many answers to this question as there are real money plans, though most still seem to follow a template that starts with the classic 60–40 stocks-bonds asset mix, combined with a rather small active risk budget. Many plans have added illiquid assets to this mix—such as private capital, real estate, and infrastructure—and some plans have included a small risk allocation to commodities and possibly inflation-linked securities, such as TIPS.

Studies show that about 90 percent of the risk and return for most plans is generated by the asset mix, with only 10 percent by value added. I would suggest, however, that only about 10 percent of the resources and intellectual effort at most plans is dedicated to the asset mix, whereas 90 percent is dedicated to the active book. This seems counterintuitive.

The vast majority of active management risk seems to be dedicated to trying to generate value through stock-picking, as well as various strategies within the fixed income arena. Many are also now expanding into other developed markets and emerging markets. While a number of the larger plans try to capture some of this alpha internally, a great deal of the active risk is farmed out to external managers. However, there are more sophisticated plans running what are effectively diversified hedge funds internally.

Finally, most plans seem trapped in dollar notional thinking despite knowing full well that the primary goal of a Maximum Sharpe Ratio (MSR) portfolio (also called a profit-seeking portfolio) is to get the best possible return on risk.

What do you mean by "dollar notional thinking"?

Dollar notional thinking refers to the common practice of allocating investments based on dollar value as opposed to allocating based on a risk budget. Oftentimes, this can lead to asset allocations that appear diversified but really are not.

To give an example, consider the common U.S.-based 60–40 stock-bond portfolio mentioned earlier. This portfolio may appear to be reasonably balanced and thus well-diversified to a dollar notional thinker. However, given that stocks are approximately five times more volatile than bonds, in risk terms the allocation equates to approximately 90 percent in stocks and 10 percent in bonds. Bonds have a negligible impact on the portfolio's returns, instead serving primarily as a risk dampener. Allocating money to economically levered equity such as private equity only makes the results more extreme. Managers got away with this asset allocation for most of the 1980s and 1990s, as it performed well in a period of rising growth and falling inflation. However, the 60–40 mix does very poorly in economic periods of falling growth, rising inflation, and deflation. For proof you need only to consider 2008, the 1970s, and Japan for the last two decades, respectively, any one of which may loom in our future.

How should real money managers go about constructing a portfolio?

The goal is to build a portfolio that produces the maximum return per unit of risk. The key is to avoid overexposing the portfolio to any one risk, instead actively pursuing as many different sources of return as possible. For example, government fixed income, including short-end rates, are a good way to diversify the equity risk premium. In fact, in the U.S., stocks and bonds have had pretty much the same return on risk for the last 80 years, during which time they have been uncorrelated, on average. A diversified portfolio would ideally have an equal risk allocation to stocks and bonds, which would suggest an allocation of about 20–80 stocks-bonds. International diversification is also very important. Within reasonable capacity constraints, I would suggest trying to equal weight most things by risk.

Once you have a diversified portfolio with stocks and bonds, your next concern should be inflation. Over the long term all assets respond to inflation. However, over the short- to medium-term many of the assets traditionally included as inflation hedges are anything but. Real estate and equities, for example, get hit hard by unexpected inflation because even though they have real cash flows, they are still businesses, and the central bank response to inflation is to raise rates to slow demand. Empirically, central banks have been quite successful at this to the detriment of these "inflation hedge" asset classes. To protect against inflation risk you need either real return bonds and/or commodities in your asset mix.

For your active mix, the same lessons apply. Avoid overinvesting in any one style, strategy or asset class. Spend your active risk budget wisely. Just because you have 60 percent of your money in equities does not mean you should have 60 percent of your active risk in equity value added programs. And just because you have a lot of money in stocks and bonds does not mean you have to try to time stocks and bonds with your active risk.

It is important to be aware of the illiquid–liquid mix in your active portfolio. If left unchecked, the illiquidity risk premium will find a way into just about everything, resulting in a significant overexposure to that risk factor. So illiquidity has to be managed as a limited resource.

A good risk system is necessary to bring all of the assets together. It will have to be able to calculate a variety of risk numbers, including long-term risk, short-term risk, and a reasonable estimate of tail risk. The risk system you use should very carefully address liquid and illiquid assets.

Finally, and perhaps most controversially, embrace leverage. If you build your Maximum Sharpe Ratio portfolio well, with many diversified assets and active programs, it might have quite a low native volatility. That is fine in a world with leverage. The key is to build that portfolio then decide how much risk you are comfortable with, and run the portfolio at that level of risk. There is no need to accept portfolios at their native volatility. The portfolio may only have a volatility of 4 percent and an excess return of 3 percent, but if you are willing to run a 10 percent volatility portfolio, a three times levered MSR portfolio is very likely to

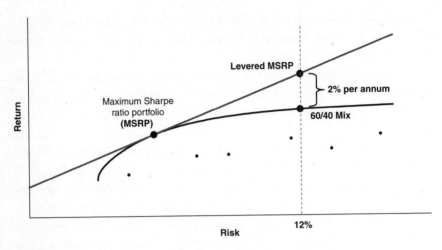

Figure 14.1   Finance 101: Leverage and the Efficient Frontier

make more money for less risk than a similarly risky 60–40 portfolio. This chart is taught in about day two of every Finance 101 class, but it is surprisingly ignored by the investment community. (See Figure 14.1.)

Moving along the frontier is only correct if you are precluded from using leverage and have a return target greater than that derived from the MSR portfolio. If that is the case, it may be helpful to reexamine the limitations on leverage, because the costs of being poorly diversified may be greater than the plan sponsor(s) may realize.

In general, if you look at plans that have done well versus plans that have not, the thing that stands out is that good plans manage a substantial portion of capital in-house. This has two benefits. First, it avoids paying high fees to managers while at the same time improving transparency. Second, plans managed in-house may be able to achieve more effective diversification in their portfolios (at a minimum it forces the issue that diversification (and returns) are in-house management's responsibility). If you do these two things well, you are probably on the road to improving the performance of the fund.

Why did the 60–40 become the standard policy portfolio?

The 60–40 portfolio became popular during a time when leverage was costly to attain. Prior to the proliferation of a liquid derivatives market in the early 1980s, there was no way for investors to lever natively low-risk assets such as bonds in a cost-effective manner. The cost of borrowing funds through conventional methods outstripped the return that could be earned on the bonds. As a result, in order for most investors to attain their required rate of return, they had to allocate more to stocks than what would otherwise be optimal. But this is obviously no longer the case.

So why has institutional money management not moved toward the optimal solution of more bonds and less stocks, despite the existence of accessible and cheap leverage for the past 30-odd years? Part of the reason might be that asset returns in the 1980s and 1990s actually validated the 60–40 approach, as stocks had a very strong run over these two decades. Stocks have paid investors everything they required and more, naturally leading to an "if it ain't broke, don't fix it" attitude. It does not help matters when luminaries such as Jeremy Siegel extol "stocks for the long run" or renowned Yale endowment manager David Swensen endorses an "equity-centric" portfolio. Why do they do this? Because stocks have historically outpaced bonds over the long term, and this is indeed true. However, what is missing in this argument is the risk side of the equation. Yes, stocks return more than bonds, but they are riskier, too. In fact, over the last 30 years, risk-adjusted bonds have significantly outperformed equities. Going forward this may or may not continue (certainly there is chatter about bonds being overvalued) but for those plans that do not comfortably try to see into the future, one approach is to build the best possible diversified portfolio by more optimally allocating risk. With easy access to leverage through the liquid derivatives market, there is no reason why 60–40 should automatically be considered the default portfolio any longer.

Lastly, there is the career risk aspect, which forces managers to conform to their peers. When the 60–40 is chugging along and everyone is happy with the returns, there is little motivation to deviate from the established consensus (even though equities are flat over the last decade). It takes a year like 2008 for everyone to step back and reassess whether their asset mix really makes sense. My hope is that investors take this opportunity to establish a new "best practice" in determining the optimal portfolio allocation.

How should real money approach risk?

Pensions should adopt a risk culture first and foremost. Risk conscious-
ness must be the cornerstone of an institutional portfolio. Once a risk
culture is established, managers will naturally identify their sources of
risk, then determine whether the associated expected returns are commensurate. Although there is no perfect solution, accepting that risk
exists is a good starting point. In other words, risk needs to be treated as
an input, not an output, to the investment process.

When establishing a risk culture, it is important to incentivize managers to be cognizant of risk. This can be done through a risk budgeting
system whereby managers are assigned a maximum amount of risk (as
determined independently by a central risk system) and are compensated
based on how much profit they can generate on their assigned risk limits. This system automatically forces managers to focus on risk-adjusted
returns, as opposed to just nominal returns. Because risk is in scarce
supply, managers must trade off between the marginal risk consumed by
an investment and the investment's expected return.

Also, total fund risk can be assessed along various dimensions. Pensions can maximize diversification, emphasize illiquidity risk, or do
something in between. I believe that maximizing diversification benefits is the easiest way to approach an institutional portfolio because it is
an approach rooted in humility. With this approach, I do not have to call
tomorrow's winners, I just need to be exposed, in the right quantities,
to as many sources of risk premia as possible and get "paid to play,"
so to speak.

In order to maximize diversification, do you specify risk premiums by estimating a forward return on all risks and then incorporate future correlations into your analysis?

There is a passive approach and an active approach, and which is the
optimal one is up for debate. The active approach favors adjusting asset
allocations away from optimal diversification when certain asset classes
are perceived to be cheap (improving the expected return). The passive
approach argues for establishing the best possible diversified portfolio,
making adjustments only to maintain diversification. I can respect both
and I would suggest that just having the conversation is a step in the right

direction. I have seen both argued very, very effectively. Some argue that it is a mug's game trying to determine whether or not stocks are cheap relative to bonds for the next few years. Other people disagree, saying that stocks can be expensive or cheap over time, and because of this, you should overweight relative to other assets when they are cheap, trying to capture the higher expected return. In my view, both approaches have merit, and I am not smart enough to know which is right. You could pick one, or employ some combination of the two. But understanding the true risk premia that you are collecting and having a thoughtful discussion about risk is a big step in the right direction. There is no magic, only more diversified and less diversified. While it may not always work out after the fact, I can expect the more diversified portfolio to give me better odds of outperforming, which is all I can ask for.

How do you approach risk versus return in the context of your portfolio?

Portfolio managers get themselves into trouble when they look at opportunities as standalone risks. The marginal contribution to overall risk is what is most important.

For example, let us assume that you have opportunities A, B and C, whereby A has a high expected return and is highly correlated to your existing portfolio, B has a medium expected return and is moderately correlated, and C has a relatively low expected return but is truly uncorrelated. Few portfolio managers choose C because it is boring and will not garner attention or represent identifiable personal achievement. But this is where people get themselves into trouble. Everybody wants the great trade A, and only a few seemingly recognize the value of the okay, but diversifying trade C. Finance is a boring discipline, and building a thoughtful, well-constructed, effective portfolio is a thankless, but absolutely essential task that requires great discipline. In the way most money management firms are set up, the big trade with the 25 percent return gets people paid at the end of the year. But this incentive structure completely misses the point—it completely neglects risk. Fund managers, pension boards, and trustees should encourage more of a risk-conscious culture by encouraging portfolio managers to choose trades based on risk profiles and diversification benefits, not on potential return.

How do you measure the illiquidity premium?

Illiquidity risk has been a hot topic in investment circles in light of what happened in 2008, and there are various considerations when it comes to the subject. First, many investors overlooked it as being a source of risk and loaded up on illiquid assets believing they were getting a free lunch—earning a few extra percent a year for no additional risk. Well, that turned out to be false. Illiquidity risk needs to be recognized for what it is, which is just another risk premium amongst many. It may have a positive expected return, but it also comes with a commensurate risk. An important rule of risk management is to never over bet on any single risk premium or process, and this rule was violated en masse when it came to the illiquidity risk premium.

There is a great deal of research on how to theoretically value the illiquidity premium, but unfortunately, the inputs are very hard to estimate. By entering into an illiquid investment you give up the option to sell at the time of your choosing, and as result, an opportunity cost is incurred. Illiquidity is essentially a short put option on opportunity cost and, if you were able to estimate the likelihood and value of all future opportunities, then you could estimate the illiquidity risk premium using standard option pricing theory. Of course, this is almost impossible in practice. As is typical with all short option (short gamma) strategies, illiquidity tends to accrue profits consistently over time, only to give it all back when volatility spikes. This payoff profile is precisely what we saw in 2008.

The cost of illiquidity is still being calculated. Because the private equity, real estate, and other illiquid investments made before 2008 are still on the books, will still do not know their ultimate value or cost. Some of the large endowments that were heavily invested in illiquids are already predicting flat returns for the next few years, presumably due to an expectation of write-downs on certain investments. Illiquidity takes years and years to work through, so again, due to opportunity costs, the true cost of illiquids is higher still.

Why was there such an overinvestment in illiquid assets?

One of the common stories of 2008 was that many liquid managers were shut down, despite excellent future prospects. This was because clients, desperate to raise capital or cut risk and unable to sell their illiquid assets, sold whatever they were able to. This pattern repeated itself throughout many plans; as the crisis hit, any and all assets that could be sold were, regardless of the cost to the plan (or the manager who originally invested in those liquid assets). This example serves to highlight an interesting feature of illiquid assets. A department within a plan that locks money away in an illiquid vehicle directly receives the benefit of the illiquidity premium in the form of lower fees or extra basis points, but, vitally, does not face the whole cost. These costs are instead spread across the whole plan and all departments. In economics, the illiquidity risk premium is called a negative externality: an economic transaction that has a negative impact on another party not directly involved in the transaction. If negative externalities are not centrally managed there is a resulting phenomenon of over investment, which is known as the "tragedy of the commons." In extension to a risk budget, managers must be given a liquidity limit or else the plan will, in aggregate, find itself participating in this "tragedy." If illiquidity is not measured, controlled, and managed, it will be overinvested in.

How do you hedge the illiquidity risk?

The only certain way to hedge it is to avoid it completely. A better method of reducing illiquidity risk is through diversification and proper portfolio construction. To do this successfully requires a very good understanding of exactly how much of it you currently have on your books and where, and then a sense of the illiquidity risk premium to the other major market exposures of your plan, such as equity, credit and volatility.

Should real money funds just avoid illiquid assets?

Not completely. Illiquid assets have a number of advantages for real money plans. First of all, assuming one is paid some sort of premium to take on the illiquidity risk, illiquids can be, at the right size, a diversifying positive return investment for a plan. As I explained earlier, it is not at all straightforward to determine the value of the opportunity costs and the riskiness of the asset in order to come up with a fair price. This is compounded by the fact that managers putting on illiquid trades did not personally face the true costs, meaning real money funds most likely did not charge enough for this in the past.

Second, many argue that the ability to control and know the cash flows makes private assets (e.g., real estate) useful liability hedges. This may or may not be true, though my inclination is that these assets can and should stand on their own risk/return merits. "Labeling" something a hedge does not necessarily make it one, leading to misspecified risks and asset weights.

Third, there are the tax shield and operational efficiency arguments for private equity, though these have to be weighed against the high management fee structure associated with most private equity funds.

Fourth, the relative lack of market pricing results in a (albeit entirely artificial) smoothing of returns, and this likely helped hide the true losses of many plans last year. There is, of course, the other side of this coin, which is the mark-to-market hangover for illiquid assets that we are likely going to face for the next few years.

Finally, and likely most importantly, illiquid assets are useful for many plans in that they act as a source of off-balance-sheet nonrecourse leverage. For plans that are precluded from using leverage by their board or risk departments, illiquid assets can be a type of workaround. A take-private LBO is simply the act of borrowing money to buy, in a highly leverage form, the cash flows of a company. This is economically similar to buying the stock using borrowed money (i.e., levering the stock), but the accounting is very different. In the case of private equity, you own what is effectively a higher volatility asset, but you don't show any leverage on your books. It is possible that the recent move toward private equity has been driven more by pension plan demand for an off-balance-sheet levered asset class than for a well-constructed strategy to capture the illiquidity premium, which really just came as part of the deal.

This, in my mind, is an excellent example of the law of unintended consequences: no matter how well-meaning, constraints generally lead to workarounds. Where there is a will, there is a way. In this case, due to imposed accounting leverage constraints, instead of building the optimal portfolio by increasing their exposure to low volatility assets and decreasing their exposure to naturally more risky assets, funds were incented to actually invest in an economically highly levered version of what is already their most risky and over allocated asset, namely equities.

The 60–40 asset mix with private equity is really more like 80–40 (with a hidden 20), which means even more of the fund's risk comes from the equity risk premium.

Do you foresee the real money world embracing leverage going forward?

Although not all investors agree, certainly some are beginning to see leverage as perhaps the most important tool at our disposal for running an optimal portfolio. When used properly it allows us to reduce the volatility of a portfolio while simultaneously increasing its returns. Of course, like anything else, when invested inappropriately it can result in significant losses. As such, a proper risk system and risk-taking culture must be in place before leverage is deployed. In my mind there are four different types of leverage usage, the first two of which fall into what I would classify as "good leverage":

1. Using leverage to hedge liabilities. This is the safest use of leverage, and it is by definition risk reducing, though not necessarily return enhancing.
2. Using leverage to improve the diversification of a portfolio. This is accomplished by levering up low-volatility assets and levering down risky assets. When done properly, leverage used in this manner can be risk reducing and return enhancing.
3. Levering risky positions to generate even higher expected returns. This is how leverage gets a dirty connotation because it often ends in tears, and should be avoided.
4. Using off-balance-sheet hidden leverage to make risky assets even riskier (i.e., private equity). This is probably the most common use of leverage in real money funds. The main advantage of this is that it is nonrecourse leverage, meaning you cannot lose more than your initial investment if the asset were to drop to zero.

As I alluded to earlier, we also need to distinguish between accounting leverage and economic leverage. Accounting leverage refers to leverage that shows up directly on a fund's balance sheet. If a fund were to repo out securities or engage in a derivative transaction, that is accounting leverage. Economic leverage, on the other hand, is leverage born indirectly by the fund through some other entity. For example, if I invest in the stock of a company, that company has itself financed its assets through borrowing. It is important to make this distinction because funds that are precluded from accounting leverage can easily circumvent this restriction by, say, buying a fund or stock that is itself leveraged (one more reason why equities tend to be over allocated to as an asset class). The point is that the constraint on leverage does not necessarily deter levered risk-taking, it just drives it off-balance sheet. As a result, leverage is not a true measure of risk.

Besides targeting returns instead of risk, why else do real money funds fail to construct optimal portfolios?

In a nutshell, people get in the way. For one reason or another, people impose constraints that make their lives easier but sacrifice risk-adjusted return in the process. All constraints have costs. Although some of these costs are hidden, the dollar impact, particularly when compounded over time, can be enormous.

Constraints come in many shapes and sizes, but the most common are constraints on the use of leverage, constraints on which assets or strategies can be invested in, and constraints on the amount that internal managers can be paid, which of course constrains the quality of in-house talent you can attract to manage your plan.

Let us discuss leverage first. Most institutional investors are precluded from using leverage for reasons that are not necessarily without their merits. Clearly, excessive leverage can lead to disaster if the institution does not have proper risk management systems in place, systems robust enough to address the assumptions of the models. Imposing leverage constraints is an effective way to mitigate operational risk (i.e., blowup risk) in the absence of a risk system that the firm can trust. I would suggest that most pension funds currently do not yet have a risk system adequate for measuring risk in the presence of leverage. The risk systems in use today are designed more for board reporting than for portfolio management. Therefore, for the vast majority of funds, investing in the 60–40 portfolio is an act of unfortunate but necessary prudence. But make no mistake, constraints on leverage lead to suboptimal portfolios. This is simply basic finance and well documented in the research. The difference in expected return at the same level of risk between the levered diversified and unlevered undiversified portfolios can be substantial, potentially 2 percent per annum under realistic assumptions.

A second constraint often faced by pension plans is on which assets or strategies managers are permitted to invest in. The reality is that the two traditional asset classes, equities and bonds, are still the ones that most institutions feel most comfortable with. They have been around for centuries and the source of their risk premia are well understood. However, the fact is that there are many alternative risk premia from other assets and risk drivers. These are often neglected due to institutional lethargy and erroneous estimation of the risk-versus-reward profile of these alternatives. The end result is that most institutional investors over-allocate to the equity risk premium because it feels safe and everyone else is doing it. Any allocation to alternative risk premiums is typically small enough to have a negligible impact on performance but just big enough to claim that progress has been made in the discovery of exciting and innovative new investments. Of course, nobody wants to put too much into these unconventional assets, since the career risk of a blow-up or temporary underperformance would be too much to bear.

Oftentimes, external agents impose constraints on assets or strategies because they lack the capacity to understand the complexity of the issues involved. This problem is particularly acute in plans (mostly public) that employ what is known as a lay board, where plan members are represented on the board. By requiring high proportions of lay representation, you are saying you want noninvestment professionals making the core decisions on billions of dollars. This can lead to grossly suboptimal decision making. To be successful, it is crucial that a plan have professional internal money management and a professional board, both ideally comprised of a wide array of professional backgrounds with some representation from the investment world. The internal managers and the board should have the singular goal of generating the optimal risk-adjusted return, which ensures the lowest level of contributions for the plan members themselves and their ultimate sponsors, both of whom are hard-working taxpayers. The lower contributions are far more valuable than the politically motivated issues often put forward to support poorly constructed boards of directors.

When it comes to the large U.S. public plans, it is not in the best interest of either the taxpayer or the pensioner to employ underpaid, underqualified people to manage these huge sums of capital. This constraint is political, as any enterprise backed by the government would be, and it completely assures that you will not have the best possible pension plan. This structural disconnect costs hundred of billions of dollars in the United States. Small differences in returns compound to become enormous sums of money over time.

Ultimately, the question of constraints boils down to one of acceptable trade-offs. If a fund wants to take advantage of the diversification benefits afforded through the prudent use of leverage, then it ought to be investing in a risk management infrastructure and more importantly, a risk culture that would allow it to do so. If the plan wants to take advantage of an expanded opportunity set in alternative investments, then it cannot be afraid to place a nonnegligible amount of risk into these new opportunities. If the plan wants the best talent managing its billions of dollars, it should be prepared to pay for top professionals.

The difficulty is that these concepts are too esoteric for the average taxpayer to understand, yet they are the ones who will ultimately bear the cost. A one or two percent difference in annual performance does not seem significant to most people, but when you compound it over a long time horizon, it is enormous.

One percent a year of underperformance over 20 years on billions of dollars of pension assets is indeed enormous. Compensation is obviously a problem in the real money world, especially relative to the external funds they hire, the latter of which have massive and often hidden associated fees. Compensation for internal staff raises questions, yet staggering sums are paid to external managers. In order to talk about how to construct the most efficient risk-adjusted portfolio, first and foremost you need to have people in the room capable of having that conversation. I want to be fair, I am not saying that you have to pay people exorbitant amounts of money. But it is self-defeating when people who manage $20, $50 or $100+ billion make state worker wages. Football coaches for state universities are some of the highest paid state employees, yet pension plan managers charged with multi-billion dollar decisions that directly affect all taxpayers make substantially less (see Table 14.1). This imposes an enormous hidden cost.

Table 14.1 Public College Football Coach Salary *vs.* Public Pension Manager Salary

Football Team	Salary	Pension	Assets	Salary	Bonus	Year
University of Texas	$2,910,000	Texas Teachers	$ 89 billion	$402,000	Up to 175% of Salary	2006
University of North Carolina	$2,100,000	North Carolina State	$ 66 billion	$340,000	$51,746	2008
University of California, Berkeley	$1,850,000	CalPERS	$181 billion	$425,000	Up to 75% of salary	2009
University of Maryland	$1,750,000	Maryland State	$ 32 billion	$239,700	none	2009

Many public pension funds site low wages as a constraint on attracting and retaining talented portfolio managers. Despite managing billions of dollars of public funds, the wages of pension fund managers is relatively low when compared to that of investment managers in the private sector. States' unwillingness to pay up for top tier professionals is not seen when it comes to college football coaches. There are 58 public schools that pay their football coaches at least $1 million.

SOURCE: "College Football—Highest Paid Coaches" *America's Best & Top Ten*, http://www.americasbestonline.net/index.php/pages/collegehighestpaidcoaches .html; Doug Halonen, "Plan Sponsors: Public plans up ante on pay," *Pensions & Investments*, January 8, 2007; http://www.pionline.com/apps/pbcs.dll/article ?AID=/20070108/PRINTSUB/701080731; Cullen Browder, "Treasurer suspends bonuses for pension managers," *WRAL.com*, June 3, 2008, http://www.wral .com/news/local/politics/story/5257415/; Maryland Department of Management and Budges, "Salary Plan," August 14, 2009, http://dbm.maryland.gov/ employees/Pages/SalaryPlan.aspx; Craig Karmin and Joann S. Lublin, "Dear Wins Job of CIO At Calpers," *Wall Street Journal*, January 22, 2009, http://online.wsj .com/article/SB123256129671103021.html; State Retirement and Pension System of Maryland, "Quarterly Investment Update Asset Class by Market Value and Allocation," September 30, 2009, http://www.sra.state.md.us/investments/Quarterly.Update-Sep09.pdf; CalPERS annual report, http://www.calpers.ca.gov/ invest/investmentreport-2008/default.htm; Lee Weisbecker, "Cowell: N.C. pension system gains 10.4%," *Triangle Business Journal*, November 9, 2009, http:// triangle.bizjournals.com/triangle/stories/2009/11/09/daily16.html; and Teacher Retirement System of Texas, "Annual Financial Report Highlights: Fiscal Year 2009," http://www.trs.state.tx.us/about/documents/cafr.highlights.pdf.

It is a fair statement to say that you get what you pay for, or perhaps in this case it might be more correct to say you don't get what you don't pay for. I am not sure what the right salary is for pension plan managers. It is probably not $100,000, although it does not have to be millions of dollars, either. Somewhere in between you can get good talent, although the number is likely high enough that it creates problems for politicians, as we have seen with the bank bailouts, Obama's pay czar, and other recent events. As politically difficult as it is, though, someone has to step up and articulate that the long-term costs associated with compensation constraints are simply not tolerable.

One way to show how material this concept can be is to consider public Canadian pension plans relative to U.S. ones. You can pull up annual reports to see what people are getting paid; it is public information. Not only can you often see a difference in salaries between the U.S. and Canadian pension plans, but you can also observe that returns for those plans are commensurate with the compensation numbers (see Table 14.2). Again, I am not saying that you have to pay people huge sums of money. But if you want someone to manage $20 billion, yet you are only willing to pay $80,000 a year, you will get what you pay for.

The 1% Effect

If CalPERS were able to generate returns of just 1 percent more per year for the past 25 years, the pension plan would currently have an additional $55 billion in assets. Since 1984, the public pension plan has grown from $28 billion to a peak of $260 billion in 2007, and at the end of 2009 it stood at about $200 billion. Given their current annual compensation expenses of about $180 million, even if CalPERS spent an additional $100 million a year for the past 25 years to attract talent capable of generating that 1%, assets would still have increased by $46.5 billion.

Is a long-term time horizon an advantage, or is it really just an excuse real money managers use for poor performance?

The long horizon of pension funds is somewhat of a misnomer. All pension plans have shorter-term reporting requirements, which create

Table 14.2 Average Wages to Returns Three Largest U.S. and Canadian Public Pensions

	U.S. Pensions	Canadian Pensions
AUM/Wages Ratio	0.07%	0.15%
5-year annualized return	2.34%	5.04%
10-year annualized return	3.05%	5.50%
10-year annualized volatility	14.53%	11.06%

SOURCE: CalPERS 2008 annual report www.calpers.ca.gov, CalSTRS 2008 Comprehensive Annual Financial Report www.calstrs.com, New York State and Local Retirement System 2009 Comprehensive Annual Financial Report www.osc.state.ny.us/retire, CPP 2009 Annual Report www.cppib.ca, OMERS 2008 Annual Report www.omers.com, OTPP 2008 Annual Report www.otpp.com.

checkpoints that can change the outcomes for some plan members over relatively short periods of time. Essentially, decisions to increase contributions or reduce benefits are made based on the shorter-term performance of the plan, so the path dependency of the plan's returns becomes a concern. I would argue that the time horizon for pension managers depends on the tolerance of plan members and sponsors for shorter term periods of poor performance. Which is to say it may be shorter than you think.

Let us assume a friend of yours just sold his company and now has $10 billion in cash. He splits the capital and gives you two different mandates. The first is totally unconstrained and has a 30-year time horizon—he is going sailing around the world, will only ask how you did in 30 years, and allow you to pay yourself and your team whatever you think is fair. The other mandate is also, in theory, unconstrained, also for 30 years, but your friend can shut you down monthly if he thinks you are not doing your job. Would you run both portfolios the same way?

I would not run them exactly the same way, although I believe the optimally diversified portfolio remains the best bet for maximizing risk-adjusted returns, whether the time horizon is long or short.

However, if I could get fired due to short-term underperformance, agency risk is introduced into the equation. As any self-optimizing individual would do, I would take measures to hedge out this agency risk, and there are several ways that this can be accomplished. One way is to optionalize the portfolio, essentially putting a floor on my interim returns. This would entail costs to the fund over the long term because I am essentially buying insurance on my job and billing my employer for the premium. Another way is to avoid potentially diversifying and lucrative investments that have negatively skewed distributions. Having a short-term floor on performance precludes taking good long-term bets that could potentially lead to large drawdowns where you could get knocked out of the game. The final, but perhaps easiest way to avoid drawdowns would be run the optimal portfolio, but at a lower level of risk. Running my portfolio at half the risk cuts all of my drawdowns in half, greatly improving my probably of not being fired. Of course, the cost of such a strategy is exactly half of my expected excess returns.

This clearly illustrates how a shorter-term focus can be a large drain on long-term performance because rational managers will inevitably act in ways to optimize their own utility at the expense of the fund.

If you were hired to run CalPERS and the "Governator" protected you from constraints, how would you manage that $200 billion plan?

You have already introduced a constraint: the size of the plan. Deploying $200 billion is not an insignificant constraint. For example, in order to maximize risk-adjusted returns, let us assume that your plan needs to make a meaningful allocation into commodities to protect against unexpected inflation. That might not be possible at this size. A $200 billion portfolio would probably look quite different from a $20 billion portfolio. On the other hand, the $200 billion portfolio might be able access certain structures and deals directly, without paying fees, and this would reduce costs and possibly increase returns. Instead of paying fees to experts and outside managers, your scale would enable you to perform most functions in-house at lower cost. Keeping in mind the size constraint, I would hire a great team, build state-of-the-art risk systems, and go about building a diversified portfolio that produces the maximum return per unit of risk. If that didn't meet my actuarially assessed return target resulting from pensioner obligations and other issues, I would modestly lever the portfolio. If needed to reach my requirements it is much better to use a well-constructed slightly levered portfolio than hidden leverage inside a poorly diversified one.

Assuming you are wildly successful at building an optimal portfolio at CalPERS, the portfolio information will be publicly available and people will want to mimic you. Soon, every pension, foundation, and endowment will be led by their consultant to pile into the "CalPERS Model."

The more people that convert to this model over time, the better it will be for the early adopters, as a repricing would take place in the assets of the "CalPERS Model" (a similar idea to talking up your book). After a while, as this model increasingly becomes the norm, those running the model will become the marginal price setters in the marketplace and will drive down expected risk-adjusted returns to some "fair value." This is inevitable, though the evolution would take a long time—possibly longer than our lifetimes. And because many plans will never be able to overcome their politically driven agency issues, I doubt this approach will ever become a standard like the 60–40 policy portfolio.

The real question in my mind is what happens to the 60–40 investor after this model increasingly becomes the norm. If the assets in the "CalPERS Model" get repriced to offer appropriate returns going forward, then the return on risk of the classic 60–40 will lag even further behind, and will face an even higher probability of falling short of its objectives.

Finally, it is important to remember that this approach or model is primarily a way of thinking about portfolio construction. There is no one method to constructing the optimal portfolio. The asset classes and risk premiums comprising the investment universe will greatly impact the construction of the final portfolio. The first step is to find as many sources of risk premia as possible, and there are always new sources of risk in the markets. Searching for new risk premia is a perpetual process.

Conclusion

I f someone told me that I would have spent the better part of 2009 studying the history and theory of pension, endowment, and real money investing, I would surely have laughed out loud, as this was arguably one of the least interesting areas of finance. But as performance reports, warnings, and stories of illiquidity began leaking out of the Yales, Harvards, and CalPERS of the world, I became intrigued. The deeper I dug, the more fascinated yet terrified I became. Although the subject matter was of critical importance, few seemed to be asking hard questions—it was shocking. For example, a full year after the crash of '08, I posed a hypothetical question to the CIO of a large U.S. public pension fund, which had just lost billions and billions of dollars. I asked if he had known in advance how the fall of 2008 was going to unfold, what would he have done differently and what could he have done to protect the portfolio? He only replied, "Good question."

As my research moved from arcane portfolio construction to uncertainties in the broader macroeconomy, I discovered linkages encompassing politics, society, philosophy, and history. I wanted to know why the extreme losses occurred, what lessons were learned, and what changes were being made. Instead of answers, I received only obfuscation and excuses: 2008 was impossible to predict; it was a perfect storm, a "black swan," a fat tail. But rationalizations and references to relative performance neither fund budgets nor honor cash liabilities.

Real money is the glue that holds together important societal functions, forming the foundation for so many of our institutions. In 2008, the glue started to come undone and the foundation cracked. The staggering losses have shed light on the true risks being assumed in these portfolios, and I hope the insights brought out by the managers in this book compel all investors to rethink their approach to portfolio management. As the risk managers in this book have stressed, all real money investors should take more of a risk-adjusted, absolute return approach in order to avoid having to force behavioral changes in the underlying institutions and constituencies they were created to support.

In short, relative performance is inadequate to address the annual cash needs of pensioners, universities, or charitable organizations. And it is irresponsible to point to 2008 as a 100-year storm and carry on with business as usual. High equity allocations have bailed out long-biased investors for the past 30 years, an extraordinary period marked by a strong tail wind of declining interest rates and inflation (not to mention globalization, technological advances, and productivity growth). Arguably, with interest rates and inflation running close to zero, that trade is over, pointing to a more challenging environment going forward.

Regardless of what the future holds, fiduciary duty obliges real money managers to at least be open to rethinking their approach if it can lead to more effective risk management, better risk-adjusted returns, and smaller drawdowns. The implications to broader society of failing to do so are far too serious to ignore. Pension funds, not banks, are the real "too big to fail" institutions.

The global macro hedge fund managers in this book, themselves examples of superior risk managers, have taken the first step toward what I hope becomes an active exploration of current methods and potential solutions for real money. To this end, I would encourage anyone who believes that he or she has something to contribute to the debate to please contact Drobny Global Advisors (www.drobny.com). We have created a business around fostering intellectually honest debate and discussion among hedge funds. In light of the events of 2008, we invite members of the real money world into our community, widening the scope of the discussion in hopes of facilitating knowledge transfer.

Obvious structural impediments exist in the real money world, but arguing for limitations will not solve the problems. For the sake of taxpayers around the world, I hope this discussion begins as quickly as possible.

Acknowledgments

This book would have not been possible without the help of my partner in crime, wordsmith extraordinaire, editorial genius, and cocreator, John Bonaccolta. John was instrumental in both *Inside the House of Money* and *The Invisible Hands,* and for that I am forever indebted. Working together dulled the pain of writing by not only having someone to collaborate with on words, but also having someone to take much needed surf breaks with. Indeed, much of the strategic vision for this book was conceived between sets.

The project remains, nevertheless, the collaborative effort of Drobny Global. Dave Berry spent many late nights providing innumerable great ideas, structural commentary, and suggestions; Lawrence Loughlin provided macro insights and important firsthand knowledge of the real money world from his time at Cambridge Associates and GAM; Tyler Hathaway provided detailed research, data, tables, and all-around support that made this book much stronger; Adam Bain created the graphs and provided many helpful suggestions that tightened the overall work. Lastly, but most importantly, I would like to thank Andres Drobny, my friend and business partner for the past decade, for his steadfast support, continual teaching, and unconditional partnership. Of course, the ability for all of us at Drobny Global to focus on this project would not have been possible without Laurence, Nicole, Lauren, Ria, April, and Kim—thanks!

Jim Leitner deserves special thanks for providing the inspiration for this book through his concept of seeking to blend the best of real money with the best of hedge fund investing, which he discussed in *Inside the House of Money*. More importantly, Jim has been a good friend and mentor, with whom I have spent countless hours discussing global markets, always walking away smarter for it.

Although Jim was the inspiration for the book, I owe part of the idea to Peter Jepsen, who, over drinks in New York, asked for another book saying: "I don't care who the managers are, I just want the ideas; I would read it if they were all anonymous." A light bulb went off.

I am also grateful to the entire membership of Drobny Global Advisors, who also regularly asked for a follow-up. Their intellectual curiosity and boundless energy in dissecting world markets at our conferences is a constant source of motivation.

Despite their anonymity, the "Invisible Hands" featured in this book took a bold step to reveal details of their work and broader thoughts for how to reshape the real money world. They and their associates (you know who you are) spent precious time sharing their views on the subjects contained herein. This book is quite simply theirs. Thank you.

At John Wiley & Sons, Pamela van Giessen provided support, most importantly in the form of consistent questioning about my next book project. Likewise, Kate "Bison" Wood, Emilie Herman, and Todd Tedesco were available to provide help and clarity when needed. I would also like to thank Darlene March, PR extraordinaire, for her help on *Inside the House of Money* and her commitment to this current work.

While my friends and former colleagues at Deutsche Bank have given tremendous support over the years, I would especially like to thank: Kenan Altunis, Zar Amrolia, Barry Bausano, Drew Bradford, Alan Cloete, Shannon Day, Rashid Hoosenally, Brian Rigney, Neehal Shaw, and Daniel Swasbrook. I would also like to extend my gratitude to Anshu Jain, who, upon hiring me into the hedge fund group in 1998, led me down this path.

A host of people provided ideas, inputs, readings, or just general support. They are: Caroline Abramo, Anders Almhem, Yaser Anwar, Jon

Bailly, Julian Barrowcliffe, Alan Boyce, John Brady, Kelly Brown, Jared Carney, Kieran Cavanna, Marc Cohen, Garry Collins, Jason Cummins, Jared Diamond, Graham Duncan, John Engskov, Adrian Fairbourn, Niall Ferguson, Richard Gladwin, Ari Gold, Chris Gorman, Bill Gruver, Grant Harrell, Brett House, Bill Marcus, Andrew Marsh, Mark McLornan, Hank Moody, Jack "Downtown" Moriarty, John Morris, Gary Mueller, Nick Nanda, Rishi Narang, Joe Nicholas, Jim Pallotta, John Porter, Jonathan Ratcliffe, Edouard Robbes, Jeffrey Sachs, Patrik Säfvenblad, Peter Sasaki, Claudio Schiavoni, Rohit Shetty, Chris Smith, Steve Solomon, David Steck, Gary Sutton, Harris Tam, Jim Tar, Rob Teeter, and Eddy Zuaiter.

Of course, I owe a great deal to numerous people who taught me about the real money world—both inside and outside of that world—many of whom have asked to remain anonymous. Others include: Chris Ailman, Michael Barry, Bob Borden, Chris Brown, John Brynjolfsson, Mark Cutis, Joe Dear, Mebane Faber, Amy Fisch, Allen Gillespie, Peter and Cathy Halstead, Jim Misdim, Jim Powers, Lee Thomas, Karyn Williams, and David Zierk.

Finally, I would like to thank my family for their unconditional support: Mom and Dad, Paige and Cody, Grandma Ruth, Rob and Maureen, Ieuan and Nia, Gwylim, and Katch, and Joe "I have a sixpack and play rugby for Wales" Davies. I would especially like to thank my son Tonton for teaching me humility, patience, and for giving me so much joy. Last but not least, the most important thank you goes to my wife, Clare, the best relative value trader I know. Thank you for all of your love and support and for being patient with all the distant stares and time spent writing and traveling. You're the best.

Steven Drobny
Manhattan Beach, California
December 2009

Bibliography

Abelsky, Paul. "Russia Moves $43.7 Billion From Wealth Fund to Cover Shortfall." *Bloomberg*, July 23, 2009.

Adamson, Loch. "Macro Investing: Masters of a New Global Order." *Institutional Investor*, April 20, 2009.

Arnott, Robert D. "Bonds: Why Bother?" *Journal of Indexes*, Rethinking Fixed Income, May–June 2009.

Arnott, Robert D, and Peter L. Bernstein. "What Risk Premium Is 'Normal'?" Social Science Research Network Electronic Paper Collection, January 10, 2002.

Avery, Helen. "Insurance—Zurich: Diversification Works." *Euromoney*, April 2009.

Baldassare, Mark. *When Government Fails: The Orange County Bankruptcy*. Berkeley and Los Angeles, CA: University of California Press, 1998.

Bailey, Eric, and Patrick McGreevy. "California Begins Printing IOUs." *Los Angeles Times*, July 3, 2009.

Barclay Hedge Ltd. "Hedge Fund Industry—Assets Under Management." Alternative Investment Databases, www.barclayhedge.com, 2009.

Bary, Andrew. "The Big Squeeze." *Barron's*, June 29, 2009.

Berkshire Hathaway Inc. "Berkshire Hathaway 2007 Shareholder Letter." www.berkshirehathaway.com.

Bernanke, Ben S. "Remarks by Governor Ben S. Bernanke: At the meeting of the Eastern Economic Association, Washington, D.C." Federal Reserve Board, www.federalreserve.gov, February 20, 2004.

Bernstein, Peter L. "The Debt Supercycle and Other Stories." *Economics & Portfolio Strategy*, Peter L. Bernstein Inc., September 1, 2008.

———. "Where Has the Long Run Run? The Policy Portfolio Reconsidered Once Again." *Economics & Portfolio Strategy*, Peter L. Bernstein Inc., February 15, 2009.

Bhaktavatsalam, Sree Vidya, and Gillian Wee. "Pimco's Gross Says Harvard, Yale May Need to Alter Investments." *Bloomberg*, May 29, 2009.

Biggs, Andrew, et al. "A Slow Burning Fuse: A Special Report on Ageing Populations." *The Economist*, June 27, 2009.

Blood, Michael R. "Protestors Gather at UCLA to Oppose UC Fee Hike." *Associated Press*, November 19, 2009.

Bloomberg L.P. Retrieved data from Bloomberg database, 2009.

Bonafede, Julia K., Steven J. Foresti, and Alexander Browning. "2009 Wilshire Report on State Retirement Systems: Funding Levels and Asset Allocation." Wilshire Associates Inc., March 3, 2009.

Browder, Cullen. "Treasurer suspends bonuses for pension managers." *WRAL.com*, June 1, 2009.

Brull, Steven. "The Big Public Pension Squeeze." *Institutional Investor*, June 2009.

Byrd, Jennifer. "Gaps in Funded Status Just Getting Bigger." *Pensions & Investments*, March 23, 2009.

CabinetOffice, Office of the Third Sector, "Real Help for Communities: Volunteers, Charities and Social Enterprises." *Cabinetoffice.gov*, December 2, 2009.

"California Dreamin' Over? Record Number of Residents Moving." *Associated Press*, January 13, 2009.

CalPERS. "CalPERS—Comprehensive Annual Financial Report: Fiscal Year End 6/30/2008." www.calpers.ca.gov.

———. "CalPERS—Facts at a Glance: General," December 2009. www.calpers.ca.gov.

———. "CalPERS—Facts at a Glance: Investments," December 2009. www.calpers.ca.gov.

"CalPERS earned 10.5 percent last year." *Sacramento Business Journal*, August 12, 2000.

CalSTRS. "CalSTRS Acts in Face of Historic Global Market Drop." July 21, 2009., www.calstrs.com.

———. "CalSTRS—Comprehensive Annual Financial Report: Fiscal Year End 6/30/2008." www.calstrs.com.

————. "CalSTRS—Investment Committee: Quarterly Activity Report as of March 31, 2009." www.calstrs.com.

————. "CalSTRS—Investment Committee: Quarterly Activity Report as of September 30, 2007." www.calstrs.com.

Capgemini and Merrill Lynch Global Wealth Management. *World Wealth Report 2009.*

Cho, David. "Steep Losses Pose Crisis for Pensions, Two Bad Choices for Funds: Cut Benefits or Take Greater Risks to Rebuild Assets." *Washington Post.* October 11, 2009.

Christie, Jim, Peter Henderson, and Jennifer Ablan. "*Laying on bets at America's biggest pension fund.*" *Reuters,* October 23, 2009.

Clark, Robert L., Lee A. Craig, and Jack W. Wilson. *A History of Public Sector Pensions in the United States.* Philadelphia: University of Pennsylvania Press, 2003.

Clowes, Michael J. *The Money Flood: How Pension Funds Revolutionized Investing.* New York: John Wiley & Sons, 2000.

"College Football—Highest Paid Coaches." America's Best & Top Ten.

Commodity Research Bureau—CRB. Retrieved data from CRB Indexes, www.crbtrader.com, 2009.

Crippen, Alex. "CNBC Transcript: Warren Buffett & Bill Gates—Keeping America Great." CNBC Inc., November 13, 2009.

Damodaran, Aswath. "Historical Returns on Stocks, Bonds and Bills—United States." Data Sets, pages.stern.nyu.edu/~adamodar, 2008.

Dear, Joseph. Meeting with Steven Drobny. September 17, 2009.

Denmark, Frances, and Julie Segal. "Lessons Learned: Colleges Lose Billions in Endowments." *Institutional Investor,* November 2009.

Dimson, Elroy, Paul Marsh, and Mike Staunton. *Triumph of the Optimists: 101 Years of Global Investment Returns.* Princeton, NJ: Princeton University Press, 2002.

Dimson, Elroy, et al. "Credit Suisse Global Investment Returns Yearbook 2009." Credit Suisse Research Institute, 2009.

Drobny, Steven. *Inside the House of Money: Top Hedge Fund Traders on Profiting in the Global Markets.* New Jersey: John Wiley & Sons, 2009.

Dow Jones. Indexes, retrieved data from Dow Jones database, www.djaverages.com, 2009.

Evans, David. "Hidden Pension Fiasco May Foment Another $1 Trillion Bailout." *Bloomberg,* March 3, 2009.

Evans, David. "The Poison in Your Pension: Banks Are Selling the Riskiest CDO Portions, Known as Toxic Waste, to Public Pensions and State Trust Funds." *Bloomberg,* July 2007.

Faber, Mebane T. "World Beta: Engineering Targeted Returns and Risk." www.mebanefaber.com, 2009.

Faber, Mebane T., and Eric W. Richardson. *The Ivy Portfolio: How to Invest Like the Top Endowments and Avoid Bear Markets.* Hoboken, NJ: John Wiley & Sons, 2009.

Federal Reserve Board, "Selected Interest Rates (H.15)," Data Download Program, August 5, 2009.

"Financial Update: Harvard Retains Triple-A Rating, Princeton Foresees Deeper Cuts." *Harvard Magazine*, Breaking News, April 8, 2009.

"Flow of Funds Accounts of the United States: Annual Flows and Outstandings." Board of Governors of the Federal Reserve System, www.federalreserve.gov, 1945–2009.

Fort Washington Capital Partners Group, "Why Over-Commitment Is Required to Achieve Target Exposures to Private Equity," April 2007.

Foundation Center. "Top Funders: Top 100 U.S. Foundations by Asset Size." *FoundationCenter.org*, November 19, 2009.

"Foundation Trusts 'Must Plan for Spending Cuts'." *Health Service Journal*, August 11, 2009.

Fornari, Fabio. "The Size of the Equity Premium." European Central Bank (ECB), January 2002.

Gilbert, Katie. "He Dare Not Speak Their Name: Just Because This Danish Pension Officer Avoids Saying 'Hedge Funds' Doesn't Mean He Doesn't Love What They Represent." *Institutional Investor's Alpha*, July–August 2009.

Golden, Daniel. "Cash Me If You Can." *Portfolio.com*, March 18, 2009.

Governance and Accountability Institute. "California Public Employees' Retirement System (CalPERS)."*INSIGHTS-edge*, November 20, 2009. www.gai-insightsedge.com.

Grantham, Jeremy. "Just Desserts and Markets Being Silly Again." GMO LLC, Quarterly Letter, October 2009.

Greenwald, John, et al. "The California Wipeout." *Time*, December 19, 1994.

Halonen, Doug. "Public Plans Up Ante on Pay: Use of Incentive Bonuses for Investment Execs Growing." *Pensions & Investments*, January 8, 2007.

Harvard Management Company Inc. *Harvard University Financial Report: Fiscal Year 2008*. www.hmc.harvard.edu.

———. *Harvard University Financial Report: Fiscal Year 2009*. www.hmc. harvard.edu.

"Harvard's Annual Financial Report Fully Details 2009 Losses." *Harvard Magazine*, October 19, 2009.

Healy, Beth. "Harvard Ignored Warnings About Investments: Advisers Told Summers, Others Not to Put so Much Cash in Market; Losses Hit $1.8b." *Boston Globe*, November 29, 2009.

Hedge Fund Research Inc. Data retrieved on HFRI Indices, 2009.

Hennessy, John. "President Hennessy Addresses the State of the University and the Economy." *Stanford University News, Stanford Report*, April 30, 2009.

Hilzenrath, David S. "2008 Leaves Pensions Underfunded: Stock Losses Leave $400 Billion Deficit; Shoring Up Funds May Be Costly." *Washington Post*, January 8, 2009.

Howson, Colin, and Peter Urback. *Scientific Reasoning: The Bayesian Approach*, 2nd ed. Chicago: Open Court Publishing, 1993.

Incapital. "Break-Even Inflation." *Inflation-Linked.com*.

"Joseph Dear: Change Agent." *Institutional Investor*, June 2009.

Karmin, Craig. "College Try: Chicago's Stock Sale." *Wall Street Journal*, August 21, 2009.

Karmin, Craig, and Joann S. Lublin. "Dear Wins Job of CIO at Calpers." *Wall Street Journal*, January 22, 2009.

Keogh, Bryan, and John Detrixhe. "Pensions Eliminating Stocks Add $40 Billion to Corporate Bonds." *Bloomberg*, December 3, 2009.

Lauerman, John. "Harvard Endowment Woes Spur Protests over Vacant Properties." *Bloomberg*, September 16, 2009.

Levin, Richard C. "Yale 2009–10 Budget Update." Yale University Office of Public Affairs, Speeches and Statements, www.opa.yale.edu, September 10, 2009.

Lorin, Janet Frankston. "Tufts Says Wealthy College Endowments Should Take Less Risk." *Bloomberg*, November 19, 2009.

Lorin, Janet Frankston, and Oliver Staley. "Yale's Swensen Model Unbroken by 30% Endowment Drop, Levin Says." *Bloomberg*, July 16, 2009.

Lowenstein, Roger. *While America Aged: How Pension Debts Ruined General Motors, Stopped the NYC Subways, Bankrupted San Diego, and Loom as the Next Financial Crisis*. New York: Penguin, 2008.

Mack, Consuelo. "Interview with Yale's David Swensen." *WealthTrack.com*, #447, May 22, 2009.

Markit Group Limited. Index data provided by Markit, 2009.

Markowitz, Andy. "Tufts President Criticizes Top Schools' Investment Strategies." *Philanthropy Today*, November 19, 2009.

Maslakovic, Marko. "Fund Management 2009." International Financial Services London, October 2009.

McGill, Dan M, et al. *Fundamentals of Private Pensions.* 8th ed. Oxford: Oxford University Press, 2005.

Mendel, Ed. "Post-crash pension fund plans." www.calpensions.com, March 13, 2009.

Mendillo, Jane L. "Harvard Management Company Endowment Report: Message from the CEO." www.hmc.harvard.edu, September 2009.

National Association of College and University Business Officers. "NACUBO Press Release on 2008 Endowment Study Results," January 27, 2009. www.nacubo.org.

———. "Table: Average Asset Class Allocation of Total Assets [2008]." *NACUBO.org.*

Nesbitt, Stephen L. "2003 Wilshire Report on State Retirement Systems: Funding Levels and Asset Allocation." Wilshire Associates Inc., March 12, 2003.

"News Briefs: Pension Funding a 'Top Risk' to Economy." *Pensions & Investments*, Alternatives, July 21, 2008.

Pension Benefit Guaranty Corporation. "PBGC Deficit Climbs to $33.5 Billion at Mid-Year, Snowbarger to Tell Senate Panel." Press Release, May 20, 2009.

Pichardo, Raquel. "CalPERS a Model of Innovation at 75: Giant Fund Shows no Sign of Complacency as it Continues to Break New Investment Ground." *Pensions & Investments*, May 12, 2007.

Quint, Michael, and Gillian Wee. "Harvard Losing AAA Benefit in Market Shows Swap Risk (Update1)." *Bloomberg*, March 3, 2009.

Reed, Chris. "CalPERS Kept Investing in Real Estate Until mid-2007, and with Borrowed Money; so Much for its Great Rep." *San Diego Union-Tribune*, December 26, 2008.

"Rich Harvard, Poor Harvard." *Vanity Fair*, June 30, 2009.

Rider, Richard. "Thinking of Leaving California? You're Not Alone." *Advisor.com*, April 17, 2008.

Rose-Smith, Imogen. "Lose the Ferrari." *Institutional Investor*, May 2009.

Rowling, Megan. "UK Government Aids Struggling Charities, as Donations Fall." *Reuters*, February 9, 2009.

Russakoff, Dale. "Human Toll of a Pension Default." *Washington Post*, June 13, 2005.

Sass, Steven A. *The Promise of Private Pensions*, Cambridge, MA: Harvard University Press, 1997.

Staley, Oliver. "Stanford Endowment Loss Prompts President to Suspend Smoothing." *Bloomberg*, October 26, 2009.

Staley, Oliver, and Gillian Wee. "Yale to Cut $150 Million Annually Through Fiscal 2014 (Update1)." *Bloomberg*, September 10, 2009.

State Retirement and Pension System of Maryland, "Quarterly Investment Update Asset Class by Market Value and Allocation," September 30, 2009. dbm.maryland.gov.

Stewart, James B. "Ivy League Schools Learn a Lesson in Liquidity." *Wall Street Journal*, August 18, 2009.

Stewart, Nyree. "Global Pension Assets Drop 18% in 2008." IPE International Publishers Limited, February 3, 2009.

Tax Foundation. "Federal Individual Income Tax Rates History, Income Years 1913–2009," January 2, 2009.

———. "State Individual Income Tax Rates, 2009," July 1, 2009.

Taylor, Dr. Bryan. "The Equity Risk Premium: An Historical Analysis." Global Financial Data, March 2, 2009.

Teacher Retirement System of Texas, "Annual Financial Report Highlights: Fiscal Year 2009," http://www.trs.state.tx.us/about/documents/cafr_highlights.pdf.

Tokyo Stock Exchange Group Inc. Retrieved data from historical Market Data, www.tse.or.jp, 2009.

"Tuft's Bacow Says Richest Endowments Should Reduce Risk: Video." *Bloomberg*, November 19, 2009.

U.S. Bureau of Labor Statistics. "Consumer Price Index," October 2009.

———. "National Unemployment Rate," October 2009.

Vardi, Nathan. "Did Harvard Sell at the Bottom?" *Forbes*, October 26, 2009.

Vickers, Marcia. "Global Guru: The Head of Harvard's $30 Billion Endowment Talks about Investing, the Market, and the Global Economy." *Fortune*, May 31, 2007.

Watson Wyatt Worldwide. *2008 Global Pension Assets Study*, January 2008.

———. *2009 Global Pension Assets Study*, January 2009.

———. "Global Pension Assets Double in Ten Years," Press Release, January 24, 2007.

———. "Global Pension Assets Fell Sharply in 2008, Watson Wyatt Study Finds." Press Release, January 26, 2009.

———. "Global Pension Fund Balance Sheet Stressed." Press Release, January 26, 2009.

Wee, Gillian. "Endowment Losses from Harvard to Yale Leave Universities Poorer." *Bloomberg*, July 22, 2009.

———. "Pimco Plots Asset Strategy to Mimic Yale Without Cash Strain." *Bloomberg*, September 1, 2009.

———. "Stanford Reports Endowment Investments Fell 26% (Update3)." *Bloomberg*, September 23, 2009.

———. "University of Pennsylvania Endowment Beats Harvard with Stocks." *Bloomberg*, August 12, 2009.

———. "University of Virginia Adds Private Equity to Meet Commitments." *Bloomberg*, July 9, 2009.

———. "Yale's Investments Fall 24.6% on Buyouts, Energy (Update2)." *Bloomberg*, September 22, 2009.

———. "Yale's Swensen Recommends TIPS to Hedge 'Substantial Inflation'." *Bloomberg*, May 23, 2009.

Weisbecker, Lee. "Cowell: N.C. Pension System Gains 10.4%." *Triangle Business Journal*, November 10, 2009.

Yale University Investments Office. *The Yale Endowment 2007 Investment Report*. www.yale.edu/investments.

———. *The Yale Endowment 2008 Investment Report*. www.yale.edu/investments.

About the Author

S teven Drobny is the cofounder of Drobny Global, an international macroeconomic research and advisory firm that counts many of the leading global hedge funds and money managers as clients. Prior to Drobny Global, Steven worked for Deutsche Bank's Hedge Fund Group in London, Singapore, and Zurich. He holds a master's degree from the London School of Economics and a bachelor's degree from Bucknell University. He is the author of *Inside the House of Money: Top Hedge Fund Traders on Profiting in the Global Market*. Please visit www.drobny.com for more information on Drobny Global and this book.

Index